STACKED

Double Your Job Interviews,
Leverage Recruiters,
Unlock LinkedIn

DR. KAREN GURNEY

Get the free video companion course to see this book in action at

www.karengurney.com/stacked

CAREER IQ LLC PUBLISHERS
CLEVELAND OH

DEDICATION

To my husband Ron who made this possible by going to work every day.

Contents

My Story and Why
This Book is for You

I have been working in the recruiting industry as an Executive Search Consultant and Career Coach since 2004, but something happened in 2015 that completely changed how I worked, literally overnight.

I had a client who was an Internet Marketing Manager and was seeking a position in E-commerce, social media marketing, or digital marketing; he could barely get a call for an interview after a year of job hunting. Before I started his job search campaign, I checked his LinkedIn.com profile to make sure it looked good.

His LinkedIn profile was absolutely horrifying. His picture was a selfie that looked like a bad mugshot after a night of drinking and a subsequent police interrogation. His profile had too much information that was irrelevant to his goals, his headline was meaningless, and he only had 24 connections. There was no way I could position someone that was supposed to be an expert in digital marketing with this repellent LinkedIn profile.

My client was absolutely desperate for a job. He was a nice guy and a good job candidate with a lot of related experience. I usually just give my clients tips to improve their profile but I knew time was of the essence and I needed to take control of his online image immediately. I got his login for LinkedIn as well as other online job boards and within two hours, I re-aligned everything, got a new professional profile picture, changed all of his online profiles to match his job search goals, and did a campaign to grow his connections over the LinkedIn 500+ connection display threshold.

Within 48 hours he had over 300 connections and one job interview. By the end of the week, he had four job interviews and had hit the 500+ connection mark and ...

He had not applied for a single job! Not one!

All the calls he got were from his online profiles.

This method is now the core of my career coaching practice.

So what is the secret? It is just one phrase: Keyword-stacking.

Once you learn how to keyword-stack your profiles in the way that recruiters search, you will get calls too.

What You Will Be Able to Do After Reading This Book
- Have recruiters come straight to you for great jobs
- Get calls for jobs without applying
- Double your interviews
- Tap unadvertised jobs in the hidden job market

You Also Get My Online Award-Winning Class - Free!
This book works hand-in-hand with my online video class which allows Q&A for targeted personal strategy questions. You can access the link by typing this into an internet browser www.karengurney.com/stacked.

With the class you get:

- Video instruction
- A resume template that beats the resume black hole
- My copyrighted "Core-3©" career assessment
- Fill-in-the-blank interview preparation scripts
- Salary negotiation scripts
- And so much more!

These methods have facilitated thousands of career changes, and now you can use them too!

I look forward to helping you achieve your career goals.

Sincerely,

Dr. Karen Gurney

Modern Hiring Manifesto:
Job Candidate
Rules of Engagement

To win the game you need to know the following rules.

- To get a job and advance in your career, you need to be **findable** by a recruiter, either online or through the employer's internal Applicant Tracking System (ATS).
- LinkedIn.com, Job Boards, and the employer's ATS virtually **work the same way**. Learn one - learn all.
- Recruiters begin their candidate search with **keywords**.
- You need to know what words they are looking for to **keyword-stack** a resume.
- **Job advertisements** on the job boards contain the keywords.
- The job board is **living breathing job market information** that allows you to plan your career and perform career changes.

Write the resume to the job ad, to
- ➢ Ensure being found by recruiters.
- ➢ Pre-qualify for jobs.
- ➢ Reduce the time to get a job.
- ➢ Make career changes easier.
- ➢ Easily create a winning resume.
- ➢ Have easier job interviews.
- ➢ Build a solid foundation for salary negotiations.

Posting the keyword-stacked resume to LinkedIn and the job boards

> ➢ Brings recruiters to you.
> ➢ Taps the hidden job market of unadvertised jobs.
> ➢ Provides social proof in background checks.

Once you post online, you will get unexpected calls for **phone screens,** 30-minute conversations where you must **prove**:

1. You want the mystery job that you know nothing about.
2. You are qualified for the mystery job.
3. You want the pay of the mystery job.
4. You will stay on the mystery job.
5. You will be happy on the mystery job.

- To be successful, a candidate must control the engagement and **avoid on-the-spot phone screens.**
- To get an in-person interview a person needs to be able to properly **quote "desired salary."**
- To get a job offer, you need to treat every job like it is your **dream job,** because employers only want to hire people that want the job.
- To make more, you need to learn how to properly perform **salary negotiations.**

Be prepared to learn the **cutting edge techniques of modern hiring** that put you in the driver's seat of your career.

How This Book is Organized

There are 11 chapters for a complete Stacked strategy that doubles your interviews.

Chapter 1: Get Recruiters to Work for You with LinkedIn
Chapter 2: Your Core-3© Career Assessment
Chapter 3: Market-Based Resume©
Chapter 4: LinkedIn and Online Profiles That Tap the Hidden Job Market
Chapter 5: "Double Your Interviews" Campaign Kickoff
Chapter 6: Phone Screens & Interview Preparation
Chapter 7: Salary Negotiations & Desired Salary Quoting
Chapter 8: Networking to Get a Job
Chapter 9: Advanced LinkedIn Strategies
Chapter 10: Unique Career Change Types & Strategies
Chapter 11: Timing and Troubleshooting the Job Search Campaign

A typical chapter includes:

- Myths Discussed and Debunked
- Section Exercises
- Homework
- Quizzes

Chapter 1:
Get Recruiters to
Work for You with LinkedIn

Recruiters are using online and company databases to seek out qualified candidates for open positions every single day. You are not getting calls on your resume because of one simple reason: the recruiters cannot find you. You are about to learn the fastest and easiest methods to get calls for the jobs you want, bringing recruiters to you using cutting edge recruiter search training via LinkedIn. Before we discuss how recruiters use the LinkedIn Recruiter Application, let's debunk some common job search myths.

This chapter includes the following lessons:
1.1 – Job Search Myths
1.2 – The 3-Step Recruiter Process
1.3 – Types of Recruiters and Why This Matters
1.4 – 'Leverage the Recruiter' Strategy Recap

1.1 Job Search Myths

Here are some of the common concerns that people have before jumping in:

Myth 1: I have to know what job I want to succeed.

No. In fact, what I am about to teach you is the most effective method of identifying job opportunities and career changes that are actually available to you right now (and, how to build a resume and online profile to get them).

Myth 2: I have to "network" to make this work.

No! This answer may be shocking; networking is actually the *last* tactic you should be using in your job search. It takes a very long time to build a network robust enough to help you find the job you want. I am not saying don't pursue networking over the life of your career. I am saying that when you are ready to get interviews there is a much faster and effective way to get job interviews (and offers).

Myth 3: I have to go "door-to-door" to get a job.

No! I know there are books that say this is the best way to get a job, but that is not the way hiring is done for professional level roles, and you risk upsetting employers and ruining your reputation. Besides, if you really *want* to do that then I can already tell you that you should be in outside sales. For the rest of the population, there is a better, easier, and more professional way to get job interviews.

Myth 4: Hiring is "all-who-you-know."

Absolutely not! The concept that hiring is based entirely on who you know is not only ineffective common wisdom, it is 100% wrong. You can double your job interviews overnight and bring recruiters straight to you for the jobs that you want, without knowing a single person at your future employer.

Myth 5: I have to spend hours and hours blasting hundreds of the same resume.

That is not an effective technique. However, I am going to teach you how to leverage some easy online methods that yield results overnight once you know what to do.

Myth 6: I have to go to Career Fairs and do some bizarre "Guerrilla Marketing."

For a non-student, career fairs are typically soul-sapping experiences that should be one of the last steps in your career search (not the first). Nothing I teach you in this book will put you in weird uncomfortable situations. The biggest irony in hiring is that the simplest and most comfortable methods yield the best results.

Myth 7: I need a paid LinkedIn Premium Account.

Not at all. At the time I am writing this, there are very few advantages to a paid "Premium" membership. However, LinkedIn plays a very important part of what I am going to teach you to do to double your interviews.

<u>Myth 8: I need to have a college degree.</u>

The techniques taught in this book are valuable for anyone who uses a resume to apply for a job.

<u>Myth 9: I need to take an online class.</u>

No, but you will want to. As a bonus for purchasing this book, I am offering my award-winning class for free at www.karengurney.com/stacked. You will want the downloadable templates I offer to make implementation of these concepts much quicker.

Now we know what does not work, let's find out what does.

1.2 The 3-Step Recruiter Process

When recruiters look for candidates via the online databases or through their employer-based Applicant Tracking System (ATS), also called the Talent Management System (TMS), most resumes do not surface even for the most qualified candidates, creating what is referred to as the "resume black hole." When you know how recruiters search, you can keyword-stack and optimize your profile so that you are produced as a qualified candidate in the recruiter search.

To understand how recruiters search for candidates we will use the most popular website for careers, LinkedIn.com, as our vehicle. Most users of LinkedIn understand that this is a free social media website for your professional lives. However, most job applicants have not been exposed to the "recruiter" app.

This search application is used by Human Resource professionals to seek out profiles for their "ready-to-fill" open jobs. In this chapter, I will show you the instructions that LinkedIn offers recruiters for this application, which also reveal the popular current job candidate search methods. The recruiter search process is the same whether it is via LinkedIn, online job boards, or an employer's internal Applicant Tracking Systems (ATS).

The #1 Way to Learn How Recruiters Work
LinkedIn Recruiter Search Application

First we will examine the core techniques that recruiters use and then we will discuss each one in greater detail.

Recruiter 3-Step Search Process

Recruiters do a three-step process within the recruiter application.
- ➢ Step 1: Keywords
- ➢ Step 2: Location
- ➢ Step 3: Narrowing Terms

Step 1: Keyword Search

When LinkedIn teaches recruiters how to use their recruiter application, their training tells recruiters to use keywords, not titles, as the first search method to identify the right candidate. This may come as a surprise to job search candidates that have been taught do to a reverse-chronology resume that focuses on title, industry, and professional category.

This disconnect between resumes and recruiter search leaves highly qualified professionals drowning in the deep dark end of the candidate pool. The last time your resume came up for air was probably only for a direct match to your most recent title, and for good reason: that is focus of most resumes. Title will indeed become important later on in the process. However, at the beginning, keywords are the primary way candidates are found. Therefore, you need to understand the in-demand keywords for your background so that you are being produced as a candidate during the recruiter search.

In the example LinkedIn gives, a recruiter is searching for the keywords "SaaS sales" (SaaS means Software as a Service). When a recruiter searches LinkedIn for this keyword combination, there are over 400,000 results! This result is similar for many other keyword searches. It is not possible or efficient for the recruiter to review 400,000 candidates so they must reduce their options. It would seem that this is where title would come in but, not yet.

Step 2: Location search

After keywords, recruiters use location to narrow down their list. Location goes beyond the direct search and affects overall hiring. There is a large and reliable statistical link between attrition (the rate at which employees quit their jobs) and a distance beyond a 30-minute commute to work. In other words, employers find that employees who have to drive farther quit their job sooner. This statistic is even higher when the job candidate has moved to a completely different metropolitan area. The quit rate of relocation employees is reported to be as high as 80% in under two years. Employers obviously do not want to hire job candidates who are going to quit. (*There is a special lesson in Chapter 9 about geographic relocation strategies*). For now, we will assume that you are seeking a job close to your home.

Step 3: Narrowing terms

The Keyword-Location search combination will still produce too many results, requiring the recruiter to narrow the search even more. The following fields are the next most popular options.

Narrowing Terms:
• Title,
• Industry,
• Rank,
• And years of experience.

The following search terms start defining the level of experience the candidate would be expected to have for the targeted positions.

Title
The fastest job move a person can make is often based on their title. One would think that this would be the first search term, not the third. However, an experienced professional may have a variety of titles that are closely related and which are often the same across many different types of positions. Therefore, as noted earlier, keywords and location are a more reliable source of quality results for the recruiter. A caveat about titles: once a candidate surfaces in the search and their profile is scrutinized in depth, a candidate's title progression as it relates to the

position will actually be the most important factor in the hire. But first, a professional must be found using the other criteria.

Industry

The industry the person has worked in can be very important to some positions, while to others it may be of limited importance. Therefore, the use of industry as a search method will vary greatly.

Rank

Rank has to do with whether a person has a lower hierarchical title, mid-manager, Director-level, Vice President or Executive. It is important to have your profile match the level of rank that is reasonable to attain based on your background so that you can surface for the most likely job opportunities.

Let me give you an example. A single entrepreneur who owns a marketing firm may title themselves as Director of Digital Marketing even if they have no team. However, in a company with 2,000 or more employees, a Director of Marketing will likely have a team with multiple direct reports. A recruiter may find this single entrepreneur and eliminate them from the pool of candidates due to company size. On the other hand, this person may have excellent experience for roles like Social Media Strategist or Digital Account Manager. Due to their Director of Marketing title they may not surface for the jobs that match their actual level of qualifications.

Years of Experience

In a search, a substitute for rank is often the number of years of experience. Employers may prefer depth of experience, versus title and rank achievement, especially in technical roles. It may seem like more years are always better but you are seeking a direct-hit match to recruiter expectations.

In summary, this LinkedIn training on the recruiter application has given you a good idea of what is important for online profiles and resumes. However, there are different types of recruiters and this makes an impact on your success. Since your career progression is depending on these professionals, it is important to understand what motivates each type of recruiter.

1.3 Types of Recruiters and Why It Matters

You may encounter multiple types of recruiters in your career. When you apply the strategies taught in this book, these various types will be calling you unexpectedly for jobs you have not even applied for, as well as from your direct applications. You want them working for _you_. So how do you do that? There is one generality that holds true for all recruiters.

Recruiters seek people for jobs, and not jobs for people.

Perhaps that seems obvious, but recruiters constantly complain that people ask them to find a job or ask the recruiter to "make them a fit." No matter what type of recruiter, they are not paid to make you, or any candidate, a fit into their open jobs. Once you know that jobs are available and that they need to find a direct-hit match, it is much easier to understand how to effectively make recruiters work for you. Now, let's explore the differences in type.

Five Types of Recruiters

1. Third party recruiters: retained or contingent
2. Internal company human resource (HR) recruiters
3. Staffing agency recruiters
4. Executive career managers
5. Head hunters

These five recruiter types can make or break your success.

Type 1. Third Party Recruiters: Retained & Contingent

Third party recruiters are major players for leadership and technical roles. In the case of accounting, finance, information technology, or any position that is management level or above, you are more likely to get a call from one of these recruiters than from an internal company recruiter who received your direct application. If a job pays over $65,000 per year a recruiter is probably seeking a professional that will best fit. These recruiters like to pick up the phone and call prospects. There are examples where a job candidate applied for a job but, instead of getting a call from the company's HR department, a third party recruiter found them online for the very same job. This means these recruiters cannot be ignored if you are in certain fields or level of employment.

Keep in mind that, no matter what level you have attained, you absolutely should want to get these calls. Many candidates tell me they only want calls from internal recruiters, however it is much faster and easier to leverage the third party recruiter than any other type.

Popular national names in third party recruiting industry are Robert Half for Accounting and TEKSystems for I.T. but there are hundreds of thousands smaller players in different locations. Do not expect a niche firm like Robert Half to place a customer service professional. Some recruiters seek out all sorts of jobs but many agencies have niches. These professionals tend to focus on identifying talent for jobs that pay over $65,000 per year, but I have seen calls on some entry-roles as well.

When you get a call unexpectedly, meaning you do not remember applying for the job or company, it is usually from a third party recruiter. These professionals mine online databases for "passive candidates." LinkedIn is the perfect place to do this because many professionals create profiles even if they are not currently seeking a new position. Making your resume and online profile attractive to these recruiters is an important strategy to make the fastest and most profitable career change.

If a third party recruiter is calling on your resume or LinkedIn profile, it is an indication your profile is properly optimized and that your skills are in hot demand; it may also indicate a short supply of talent in the market. In other words, you are doing your career, resume, profile, and job search correctly.

What are the differences between the third party recruiter types?

Employers pay an outside agency to help locate talent. There are two primary types:
1. Retained
2. Contingent

With retained recruiting agreements, the company regularly pays to have a recruiter source for particular positions and they only hire through that agreement. Contingent recruiters have no agreement with the company. This group can sometimes create a painful experience for candidates because they call on jobs that they do not formally represent. The only reliable way to spot a contingent recruiter is if they ask you to sign a contract to work with them. There are fewer and fewer of these types of recruiters. It is best to keep working the job search and not focus on the type of recruiter you may encounter.

In both cases, the recruiters are paid about 20% of the job candidate's annual salary. For someone making $100,000 that is a $20,000 commission. The employer pays the fee, which excites job candidates. They feel like they have an "agent" working for them at no cost.

Why would a company pay so much for a candidate they can find on their own?

There are a variety of reasons that the third party recruiting industry exists:
1. The employer's clunky Applicant Tracking System (ATS)
2. Applicant overwhelm
3. Genuinely hard-to-fill jobs

1. The clunky ATS

The ATS, which is commonly referred to as the "resume black hole," negatively affects an employer's ability to find applicants in their own database. Believe it or not, employers have a hard time mining their own ATS which creates a false impression that there are no qualified applicants. The ATS is technologically inferior to online job boards because it does not receive as much constant investment into programming compared to LinkedIn and other online databases. If you think of how Google search has evolved over the years and the artificial intelligence required to figure out what you are searching for, it will make sense. The ATS programs are, in a word, clunky.

2. Applicant overwhelm

In addition to the ATS problem, the ease of applying for jobs online has created an overwhelming amount of applicants for open positions. Many employers, especially the top tier ones that everyone wants to work for, complain that they get over 1,000 applications per advertised job. Sometimes, it is just easier and more cost-effective to hire an outside recruiter.

3. Hard-to-fill jobs

The third party recruiting industry originally began for professional niche hard-to-fill positions. Some positions really are difficult to fill with a limited number of qualified candidates, and it requires an extensive and lengthy internet search to find the right person. Some recruiting agencies have professional category specializations allowing them to identify qualified candidates more quickly. Their finger is on the pulse, so to speak.

Some businesses are either too big or too small to be able to source the right candidates. Some companies have more money than time and it makes sense to pay agency fees. As in all things with business, sometimes it is cheaper or more effective to outsource for a specialized activity, and recruiting is one of those activities.

Shouldn't a depressed economy increase the supply of qualified applicants and reduce the need to hire a third party recruiter to source talent?

This is an interesting question and a completely logical assumption. However something very different has happened. Because we have been in a depressed economy since about 2000, the employers believe they can get whatever they want. This is referred to as "seeking the unicorn."

This situation can get really absurd. A recent conversation with a third party recruiter uncovered that one of their candidates, with an Ivy-league MBA and over 10 years of work experience, was a finalist for a position. The candidate was not extended an offer because they did not have a 4.0 GPA in the Bachelor's degree program. This is the type of ridiculous hiring behavior that drives third party recruiters and job candidates crazy. However, the "seeking the unicorn" strategy opens the door to two things: 1) third party recruiters who use much more effective talent sourcing methods and 2) the strategies in this book which help you win at their game.

Why are third party recruiters so much more effective at recruiting?

They are the sales people of the HR industry and they are driven by a juicy commission.

- Job candidates are their product and they want to talk to as many as possible.
- They do not use technologically inferior ATS programs as the internal recruiters do.
- They often list their personal email and telephone number in a job advertisement to increase how many people they talk to.
- Because there is no ATS, a <u>human being</u> will review your resume submission.
- As sales people, they jump on the phone to talk to a candidate with no hesitation, sometimes within hours of submitting the resume.
- They read newspapers to see which companies are laying off, thus creating a new stream of qualified candidates that they can sell to hiring companies.
- They will call everyone on their list to source new candidates because a qualified person is likely to know another qualified person.
- They have started taking qualified people out to lunch even if they are not actively seeking work, for the sole purpose of finding new candidates through networking.

In conclusion, third party recruiters are successful because they do recruiting the way it used to be done, **live human interaction.**

<u>How does this affect me as a candidate?</u>

The current environment has created a highly competitive free-for-all environment, and unsuspecting job candidates are literally feeling victimized by third party recruiters. Some job candidates have even described these individuals as "evil" and expressed a high-degree of disgust with the field. We can offset this by actively understanding and managing these relationships.

Dealing with third party recruiters can be both exhilarating and depressing. Nothing is worse than getting a call from a pumped up recruiter telling you how great you are for a job and then never hearing back. However, you do want these calls! They are one of the best indicators of a perfectly optimized job search and there are some professions almost exclusively hiring this way. These recruiters cannot be ignored by the job seeker.

Type 2. Internal Company HR Recruiters

Many job candidates only want calls from companies and positions they have applied to directly. This significantly extends the amount of time it takes to get a great job. You already know that the ATS, the tool an internal recruiter uses, is technologically inferior. But in addition, internal HR recruiters are not sales people; they are motivated by screening out as many candidates as possible and typically seek to only bring in about three people for the time-consuming in-person interviews. It is very resource-intensive to hire and recruiters often have competing interests for their time.

Most companies hire by committee to protect from biased decisions. It is difficult to put busy employees in the room for something that is not a priority in their work. This is a sharp contrast to the third party recruiter whose one and only job is to screen in candidates.

Another reason candidates are getting so few interviews is that it takes a long time to apply for jobs through the ATS software. However, this book will double your interviews by shifting you away from the direct-application-only job search method.

Type 3. Staffing Agency Recruiters

A staffing agency is a type of business that employers use to fill their short-term assignments. Some employers also like to "try before they buy" and place many different types of positions with temp-to-hire employees. However, many agencies are now working in the third party recruiter space for professional-level roles. I like to use staffing agencies to help candidates who have experienced a long period of unemployment or are returning to a profession they were in a long time ago. The interview process for these roles is less rigorous (sometimes non-existent) which can help a job candidate get back to work who is super capable but has recently experienced a challenging period in life. Staffing agents typically only call candidates who apply directly into their system, so they are not out mining the online job boards for passive candidates. A job applicant has to apply to their jobs and database to be found. Adecco and Kelly are well-known agencies, but there are many more local ones as well.

Type 4. Executive Career Managers

You know now that recruiters and staffing agencies seek people for jobs, not jobs for people. A company pays a recruiter $10,000 to $20,000 or more to get a qualified hire. Would you pay that to someone to find you a job? Perhaps, but read on.

This is where we meet an unusual type of business called the "executive career management" firm. The career management firm appears to be a staffing agency or third party recruiting firm that will act as an "agent" and call on businesses to negotiate a new job for the candidate. They work for, and are paid by, the candidate.

These companies are exactly like me, your author; they are career coaches and consultants. That is not a bad thing, except they create an impression that they are more than career coaches. You might pay $10,000 to have someone find you a job but you may not be willing to pay even $1,500 to hire a career coach. Some people receive the coaching they need from these firms and it results in a job. However, many times job candidates that pay these firms later feel like they were scammed. My issue is the impression they create of being an agency.

These are the ways to identify if a company is an "executive career management" firm.

- They typically advertise online as if they have executive positions. (This is their primary lead generation system or sales marketing method.)
- Upon clicking on these job advertisements, there will be a general description but no employer name.
- A visit to their office will result in a highly satisfying career analysis where the candidate feels like a million bucks. (This is one of their primary sales-closing tactics.)

- The person working at this firm will discuss the "hidden" job market and how they can help tap their network to uncover opportunities.
- The job candidate receives a rigorous accomplishment inventory for homework and then must come back in a week.
- They will review the homework and then pitch a $1,500+ contract to help the candidate find a job.
- The job candidate may have the feeling that the firm will act as an "agent." (This is the other primary sales tactic.)
- The candidate may or may not get a job from the work product done by the firm.
- There is a "no refund" policy.

There is no candidate on earth that would not be excited about the potential to have someone go out and sell them for opportunities. However these firms are not recruiters, staffing agencies, or agents – they are career coaches, strategists, and search consultants.

Unfortunately, there is no agency in the hiring industry that represents the candidate.

Career management firms are not "bad" because they do perform a service to help the candidate package and present themselves for new opportunities. However, the way they sell their service leads candidates to believe one of two things: 1) that their background is more in-demand than it really is and 2) that the firm will act as a recruiter and seek out or create job opportunities for the candidate. Just know that you are paying for career coaching and not for job placement.

Type 5. Head Hunter

As a final discussion of recruiter types, we will talk about head hunters. Most job candidates believe that recruiters find jobs for people. It is a general belief that a 'head hunter' helps people get jobs.

There is no such thing as a head hunter!

They are a mythic beast made up by hopeful job candidates who misunderstand how hiring is done. Someone could technically call any type of recruiter a head hunter. The reason I do not like the term is because, in most cases, that person completely misunderstands what a recruiter does for a living.

The only agents for hiring are for sports and entertainment. Unless you have won the Heisman Trophy for football, or an Emmy award for acting, there is no agent out there that is going to call to find you a high-paying opportunity. Let me say it again: agency does not exist on the candidate side of hiring. If that is what you, like many others, think about head hunters, then you will have bought into the mythic beast concept of this field.

1.4 "Leverage the Recruiter" Strategy Recap

Recruiters are seeking qualified people for their open job requisitions.

If the recruiters are of the "third party recruiter" variety, they are going to receive a juicy commission by sending a 100%

super-qualified direct-hit match, square-peg, square-hole candidate to the employer paying their contract. They intend to talk to a lot of people to find their golden egg but, ultimately, will only send a few people that they know the employer will pay them for.

If they are internal company recruiters, they are seeking to look at, and contact, <u>as few of people as possible</u> because they are busy and no one is going to pay them a big fat commission check for doing more work. The less people they need to talk to the better because they do not want to create a mob of angry, depressed, and rejected job candidates who think they are perfect for the stated job. The Human Resources department recruiter wants to talk to at most ten 100% super qualified direct-hit match square-peg, square-hole candidates.

The staffing agency sits somewhere in between the company and third party recruiter, with a focus on temporary or temp-to-hire jobs. They increasingly play the role of third party recruiters because companies already use them for other types of recruiting. The staffing agency can be helpful in moving a candidate who has been out of work for a while.

With all recruiters, your job is to present yourself as a 100% super-qualified direct-hit match, square-peg, square-hole candidate for open positions using the job advertisements as a clue as to what they are seeking. You can then surface at the top of their search, so that they can get the best results, while talking to the least amount of people in the shortest amount of time.

> Homework

For clarity on this chapter, get the online class at www.karengurney.com/stacked and review the video lesson on LinkedIn Recruiter Search. This is a critical concept to understanding what you must do to be found by recruiters.

Quiz 1: Recruiters (T/F)

1. ___ Recruiters only call on actively applying professionals.
2. ___ The best way to be found by recruiters is keyword-stacking.
3. ___ In Recruiter search, title is more important than keywords.
4. ___ Where you live is not important to recruiter search.
5. ___ Recruiters search LinkedIn differently than internal company databases.
6. ___ There is only one type of recruiter.
7. ___ Head hunters find jobs for people.
8. ___ Calls from direct applications are better than 'out of the blue' calls.
9. ___ There are agents that seek jobs for people.
10. ___ It is possible to tap the hidden job market and get calls for unadvertised jobs.

Chapter 1: Answer Key (T/F)

1) False: Recruiters call on "passive" candidates every day.
2) True: Keywords are critical to being found.
3) False: Titles are important in hiring but less important in the search process.
4) False: Location is a primary method to search for candidates.
5) False: LinkedIn searches and database searches are basically the same.
6) False: There are four real and one mythical types.
7) False: Head hunters are mythical. Recruiters find people for jobs.
8) False: Both are important and 'out of the blue' calls will double your interviews.
9) False: Candidate-driven Agents only exist in sports or entertainment.
10) True: Yes, this book's strategy taps the hidden job market and doubles interviews.

Chapter 2:
Your Core-3©
Career Assessment

You now know that recruiters seek jobs for people, so to get them to work for you, you need to be a direct-hit square-peg square-hole match "on paper" based on their keyword search. How do you find these keywords? The job market!

The method I use to help determine the right keywords to bring recruiters to my clients is the same strategy I use to help candidates who tell me they are hungry for a more rewarding role, want a change, or need to do something different.

There is a significant lack of information in the job market. Most people go about their career bumping into figurative walls because no one ever told them exactly how to effectively search for a job. Some find a mentor or obtain a great job straight out of college and their career grows at a steady rate. For others, their career does not match their lifestyle or work interests. In other cases, professionals may find themselves stagnating or even falling apart.

When a candidate does not know what to do or how to solve a career problem, where do they turn for information?

It is very common for professionals to use personality assessments like the Myers-Briggs Type Indicator (MBTI©), Gallup's Strengthsfinder©, or some other popular personality-career analysis tool. I will be the first to tell you that I love personality assessments. In fact, when I take them, I am usually listed in the category of people that love them! (Yes, there is a category for that. There is also a category for those that despise them.)

The problem is, no matter how you feel about personality assessments, they will not tell you how to get from where you are to where you want to go. However, each candidate has a Core-3© set of job changes based on their skills. Let's first explore some myths about career and job changing as they relate to personality assessments before investigating your Core-3©.

This chapter includes the following lessons:
2.1 – Career, Jobs, and Personality Test Myths
2.2 – The Core-3© Career Assessment
2.3 – Finding Your Dream Job
2.4 – Targeted Job Alerts

2.1 Career, Jobs, and Personality Test Myths

If you think one of the popular personality or skill assessments is going to help you identify what you should be doing, studying, applying for, or working towards, think again.

<u>Myth 1: Personality tests will help me identify rewarding work.</u>

This is just not true. When I first graduated from my Bachelor's program, I had a degree in Political Science and Spanish. I did not realize it at the time, but the job market for those skills was extremely limited. Silly me, I incorrectly thought that if a

University offered a program, there was a good job potential for that degree. Following graduation, I held a job collecting on credit cards (bummer). I quit that job after two years and then sold insurance for two years (major bummer), and then I worked on a software Help Desk for three years (better but still a bummer).

From my perspective, my career was in a shambles. I felt like I was stuck in dead-end jobs with no hope of leadership roles, and I really disliked my life. I had no idea where to turn and that is when I decided to take two different personality assessments. The MBTI® told me I was an ENFP and Strengthsfinder© determined I was an Ideator that liked to relate to people and woo them. Please tell me, how could I move from dead end call center jobs into a great new position with this information????

Personality assessments do not help you change careers, jobs, or lives … but what I am about to show you will.

Myth 2: Personality/skill assessments will tell me which fields need my abilities.

Personality and skill assessments help you become aware of your inherent *and* learned abilities. Reputable experts in psychology know that an assessment will essentially tell you what you already know. The assessments definitely will not match you to positions that are open in the market right now for your greatest skills. They also will not help you identify the skills and abilities that are in demand right now or where demand exceeds supply of workers. Only the job market can tell you that - and I am going to teach you how to tap that information.

Myth 3: Personality tests will help me identify the education or training I need to get a job.

Personality tests are woefully inadequate for identifying education programs that will result in a job. For instance, one of my clients was a Biomedical Engineer. This should be an excellent career, right? She studied for over 24 years, and worked for 10 years with another researcher. She reached the point in her career where she had to create her own funded research or she literally would be out of a job. No one told her about that when she studied for her degree. Biomedical research and STEM programs were supposed to be in-demand. Was a personality test going to help her identify new career paths for her background? No! To put her on a different career path, I used the Core-3© Career Assessment.

Myth 4: Employers do not reveal what they are looking for.

It is true that there are information shortcomings in the job market that limit great career planning. However, employers do reveal what they want, and I will teach you how to crack the code. As a coach, I get calls every day from candidates working in professional categories which I have not been exposed to in my own professional life or with previous clients. I developed my own process to assist them in understanding what their core strengths are by tapping the job market. What is great about this process is that it not only helps me understand the strengths of the candidate, it also helps my clients understand where the demand is for what they know. There is a third important benefit to using the job market as a "personality assessment," it also identifies potential jobs. This method is the most holistic way to make a career change. You have something that employers want and it can result in a complete shift.

There is one more thing to remember. After you build this list and start looking for a job, the job ads will also give you additional keywords for your job search and resume profile.

Myth 5: There is only one career change available to me.

Not true. At any given time, a person typically has at least three core moves they can make that, from an employer standpoint, are considered lateral. But for the candidate, a lateral move can mean big shifts in money, title, career trajectory, or lifestyle. The "lateral" part does not necessarily mean doing the same work; it means that the person matches at least 75% of what the employer is seeking. This should come as a relief to job candidates who think they are pigeon-holed in their career, a "jack-of-all-trades and master-of-none," those who feel they have no skills, or candidates who feel their challenges are insurmountable. Of course each person's career is linked to personal and financial interests, which adds to the complexity of the situation. My goal is to help you identify the jobs available that want what you know, and to help you position yourself for them.

2.2 The Core-3© Career Assessment

Before you jump into your assessment, let's spend some time defining the Core-3©.

Core-3© Definition

Your Core-3© are the <u>three primary career changes</u> available to you based on the following attributes:

- You will be able to read the job description and say, 'Yes, I have done that" to at least 75% of the line items in a job advertisement.
- You will have close to 100% of the mandatory requirements.
- Even if you are missing many line items, you will have a combination of one to three very hard-to-find skills, like a second language or technical skill.

Your Core-3© are not:

- Your three primary skill sets, or
- Your last three job titles.

Your Core-3© will change over time based on the following attributes:

- The skills you have gained, and
- The changes in job market demand.

<u>Your Core-3© Assessment is the job market demand for your keyword skills.</u>

The Core-3© can also be used to identify streams of jobs that support specific lifestyle interests. For example, a millennial seeking to climb the ladder into executive positions, a professional mom who has worked for 10+ years and wants a part-time job, or a 55-year old professional who wants to semi-retire.

Once you have identified the stream of jobs for your background, the goal is to then use this information to create a Market-Based Resume© and an online profile that capture your matching skills, thus creating the look and feel of a "lateral" career move. "Lateral" does not mean the same job, title, pay, and industry. These job moves can result in promotions or pay increases, achieve some life or work goal, or be radically different from your most recent position, while still appearing to the employer as if it was the exact work you have been doing in the recent or even distant past.

Exercise 2.2 Core-3© Career Assessment

To perform the Core-3© Career Assessment, grab a piece of paper or open a document and write the following down with spaces in between to fill in your answers. The class has a downloadable form of the exercise. (www.karengurney.com/stacked)

- Professional/industry acronyms or phrases
- Certifications
- Software
- Industry "players"
- Titles
- Languages
- Target geographic market
- Titles and employers of promoted or job changing colleagues
- Jobs you have already had calls on

Job Search Market Parameters

To identify the right positions for you, you need to start with the search terms you just listed. The job market itself will reveal additional parameters. Begin the search, add more, and try different combinations to identify your Core-3© stream of jobs.

The key to building a great list is to start with a few items, try some combinations, and then use the job advertisements to continue building out your list. This is not a perfect science. Trial and error will be required by combining different items on your list to find great jobs.

Professional/Industry Acronyms or Phrases

There are certain industry phrases or acronyms that may be popular in your profession or industry. These do not have to be complex to reward you with great hits on your job search.

For instance, in the online class, I demonstrate the job search process of an Accountant. She really enjoyed forecasting. When we searched for that word, the majority of the positions were actually titled in the Finance profession, not Accounting. This was a complete game changer for that candidate. In your list, if you cannot think of any specific acronyms or phrases, move on to the next category.

Certifications

In certain professions a certification is mandatory, which makes identifying jobs very easy (for example, Project Management Professional (PMP)). If you have certifications, list and search by them. If not, move on to the next category.

Software

The software you use can create opportunities for many new types of jobs. This is the #1 method I use to facilitate a career change for my clients. It is especially helpful when the person has used or interacted with ubiquitous software pieces which are popular across an industry. Below is a list of common programs:

• SAP (Manufacturing),
• EMR (Hospital Software),
• SQL (Database Software),
• Oracle (Database & Reporting Software),
• Crystal (Reporting Software),
• Peoplesoft (Human Resources),
• and, Intermediate MS Excel (Database).

The more broadly used the software, the better for the career, but even niche software can offer some interesting streams of jobs. For those in entry or even lower-level positions, software skills can assist in making moves into analyst, sales, or account management roles, which become gateways into new professional paths which may not have been open to the individual had they not had the software experience. List the software you have touched and use the job ads to continue expanding your list.

Industry "Players"

Professionals who work with vendors or customers may be able to open doors to new career pathways based on their deep knowledge of those businesses. In addition, competitors or other businesses in the same or a similar industry may be interested in your background. For example, a marketing professional worked in paint (chemicals), and discovered that different chemical company selling through a similar distribution and store network was interested in her work. As a result she achieved a promotion in title and salary.

Titles

As you know this is not the first search term recruiters use to find talent. However, if you can define nothing else about your career, you do know your title. Also, if you need a job quickly, the same title in the same profession is one of the fastest ways to change positions. This can actually also result in more money, sometimes $10,000 or more, because employers pay a premium for experienced workers.

Another strategy to consider is a "'return to an old profession." Do not forget about previous titles as well. Perhaps you were on a better path in your previous position than you are now and can return to it.

A title communicates a few things to an employer. It lets them know what you have been doing recently, whether you have had an upward logical progression, your "apparent" goals based on the choices you have made, the industries you have worked in, the level of responsibility you have had, your skill level, and an approximation of your current pay rate. In other words, there is a lot of information loaded into a job title that you can leverage (or overcome) to move if you want to go in a different direction or get a promotion.

If a fast job change is the ultimate goal, look for jobs with the same title in the same industry. If the goal is a much larger change, the title is just a "jumping off" point in your search.

Add to your list the following:
- Most recent title
- Previous titles
- The title representing the most likely promotion from most recent title
- Level of responsibility: coordinator, manager, director, etc.
  Profession: accounting, finance, engineering, sales, marketing, etc.
- Industry: banking, manufacturing, healthcare, software, etc.
- Years of experience: entry (0-2 years), mid (2-5 years), experienced (5+ years)

Languages

The ability to speak a second language can often open up opportunities you might not otherwise have been qualified for, especially when combined with one or two other skills. Native or intermediate language skills are not something a person can pick up on the job. Spanish and Portuguese are in particularly high demand in certain geographies, and these skills can spur career changes that overcome other skill gaps. Search for languages first in your target geography, and then add different skills to narrow down the list.

Target Geographic Market

The most likely location to get a job is within 30 miles of your current home location. As discussed in the previous chapter on LinkedIn Recruiter searches, location is one of the primary ways recruiters narrow down their list. There is a negative statistical relationship between distance to work and the likelihood of a person quitting their job soon after starting. However, the United States has the most mobile labor force in the world. Around 1% of the population (or over 300,000 people) move to new areas every year for a job.

First, write down the general large city area you are interested in. Then think about secondary areas, especially the next closest cities or large locations where you have a support system. The strategy to make these moves is dramatically easier if a person is within driving distance to interview. Geography, and the impact of a move, is less of an issue as a professional attains a "Director-level" or above position.

Titles, Industries, and Employers of Promoted or Job Changing Colleagues

When job candidates think about making a career change, they often think about a total shift of profession and industry, sometimes ignoring the next logical step in their career progression. A career change that leverages what you know can move you into training, quality assurance, management, implementation, doing the same job you are doing but remotely from home, doing the same job but with travel, or seeking out that next-step senior-level promotion. These types of step-up or step-over roles in the same profession and industry look like lateral moves. But, these roles often feel dramatically different than the current role you have held in an organization.

If you are frustrated with your current role do not ignore the next step up or over as a method to change your life. The best way to identify these roles is to examine the positions, titles, and industries of your previous colleagues. If you are lost, this is a good place to start to identify the market demand for your skills which can result in a much different position and which also matches your lifestyle goals.

Jobs You Have Had Calls on Without Applying

If you are already getting calls for jobs "out of the blue," this is an indication of where the demand is for your skills in the market. It also indicates how your profiles are optimized. If these jobs do not match your goals, then it is time to change your profiles to reflect where you are going versus where you have been. However, you may want to consider one of these potential jobs. The market is telling you how your current profile is being perceived; do not ignore these signals. If this is what you want, promote it more. If it is not what you want, change your resumes and profiles.

Education

Your degree or education is also a good additional search term. In some industries, like engineering, the right degree is absolutely mandatory; however, for many roles the type of degree is less important. For instance, a professional can work in Marketing but have an Accounting degree.

2.3 Finding Your Dream Job

Now it is time to search for the items on your list to find the streams of jobs available to you based on your background. For this task, I recommend Indeed.com. This job board has silently overtaken major competitors like Monster.com and LinkedIn.com to become the most robust job board, online resume posting, and recruiter talent search website in the United States. Because it is an aggregator, pulling jobs from multiple databases, it offers the most global view of the job market.

In 2015, the majority of my candidates who received calls from recruiter searchers came from either Monster.com or LinkedIn.com. In 2016, although I saw an almost total shift away from Monster.com in particular, I still recommend posting to at least four general job boards and to any applicable third party sites.

However you are not at that point yet in this process. The first thing you need to do is survey the job marketing to identify your Core 3©. The job market survey will uncover additional skill sets to add to your list. This will require many searches.

The job search can be as broad as the entire country or for a select city. Once several searches are made and the stream of jobs presents itself, the next stage is to set up job alerts.

Exercise 2.3 Survey the Job Market

Begin the survey by going to www.Indeed.com and then follow these steps:

- Enter one skill word at a time to get a broad overview
- Select a geographic market
- Start with single-word specialized certification or software words first
- Assess the results and determine additional words to add
- Try search-term combinations from your list
- Keep narrowing the list until you identify a stream of job titles that have 100% of your mandatory qualifications, 75% of the line items, or a rare set of combined skills.

Once a promising single or combined group of skills is identified, create a job alert to stay abreast of new postings.

2.4 Targeted Job Alerts

Most job boards have an automatic function to send you alerts based on previous job searches. However, they are usually very title driven. This can result in some pretty bizarre job suggestions. One example is for the title Account Manager, who can work across a variety of industries from advertising agencies to manufacturers. Although there is a tendency for these roles to be involved in expanding sales for existing customers, that is where the commonality ends. The algorithms in the job boards are not going to be able to easily differentiate the right jobs as efficiently as a professional who knows their own skills and experience. Use Indeed.com and the other job boards to set your own job alerts. There are multiple delivery options and they can be cancelled when you choose.

Job alerts can be set on proprietary systems or for specific employers. This can be very helpful for positions in government or universities that tend to have limited job advertising budgets. It is a good idea to set up accounts and alerts for special organizations of interest.

Job alerts can also be used for ongoing research or a long-term career planning goal. For instance, some professionals are interested in understanding what is happening in their profession or industry and do not want to miss great jobs that may pop up, now or in the future. Job alerts are also helpful if a busy professional only has one day a week to review and apply for positions. Use job alerts to your benefit and do not miss anything happening in your field.

Exercise 2.4 Job Alerts

Once you test different search terms, a certain word or skill combination should produce good results. It is easiest to manage job alerts when you have an account with Indeed.com (which you will need anyway for online profile posting). After you identify a promising search, enter your email in the job alert bar on the top right hand section of the Indeed.com search page.

>Homework

Create your list, perform the survey, and set up the job alerts. If you need further inspiration, visit the free video class to watch me perform a Core 3© assessment. (www.karengurney.com/stacked)

Once a stream of jobs has been identified, it is time to build a "composite" profile that pulls the keywords from multiple job ads targeting that one position. Our next step is breaking down the job ad to create a keyword-stacked market-based resume.

Quiz 2: Career Assessment (T/F)

1. ___ Personality tests help you change careers.
2. ___ Personality tests help identify educational programs that result in a great career.
3. ___ There are at least three different career changes available to you.
4. ___ You can career change based on skills even without a matching job title.
5. ___ Software skills can present completely new career avenues.
6. ___ Just one search term is all you need to find great jobs.
7. ___ A second language can overcome missing skills.
8. ___ Indeed.com is the best job board to start your search.
9. ___ The online job boards are effective at sending you new job leads.
10. ___ Indeed.com is the only job board you will need during your job search.

Chapter 2: Answer Key (T/F)

1) False: No, personality tests help you understand inherent or learned abilities.
2) False: No, personality tests do not help in picking degrees for in-demand professions.
3) True: There are at least three career changes available to you.
4) True: Skills are the #1 way of changing directions.
5) True: Software knowledge can really open new doors.
6) False: Many single and combination search terms will be needed.
7) True: Language can be a strong competitive advantage that overcomes skill gaps.
8) True: Indeed.com is a job search aggregator and offers the best job market overview.
9) False: Set up your own job alerts because the job board's automatic leads are ineffective.
10) False: Indeed.com is the best place to start to identify your Core 3© career changes; other job boards will be needed to perform your entire search.

Chapter 3:
Market-Based
Resume© Template

So far, you have uncovered how recruiters search for candidates and you have used the job market to identify your Core-3© power job moves. Now you need to learn how to use job ads to keyword-stack your resumes and online profiles to attract recruiters for the jobs that you want.

One of the challenges of writing a career book is to offer a resume strategy that can work for every single person at all professional levels and across different industries without having hundreds of resume examples. This method does just that by letting the job advertisement and market drive your resume creation. I will be offering an example of one candidate with three different resume changes. My online video class showcases a different example for variety. (www.karengurney.com/stacked)

How can one resume strategy work for everyone? This may sound a little bit controversial but ... the first part of the resume has NOTHING to do with your personal experience!!

I know that sounds crazy but if you had to write a paper about Shakespeare's *Romeo and Juliet*, would you start the essay discussing your own love-life? No, of course not. And the same is true with a great resume. Your resume (and your online profile) is based on the typical job requirements of your goal position. Once you have done the Core-3© Career Assessment and have identified your power career changes, you will have already matched your background to job market need.

To start a great resume, you literally set aside your work experience for a moment and focus on the top of the resume, which is a re-write of the related job advertisements that you have found. Once that is done, then you add your *matching* background. Going back to the *Romeo and Juliet* example, would you write about *Macbeth* if the paper was supposed to be about a different play? Use the job advertisements to drive the resume, not the other way around.

The #1 Resume Hack: Write the Resume to the Job Advertisement.

This resume style takes all the hard work you did identifying different career paths for your skills, and makes a resume out of the resulting job advertisements. At this stage you optimize the resume based on the keywords necessary to allow recruiters to find you based on their search parameters. By specifically creating a resume based on the job advertisement's required and desired skills, years of experience, job title, education, and accomplishments, your resume surfaces to the top. This document is also used as a template to build your online profiles on LinkedIn.com, Indeed.com, Monster.com, staffing agencies, and niche professional job boards. An aligned profile helps the recruiter to assist you because it is easier for them to sell a direct-hit match candidate to the hiring manager.

With the Market-Based Resume©, <u>what matters is what matches</u>; all other material is minimized or removed. By the time you are done with this section you may ask yourself the following question: *"Why don't I just copy and paste the job advertisement into my resume?"* My dear readers, it is almost that simple!

Before you learn this powerful resume style, let's review and debunk some myths about modern resume writing.

This chapter includes the following lessons:
3.1 – Modern Resume Myths
3.2 – The 4-Easy Steps to a Resume that Gets Calls
3.3 – Cover Letters

3.1: Modern Resume Myths

A resume format that works for online profiles and internal Applicant Tracking Systems (ATS) is not the same as the old resume style. This lesson discusses or debunks many myths and common beliefs about resumes.

Myth 1: The look of the resume is as important as the content.

This is not true. There are some amazing and quite beautiful templates out there for resumes that do absolutely nothing to tell the recruiter that you are qualified for the job. In addition, some of the graphic rich, grid-like resume formats can really be hurting your chances of being found because the ATS cannot read them.

To do a quick check on how your resume is being read, log in to Indeed.com and upload your resume. Also, open your Notepad on any PC, and copy and paste the resume into Notepad, which will strip the formatting. That stripped-down version is the actual output that a recruiter has from Indeed.com. It is not pretty, and some systems are designed to boot out resumes that cannot be read properly.

The look of the resume is less important than ...
- Matching content
- Matching keywords
- Matching accomplishments

Myth 2: Modern resumes should be submitted as a PDF not a Word Document

The industry standard in resume creation and submission is a Microsoft Word Document (.doc or .docx). Even the most cursory review of the job market will indicate immediately that MS Word is the mandatory resume submission format. This is true because although Adobe PDF is popular and better at retaining its format shape, the Applicant Tracking Systems cannot read a PDF document. Instead, create and submit using MSWord. (I do like to review a PDF version of a resume to catch any strange formatting issues - a great way to proofread.)

Myth 3: Resumes should be pretty to stand out.

MS Word offers some really attractive looking resume templates. Even I think they look great. BUT, these resumes do not help you stand out with online submission. In fact, they may be hurting your chances of being found by recruiters due to issues that the ATS has with grids and images. Consider keeping a "pretty" version for your in-person networking and for online use. The goal is a resume style that focuses on matching information and keywords that the systems can read.

Myth 4: Modern resumes do not need whitespace - more information is better.

The human brain needs "white space" to discern words and images. For this reason, it is critical to maintain at least a half inch margin; .75 inch is also good. If your resume is too crammed with words, the recruiter will not be able to read it. A recruiter will read the resume from left to right with the top half of the page being the most important visual space. Create a resume that presents the most important matching information first.

Myth 5: Solid lines that go from one side of the page to another are useful.

The use of lines to create visual separations is generally discouraged because the old type of ATS, which many companies still use, cannot read them. It is better to use center justifications, ALL CAPS, **bold**, and different font styles to create visual separation.

Myth 6: Dates of employment have to be month and year.

Because many candidates have dates of employment spanning less than two years, it is recommended to tab the dates over the right and use a year-to-year date format. You will, however, be required to use the month/year (xx/xxxx) format on your job applications. I recommend year-to-year on the resume and a separate document that has month/year for employment applications. Eventually, you will need it.

Myth 7: Fancy bullets are fun!

Fancy bullets are generally unnecessary for the resume. Use the standard "•". Use tabs to move copy horizontally on the page. Note that to get dates and other information justified properly on the right, the use of tabs and spaces will also be needed to get the correct alignment.

Myth 8: I can copy lines from the internet into my MS Word document with no problem.

When material is copied and pasted from the Internet, paste it into "Notepad" first to strip any background formatting and graphics, and then copy and paste into the Word document. If the formatting within an MS Word document gets difficult, select the entire document and change your paragraph spacing to "no spacing" (in the 2010 version of the program) to remove all paragraph spacing. Sometimes it is best to start over instead of fussing.

Myth 9: Tables and graphics are great!

They may be great but the ATS cannot read them. Do not put them on your resume. Use tabs instead to create columns and spacing on resumes.

Myth 10: Times New Roman Font Size 12 is the best ever!

I love the Times New Roman font but it is no longer acceptable, because "sans serif" fonts are considered the most readable modern fonts for this computer age. The recommended fonts and sizes are Arial-11, Calibri-12, Tahoma-11, and Verdana-10. The template on the video class is Verdana-10. Sometimes if I want to be fancy, I will use Garamond-14, but for headers only. (Get the template and class at www.karengurney.com/stacked)

Myth 11: The header and footer are a great place to put my contact information!

The ATS cannot read information in the headers or footers so do not use these.

Myth 12: I need my contact information on both pages.

Usually, this means putting the contact information in the header, which as I said can't be read by the ATS. It is not necessary to have your contact information on all pages of your resume.

Myth 13: It's OK to have a resume over two pages long.

The answer is no, unless it is a C.V. for an academic or scientific position that includes publications and consortium events. Studies have shown that the recruiter tends to look at the top of the resume and scan for education at the bottom on the first page. If they do not find it on the first page, they will look for it on the bottom of the second page. If they have to search, your resume goes in the trash bin. The recruiter is not going to review multiple pages of experience. The goal is to quickly show them you are a match and to get the call for an interview, not to review your entire history.

Myth 14: I need to list all 20 years of work history.

Generally speaking, you should only be listing the last ten years of work history. This can be pushed to 15 years but it is not advisable. More history tends to age the candidate and the older worker tends to have a lot of redundant or irrelevant history as well. Only keep older information if it is critical for the next job.

Here is a recap of general formatting recommendations.
- Document program: MS Word (.doc or .docx), not Adobe PDF
- Margins: One-inch standard, .75 inch, or .5 inch. Do not go too narrow
- Lines that span the page: Do not use
- Fonts and sizes: Arial-11, Calibri-12, Tahoma-11, or Verdana-10
- Spacing: Single or 1.15
- Highlights: **Bold**, CAPS, *italics*, different fonts
- Justification: Left or center
- Listing: Standard round bullets
- Indentation: Tabs and return
- Tables and pictures: Do not use
- Colors: Do not use
- Page Numbers: Do not use
- Header and Footer: Do not use

The online class has a downloadable resume example that has the correct formatting. This can be used to create your own resume. (www.karengurney.com/stacked)

<u>Myth 15. Reverse Chronology is the only way to build a resume.</u>

This one is partially true. In the classic reverse chronology resume, the recruiter focuses on the following items: Employer/Industry, Job Title, Dates of Employment. This is an issue for professionals who want or need to move out of their industry or job title, or that have gaps, too much job jumping, or even too long a tenure at a specific job. A candidate who needs to change careers often turn to the classic functional resume that focused on the skills and accomplishments. These resumes minimize mismatching industry, titles, and dates of employment.

Recruiters tend to dislike or (I will say it more strongly) *hate* functional resumes. The recruiter wants to see immediately if the candidate's most recent work experience matches the job for which the recruiter is hiring. Unfortunately, the recruiter believes that the most recent work experience is more important than the job candidate's related skills and accomplishments. Because of this, hiring practices typically reinforce square-peg, square-hole lateral moves.

The ATS-friendly Market-Based Resume Profile© combines the reverse-chronology resume with the qualities of a functional resume in a way that does not appear to hide anything.

Below is the format difference between a classic reverse-chronology resume compared to the Market-Based Resume© style. There are four differences: 1) the use of a Title Bar, 2) a Summary of Skills, 3) skill highlights, and 4) matching line items and accomplishments.

CLASSIC RESUME
- Contact information
- Objective
- Reverse-chronology work experience: highlighting job duties
- Education

MARKET-BASED RESUME©
- Contact information
- Title Bar
- Summary of Skills
- Skill Highlights
- Reverse-chronology work experience: line item accomplishments
- Education

Myth 16: I need to list every possible contact method to reach me.

The contact information includes your name, mailing address, one telephone number, and one email address. More than one of anything just clutters and does not help.

Myth 17: My email address from when I was 20 years old will work great.

Old email addresses pose a few problems. The account "handle-name" and email provider you chose 15 years ago may appear very unprofessional and outdated now. I recommend that you create an email specifically for your job hunt. Most of us are inundated with spam or even solicitations that you have signed up for, but because many employers use email now to set up a phone interview or to send you a written pre-screen, it is very easy to miss an email from an employer or the Applicant Tracking System. Make sure the email address you use is neutral sounding and is something you reliably check every day. Gmail is recommended.

Myth 18: I have to list my LinkedIn account on the resume.

This is still optional. If a LinkedIn account is listed, the profile must be optimized to support the desired position.

Myth 19: Objective or no objective?

The Title Bar, Summary of Skills, and Skill Highlights section taught in this program replace the objective and are a primary tool to beat the ATS system.

Myth 20: One resume style will make everyone happy.

One resume style and strategy gets you past the ATS to get a call for an interview, but do not expect to get great feedback about it. Resumes are extremely personal, like a work of art.

Ten people can look at one piece of artwork and have different feelings about it. Do not be surprised if a recruiter calls you on your resume and provides negative feedback about length and formatting.

The truth is if the resume got you a call, it was successful!

Welcome the feedback respectfully; potentially even make changes if the recruiter suggests it will help with continued candidacy. But in many cases the feedback is the personal taste of the recruiter. If the resume got the call, it did its #1 primary job! Its second job is to make the interview conversation easier. If the format is hampering the interview conversation, or not presenting all the relevant information in an easy-to-follow format, then it may be a signal to alter the profile.

Now it is time to start looking at resumes to see how market-based profiling works. I recommend visiting the online class to not only watch the modules but grab the example and use it as a template. (www.karengurney.com/stacked)

3.2 The 4-Easy Steps to a Resume that Gets Calls

This resume format optimizes for keywords and *skyrockets* your chances of being found in employers' systems and online by recruiters searching for you right now.

Market-Based Resume©
1. Title Bars
2. Summary of Skills
3. Skill Highlights
4. Line Item Accomplishments

3.2.1 Title Bars

This lesson could also be called **"how to include title and industry on your resume regardless of your most recent position."**

In the classic version of a resume, the "objective" section is an area right under the contact information that gives a job candidate an opportunity to state their goal in applying for a certain job. These objectives were typically weak statements that usually had nothing to do with the job advertisement. This section is completely replaced by the Title Bar, Summary of Skills, and Skill Highlights.

Title Bar Definition

A three- to six-word re-write of the goal job title typically written in bold and ALL CAPS that creates a framework for the resume profile.

The Title Bar serves the following functions:
- It uses the target job title in the resume for keyword optimization whether or not the candidate has held that title.
- It allows the resume to surface in the Recruiter's search because it is entirely based on the keywords used to find the targeted candidate.
- Once the resume surfaces, it also instantly sends a signal to the recruiter's brain that the candidate is qualified for the job.

- It allows the job applicant a method of stating the job title from the advertisement even if they have not specifically held that title.

Your most recent job title and industry is one of the primary methods that employers use to qualify a candidate for positions. Many candidates do not have a job title that is an exact fit for the position. The simple but powerful step of using a Title Bar creates a profile theme and uses the keywords that are critical to get through to the recruiter. Title bars also remind the candidate to focus on writing a matching profile for the particular job.

In the following section, I will present a recently graduated job candidate that is applying for three different positions. Based on this candidate's Core-3©, there were three great options. The item listed before the colon is the job title of the ad, and the item after the colon is the Title Bar used for the respective resume.

This candidate was a 40-year old new graduate seeking to either leverage many years of retail management for a promotion or to move in a completely new direction into Human Resources. Technically, the candidate had only one relevant title in their previous work history - Retail Manager. One of the job advertisements was seeking a Multi-Store Regional Loss Prevention Manager. The candidate had never held a position with that exact title but had done the loss prevention work. The candidate had also not held a Human Resource title but had done a lot of related work and was trying out internships as a way to break into a new field following graduation.

The process of restating the job title tells the recruiter what the resume is about and that the candidate has done this type of work. It also keyword-stacks the resume with the targeting job title so it can be found.

1. Regional Loss Prevention Manager: MULTI-STORE LOSS PREVENTION PROGRAMS
2. Human Resources Internship: HUMAN RESOURCE INTERNSHIP PROFILE
3. Retail Store Manager: RETAIL MANAGEMENT ACCOMPLISHMENTS

Exercise 3.2.1: Title Bars

In the following exercise, apply the concept of Title Bar to jobs you identified in the Core-3© Assessment.

Write the Title Bars for the start of three different resumes.
Title Bar 1 for Resume 1:_____
Title Bar 2 for Resume 2:_____
Title Bar 3 for Resume 3:_____

3.2.2 Summary of Skills

The Title Bar is the first of four steps in an ATS-friendly Market-Based Resume© Template customization. The second is the Summary of Skills section, which is the area directly under the Title Bar. When applying for jobs, the applicant should meet the following minimum thresholds to be considered qualified for the position: 1) match close to 100% of the mandated qualifications and 2) have at least 75% of the line items in the job advertisement. This second step offers an opportunity to repeat the important mandatory qualifications of the position including years of experience, the level of responsibility, and skills.

Summary of Skills Definition:
Summary of Skills is a rewrite of the <u>REQUIRED QUALIFICATIONS</u> section of the job advertisement which should include:

- Position title
- Education level
- Requested years of experience (each request)
- Level of responsibility
- Matching industry and profession focus

This serves as a direct-hit match to the required qualifications at the top of the resume where it will be read immediately.

Sometimes a job advertisement will say "3 years of 'x'" or "5 years of 'x'." You should literally write that out. This works - I have had recruiters read the Summary of Skills right back to the job candidate. Remember that these recruiters are going through hundreds of resumes a day so make it easy on them. The next exercises provide examples of appropriate Summary of Skills writing and scripts based on the three Title Bars from the previous lesson.

Exercise 3.2.2 A Summary of Skills Example Review

Use the following examples to help guide the creation of your Summary of Skills sections. Select the script that fits your situation the best for the three Market-Based Resumes© that you have started.

MULTI-STORE LOSS PREVENTION PROGRAMS
Degreed regional manager with 5+ years in drug-store loss prevention programs and 3+ years of experience specializing in employee-oriented theft, the design of sting programs, store audits, and court representation at offender prosecutions.

HUMAN RESOURCE INTERNSHIP PROFILE
New graduate with a Bachelor's degree in Business and concentration on Human Resources with 2+ years of curriculum development and 3+ years of additional recruiting, hiring and employee relations experience as a retail assistant manager, which would allow me to support the HR team immediately while also learning.

RETAIL MANAGEMENT ACCOMPLISHMENTS
Experienced retail manager with 10+ years of profit and loss responsibilities has recently graduated with a Bachelor's in Business Administration. My stores have consistently made a profit with effective merchandising, staffing, and training. In addition, I have saved money for the store through the implementation of loss prevention programs.

Exercise 3.2.2b Scripts for Creating Summary of Skills

Use the following scripts to help guide the creation of your summary of skills sections. Select the script that fits your situation the best for the three Market-Based Resumes© that you have started. This is a re-write of the mandatory requirements section of the job advertisement.

Script 1:

Degreed_____ (*position title written as a skill*) experience in _____ (*industry*) with _____ (*amount of years in the job ad*) of targeted experience in _____ (*skill 1*), _____ (*skill 2*), _____ (*skill 3*). My experience includes the _____ (*list of other skills*).

Script 2:

New Graduate_____(*level of responsibility*) with a _____ (*mandated degree*) with ___ (*years*) of _____ (*skill 1*) and also_____ (*years*) of _____ (*skill 2*).

Script 3:

Experienced _____ (*level of responsibility*) _____ (*job title*) with experience in _____ (*skill 1*). I am seeking to obtain a _____ (*job title objective*). In my work, I have _____ (*state an accomplishment that matches desired qualifications*).

*Note: this is the only place on a resume where using the first-person 'I' may be considered acceptable.

3.2.3 Skill Highlights

The Skill Highlights section is the third method that tells the recruiter a candidate is a direct-hit match to the job advertisement. This method helps preserve the classic reverse-chronology version that they prefer while still directing their attention to matching qualifications.

Skill Highlights Definition

Condensing the line items and mandatory qualifications down to two- to four-word statements focused on "hard-skills," in a 2-column format under the Summary of Skills.

This serves to repeat the "hard-skill" line items and tells the recruiter that the applicant is qualified for the job immediately.

One of the more challenging things for a candidate to do is to create and differentiate these "hard-skill" power statements when job advertisements are chock full of "soft-skill" statements. Soft-skills are important but they will not get you a call for an interview. To get found and get a job offer you need to simplify your matching technical dominance. Below is a list of soft-skills and a corresponding hard-skill list to demonstrate the difference.

Soft-Skill versus Hard-Skill Comparison	
Soft-Skills List	Corresponding Hard-Skill List
Leadership Problem Solving Technical Expertise Analytical Dependable	Multi-Unit District Manager Support Store Audit Compliance & Reporting Payroll Calculations & Submissions Inventory Management & Analysis Store Revenue Growth

The soft-skills are very important qualities but they must be demonstrated throughout the resume with hard-skill accomplishments, length of time at various jobs, job titles, and software or technical expertise. The soft-skills words are rather meaningless compared to the matching hard-skill list.

To examine this process, the book will refer back to the three resume examples. The skill highlights used for each resume are reduced to powerful keyword-stacked statements.

Exercise 3.2.3 Skill Highlights: Examples with Title Bar and Summary of Skills

MULTI-STORE LOSS PREVENTION PROGRAMS
Degreed regional manager with 5+ years in drug-store loss prevention programs and 3+ years of experience specializing in employee-oriented theft, the design of sting programs, store audits, and court representation at offender prosecutions.

Skill Highlight
Shrinkage Sting Operations
Loss Prevention Court Representation
Store Audits & Compliance
Store Revenue Growth
Inventory Management & Analysis
Staff Management & Scheduling
Hiring, Training & Development
Payroll Calculations & Accurate Submissions
Multi-Unit District Manager Support

HUMAN RESOURCE INTERNSHIP PROFILE
New graduate with a Bachelor's degree in Business and concentration in Human Resources with 2+ years of curriculum development and 3+ yeas of additional recruiting, hiring and employee relations experience as a retail assistant manager,

allowing me to support the HR team immediately while also learning.

Skill Highlight
President of Society of Human Resources (SHRM)
Human Resource Classwork
Curriculum Development
Recruiting & Staffing

RETAIL MANAGEMENT ACCOMPLISHMENTS
Experienced retail manager with 10+ years of profit and loss responsibilities, recently graduated with a Bachelor's in Business Administration. My stores have consistently made a profit with effective merchandising, staffing, and training. In addition, I have saved money for the store through the implementation of loss prevention programs.

Skill Highlight
Store Revenue Growth
Store Audits & Compliance
Staff Management & Scheduling
Hiring, Training & Development
Payroll Calculations & Accurate Submission
Inventory Management & Analysis

Exercise 3.2.3 Creating Skill Highlights: Step Three in Market-Based Resume Profile©

To create Skill Highlights follow the following steps:

1. Copy and paste the job advertisement into Notepad to strip any formatting issues.
2. Take each line item of the advertisement and look for "hard-skills."
3. Discard any "soft-skills."
4. Create a 3-word to 4-word phrase that describes each "hard-skill."
5. Use tabs to create a 2-column list of a block of skills. (Do not use the split-page or column feature in word. Use the tab key.)
6. Keep a single line for online job posting on Indeed.com and other sites that cannot preserve this formatting.
7. Use the video class to watch me break down an ad. Use the example resume as an already-formatted template for your use. (www.karengurney.com/stacked)

3.2.4   Line-Item Accomplishments

It is common for job candidates to create a list of job duties for their resume and leave it the same for each resume – this is not a good practice.

Line-Item Accomplishments Definition:

A rewrite of the line-item accomplishments in the job advertisement, ideally with quantified accomplishments.

This serves the following functions:

- The Line-Item Accomplishments are, at a minimum, a list of matching duties stripped right from the job advertisement.
- In the best scenario, the Line-Item Accomplishments are quantified statements that match the job advertisement.

In some cases, re-writing the line items from the job ad is all that is needed to get a call on the resume. It is certainly better than a list of duties that have nothing to do with the job. As a career coach, I consistently work with professionals for positions I have never worked with before. To assist those clients, I created a work-around hack to help develop their resume content.

Tip: Use another job advertisement in another city to build your resume.

Some job ads have very few line items listed. To help create your resume, search for the same title in another city. Find a job that that has a robust set of line items. Copy, paste, and re-write the list of duties. This helps to avoid plagiarism for the position you are applying for yet offers the most content to work from.

Sooner or later, you will need to learn how to quantify your accomplishments. For readers who bristle and say "my work is not quantifiable" then, at a minimum, make sure your job duties match the line items of the advertisement. Matching accomplishments will later be needed for both the interview and salary negotiation process. Therefore, it is beneficial to develop a list of accomplishments for the resume. This skill is also critical for garnering higher incomes throughout your career.

For the Retail Manager and Loss Prevention resume examples, the job candidate will review the requested line items and then capture and communicate their value for the positions based on their past roles. Below is an example of quantified accomplishments:

- Improved C-Store revenue from an average of $65,000 to $90,000 revenue per month.
- Reduced shrinkage by 15%, controlling $90,000 of C-store Inventory.
- Supervised and scheduled nine customer service hourly employees for a 24-hour business over 5 shifts: 1st, 2nd, 3rd, and two middle or carry-over shifts.
- Increased safety and health inspection passing grades by 15%.
- Prepared payroll based on a total of 365 allowed hours with a formula that is calculated to be no more than 13% of typical monthly income for a high volume store and 9 to 10% for slower stores.
- Assisted district supervisors in managing operations of 37 district stores ranging from $30,000- $90,000 per month per store in revenue.

Line-item Accomplishment statements tend to have a few things in common:

1. They have numbers that quantify the related work.
2. They focus on the end result, not the duties done, to demonstrate success.
3. They tend to be "big picture" and relate to how the accomplishment drew more revenue or saved on expenses for the organization.
4. They create a comparison of some kind to help the reader understand why this was an accomplishment.

Providing evidence, or proof of success, can translate to more calls on the resume, more offers in the interview, and more money in salary negotiations.

Exercise 3.2.4 Creating Accomplishment Statements

Follow the steps below to begin writing accomplishment statements. At a very minimum, re-write the job advertisement line items to describe your work background.

1. Copy and paste the job advertisements into Notepad.
2. Create a line under each job requirement.
3. Underneath each line write the question: "tell me about a time when you did <u>(fill in whatever the line item on the job advertisement is about)</u>."
4. Accomplishment Script: Use the following script to create accomplishment phrases.
   "I performed _____, which made or saved _____ (*money, time, or some other performance unit*). This was done better than _____ (*coworker, other teams, industry standard*) and impacted my employer positively by resulting in _____ (*achieving the employer's goal*).
5. Use growth rate percentages instead of whole numbers when the amount of units is not impressive. For instance, an increase of 10 units to 15 does not sound as impressive as a 50% increase. The growth rate equation is as follows:

Growth Rate Equation
Growth Rate (%) = ((New-Old)/Old) * 100 or

((Present-Past)/Past))*100

In our example of moving from 10 units to 15, the equation would look like the following:
((15-10)/10)*100 = 50%

6. Reduce the scripts down to simple statements.

"Improved _____ revenue from an average of $_____ to $_____ revenue per month."

"Reduced _____ by ___% controlling for $_____."

"Increased _____ by ___%."

Many candidates believe the resume and cover letter are inseparable in the job application process. A large percentage of job applicants spend more time on the cover letter than the resume. Cover Letters should not be your focus! Lesson 3.3 discusses the topic of cover letters and its relationship to the resume and job search.

3.3 Cover Letters

Cover letters have been greatly impacted by the use of online job boards and Applicant Tracking Systems. For instance, when recruiters search for a candidate, whether internally or online, a cover letter is not scanned for keywords. Since the goal here is to "double your interviews" and leverage recruiters, this means spending more time customizing the cover letter than the resume will jeopardize the ability to be found. The following section discusses and debunks myths related to their use in modern career changing.

3.3.1 Cover Letter Myths

Myth 1: Cover letters are mandatory.

Career advisors will tell you that a cover letter is necessary with every job application 100% of the time. This is not true. Research has found that 80% of candidates customize their cover letter and not their resume, yet experts estimate that less than 20% of recruiters actually read cover letters.

The rise of the ATS is reducing the importance of cover letters every single day.

The majority of job candidates who have used the methods covered in this book obtain positions without ever submitting a cover letter. Even if there is a field in the ATS to upload, that cover letter will not be scanned during a candidate search or read later by the recruiter.

Myth 2: I need to add the cover letter to the resume document if there is no space for it.

Sometimes candidates will put the cover letter in the same document as the resume. This is not a good practice unless specifically requested by the employer. The ATS may parse data to prefill fields in the application, which will not work with the cover letter potentially damaging your submission.

Myth 3: The employer adds space for an optional cover letter so they must want one.

No, when it is noted as optional it is just a reflection of employee expectations. If the employer wants one, they will tell you.

Myth 4: The Cover letter is a second opportunity to "keyword-stack."

No – because the cover letter is not scanned, use the Summary of Skills and Skill Highlights section as a great substitute for a cover letter. It is more important to make changes to the Summary of Skills section to match the job advertisement than it is to submit a cover letter, because the software will always scan the resume. Even if a cover letter is mandated, the Summary of Skills section along with the most relevant bullet points and keywords can be slightly reworded to form the cover letter.

Myth 5: If the job advertisement requires a cover letter and I do not send one, I will still be considered as a viable candidate.

Some employers do still use mandatory cover letters as an extra exercise to help weed out candidates. When a job advertisement specifically requires a cover letter, you must submit one to be considered as a candidate.

Also, if the job is something you are very interested in, a carefully customized cover letter may indicate a higher level of interest. The great news is that a good Market-Based Resume Profile© can help quickly create the cover letter.

Because cover letters extend the time it to apply for a position, they are considered part of a "quality" strategy in this program. In the job search process, a candidate should be submitting both high quality customized materials and a large quantity of general market-based profiles. As noted above, you should submit one only if it is mandated for the position.

I will be completely transparent here. A cover letter is one of the single greatest wastes of time when it comes to applying for jobs in today's hiring climate. Any information you feel is important for the cover letter should already be on the resume. It is far more important to tailor your resume to the job than to tailor a cover letter that no one will ever read.

The exercise on the next page presents a cover letter template. Change the bulleted items in the resume to read more like a composed paper instead of resume statements. The cover letter template is also available on the video class free link. (www.karengurney.com/stacked)

3.3.2 Cover Letter Template

NAME
Address
Phone • Email

Date

Employer
Employer Address

RE: (Job Title and Job ID Number if Listed)

Dear Hiring Manager,

Please accept this cover letter and resume as my application for _____ (*Job Title*) position. With over ___ years (*use the years from the job ad*) of _____ (*state the primary skill listed in the job title*) experience and _____ (*list the second more important skill or industry qualification*) I am uniquely qualified for this position.

Insert the Resume Summary of Skill Section reworded
Insert the Resume Skill Highlight 1 and Accomplishment reworded
Insert the Resume Skill Highlight 2 and Accomplishment reworded

I believe that my _____ (*state the primary skill listed in the job title*) experience combined with _____ (*list the second more important skill or industry qualification*) can make an impact on your initiatives. I look forward to speaking with you over the phone at _____ (*telephone*) or by email _____ (*a neutral sounding Gmail address used for your job hunt*).

Sincerely,

(*Your Name*)

> Homework

Download the cover letter template in this lesson from the online class. (www.karengurney.com/stacked)

- Take one job ad and write the Title Bar, Summary of Skills, and Skill Highlights to create the top of your resume.
- Add your work history only after you have created the framework for the resume from the job advertisement.
- Create a simple pre-formatted cover letter for use only when required by the employer.

Quiz 3: Resume & Cover Letter (T/F)

1. ___ The first part of the resume is about your work or education.
2. ___ The best way to submit a resume is in the Adobe PDF format.
3. ___ The resume's job is to get calls, not satisfy the recruiter's stylistic resume ideals.
4. ___ The Title Bar, Summary of Skills, and Skill Highlights replace the "Objective" line.
5. ___ Your work history should cover the line items in the job ad.
6. ___ A resume should be no more than two pages.
7. ___ Quantified accomplishments need to be on the resume.
8. ___ A single resume will work to get you hired.
9. ___ A customized cover letter and template resume is best.
10. ___ A cover letter is needed for most submissions.

Chapter 3: Answer Key (T/F)

1) False: The first part of the resume is a re-write of the job advertisement. Yes, it needs to be true to you, but it should be about the job advertisement, not you.
2) False: No, no, no, no - stop submitting PDF resumes.
3) True: If the resume got you the call it did its job no matter how the recruiter feels about the style.
4) True: The objective line is dead and even joked about among HR and resume writers.
5) True: Copy, paste, re-word, and add accomplishments matching the line items.
6) True: Your resume should not exceed two pages in most cases.
7) True: Numbers typically play well on the resume. Eventually you will have to quantify.
8) False: Ideally you customize the top of each one and have three core resumes.
9) False: Customize the resume as often as feasible and have a templated cover letter (only when requested). The resume is always scanned or read; the cover letter is never scanned and rarely read.
10) False: If a cover letter is not mandatory, do not submit one.

Chapter 4:
LinkedIn and Online Profiles That Tap the Hidden Job Market

LinkedIn and the online job boards are the engine that drives the "double your interviews and leverage the recruiters" strategy. Once the profiles we discussed earlier are optimized according to the Core 3©, then the LinkedIn profile can be created.

Recruiters are searching these databases every day to fill their open positions. In addition, most offer "quick apply" options using your profile which can ramp up your job search immediately.

LinkedIn and the online job boards allow a job candidate to tap the hidden job market in a way that has never existed before in history. When jobs were primarily advertised through the newspaper, there was no way for employers to access a database of talent for their positions. As well, before the turn of this century, to access the hidden job market of unadvertised jobs the candidate was forced to develop and maintain a network of contacts. Now employers and candidates alike can succeed by searching these databases.

Before we discuss the strategy, let's review some myths.

This chapter includes the following lessons:
4.1 – LinkedIn and online job board myths
4.2 – LinkedIn profile optimization

4.1 LinkedIn and Online Job Board Myths

Myth 1: The ATS, LinkedIn, and Online Job Boards are programmed differently.

No. The software programming of all the hiring software systems and the way recruiters search for candidates are essentially the same. However, the online job boards receive more consistent investment to help improve search results. In addition, because third party recruiters cannot tap internal company databases the amount of searching done with the online job boards is more extensive.

Myth 2: The resumes for direct application and the online profiles are different.

No. The resume you create will be used for both direct application and the online job board profiles. There are some unique aspects of LinkedIn, Indeed.com, and Monster.com (how attention is drawn to keywords, and some pre-populated box formatting issues with the resume upload) but, in essence, they are the same.

Myth 3: LinkedIn is the primary online database that recruiters use to find talent.

No, not yet. LinkedIn began as social media tool for professionals before it became heavily used for recruiting. As more and more professionals used the job board, LinkedIn started leveraging the website for revenue-generation by selling the recruiter app and employer job posting. It is the #1 job board for I.T. positions if for no other reason than because it is easy to search for certifications that are used throughout the I.T. profession. But professionals will need to leverage more than one job board to double their interviews.

Myth 4: Online job boards are better than networking for tapping the hidden job market of unadvertised jobs.

This one is actually true! Recruiters are searching these job boards every day for un-advertised jobs. A highly optimized profile on the job boards, including LinkedIn, is the most effective method an active or passive job search candidate can use to be targeted for the hidden job market. It is much easier, faster, and efficient than networking to tap this market.

Myth 5: LinkedIn is not used in a background check.

LinkedIn is used to screen, but not after an offer is made. It is more common for the recruiter to scan the LinkedIn page before even calling for an interview, so it is very important to control your professional image before you apply. LinkedIn is very important in this process, but it should not be your last stop in creating your campaign.

Each of these systems is unique in how it harnesses the power of keyword-optimization. I will discuss my three current favorites: Monster.com, LinkedIn.com, and Indeed.com. I also recommend creating profiles for niche websites like Roberthalf.com for Accounting and Finance or Teksystems for Information Technology.

4.2 Monster.com and Professional Categories

Monster.com is the original online job search database that fine-tuned the concept of professional category assignment search. Before there was keyword-search, recruiters would use professional categorization offered by Monster. What is great about Monster.com is it offers a glimpse into how the recruiter perceives the candidate. As an effective job board for your resume, Monster.com has declined in the United States but it is still hot in Canada and offers some important lessons.

Let's review some concepts that we have covered thus far. You know now that you have to help recruiters find you by optimizing your resumes and profiles for keywords and popular recruiting search terms. As a professional, you cannot be defined with just one term. Most of us do multiple duties using various skills within a single position. Most professionals are well-qualified for at least three power moves which are often in different job categories, the Core-3©. In addition, a candidate may be qualified for a step-up, step-down, or a step-over into a different industry which is another Core-3©. Let's use Monster.com to demonstrate how this operates, because it is the most robust job search database in regards to professional categorization.

When creating a profile in Monster, one of the first selections to make is that of professional categories and sub-categories. Here is the first Category and Subcategory you will find on Monster.com.

Category 1: Accounting/Finance/Insurance

Subcategories:

1. Accounts Payable/Receivable
2. Actuarial Analysis
3. Audit
4. Bookkeeping
5. Claims Review and Adjusting
6. Collections
7. Corporate Accounting
8. Corporate Finance
9. Credit review/Analysis
10. Financial Analysis/Research/Reporting
11. Financial Control
12. Financial Planning/Advising
13. Financial Products Sales/Brokerage
14. Fund Accounting
15. General/Other: Accounting/Finance
16. Investment Management
17. Policy Underwriting
18. Real Estate Appraisal
19. Real Estate Leasing/Acquisition
20. Risk Management/Compliance
21. Securities Analysis/Research
22. Tax Accounting
23. Tax Assessment and Collections

As you can see, in the **Accounting/Finance/Insurance** category there are 23 subcategories that are specialized skill sets for the candidate. An applicant will likely fit into at least three of these subcategories. Each subcategory can be Core-3©. In addition to subcategories, a job candidate may have worked across more than one primary category.

On Monster.com there are 25 categories. Listed in parentheses is the number of subcategories for each primary category.

1. Accounting /Finance/Insurance (23)
2. Administrative/Clerical (11)
3. Banking/Real Estate/Mortgage Professionals (11)
4. Biotech/R&D/Science (8)
5. Building Construction/Skilled Trades (14)
6. Business/Strategic Management (15)
7. Creative/Design (10)
8. Customer Support/Client Care (10)
9. Editorial/Writing (6)
10. Education/Training (13)
11. Engineering (14)
12. Food Services/Hospitality (9)
13. Human Resources (8)
14. Installation/Maintenance/Repair (16)
15. IT/Software Development (13)
16. Legal (9)
17. Logistics/Transportation (17)
18. Manufacturing/Production/Operations (16)
19. Marketing/Product (13)
20. Medical/Health (15)
21. Other (3)
22. Project/Program Management (5)
23. Quality Assurance/Safety(11)
24. Sales/Retail/Business Development (19)
25. Security/Protective Services (9)

A professional in Category 1: Accounting/Finance/Insurance may work on the Category 15: IT/Software, Category 16: Legal, or Category 22: Project/Program Management. The Monster database really demonstrates how many categories and sub-categories one professional can belong to. If you have been feeling pigeon-holed in your career, this should give you hope that a job or career change is possible across a span of your skills and abilities by understanding how to re-orient your profile to different categories.

Let's stop for a moment and think about this. If the recruiter is looking for an Accountant that has worked in Audit but the job candidate's current resume is focused more on their financial analysis and reporting work, the recruiter cannot find that candidate in the database even though they may want that job and are qualified. You can help the recruiter find you by making their job easier, versus hoping an employer will come across your resume and spend time figuring out if you are qualified. The easier you make it for them, the easier it will be for you.

You can double your interviews by picking the right categories, aligning the resume, and matching the profile, sometimes in less than 24 hours. The online class presents a candidate named Lisa, and we will discuss her example here. To see how I optimized her Monster.com, LinkedIn.com, and Indeed.com profiles, use your free video course link. (www.karengurney.com/stacked)

Monster.com Professional Categorization: Lisa's Example

Lisa is an accountant who worked in many accounting roles. Her latest role was as controller, one of the highest accounting titles, but the organization was small with only $4M in revenue. Lisa was willing to consider several accounting titles as long as she made over $70,000 per year. Based on her experience, that was not an issue. What was an issue, however, is that anything less than controller looked like a step back for Lisa. (We will discuss step-back strategies in Chapter 9.) However, in this case, we will focus on the ways I optimized her Monster.com profile based on the different aspects of her background.

On Monster.com, for Lisa's resume there are a number of selections under Accounting that I could pick but, like your Core-3©, Monster.com only allows you to select three at a time.

The recruiter is going to use these to narrow down their list of candidates, so it is important to try three and then rotate among your different Core-3© resume profiles (assuming that you want to do three different campaigns). For Lisa, she has done all of these subcategory options:

- Audit
- Corporate Accounting
- Corporate Finance
- Financial Analysis/Research/Reporting
- General/Other: Accounting/Finance
- Tax Accounting

For her first campaign, I focused on financial analysis and audit. So I selected Audit, Financial Analysis/Research/Reporting, and to be sure I caught all possible inquiries, also General/Other: Accounting/Finance. Lisa has worked in different categories that are unique to an industry, like product licensing. If the market was good for those skills, I would try a later campaign focused on subcategories of her other qualifications. Monster.com has the most developed method of all the job boards of narrowing down a job candidate's skills for professional categorization. Even though Indeed.com is more popular than Monster.com in the United States, this particular job board really emphasizes the importance of "categorizing" your resume so that the recruiter can find you and say "this person is qualified."

I do need to add one last caveat: Monster.com, and increasingly Indeed.com, tends to generate a lot of spam emails. No matter the profile, a professional will get calls for sales positions. Ignore any emails or calls that do not specify a title related to your resume.

4.3 LinkedIn.com Profile Optimization

LinkedIn is best known as a social network representing your professional life. However, as we know now, recruiters are using it to source passive and active job candidates. To increase the likelihood of being found, and to also properly represent your career, LinkedIn offers many sections you can add to your profile. Some of these qualifications are important for recruiters to find you and, after they find you, pre-qualify you as a candidate. This is a listing of sections that require your attention.

1. Profile picture
2. Headline
3. Geographic setting (i.e. City)
4. Industry
5. Connections

6. Summary of Skills
7. Work history
8. Education
9. Certifications
10. Skills (Recommendations)
11. Endorsements
12. LinkedIn job alert preferences
13. Recruiter push

In the following section, I will review each of these, and will offer a strategy and compare it to what I did for Lisa. You may not want your current employer or network to be notified of what changes you have made to your profile; you can turn the "Notifications" off. The changes will still be public but an alert will not be sent to your network.

Profile Picture

Needless to say, your profile picture is the first impression that a recruiter uses to understand who you are across a broad dimension of demographics. In the United States, we do not put pictures on our resumes as happens in other countries. Because of this, LinkedIn is often cross-referenced by recruiters even when a candidate has directly applied to the employer. Technically this increases the type of demographic bias that U.S. employers are supposed to avoid. However, the option is to either have no profile at all or to control your online image using LinkedIn.

My recommendation is to find a local photographer that specializes in talent headshots to take your picture. This means no JCPenney and Sears photography, or friends taking your picture at the local park. When Googling to find the right photographer, search for the word "headshots" or "talent photography" in your city. An appointment with a true headshot or talent professional will include a makeup artist/hair stylist and numerous outfit changes. Do not leave the face of your professional career to a selfie on your phone. Get professional hair, makeup, and photography.

I also use a free profiling tool, Carol Tuttle's *Dressing Your Truth*, to identify my client's power-colors and style. Google her program. This image coach has built an impressive free analysis tool that will help you identify your power color and style. You do not need to join her program to identify your type, but you may want to for additional information. For my clients who do not want to join this program, I Google their "type" with the word "Pinterest." There are other people who share your type and who have created boards for different styling. There are Pinterest boards for both men and women, and Tuttle's program applies to both.

Headline

Your headline should be very similar to the Title Bar on your resume. LinkedIn will generate a headline from your most current position, but that is not what you want to use. Unless it is "Product Manager" at General Electric or some other well-respected business, it is best to create this on your own.

After you perform the Core-3© assessment, identify a stream of jobs, and write the resume to the job, you will have the right headline for LinkedIn sitting right at the top of your resume. This can be typed in CAPS or first word capitalization. Play around until it displays the way you want. Note: LinkedIn will override what you put in with your most recent position unless you uncheck the box. This can be annoying, so you may want to wait until you input your work experience to do the final tweak on the LinkedIn profile.

Lisa Headline Example on the Online Class:

In the class, Lisa's headline is "Financial Forecasting Analyst." This is good because that matches the direction she wants to go in, however if she decided to focus on Controller jobs, she might use Controller, Financial Planning and Analysis (FP&A) and/or Audit headlines. You always want to focus on a headline that matches your primary goal position for your campaign. This can always be changed and rotated for different campaigns.

Geographic Setting

At the top of your profile, under your headline, there is an option to set your city. As you know, where you live is an important search keyword for the recruiter. If you want to get calls choose the city where you want to work, not where you live. You may feel this is dishonest and I know this is not ideal, but on a base strategic level, to double your interviews where you want to work you have to match the selections made by the recruiter.

Industry

The industry selection is the one I dislike the most on LinkedIn for many of the same reasons as the geographic selection. If you recall from the Monster.com training, Monster offers hundreds of professional subcategories as well as industry settings, which I largely ignore. What *you* actually do is your professional category. What your *company* does is your industry. These are totally different aspects of your qualifications, but LinkedIn only offers one selection, which makes recruiter search by category difficult, if not impossible. My recommendation is to choose the closest selection to what you want to be doing professionally (professional category) not the type of industry you want to be working in. For instance, I selected Human Resources because that is how the market perceives my work. Technically, from my perspective, my work falls more under Professional Training and Coaching. This is a balancing act - you must think about the most likely selection by the recruiter. In the case of LinkedIn, most recruiters bypass industry and focus on keywords and the other selections anyway.

Connections

LinkedIn is about being social, which means connecting with the people you know. There is a baseline of connections of 500+. My recommendation is to get to 500+ as quickly as possible. This means loading your email lists and then, as people connect with you, using the LinkedIn "recommended connection" opportunity to connect with many more cross-connections. When performing a connection campaign, you may get an interview if the headline is set correctly, especially for digital marketing and sales people. However, my goal here is primarily to make you appear "highly-connected" or popular. You may not in general be interested in "being popular," but for your job search, this indicates a networked person that is dedicated to developing professionally. That is the message you want to send.

Summary of Skills

LinkedIn offers a Summary of Skills section. Copy and paste the top part of your carefully crafted resume to attract a certain type of job. The goal of this section is to keep the recruiter focused on your matching skills when their search produces you as a candidate. In our online class example, Lisa wants to focus on financial analyst and forecasting roles versus "Controller" positions. Therefore, she pasted the top of her resume right into the summary of skills along with the headline for the resume. You will need to do some formatting to make sure it looks correct.

Lisa's Summary of Skills Example from the Online Class

FINANCIAL FORECASTING ANALYST PROFILE
From working in managerial accounting, financial accounting, and financial analyst roles, I have developed a strong acumen for analyzing, forecasting, and budgeting organizational finances specifically for system implementation, process improvement, new product development, lending, cash flow, and expenses. I specifically did the work with Mitsubishi Caterpillar Forklift America, the most related industry to this position. In every position I have held, I presented the most detailed forecasted comparisons for evidence-based managerial decision-making that generates revenue and saves money.

Forecasting: Sales & Cost of Goods Sold
Internal Control Systems

Internal Reporting: P&L and Balance Sheet
Daily & Annual Cash Flow Analysis
Cost Analysis
Bank Financing
Internal Audit
Variance Identification
Systems Evaluation & Implementation
International Billing Policy
Month End Close

Lisa's Summary of Skills tends to be more simplified but, in this case, I really wanted to point the employer's attention to her Mitsubishi work that was closely related. Since it was at least three positions in the past, they might have missed it. You can use this top portion of your resume and the Summary on LinkedIn to laser-focus the recruiter's attention. You can also make this general to fit into different companies that may view your profile.

Work History

There are two aspects of the work history that are important: The LinkedIn "generated title" selections and "years of experience."

Title Selection

The LinkedIn system generates title options that will be slightly different from the title you have. Use the closest-match LinkedIn pre-formulated titles to improve your ability to be found. Consider selecting titles that reflect your goal position versus your actual title (within reason). Your LinkedIn profile is not a legally binding application; the goal is to be found, and using the system the way it is designed improves those chances.

The next area of concern is "years of experience." If the job advertisements are requesting five or ten years of experience, it may make sense to consolidate all of your experience with one company under the most recent title. To improve honesty in representation, create a "title transition history," a list of your title progression with dates, under the one title. In most cases, it is better to have one single employer with all years of experience in one post and list the title transition under that post, rather than to separate them out.

The one exception would be if you have only worked for one employer. In that case, showing a promotion history breaks up the profile and shows upward progression, which may be a more positive tactic. Whichever strategy is selected, remember to present what matches your goal position. Any random or unrelated positions, short term temporary positions, or even work detail that does not support your goal position should be left off the profile. The overall strategy: think of LinkedIn as a brochure for the job you want versus a legally binding job application. What would you put on that brochure?

Education

Do not include your high school education. Once you have your Bachelor's degree, it is no longer important to display an Associate's, unless that program is directly related to the goal position. Education is not a primary search term, but a baseline degree is a pre-requisite for most professional positions. For the most part, it is not necessary or even desirable to list anything below a Bachelor's degree.

Certifications

Certifications are critically important to hiring and also serve as a keyword search item. Make sure your certifications are listed on your LinkedIn profile and your resume. When seeking jobs, use certifications as a primary search term to uncover new streams of opportunities. You may also consider adding an important certification to your last name space on LinkedIn so that it displays immediately. You can do the same with the resume. This is ideal for a Certified Public Accountant (CPA) or any role that requires mandated licensing to perform the work.

Skills & Endorsements

LinkedIn offers an opportunity to list skills that people can easily endorse. Endorsements are not recommendations, which are a more detailed write-up; these are "hard" skills that are likely to be searched as a keyword. The system allows you to input them and periodically will ask connections to endorse those skills. The best way to get more endorsements on a skill is to endorse someone else's skill. This prompts a system email to request the person that you endorsed to in turn endorse you. Do not let LinkedIn generate these and leave it to chance! Create "hard skill" endorsements that match the job you want and then start endorsing your friends so they will be prompted to endorse your skills.

Recommendations

After the profile is created, invite people to write recommendations. As a consultant, these have been extremely valuable to me and they are also quite effective for candidates. Although recommendations will not necessarily help the recruiter find you, they do help recruiters evaluate you as a candidate during the selection process. In 2017, Linkedin rolled out a new version which temporarily eliminated this section. The plan is to bring it back at a later date.

Set Your Job Alert Preferences

Indeed.com is the most important website to set up customized job alerts because it aggregates job postings from multiple websites offering the most robust job market information. However, more companies are posting jobs on LinkedIn, and Indeed.com at this time does not pull those jobs. In LinkedIn, click on Jobs and then Preferences to set up job alerts for positions posted by companies.

Set the locations of interest, the range of your level of professional ability, and in the section that asks for industry, select your professional ability as well as industry. If LinkedIn does not have an item as a category, you will not be able to add it. This section is limited and honestly, not my favorite. LinkedIn's industry list is not as robust as it should be but you can still select as many professions and industries that make sense.

Set Up Recruiter Push "Let Your Next Job Find You"

Buried underneath the job alert preferences is a handy little hidden section that allows you to notify recruiters of your job interests for 90 days.

Go to the Jobs and then Preferences on LinkedIn and then under the job alerts is a section that says "Let Your Next Job Find You."

- *Share career interests with recruiters?* Switch this to "On."
- *What field are you interested in?* Choose the best option from the list that matches your professional background. Choices are limited - do your best.
- *What roles would you like to be considered for?* Pick at least three titles that surfaced from your Core 3©. (LinkedIn has to have the title in its database for this to work. Start typing and select from the auto-generated titles.)
- *What job types are you interested in (Check all that apply)?* Full-time, Part-time, Contract, Internship, Remote, Freelance
- *When can you start?* Anytime
- *Share your job preferences?* On

There are more advanced features for LinkedIn that are explored in later chapters but they take much longer. The goal in this chapter is to get a highly optimized job search campaign up and running as fast as possible that will draw recruiters to you and, when you apply for jobs, will provide a profile that matches the resume.

4.4 Indeed.com and the Top of Your Resume

It is no secret by now that Indeed.com is a career coach's best friend. Because the database aggregates from other websites along with employers posting into the system directly, Indeed.com is the database of choice for job research. There are many reasons that a job applicant needs to be on this site:

- Job research,
- Job alerts,
- Salary survey,
- Posting a searchable resume that recruiters can find, and
- Indeed "quick-apply" job submissions.

Job Research

In chapters one and two, we discussed the importance of aligning resumes and profiles with core skill sets sought by recruiters. The goal is to get calls for jobs without applying, double your interviews, make easier career transitions, experience reduced periods of unemployment, obtain pay increases, and find more rewarding work by matching background to market need. Indeed.com can help with this and more.

Job Alerts

There is an email bar on the upper right hand side of the page where you can enter your email and it will send alerts for new jobs fitting the criteria you set. Your own self-generated job alerts (using the right search terms for the stream of jobs in your Core-3©) are much more reliable than the system-generated ones.

Salary Survey

In Chapter 7 on salary negotiation, I will cover how to use Indeed.com to perform a salary survey, a critical skill in salary quoting and negotiations.

Resume Posting

In addition to seeking jobs and market information, you can also post resumes which are searchable by employers. My candidates are increasingly getting job interviews from recruiters that are identified through a search of the Indeed.com database. In 2016, it appears that recruiters are leaving Monster.com and moving quickly to Indeed.com. The more job applicants using a database, the more attractive it is to recruiters.

Whether you are in an active or passive job search, your resume needs to be on Indeed.com. One of the great things about Indeed.com is that an applicant can really see how an Applicant Tracking System parses data. When a system user uploads a resume, the ATS pre-populates fields just as employer's tracking software does. This is one great method to identify resume formats that may not work well in the system.

There are a few things to be aware of with resume posting on Indeed.com. The output that the employer sees is absolutely awful. To see what an employer sees, open notepad, then go into your resume and click CTRL-A to highlight everything, CTRL-

C to copy everything, and then go back to notepad and select CTRL-V for paste. This will demonstrate exactly what an employer sees. Because of that, once an employer identifies a candidate, they will often request a resume formatted in a readable manner.

There is one more drawback to the Indeed.com resume upload system. The top of the resume as taught in this book gets removed or pushed to a bottom section, and the skills or certifications are not broken out by the system. Therefore, extra work will be needed to make sure all of the correct information is present. Copy and paste your Summary of Skills and put it under the headline section by your contact information. It will also be necessary to break out each skill and add how many years you have done it.

All of this work is definitely worth it. Once the resume is uploaded correctly and the skills and certifications are broken out, a recruiter can find you more easily in the system based on keyword-search.

Indeed.com "Quick-Apply"

The Quick Apply option is one of the most effective ways to get calls quickly. Many employers allow the user to rapidly apply using their Indeed.com profile or by doing a simple upload of a resume. The higher level the position, the less likely for this option to be available, but for most positions under $80,000 per year this is often an option. There is no faster way to get the calls rolling in right away.

4.5 Other Job Boards & Niche Staffing Websites

Other job boards tend to have fewer options to ensure a recruiter can identify a candidate. It is a good idea to search for and use databases that may be hot in your geographic area. Even more important than other job boards are niche sites based on profession.

Niche Staffing Firms and Professional Organization Websites

There are certain fields that have entire staffing firms dedicated to professional placement or that have professional organizations with a career section. For instance, when I have an applicant in Accounting and Finance, I use the Core-3©, determine which stream of jobs we want to go for, write the resume to that profile, adjust LinkedIn, Monster, Indeed and then I post their resume on www.roberthalf.com or other local recruiting firms specializing in the profession.

Another example of a niche site is the "New England Journal of Medicine" for physicians, or the American Society of Training and Development for the corporate Organizational Development (O.D.) fields. As you search for jobs, the various staffing firms that represent different jobs will pop up. Do not overlook these powerful sources of jobs.

Government and Universities

Most local, state, and federal government positions are not advertised on the popular job boards. Since most universities are public institutions within the government retirement system, they are included in this list. My public institution colleagues indicate the reason that these jobs do not appear on Indeed.com, LinkedIn.com, or other popular websites is because there are limited funds for posting jobs, and sometimes there are even regulations prohibiting paid advertising. Whatever the reason, if you want a public job you will need to create a profile and job alert on www.usajobs.gov and/or www.governmentjobs.com.

There is no great 'universal website' for jobs in higher education that every institution uses for all of their open positions. Therefore, it takes more effort to identify the potential jobs at community colleges and universities. For this strategy, create separate accounts with each target institution.

>Homework

- Review the video class for LinkedIn and Job Board optimization. (www.karegurney.com/stacked)
- Identify your job boards and open accounts with same login.
- Create the LinkedIn.com profile by hand.
- Post your resume and optimize the accounts.

Quiz 4: LinkedIn and Online Job Portals (T/F)

1. ___ Recruiters only call on actively applying professionals.
2. ___ Professional Category and Industry are the same thing.
3. ___ The online job boards are the "engine" of the double your interview strategy.
4. ___ The advantage to Monster.com is superior professional categorization options.
5. ___ Monster's disadvantage is spammy emails.
6. ___ LinkedIn is the most popular site for recruiters.
7. ___ Indeed.com is becoming more popular because more job applicants are using it.
8. ___ Indeed.com does not need to be tweaked, just upload the resume and apply.
9. ___ System-generated job alerts are as good as manually-created ones.
10. ___ "Quick Applies" in Indeed.com kick off the campaign.

Chapter 4: Answer Key (T/F)

1) False: Recruiters call on "passive" candidates every day.

2) False: What you do is profession. What your company does is industry.

3) True: The online job boards, when optimized, get you more calls.

4) True: Monster.com has the best professional categorization for recruiter search.

5) True: Unfortunately, a job candidate will need to manage some spam.

6) False: LinkedIn is the most popular source for I.T. recruiting. Indeed is very popular for other professions but an applicant needs to leverage multiple job boards.

7) True: Recruiters naturally gravitate towards the most populated active job boards.

8) False: Indeed.com needs two tweaks: 1) Add the Title Bar, Summary of Skills, and Skill Highlights to the job detail of the most recent position so that the output will reflect your actual resume and 2) add unique skills.

9) False: Always create your own alerts based on your Core-3© strategy.

10) True: Yes, use the "Quick-Applies" to get things going.

Chapter 5
"Double Your Interviews"
Campaign Kickoff

The goal of this chapter is to set up the exercises in order of completion, to create an effective campaign within a few hours. This is also a recap and complete strategy to double your interviews in the shortest amount of time possible.

For the purpose of this section, we will skip the myths and get right to the strategy.

This chapter includes the following lessons:

The 10-Steps to the "Double Your Interviews" Campaign Kickoff
5.1 – Core-3© Assessment
5.2 – Setup Job Alerts
5.3 – Breakdown Job Ads
5.4 – Line Item Accomplishments
5.5 – LinkedIn Profile
5.6 – Post Resume to Job Boards
5.7 – User Indeed.com and LinkedIn 'Quick-Apply'
5.8 – Apply to at least 10 Jobs
5.9 – Ongoing Applications
5.10 – Manage Phone & Email Screens

Exercise 5.1 Core-3© Assessment

Select a few search terms from your background on Indeed.com. Common terms relate to software, certifications, industry phrases, and titles. Use the job ads to identify more search terms that were not on your original list. Search by the new terms and expand the list of possible power career changes. Once you identify the search terms that produce the best stream of jobs, create your own job alerts.

Exercise 5.2 Set Up Job Alerts

Set up your own job alerts to stay current on new job postings.
1. Perform a search of your terms and verify that the results support your goals.
2. Enter your email to set up job alerts.
3. You will be sent a confirmation email.
4. The alert can be cancelled at any time.
5. Use these alerts to stay on top of new potential jobs within your parameters versus the unreliable system-generated alerts.

Exercise 5.3 Breakdown Job Ads and Create Top of Resume

From similar jobs, create a composite Market-Based Resume© to one stream or multiple streams of jobs.
1. Break down the job ads into core keywords, phrases, and qualifications.
2. Write a Resume Title Bar/Headline.
3. Write a one- to three-line Summary of Skills straight from the mandatory qualifications.

4. Create a list of matching "Skill Highlights" that are two- to four-word breakdowns of the line items and mandatory qualifications.
5. Do this for each resume matching the Core-3© strategy.

Exercise 5.4 Line Item Accomplishment Work History & Education

Complete the resume by inserting your work history and education for each profile.

1. Rewrite each line item in the job and when possible add a quantified accomplishment related to each line item.
2. Write about the relevant work experience over about 10 years.
3. Leave out unrelated work unless this creates a gap.
4. Add your education towards the bottom of the resume.
5. What matters is what matches the requirements. Avoid unrelated details.

Exercise 5.5 LinkedIn Profile

Now use the resume to create the LinkedIn profile.

1. Use the resume's Title Bar to make the LinkedIn profile headline.
2. Select the goal city.
3. Select your profession (not industry) from the industry setting.
4. Copy and paste the resume's Summary of Skills into the LinkedIn Summary of Skills (correct any alignment issues).
5. Create work history, but consider consolidating positions within one company into one posting.

6. Let the system present the closest matching title to your goal title. (LinkedIn is more like a brochure than legally-binding application.)

7. Enter your Bachelor's degree and higher (or your Associate's degree if you have no Bachelor's degree). Do not add high school.

8. Enter Certifications.

9. Create individual skills that other people can endorse.

10. Connect with over 500 people using your email and suggested connections.

11. Endorse other people's skills so that they will be prompted to endorse yours.

12. Seek out detailed recommendations.

13. Set up custom job alerts.

14. Set up recruiter push.

Exercise 5.6 Post Resume to Job Boards and Tweak

In the following exercise, follow the steps to post your resume to multiple job boards.

1. Identify the job boards that are popular to your area or industry field. As stated earlier, the most popular national websites are:
   - www.Indeed.com
   - www.Monster.com

2. Tweak the resume to make sure it looks good and keyword-stack the Indeed.com profile by breaking out skills.

3. Identify niche job boards, professional organizations, and staffing agencies.

Exercise 5.7 Use Indeed.com or LinkedIn 'Quick-Apply'

Once the LinkedIn and Indeed.com profiles are created:

1. Search for jobs and apply for all of the "Apply through LinkedIn" or "Easily Apply with Indeed" to get as many applications out there quickly as possible.
2. Customize the top of your resume when a job is of particular interest.

Exercise 5.8 Apply to at least 10 Jobs Immediately

The auto-apply function allows a job candidate to get the ball rolling immediately. There will be a number of great jobs that do not have a "quick-apply" option. The goal for the initial job search boost should be at least ten matching jobs for the campaign kick-off.

Exercise 5.9 Ongoing Applications

1. The manually created job alerts will continue to send new jobs as they become available.
1. Your online profiles will be available for recruiters to locate when they are searching for jobs related to the keywords in the position.
2. Perform "quick-apply" and manual applications every two weeks.
3. Applying for jobs takes both quality and quantity. Plan on applying for many, but with a matching profile.

Exercise 5.10 Manage Phone & Email Screens

The campaign kick-off will generate emails and calls from your direct application and also from recruiters searching your type of profile. You need to control these calls.

1. Prepare for every phone screen as if it were an in-person interview.
2. The following chapter will cover phone screen preparation and the rest of the job acquisition process.

>Homework

Complete the steps in the Campaign Kickoff.

Quiz 5: Double Your Interview Campaign (T/F)

1. ___ The first step to doubling your interviews is the Core-3© Assessment.

2. ___ System-generated job alerts are as good as the ones you manually create.

3. ___ The top of the Market-Based Resume© leverages the job advertisement.

4. ___ Your work experience should be a re-write of the line items of the targeted job.

5. ___ The resume you create is used to build the LinkedIn profile.

6. ___ You can post the resume to the job boards with no tweaks.

7. ___ The "quick-applies" on Indeed.com and LinkedIn.com do not work well.

8. ___ Quality is more important than quantity of applications.

9. ___ You can rely solely on recruiter search and not worry about direct-applications.

10. ___ You will only get calls for the jobs you apply for.

Chapter 5: Answer Key (T/F)

1) True: Your success begins with finding the right job ads for your background.

2) False: A human is still more intuitive than a computer. Create your own alerts.

3) True: The top of the Market-Based Resume© is a rewrite of the job advertisement and it is CRITICAL to doubling your interviews.

4) True: Forget "job duties" and focus on re-writing and capturing accomplishments that directly match the line items of various related jobs.

5) True: The Market-based Resume© is used to build the LinkedIn profile.

6) False: Most job boards, especially Indeed.com, will require some tweaking.

7) False: Quick-applies spur the job search.

8) False: You need both a quantity and quality strategy.

9) False: You will need to perform on-going applications to keep your campaign alive.

10) False: You will get calls for all sort of jobs and it is very important to control these telephone calls and emails using the information in this book.

Chapter 6:
Phone Screens &
Interview Preparation

The methods taught in this book will stimulate calls that require cutting edge interview and salary negotiation strategies. This section explores the common myths and beliefs about the interview process.

*Note: This section works in conjunction with Chapter 7: Salary Negotiations. Both chapters should be reviewed prior to taking a phone screen or even before applying for jobs.

This module includes the following lessons:
6.1 – Interview Myths
6.2 – Phone Screen Interview
6.3 – Common Phone Screen & Interview Questions
6.4 – Reason for Each Question & Strategy
6.5 – Phone Screen Question Turn-Around Cheat Sheet
6.6 – Interview Worksheet Scripts
6.7 – Explaining Terminations and Dismissals
6.8 – Behavioral Interview Questions
6.9 – Questions for Them
6.10 – What Not to Say
6.11 – Building an Interview Portfolio or Project
6.12 – "Thank You" Letter

6.1 Interview Myths

Myth 1: The ability to do the job is the primary focus of phone screen interview questions.

No - the resume has already pre-qualified the candidate. Although these skills will be verified, there are two other primary questions on the mind of the recruiter.

1. Will this candidate be a happy, productive, and non-disruptive employee?
2. Is this candidate stable and willing to remain in the position for at least two years?

To get these answers, the recruiter will ask a list of common interview questions that seem innocent but are the source of most candidate rejection. The phone screen has little to do with your ability to do the job.

Myth 2: The most capable employee is the one that gets the job offers.

The reality is that the person who wins the job is not always the most capable job candidate. The winner is the candidate who performs the best in the interview, and the majority of that performance is based on the content of their answers.

Myth 3: You can get a job that you are not sure you want.

Job candidates tend to talk themselves out of applying or interviewing for jobs because they are unsure about the position. If they are unprepared to interview, they will naturally want to know more about the job before saying they want the position. Uncertainty kills great career moves because employers only want to hire people who want the job.

Tip: My recommendation is to treat every job as if it were your dream job until you have enough information to determine otherwise.

The hiring process may be easier to understand for those readers who have done sales. Hiring is similar to sales in that the candidate needs a pipeline of opportunities. The rule of thumb in sales is closing 4% of opportunities. Although the pipeline for hiring does not need to be as wide and deep, it is more advantageous if the job candidate is talking to more recruiters, hiring managers, and employers versus focusing on one single lead (company and position).

Once you get the job offer, then you can decide to decline or accept based on the offer and interview experience. Go for it, be excited, and be flexible, and then when the job offer rolls in, negotiate, accept, or walk away.

Myth 4. Interviewers ask you what they want to know.

No. There are few times when the recruiter asks straightforward questions about a person's background and tells the applicant their concerns about their candidacy.

The majority of the time, the interviewer will ask other common questions to uncover the true goals and attitude of the job candidate. That is why so many interview questions are strange and seem like they have nothing to do with your work experience. The more conscious, aware, and prepared you are for these questions, the more likely you are to get a job offer from the interview.

Myth 5. The phone screen is a "nothing" interview

The phone screen is actually the most challenging of all interviews because the employer is actively using the call to remove candidates. You as the candidate have to perform well and be excited about a job that you know little or nothing about, and you typically are forced to perform these interviews in a distracted state - while driving, working, during childcare, or even when resting. An unprepared, distracted, or uncertain job candidate does not move forward.

Myth 6. The recruiter has been trained how to interview.

Even though there are books and consultancies dedicated to helping hiring managers to overcome making decisions based on their unconscious emotional reactions to candidates, in most cases, the interviewer will have had little formal training. This module teaches you how to control the interviewer's unconscious reactions to give them what they need to choose you!

Myth 7. If I am applying for the job, then it is obvious that I will stay in it.

No, your application does not mean you will stay. Your job transitions tell the employer how likely it is that you will stay on the job. No matter what you actually say, they will use your transition history as the "truth."

Early in your career it is acceptable to have two up to even five two-year positions. However, by the time you are in your thirties, you are expected to have "found" yourself. The employer will rely on your job transition history to predict the length of time you will stay in the job unless you make an exceptional effort to explain why this job will be different. That is why job transitions are silent job killers, and why we see questions about your reason for leaving during the applications, phone screens, and interviews. It is a never-ending process to explain yourself.

The resume already presents a story to the recruiter. If a candidate switches jobs frequently, or even at regular intervals, this indicates to the recruiter that the candidate will leave in a similar timeframe. If this is a step down, meaning the candidate appears overqualified for the job, the recruiter is almost always worried about the candidate leaving when they find a job of greater responsibility or pay. If the career change is completely different, the recruiter may feel they have no evidence at all that the candidate will remain in the position. The more work you do to create a storyline that explains your job transitions in a way that supports the position you are interviewing for, the better the job hunt will be.

Myth 8. Work happiness and joyful happiness are the same thing.

This is definitely not true. The recruiter is concerned about whether the candidate will be happy on the job. Being happy does not mean being joyful. In this case, it means being a consistent producer that does not make trouble for the managers or team members. If the job candidate states that their most difficult person or challenge is similar to the current team environment, this may indicate that the employee will not be happy. If the candidate is accustomed to working for a large organization and is applying at a small one, this may cause the employee unhappiness. Any answer or previous background that does not match the new job can be a signal to the employer that the candidate will be unhappy, unproductive, and disruptive. To diffuse this issue, your answers should indicate how you solved problems and worked with a wide range of people. In addition, it is important to not become rattled or upset during the interview.

<u>Myth 9: The in-person interview will focus on technical questions related to the job.</u>

Yes, but technical questions tend to come after the common interview questions. There is a portion of the interview that will focus on all the reasons not to hire you. These are the three silent job killers: job transitions, goals, and salary. All of the common interview questions are designed to determine what is "wrong" with the candidate. The other portion will examine your technical abilities (which can include a review of work history) and increasingly also behavioral questions.

Behavioral questions are a psychological blend of interview methodologies to uncover if you are capable but also indicate if you will stay and be a happy employee. Instead of asking, "Tell me about a time you did (technical ability)", the interviewer will ask you something like, "Tell me about a time you had to solve a problem related to (technical ability)."

131

These questions tend to put the candidate in a defensive position and often leave a great, qualified candidate stumped. This should not be the goal of an employer who is seeking top talent, but this trend is not going to change any time soon. The key to successful behavioral interviews is to take the line items of the job ad and plug them right into the behavioral questions to come up with great work samples. These robust and targeted work examples win jobs. Even if behavioral interview questions are not asked, this preparation will give you the type of content employers love.

Myth 10. I only need to prepare and practice my answers.

There are two aspects of interview preparation: 1) content for answers and 2) performance related to appearance, speech, and physical mannerisms. Every case is highly individualized, but the best advice is to "look" like the job you are going for, even if that means sitting outside the offices before your interview to see what people wear to work. A good program to search and sign up for is Carol Tuttle's free "Dressing Your Truth" which teaches you your power colors, clothes, and more.

Myth 11: I can wear the same clothes to an interview that I typically wear to work.

This is often not true. Once we have been at an employer for a long time our image tends to decline. It is the same thing as when we go to sell a house - it often looks cleaner and better decorated the day we put it on the market than any day that we lived in it.

Wear a suit that is reflective of the professional environment. Dress better, but not too much better, than the people coming out of the office. If the organization is casual, wear a casual suit anyway, just to be safe.

Tip: Buy new clothes to interview in, visit the salon or barber, and make sure you look almost as good as you would on your wedding day.

The interview is like dating for a work marriage. Make sure you look better than you normally would for a day at the office. If you are not feeling good about yourself, then you will need to "fake it 'til you make it."

<u>Myth 12. I can be honest about the negative things that happened at my previous job. The interviewer asked me, so I need to be honest.</u>

Candidates want to be able to reveal all the bad things that have happened to them and still get hired. Companies want to eliminate candidates with "bad things" in their background. What is ironic about the "honesty" issue is that employers are afraid of being lied to, and in most cases, candidates tend to be ultra-honest and discuss things that have no place in the interview.

The interview is a not a "tell-all" session; it is a performance. Know that you cannot be angry or say negative things in an interview and get an offer for a job.

Even though you will be asked about having a difficult time with a coworker, supervisor, or with work performance, it is important to create and practice specific answers that are true but may not be the first ones you would like to talk about with the prospective employer. Focus on great work examples that show problem solving based on the recommendations in the following lessons.

Myth 13. Practicing and memorizing interview answers sounds robotic.

Conventional wisdom might say that practicing interview answers sounds robotic, however Human Resource and hiring managers often share that if candidates take time to prepare for their interviews it translates to being interested in the position. Just as you would prepare for a presentation at school or work, so must you prepare for this important one-time performance. Record yourself on a webcam and practice with a friend or college career office. Practice, practice, practice!

Myth 15. I can prepare for every single possible interview question.

Unfortunately, this is impossible. This interview preparation course is not designed to include a comprehensive listing of every interview situation. If you pick up an interview book, you will find hundreds of questions listed. The goal of preparation is to have a strategy for the biggest problem areas candidates experience and the most challenging questions, in order to be prepared for surprise questions with grace and ease.

Myth 16. The interview is a 2-way evaluation where the candidate also assesses the company, the position, the salary, and the benefits package.

No, the interview is not a 2-way evaluation. It is a sales pitch by the candidate about how they match what the company wants so they can get the offer. Only when the candidate achieves the offer does this turn into a 2-way discussion.

Myth 17. I am my own worst enemy in my interview.

Yes, this one is unfortunately true. It is not just in the interview - job candidates sabotage their own job search progress every day in the following ways:

1. Pre-deciding whether a role is good or bad before applying.
2. Pitting one job offer against another to appear more attractive.
3. Taking the stance that "you are interviewing the employer as much as they are interviewing you."
4. Not preparing for job interviews using the strategies I will teach you.
5. Think about your job search as if it were online dating.

These tactics do not result in a great dating relationship and they will not get you hired either.

- Will you meet someone if you sit in your home and not reach out to anyone?
- Can you tell if someone is great just by looking at their picture or reading a brief profile?

- Once you do reach out, would you tell a prospective date that you are playing the field?
- Would you tell a good prospect that you might have a better option waiting in the wings if they make you a better offer?
- Would you tell your current spouse (i.e. your current employer) that someone is more interesting to you and they need to come up with reasons for you to stay?

Apply, be open, tell each employer they are your "preferred option," and remain enthusiastic until they propose (make an offer). Then, and only then, can you evaluate the option based on everything you have seen and heard.

6.2 Phone Screen Interview

So far we have covered how recruiters use electronic systems, both their internal software and also the online job boards, to source candidates. You also know that you can use these systems to your advantage to double your job interviews with the campaign kickoff process.

All of this work leads to one thing: phone screens (and increasingly email, written, and video screens).

Have you ever had a phone interview that seemed to go so well you were a shoe-in for the position, and then you never got a call back? We are about to explore the human psychology around interviewing and how to turn a lackluster performance into an interview performance that lights up the recruiter's mind so that they are silently saying "yes, yes, yes."

If you knew how many unprepared, nonresponsive candidates a recruiter talks to every day, it would be easy to see that it is very exciting to talk to a professional that ticks all their boxes, that is enthusiastic, that absolutely wants the experience. Before we get into what works, we need to look at the contributing factor in phone screen failures on both the candidate and the recruiter side.

Candidate Side of Phone Screen Failures:

Job candidates fail at phone screens all of the time because:
1. They are not able to create winning answers for a job they knew nothing about 5 seconds ago.
2. They are not sure what to quote for pay, what the job actually pays, what they are willing to accept, or how the job could be leveraged for long-term salary growth.
3. They are not sure they even want the job or will stay with it since they just got the call.

Most candidates either think these phone screens are not important, or they start to hate them because they are not moving forward for jobs they are qualified for and, upon reflection, that they would want to consider if given more time to evaluate the option.

Recruiter Side of Phone Screen Failures:

Recruiters fail to find the best candidates for their jobs because:
1. They expect busy job candidates to do well on these interviews, even though they did not know a single thing about the job 5 seconds before the call came in.

2. They assume the candidate has one salary figure they will work for and if it fits, great; if not they boot the candidate.
3. They assume the candidate can determine, in a very short span of time, if they will be happy and stay.

Recruiters love phone screens because they can really boil the pool of applicants down quickly but they dislike them because they inherently know there are great candidates that they are rejecting quickly. They just don't have time to think about that.

To be successful a recruiter must call many candidates in a short period of time, and they tend to be sourcing for many positions at one time, not just the one job. To maximize their time, they want to talk to you right then and not schedule into the future.

Phone screens tend to be a only a scheduled part of an internal recruiter's day, while this is literally the job of third party recruiters. If a recruiter has to schedule a call, especially an internal recruiter, they will often miss the call because they get sidetracked by other priorities. This upsets candidates and creates a feeling that the recruiter is unprofessional. This is an unfortunate part of the process but keep in mind that one missed phone screen does not necessarily reflect poorly on the company. Two or three misses and you may want to move on.

Remember that the goal of the recruiter is to find a qualified match for their position who will also be happy with the job, the pay, the location, and the work. The recruiter needs to hear one word – "yes." When they hear a lot of "yes" and "I have that experience" responses from the candidate, it creates a "yes" reaction in their mind. When a candidate says "no" or "I do not have that experience," or "I am not sure I want to do that," it creates a "rejection" reaction in their mind.

A candidate needs to say "yes" as much as possible and use a deflection technique for a "no" response.

Winning Phone Screen Responses

There are three ways to improve your phone screen and interview performance:
1. Say "Yes!" to all non-skill based questions,
2. Take a message, ask for the job ad, schedule for a later date, and prepare,
3. And learn how to deflect, substitute, and re-direct a "no" or "I do not have it" for skill-based questions.

Remember, you can always cancel an in-person interview later if it really is not something you want, assuming you, like many candidates, want to keep your choices open and allow yourself time to consider the option.

Create the Yes Reaction to Non-Skill Based Questions

<u>Non-skill based conditional response examples that kill jobs.</u>

Recruiter Question: I have a job that is a lower title than your current position - would you be interested?
> Job Candidate Response: I am not sure but I would like to hear more.

Recruiter Question: I have a "road warrior" job that requires 90% travel - would you be able to do that?
> Job Candidate Response: Hmmm, I don't think all that travel fits into my lifestyle but for the right opportunity I would consider it.

Recruiter Question: I have a job that is a 3-month contract - would you be willing to leave your full-time job to consider it?

> Job Candidate Response: Why would I ever leave a full-time job for a 3-month contract? No, but keep me in mind for full-time work.

Recruiter Question: I have a job that would require relocation to a city that you could not even place on a map - do you want it?

> Job Candidate Response: I might consider moving but only to "x" city.

Non-skill based examples that get an internal 'yes' response inside the recruiter's brain.

Recruiter Question: I have a job that is a lower title than your current position - would you be interested?

> Job Candidate Response: Yes! (no, matter what.)

Recruiter Question: I have a "road warrior" job that requires 90% travel - would you be able to do that?

> Job Candidate Response: Yes! (no, matter what.)

Recruiter Question: I have a job that is a 3-month contract - would you be willing to leave your full-time job to consider it?

> Job Candidate Response: Yes! (no, matter what.)

Recruiter Question: I have a job that would require relocation to a city that you could not even place on a map - do you want it?

> Job Candidate Response: Yes! (no, matter what.)

The goal in the phone screen is to keep the "ball in the air" so you can actually compete for the job. If you offer conditional responses, you are eliminating yourself from the pool of candidates. Your second option is to take a message and prepare your answers.

Matching-answer preparation for schedule phone screens

The following set of lessons will explain how to build matching answers that get results. Controlling the time and place of the phone screen increases your success rate, therefore it is recommended that the first few phone screens be scheduled. Take a message, get the job advertisement, prepare the matching answers, and schedule the screen.

Managing a true "no" about a skill-based question

Sometimes you will be asked if you have a skill and it will be impossible to say yes. We now know in hiring psychology if you say "no" or "I do not have it," a disqualification response is created in the mind of the interviewer. So what is the option if you truly do not have experience with something? Deflection, substitution, and re-direction. I will use the role of an accountant to demonstrate.

Recruiter Question: Do you have a Certified Public Accounting (CPA) license?
  ➢ Job Candidate Response: In my current and past accounting roles I have performed audits and worked with public accounting firms as required for this position. I can also study and sit for my certification over the next two years.

Recruiter Question: We are seeking an Accountant with experience with the Big 4 Accounting firms; I do not see that on your resume.

> Job Candidate Response: I have 20 years of experience working on audits as required for this role.

Recruiter Question: This position requires a Bachelor's degree in Accounting but I see you only have an Associate's.

> Job Candidate Response: I have an Associate's and five years of experience directly matching the requirements of this role. I can also study and complete my Bachelor's in Accounting.

Recruiter Question: We are looking for direct experience with the SAP ERP.

> Job Candidate Response: I have 10 years of experience and have worked on the large accounting software suites.

The answers deflect, substitute, and re-direct the interviewers towards your matching qualifications. This avoids the silent disqualification process and forces the recruiter's mind into a "yes" position.

6.3 Common Phone Screen & Interview Questions

As stated earlier, phone screen questions are designed to eliminate candidates. The following questions will pop up throughout the interview process but they are very common for the phone screen. First, I will present the question and explain the reason for it, and then will provide a strategy.

Common Phone Screen Questions List

1. So tell me about yourself.
2. Why this job?
3. Why did you transition from one job to another or why do you want to leave where you are?
4. What are your greatest strengths and what makes you a good fit for this role specifically?
5. What are your weaknesses?
6. What is your greatest accomplishment?
7. What are your 1-, 2- and 5-year goals?
8. Are you thinking about pursuing additional education?
9. What would be your dream job?
10. What are your salary expectations?

If you took a message and scheduled the phone screen, you can prepare matching answers to each one of these. Use the next lesson to understand the psychology behind each question and the strategy to respond to each.

6.4 Reason for Each Question and Strategy

The goal of each answer is to trip the internal "yes" response in the recruiter's mind. We want them "firing on all cylinders." If there are obvious "no" issues like a missing skill, certification, non-matching industry, or seemingly illogical job transition, this is an opportunity to turn that "no" into a "yes." The way to do this is to reiterate over and over that you are a match for the job, that you want the job, that this job matches your goals -

yes, yes, yes! Each question below has a tip that works in most scenarios.

Q#1: So tell me about yourself.

This is an open-ended question that many candidates do not know how to answer. You may ask yourself "Should I talk about my family, my personal health regimen, my last job, my current employer, my life story, or what?" The answer to this question is easier than you might think.

Tip: The Summary of Skills portion of the resume is the primary answer to this question, with a few added touches.

In one to three sentences, describe how you have the required skills and background of the job advertisement. Select additional positive personal and family information that demonstrates your stability as a candidate and as a person. End the answer with the reason you are leaving, or left, your most recent employer.

This open-ended question is the first great opportunity to send the message: "I am qualified, I will be happy, and I will stay in this job."

Q#2: Why this job?

The employer looks at the position they are offering as their priceless gift. Even though a job candidate is exchanging their time for that position, the employer does not quite view it that way. Like a gift giver, the employer wants to hear that this gift of a job will be appreciated, that you will use it well, and that it is the most important thing that could happen to you. Employers do not want to give their gift to anyone that does not want the present.

Tip: Say "This job is a perfect blend of skills and experience that I have and enjoy using the most."

When we tell the employer why we want this job we have to express three things: 1) that this is the next logical step in our career progression and 2) that we can do the job (matching strengths and qualifications), and 3) a unique list of items that employers like to hear about their company (listed below).

- Growth (if there is growth)
- It is an industry leader
- New developments in _____ (state new developments in the organization, industry, or field)
- The work environment
- Better hours and schedule
- It is closer to home
- Larger or growing organization that has greater long term opportunity
- Smaller organization that is more to my style
- Stability
- Better overall package (versus just more money)
- New industry that offers a new trajectory for my skills.

Be careful using the following:
- More money (they will be concerned that you will leave when you find more)

- Less stress or better work-life balance (suggests you are having psycho-emotional issues)
- Getting back into the work force (in most cases you don't want to shift the focus of the interview to current unemployment)

Q#3: Why did you transition from one job to another and why are you looking to leave where you are?

Other than title and industry, one of the primary items recruiters use to evaluate a good candidate is their "reason for leaving" answer. This can first appear on the job application, phone screen, or in-person interview. This is the #1 silent job killer. The interviewer is really attempting to predict whether you will stay and be happy based on your previous behavior.

Tip: The top four most acceptable answers for reason for leaving are the following words:1) promotion, 2) relocation, 3) back-to-school, and 4) reorganization/shift in company priorities.

Why you move from one job to the next and how long you stay in a job is one of the most important and overlooked aspects of a good interview strategy. The solution is to make each transition appear like a positive cohesive career strategy that has led up to the next job interview.

Promotion does not necessarily mean more money or a higher title. This catch-all word can be used to leverage anything that meant a step in a better direction.

Relocation is a great option if a person moved to another city, but only use it once or twice as the reason for leaving or you may appear "lost."

Reorganization as a reason for leaving can work even when there was not a huge layoff; if the employer decided you were not worth retaining, they "reorganized." It is important not to reveal negative information related to a previous employer, become emotional, or to appear as if you are wandering aimlessly through your career.

Q#4: What are your greatest strengths?

Candidates often state qualities that are difficult to prove and sound relatively meaningless like "I am a hard worker, dedicated, and experienced." Instead, use the list of matching skills from the job advertisement that you used to build the Market-Based Resume©.

Tip: Your greatest strengths are everything in the job advertisement that you have.

Choose accomplishments that demonstrate your related skills. Reiterate that you are a match for this job.

Q#5: What are your weaknesses?

This question seems like a no-win situation for job candidates. To manage the potential negative impact of this question, job candidates will often give an answer like "I am intense, a perfectionist, or a workaholic." Those answers are better than a truly negative answer like "I am frequently late for work," but that is still not good enough.

Tip: If the industry is different for you, state "I have not worked in this industry but I have done all of the tasks and do not feel it will be an issue." If there are mandatory requirements from the job ad that you do not have, tell the employer that you have other skills that balance any missing items. Do not say you are a quick learner! Instead, give an example of how you picked up a skill or industry quickly.

Only give the recruiter more than one weakness if they ask for it. The most common weakness is a lack of industry experience. Select missing line items versus mandatory requirements for this answer unless the missing item is very obvious. It is better to manage these issues head on and turn a silent "no" into a "yes."

Q#6: What is your greatest accomplishment?

This question is critical because you want your accomplishment to match the job's need and be a powerful statement of your qualifications. Unfortunately, many people do not believe they have a greatest accomplishment.

Tip: Find a work example (or school example if you really do not have one with work) that supports your candidacy for that particular job.

If you have done the work to build a strong accomplishment inventory and that matches the position, then this question will be easy to answer.

Q#7: What are your 1-, 2- and 5-year goals?

The correct answer to this question is surprisingly not creative. Remember, the recruiter wants to know that you want the job you are applying for, that you will be happy in the position, and that you will stay in it for a period of time, usually at least two years. However, there are some cases in which a job requires ambitious candidates that want fast movement. In other positions there is no growth and the recruiter is seeking a candidate that wants no or limited advancement. For the first one to two years, "the job you want" needs to be this job, not one higher, lower, or different. An employer is not going to hire you for a job if you tell them you really want a different position.

Commons reasons candidates do not get an offer is by stating a desire for growth when there is none, or stating the desire to stay at a certain level when the recruiter is looking for someone who wants to grow.

Tip: Use the formula below 99.9% of the time.
The majority of the time this is the answer:
1-year goal: Get this job.
2-year goal: Excel in this job.
5-year goal: Grow as the organization needs my skills.

The five-year answer can be a little more complicated. If this is a high growth organization, say you would like to grow and let the organization use your skills as needed. Be careful of sending the message that you want your boss's job. If the organization is small or there is no room for movement, then state that you are happy to stay in the position. Even if you do not actually want to work at that level for the rest of your career, it is important to state that you will be happy if you want the job offer. Then you will need to move on once you get experience.

Q#8: Are you thinking about pursuing additional education and certificates?

Sometimes an employer will find a candidate they are excited about that is missing important qualifications for the job. Many candidates may be tired of studying or amassing more skills and want to just "learn on the job."

Tip: Always answer "yes" to re-education.

This question is an excellent signal that the employer is interested in the candidate. If a candidate answers no, they are essentially telling the employer that they are not interested in doing what is necessary to succeed in the role.

Q#9: What would be your dream job?

In most cases, the job you are interviewing for has to be your dream job. There are some exceptions where the employer understands you will be moving on but is willing to hire you. For instance, if you just graduated and are working at a job unrelated to your degree, your employer may say, "I know you are just with us until you find a professional-level job."

Tip: Every job is your dream job to continue interviewing and get a job offer.

With few exceptions there is only one answer to this question. You need to tell the employer, "This job is my dream job because it leverages my skills and abilities and (the other benefits it offers)."

Q#10: What are your salary expectations?

There is an entire lesson in the book and online program dedicated to salary negotiations. It is important to reiterate that a candidate must match what the employer is willing to pay to get a job offer.

Tip: This salary quote is the amount needed to "keep the ball in the air." It is not necessarily your overall salary goal; it is the amount assigned to the position by the company. Learn how to guess what that is based on title and job description.

We all want the most money we can get but we may be happy with what the employer is offering, if we only knew what that was. The first part of the salary negotiation module teaches you how to predict what a job pays so that you can quote "desired salary." If the employer stated a salary range in the job advertisement, then that is what they are willing to pay. If they have not, then you need to perform a salary survey either through knowing someone inside of the organization or through the internet. In addition, you need to understand the value the employer has placed on the job based on the written job requirements. Common advice in salary negotiations is to have the employer name the first figure, but sometimes that is just not possible or likely. It is best to be armed with a strategy and to be prepared to negotiate.

6.5 Phone Screen Question Turn-around Cheat Sheet

This "Interview Questions Turnaround Cheat Sheet" changes problematic questions that tend to disqualify the candidate into questions that will help the candidate create the best answer for the best results.

Common Interview Question	*Question Turnaround*
1. So tell me about yourself.	What qualifications do I have that they need? What about my personal life sends a positive message to an employer?
2. Why this job?	What are all the attributes of this job that are positive and how is it the next logical step in my career?
3. Explain your job transitions.	How has each job I have had contributed skills leading up to this position? If I were hiring for this job and looking at me as a candidate, what would be the most positive true explanation?
4. What are your greatest strengths?	What are the line items in the job advertisement that I have?
5. What are your greatest weaknesses?	What are the line items in the job advertisement that I do not have? What do I have that makes up for the lack?
6. What is your greatest	What is one thing I have done

accomplishment?	related to this job that will impress them?
7. What are your 1-, 2-, and 5-year goals?	*(this is a formula)* Year 1: Get this job, Year-2: excel, and Year-5: continue contributing and growing with the organization as needed (unless you know for certain they want fast growth).
8. Will you accept more education or training?	Yes - I am a lifelong learner and will pursue whatever training and education required for this role.
9. What is your dream job?	This is my dream job and is a great use of my skills and background … (Every job you apply for has to be your dream job to get an in-person meeting or an offer.)
10. What are your salary expectations?	Based on a salary survey of a similar position, my years of work experience, knowledge of the field, educational background, and that I have these skills _____ (list the relevant skills), I feel that this position's range is between $_____ to $_____. (Tip: See salary negotiation lesson in Chapter 7.)

6.6 Interview Worksheet Scripts

Fill in these scripts to prepare answers to the most disqualifying interview questions.

Common Interview Question #1: So tell me about yourself.

"I am a _____ (select the title of the job) *professional with* ___ (state the number of years they list in the position) *in the following areas:* _____ (list one to three skills from the job advertisement) *in* _____ (list the related industry).

"I also possess ___ (list an extra skill or accomplishment). *I am interested in this company because of* _____ (research the company or industry and list the reason for interest)."

Then, make an expression of personal life stability:

"I am from this area" and/or *"I have a strong support system here."*

Then state the reason for leaving the most recent position:

"I am leaving my current position and seeking to work in this role because _____ (state the reason for leaving.)"

Tip: This is similar to the Summary of Skills.

Common Interview Question #2: Why this job?

This job is exactly what I am looking for because it is a great use of my existing skills. The job is seeking the following qualifications which I have: (list of job ad items, especially required qualifications, that you have.)

My current position has shifted and is not using the core skills that I have, that you (the new employer) *are seeking. You are seeking someone to perform the types of things I enjoy doing.*
"This is the exact work I have been doing, so I know that I can be effective. I am interested in this organization because of _____ *"*

- *Growth* (if there is growth)
- *The company is an industry leader*
- *New developments in* _____ (state new developments in the organization, industry, or field), or
- *The work environment*
- *Better hours and schedule*
- *It is closer to home*
- *Larger or growing organization that has greater long term opportunity*
- *Smaller organization that is more to my style*
- *Stability*
- *Better overall package (versus just more money)*
- *New industry that offers a new trajectory for my skills*

Be careful using the following:
- *More money* (they will be concerned that you will leave when you find more)
- *Less stress or better work-life balance* (suggests you are having psycho-emotional issues)
- *Getting back-to-work* (we don't want to shift the focus to unemployment in most cases)

Common Interview Question #3: Why did you transition from one job to another, and/or why are you looking to leave where you are?

"I moved from my employer because _____. (Select one or a combination of the following options.")

- *The next position was the next step in my career path of* _____ (a skill that the next job has)
- *I moved because I enjoy doing* ____ (a skill that the next job has)
- *A better use of* ____ (a skill that the next job has)
- *A return to an industry*
- *Closer to home*
- *Better hours*
- *Some unique aspect of the future work environment*

Tip: It is rarely good to say you are moving for money because the employer may feel you will just leave when the next better offer comes along. See Section 6.7 for a script for managing terminations and dismissals.

Common Interview Question #4: What are your greatest strengths?

"I am a great fit for this position because _____ (list all of the aspects of the job ad that you have)."

Common Interview Question #5: What are your weaknesses?

"My greatest weakness for this position is that I do not have _____ (make a list of requirements listed in the job ad that you do not have but only discuss one or two), *but I do have*

_____ (list something in your background that is similar and demonstrates that this missing quality is not going to hinder your ability to do the job), *and with my other skills in* _____ (list other strengths), *I do not believe this will be an issue."*

Tip: One of the best options is to say "I have not worked in this industry but I have worked in other industries where I have gained relevant professional experience." However, there may be serious weaknesses or missing qualifications that should be dealt with head-on.

Common Interview Question #6: What is your greatest accomplishment?

"I have increased _____ (revenue, time, or units of production) *by doing* _____ (list a skill related to job)."
or

"I reduced _____ (money, time, or units of production) *by doing* _____ (list a skill related to job)."

Tip: Choose an accomplishment related to the work you will be doing in this future position if you have one.

Common Interview Question #7: What are your 1-, 2- and 5-year goals?

1-Year Strategy: *"Get* this *job, learn my job, and be effective."*
2-Year Strategy: *"Exceeding expectations in* this job.*"*
5-Year Strategy: *"Grow according to the needs of the organization."*

"Move up (if there is a high expectation of growth or a large organization)."

"Stay happy where I am (no growth or small organization)."

Tip: You need to want the job you are interviewing for to get an offer. In most cases, you need to want it for at least two years.

Common Interview Question #8: Are you thinking about more education/training?

"Yes, I want to pursue any training, certification, or additional education required by my future role."

Tip: If the employer asks about training and education, you need to say yes to be considered as a candidate.

Common Interview Question #9: What would be your dream job?

"This _____ (state the position title) *is my dream job."* or

"Working in this field and using _____ (list of skills related to this position)."*

Tip: You need to want the job you are interviewing for to get an offer.

Common Interview Question #10: What are your salary expectations?

"Based on a salary survey of similar positions, my years of work experience, knowledge of the field, educational background, and that I have these skills _____ (list the relevant skills), *I feel that*

this position's range is between $_____ to $_____." (State a ten thousand dollar range.)

Tip: See the Salary Negotiation Section.

6.7 Explaining Terminations/Dismissals/Gaps as a Reason for Leaving

You know now that "reason for leaving" is one of most asked questions on the application, during the phone screen, and during in-person interviews. This can be problematic if you have been fired from a job. The likelihood of being hired is very low if you say you were fired for cause, something you did to upset the employer.

Tip: Never say the words fired, dismissed, or terminated.

Not all situations are the same. In many cases, you can manage the situation without indicating that anything negative happened. At the very worst, the candidate will indicate reorganization or shift in business priorities. On the application use the following strategy for the "reason for leaving" boxes that are so common now.

Answers for "Reason for Leaving" Boxes on the Application
- If there was no gap in time between positions: Promotion.
- If the gap in employment less than 3 months: Promotion.
- If you moved during the transition period: Relocation.

- If you went back to school during the transition: Back to school.
- If many people were let go at one time: Reorganization.

Try to use the word "reorganization" only once for transitions in the past five years. If reorganization is used too often the employer will assume you are a problem employee. During the interview, explanations will require more than a one-word answer, but keep it brief. Use the following selection to understand how to frame each response.

More Elaborate Interview Answers for "Reason for Leaving"

Promotion Option:

Employers want to hire people that are in-demand, experienced, and easy to work with. They also want to hire a person that understands how to build and maintain a career. A promotion will need to be explained in greater detail during the interview. This is not necessarily an increase in title; it can also be an increase in or focus on different skills, a better work environment, schedule, or pay.

Relocation Option: Move to a Different City Following a Termination

It is common for job candidates to move back to their hometown or away from their current location following a dismissal. You can use this move to your advantage by focusing on the move to a different city and not the termination itself as your "reason for leaving." If you moved back to your hometown, then state that you had a need or desire to be near family. If this move is because your spouse got a job in a new job market, then state that the career transition was due to spousal relocation. If you moved to another job market in order to seek new opportunities, then state that you moved because your old market had limited opportunities compared to the new market. Moving to and from markets sounds good to an employer and can help avoid more difficult discussions like terminations. Make sure to say that you have a strong support system where you moved because a lack of support can make an employer nervous.

Back-to-School Option: If You Were in School or Went Back to School

Employers respond well to an employee that went back to school to gain new education as a positive career transition explanation. If you have gone back to school following a termination, then state the following: "My long term goal was to go back to school, so I decided to take this time to pursue my education." Education almost always sounds great to the employer.

Option 4: Re-organization

The economy and companies shift their priorities every single day. If the company decided you were not worth saving, say they reorganized the department. Explaining that the employer's changing priorities resulted in a dismissal is fairly common. This also applies when an organization has gone through a large, well-publicized re-organization.

State that the company reorganized or shifted their priorities, or your position's priorities changed and moved away from the important skill sets that this new employer needs. It is important to state that there was a business change, or change in management priorities, that resulted in the termination.

The exercise below includes scripts to aid in explaining terminations to future employers and to your network. First, a scenario is presented with a script that is better than saying "I was fired from that job." These scenarios and explanations are listed in order of preference. If the scenario is true, use the script provided. If not, move to the next option in the list. The final explanation is the least desirable but, if no other scenario fits it is better than the alternative. Feel free to combine scripts if multiple scenarios exist.

Scripts for Explaining Terminations

Select the scenario that most closely matches your situation and use the corresponding script.

Promotion: small gaps between jobs
(This method completely avoids discussing the loss of the job by focusing on the job that quickly followed).

"I moved from my employer because _____*.* (Select one or a combination of the following options.")
- *The next position was the next step in my career path of* _____ (a skill that the next job has).
- *I moved because I enjoy doing* ____ (a skill that the next job has).
- *A better use of* ____ (a skill that the next job has).

- *A return to an industry.*
- *Closer to home.*
- *Better hours.*
- Some unique aspect of the future work environment.

Relocation: move to a different city following a termination
- *"I wanted to move back home to be near my family."*
- *"I moved to this location because my spouse found (or was relocated for) a job here."*
- *"I moved to this location for better opportunities and I have always wanted to live here."*

Back to School: if you were in school or went back to school
- *"I was in school and I decided to focus on completing my education."*
- *"I had wanted to go back to school and I took the opportunity when it presented itself."*

Reorganization:
- *"This employer promised me the job would use _____* (name a skill that the new job has), *but that was not the reality, and because that is what I want to do I am applying for this position."*
- *"There was a large reorganization and multiple people we let go (or a whole site was shut down)."*
- *"The company reorganized or shifted or my position's priorities away from _____"* (state a job skill that the new job offers or some other business or industry change resulting in the termination). *I enjoy using my skill sets in _____* (state the skill sets the new job will use), *so that is why I am applying for this new position."*

- *"The company reorganized or shifted their priorities. I realized in that position that I really enjoyed doing _____ (skill the new job offers) and/or I really enjoyed working in _____ (industry of the new job), so that is why I am applying for this new position."*

6.8 Behavioral Interview Scripting

There has been a rise in behavioral interview questions during interviews. Once you get past the phone screen, the employer will start asking questions that test your capability to do the job. The behavioral questions are a way of actually combining all three questions (are you capable, will you be happy, and will you stay) into one question. Behavioral interview questions are more common for in-person interviews and less so for the telephone screens.

Tip: For the behavioral questions, create one very specific problem-solving example for every line item in the job advertisement.

Do not leave a single question unanswered. Include even interpersonal dynamic issues because the employer will be focused on who you can and cannot deal with. For instance, take a line item and create a problem solving example in which you had a disagreement with a boss, vendor, or client. It may have been a very personal issue for you, but for the purpose of the interview, think of it more as one-time operational disagreement. Do not select answers about things related to your work hours, pay, or benefits. These questions are about problem solving related to the position.

For instance, if you are applying for a project coordinator position for tradeshows, select two tradeshow projects and answer all of these questions in the framework of that example to provide an in depth presentation of your experience. Maybe for example your boss felt that things should be done differently. Provide evidence of how you managed this issue.

Sometimes these questions may appear redundant and you may want to say, "I just answered that." This is common in a panel interview or a series of one-on-one interviews when multiple people are not listening to what other people are asking the candidate. It is important to not say, "I just answered that question," since that will trigger a strong 'No' response in the mind of the interviewer. Be ready to answer the same basic questions over and over.

The exercise below includes common behavioral questions and scripts for suggested answers.

Behavioral Interview Scripts

Create examples for every line item of the job advertisement. Be specific and choose examples that show you know how to do *this* job even if they are not from the most recent employer. Use the sample scripts to get your creative juices flowing.

With each question and answer, check in and ask yourself: "Is this answer showing them a great example of how I operated on a daily basis with this type of work? Can I show a great accomplishment related to this type of work from the perspective of problem-solving?"

1. Copy and paste the line items of the job into this preparation sheet.
2. Relate each line item with one of the behavioral questions below.
3. Create a powerful work example that shows how you solve problems related to this job.

Q1. Give an example of an occasion when you used logic to solve a problem (insert a line item in the job ad).

One day while doing _____ (state a business, client, or departmental problem that you were dealing with that pertains to a line item), I faced a problem where I lacked _____ (state a situation, process, or issue). To fix it, I did the following _____ (describe your process to solve the problem).

Q2. Give an example of a goal that you did not meet and how you handled it (insert a line item in the job ad).

One day while doing _____ (state a business, client, or departmental problem that you were dealing with that pertains to a line item), I faced a problem where I lacked _____ (state a situation, process, or issue). I was unable to fix the problem because of _____ (describe the barriers to problem resolution), so I did the following instead _____ (describe your process to work around the barriers and manage the problem).

Q3. Describe a stressful situation at work and how you handled it (insert a line item in the job ad).

One day while doing _____ (state a business, client or departmental problem that you were dealing with that pertains to a line item), I encountered a stressful situation. The problem was that the _____ (state a client or departmental problem that you were dealing with). I was stressed out due to the following _____ (state the stressors). To manage the process, I did the following _____ (Describe your process to successfully resolve your stressors. Suggestions include: I took a step back to gain perspective. I spoke with each person involved to determine a solution. I got buy-in from different people by explaining the importance of the issues.)

Q4. Have you ever made a mistake? How did you handle it?

Change this question to "When did you make a mistake (insert a line item in the job ad) and how did you handle it?" (Just because it is framed as a question, do not think it is optional to answer.)

One day while I was working on _____ (state a client or departmental problem that you were dealing with), I made a mistake doing _____ (state a mistake but make sure it is not too bad). This mistake resulted in reduced efficiency in completing the task. I corrected the problem by doing _____ (describe your process to work around the barriers and manage the problem). I have learned from what happened and, as a result, have had many positive resolutions after that one mistake.

Q5. Did you ever not meet your goals? Why?

Sometime a question seems optional. You may be tempted to say 'I have met all my goals.' To help facilitate the best answers, change this question to "When did you not meet a goal (insert a line item in the job ad), why, and how did you handle it?"

At one point in the project (state a client or departmental problem that you were dealing with), I did not reach the goal of _____ (state a goal, milestone, or deadline). The reason I did not reach the goal was because (state business reasons for not reaching the goal. Suggestions include: I needed information or assistance from other departments and, since I was not in control of that aspect, I had to communicate the missed deadline with the client/department/managers and attempt to find a workaround solution.) I was able to overcome this, which has resulted in _____ (state the result).

Q6. Give an example of a goal you reached and tell me how you achieved it (insert a line item in the job ad).

"I succeeded in doing _____ (an item listed in the job ad) by doing this _____ (using skills from job ad - This should be your greatest accomplishment for this position)."

Q7. When have you gone above and beyond the call of duty (insert a line item in the job ad)?

I put in more effort and hours to help a colleague/supervisor/department solve or achieve the following _____ (describe something that was outside of your professional duties).

Q8. How did you handle a difficult situation with a supervisor (insert a line item in the job ad)?

At one point during a project, my supervisor asked me to work on something else. But my performance was evaluated by the completion of the _____ (describe how you went above and beyond by working on and resolving both issues).

Q9. Have you handled a difficult situation with another department (insert a line item in the job ad)?

Change this question to "When did you handle a difficult situation with another department (insert a line item in the job ad) and how did you handle it?"

One day while working on _____ (state a departmental problem that you were dealing with). To manage the problem, I did the following _____ (describe your process to solve the problem).

Q10. How did you handle a difficult situation with a client or vendor (insert a line item in the job ad)?

One day while working on _____ (state a client problem that you were dealing with). To solve this problem I did the following _____. (State your problem solving process. Suggestions include: Because their expectations were vastly different than what we could accomplish, I explained what could be done in regards to the issue and was honest about resolution times as well. The explanation and honesty turned them into one of my biggest fans.)

Q11. Describe a decision you made that was unpopular (insert a line item in the job ad) and how you handled implementing it.

At one point in the project _____ (state a business, client, or departmental problem that you were dealing with), I had to make an unpopular decision. To implement my concept, I got buy-in by doing the following _____ (explain your process).

Q12. Describe a time you made a risky decision (insert a line item in the job ad)?

At one point in the project _____ (state a business, client, or departmental problem that you were dealing with), I had to make a decision that I knew I was going to take ownership of or that my boss would not fully agree with _____ (describe the risky decision and why it was risky). This decision or experiment was _____ (state the ways it was a successful and unsuccessful decision). Through this decision, the business or I grew in the following ways _____ (state skills and experiences gained).

Q13. Did you ever postpone making a decision (insert a line item in the job ad)? Why?

Change this question to "When did you postpone a decision (insert a line item in the job ad), why, and how did you handle it?"

While working on _____ (state a business, client, or departmental problem that you were dealing with), I had to postpone implementing _____ (state what was postponed) because of _____ (state why you had to postpone it). The result improved _____ (state how the postponement improved the result).

Q14. Have you had to convince a team to work on a project (insert a line item in the job ad) they weren't thrilled about? How did you do it?

Change this question to "When did you convince a team to work on a project they weren't thrilled about (insert a line item in the job ad) and how did you handle it?"

While working on _____ (state a business, client, or departmental problem that you were dealing with), I had to convince the team to do _____ (state what had to be done). The team was not thrilled about this because of _____ (State the business reasons they were not happy. Suggestions include: The change would ask for a lot more from each team-member. To get the best results we worked on prioritizing and also focusing on the time frames so we could see an end to the extra demands. We also worked as a team to ensure completion of everything on our plate.)

Q15. Have you ever dealt with company policy you weren't in agreement with? How?

Change this question to "when did you deal with company policy you weren't in agreement with (insert a line item in the job ad) and how did you handle it?"

While working on _____ (state a business, client, or departmental problem that you were dealing with), one of my employers in particular asked me to do _____ (state something that you did not agree with from a business perspective). To deal with the situation, I ____ (state how you worked this out with the manager or performed it anyway even if you did not agree).

Q16. Were you ever asked to break the law? What did you do?

No, and if I was asked, I would never do it. (This is the answer in most cases and you need to seriously consider if you want the job if it is not the right answer.)

Q17. Give an example of when you did or when you didn't listen.

I did not listen to my _____ (state who you did not listen to. Suggestions include a client, coworker, vendor, boss, department, or student) and it resulted in problems with _____ (state an issue relevant to the job that occurred from not listening). I realized from then on that I needed to listen when _____ (state a business situation where improved listening resulted in performance on future projects.)

Q18. What do you do if you disagree with your boss?

Change to "When did you disagree with your boss over a change in procedure and why? What was the outcome?"

At one point while working on _____ (state a business, client or departmental problem that you were dealing with), I did not agree with my boss on how to proceed with _____ (state a goal, milestone, or deadline). The reason I did not agree was because _____ (state business reasons for not agreeing with your boss). The result of this disagreement was _____ (state whether you went with your boss's decision or if your boss went with your decision). By taking the time to work through the problem together, we were able to achieve____ (state reaching a goal).

6.9 Questions for the Employer

Candidates need to ask great questions of the employer to ensure that they are selected for the position. These questions can really excite the employer. It is not just the questions that are important; your specific responses can really set you apart from the competition.

TIP: This is one of your greatest and final chances to create a "yes" reaction in the mind of the recruiter.

Sometimes these questions can make or break your chances at the job because:

- Some interviewers are bad at their job and you will need to take over the interview anyway.
- If you create a conversation and identify the needed skills, you can offer answers that match their needs.
- Questions show your interest in the position and organization.
- Recruiters love great questions.
- They can set you apart from other applicants.

Some recruiters are not very skilled at interviewing. You may have to take over the interview to express your qualifications. These questions can allow you to uncover additional needs or address any lingering concerns. Any answer and example you have prepared should be used if the interviewer does not seem capable of asking the right questions. In the case of a bad interviewer, ask and answer your own interview questions by telling the recruiter "I want to tell you about this experience I had."

The most important aspect of these questions is that they must be in the form of a conversation, an opportunity to re-affirm your candidacy. Every time the recruiter provides an answer, you need to say, "I have done this exact work" or "I have faced this exact challenge and here is an example." If the recruiter is not asking many questions, this is the opportunity for you to say, "I have some great examples you may want to hear about." Then, proceed by telling the recruiter, "This is the exact work that I have done."

The exercise below includes the questions to ask an employer and your suggested response.

6.9.1 Exercise: Questions for Them

After every response the recruiter gives to the questions below, say one of three things:

- *"I have done this exact work; here is an example..."*
- *"That is the exact work I am doing right now; here is an example.."*

- *"I have faced this exact challenge and here is what I did to solve it..."* ... and explain when and where this has occurred in your work history.

Questions about the position:
- What are the three top priorities you have identified for this position?
- What does the organization feel is the most important thing I can do to be effective in the first 90 days of my employment?
- Is there an annual performance review and what are the performance metrics for this position?
- What structure does the organization foresee for this role and by when?

About the company or team:
- What are trends for this team and how does it impact the company?
- What do the team and organization value the most?
- How has this team and organization been received by customers/departments?
- How does this role fit into the team?
- In the most recent press release from the company_____; how does that affect the company's trajectory?

About the industry:
- What new trends are affecting the company?
- What does the organization value the most?
- How has this organization been received by customers?

About the recruiter:
- How did you find your way into the company?
- What about this work have you enjoyed most?

The Close (for each interview segment):
- Based on this interview do you have any lingering concerns about my candidacy that I can address?

Then respond to their concerns and select one of the following closings.

- I am very excited about this opportunity and look forward to hearing back from you. I want this position and to work for this company.
- I hope that I have demonstrated that this is the exact work that I have been doing. I would like this position and look forward to contributing to the organization (or team).
- I know that you are just as interested as I am in finding the right fit. Based on our conversations about the role, I know that this fits my background and goals and that this position and organization is the right fit for me.

With this set of questions, it may not be necessary to personally identify with the recruiter because this question is not about you, it is about them. Be thoughtful and curious about their life.

Tip: Remember, whatever the recruiter says, it is important to say
"I have done this exact work"
or
"I have faced this exact problem"

and explain when and where this has occurred in your work history.
This method gets job offers.

6.10 What Not to Say in an Interview

Although recruiters often express concerns about a candidate lying about their background, most people are incredibly honest (sometimes painfully honest). Some candidates treat the interview as a tell-all breaking news event. Sometimes, they accidentally reveal negative information that they may think is positive.

Remember, there are three primary questions on the mind of the recruiter:

1. Will the job candidate stay in the position for at least two years?
2. Will the job candidate be happy or least not disrupt the team dynamic?
3. Can the job candidate do the work?

Do not accidentally release any information that may tell the recruiter that your life is being disrupted or unstable. Here is a list of information that is best to keep to yourself.

Poor Health or Death of a Loved One

Any mention of poor health from either you or a family member has no place in the interview. This extends to your parents, siblings, spouse, and children. When you walk into an interview, everyone needs to be healthy at that moment. Discussions

179

about health and death are depressing and can potentially indicate to the employer that you are not healthy or that you have problems at home that will take your focus away from the job. However, a strong fitness regime or physically active family can send a positive message to the interviewer. Focus on presenting information that states, "I am healthy and my family is healthy."

Hobbies & Affiliations

Sometimes there are unusual hobbies or affiliations that are better left out of the discussion (depending on the job and interview). Sometimes associations can be a deciding positive factor in a hire if the recruiter has similar interests. It is important to look at clues but to tread carefully about unusual hobbies. Focus on presenting information that states "I am normal and not into 'weird' activities."

Family Laundry

Your network influences your image. Like health issues, do not mention family members with criminal records, children out of wedlock, divorce, unemployed, poor health, mental issues, and congenital disorders. Also, do not mention if you have no family or friends in the area. Sometimes there is positive family information like a brother in the military or an aunt that is an elected official. This information contributes to the "pillar of society concept." Focus on presenting information that states, "I have a strong, stable healthy network of family and friends."

Children

This is probably one of the most difficult issues. Children are not a "negative" in general, but for the interview, they are problematic because childcare can distract an employee from their work. Talking about children too much tells the employer that the job is not the most important thing in the person's life. For men, this can be different because culturally there is an accepted notion that children spur the man to provide, which means the job should be his primary consideration.

When asked directly about children, of course answer honestly. However, also mention how much support you have, how healthy they are, or how you have worked while raising them with no problem. Focus on presenting information that states, "I have been a stable top performer in school and at work while I have raised my children and I have a strong support network."

Weddings

Men are not likely to talk about weddings other than to announce their status, but for women this can be a real negative. Younger women can become obsessed about their weddings, which can mean that they will be distracted at work. In addition, a wedding may mean time away from work for the event, the honeymoon, and the possibility of pending children for childbearing-aged women. Overall, men should mention an upcoming marriage, but women should avoid this issue or downplay it. Focus on presenting information that states, "I am available to work and this job (and my career) is my priority."

INTERVIEW "WHAT TO SAY AND NOT SAY" CHECKLIST

Use the following as "rules of thumb" about the personal information you reveal.

AVOID	MENTION
<ul><li>Death of a family member</li><li>Illness of family member</li><li>Personal illness</li><li>Criminal records</li><li>Non-mainstream hobbies</li><li>Children out of wedlock</li><li>Unhealthy children</li><li>Personal or family unemployment</li><li>Mental health issues</li><li>Drug use</li><li>Congenital disorders</li><li>Childcare issues</li><li>Issues with divorced spouse</li><li>Divorce</li><li>Getting married soon (women)</li></ul>	<ul><li>Personal fitness routines</li><li>Family members with strong fitness routines</li><li>A strong base of friends and family in the area</li><li>A strong support system for childcare</li><li>Successfully educated family members</li><li>Successful business owners of legal enterprises</li><li>Mainstream, interesting, or relevant hobbies</li><li>Children, but also mention strong support system with childcare</li><li>Children who are active in sports or school activities to underscore healthiness</li><li>Gainful employment of spouse and family members</li><li>Stable engagements, marriages, and relationships</li></ul>

6.11 Interview Portfolio

An interview portfolio is a method the job applicant can use to demonstrate evidence or proof of abilities to the recruiter. The portfolio is especially important in situations where the candidate needs to express ambition and high productivity. Most candidates do not make this extra effort, but it can make the difference between a job offer and a salary increase.

For instance, if you are a web designer, you might evaluate the company's webpage and discuss recommendations. Some employers are actually requesting projects or written case studies instead of a first interview. The following exercise is an additional way to get noticed by employers.

The employer will be very impressed if this is a growth-oriented position or one that is sales or marketing-oriented. It may be best to hold off on using this method for low growth positions because it may frighten the employer, sending the message that the candidate wants more than the position can offer, unless it is directly related. In addition, for someone with limited experience like a new graduate, it can appear boastful. However, it is good to learn this method as soon as possible because you will need it for your annual performance reviews and salary increases.

This exercise presents a checklist of items to include in a portfolio.

Interview and Performance Appraisal Portfolio Checklist

Create a binder or make a spiral bound presentation. Check off and include these items.

Checklist:

_____ Emails and positive feedback from customers, vendors, coworkers, and staff.

_____ Picture of awards granted and certificates.

_____ A portfolio of projects and personal contributions in the process.

_____ A list of publications and work-related social media and blog items, if applicable.

_____ List of met or exceeded accomplishments per performance metrics.

_____ Exceptional performance reviews.

6.12 Thank You Letter

Sometimes a candidate would like to submit a thank you letter following an interview. This may or may not help and there is no way to tell if one of your interviewers enjoys this special touch. A poorly written or illegible personal note can actually hurt a candidate. If the applicant was not a strong candidate for the position, a note could tip the scales for this particular boss, but in many cases this will not be a deciding factor for a candidate. Since there is no way to determine if a post-interview "thank you" can help, the following rules will at least ensure it does not hurt your chances of continued progression.

Rule 1: Get Business Cards

It will not be possible to send a note if you do not have contact information for the interviewer. In most cases, business cards are presented at the beginning of an interview or you may request it at the end. If the interviewer does not seem receptive to you, do not press them for their card.

Rule 2: History of Bad Grammar/Poor Writing

If your English papers from school were heavily marked up by your teacher, or if you received low scores for writing, do not write a letter.

Rule 3: Poor Handwriting

If your handwriting is not legible, send an email the same day as the interview to everyone you interviewed with. Follow the letter template below, and use email unless you have great hand-writing.

Rule 4: Great Handwriting

If your handwriting has received comments for its beauty or readability, send a hand-written note. Buy beautiful stationary, potentially with your initials in script or something that is professional and sharp. Have your notecards with you prior to going into the interview. If this is a large organization, find a location (your car for instance) to write the cards immediately for each person. If you did not get their business card, record each interviewer's name at the top of your "questions for them" sheet or on a tablet. Write a three to five sentence note following the template below. Walk back into the building and offer the cards to the receptionist. If this is a small organization, there is no receptionist or walking back in does not make sense, have your stamps ready and drop the notes in the mailbox the same day as the interview.

Rule 5: Content

During the interview, take some notes and mark down areas of concern for the interviewer. What were they focused on? What questions did they have that were different from other interviewers? Who is the actual hiring manager you would be working under? That person is the most important one to impress but all interviewers should be addressed.

With your list of notes about the type of skill(s), needs, and concerns that each person stressed during the interview, speak directly to those issues on the "thank you" letter. You can write the same note for each person, but it will be far more effective to show a personalized approach. At the very least, the most important person to write to is your direct hiring manager. In the letter, briefly address one to three skills, needs, or concerns you discussed. Finish the note by re-affirming your interest in the position.

Use the following template to assist in writing your notes.

6.12.1 Thank You Letter Template

(Name of Contact),

Thank you for meeting with me to discuss your needs for the _____ (Title) position. Based on our meeting, I felt the strong sense of urgency in finding a dedicated team member that will take care _____ (Skill/Need/Concern 1), _____ (Skill/Need/Concern 2), and _____ (Skill/Need/Concern 3). I possess those skills.

I am very interested in this position and I am ready to contribute to the team and organization.

Sincerely,

Name

>Homework

Prepare for interviews and control the engagement, especially the timing of phone interviews. Getting a job offer is as much about demonstrating that you will be a happy, non-disruptive team member that will stay on the job as it is about skills. Only when these issues have been satisfied will a candidate be judged on their technical capabilities.

Quiz 6: Interviewing (T/F)

1. ____ A great phone screen is about saying "yes" as much as possible.

2. ____ Phone screens are focused on your ability to do the job.

3. ____ You can quote the same "desired salary" for all jobs.

4. ____ Your "reasons for leaving" past jobs are critical to interview success.

5. ____ The phone screens are casual and are primarily for appointment-setting.

6. ____ Behavioral interview questions are specific problem solving examples.

7. ____ "Questions for them" should focus on company history

8. ____ I can get a job offer if I say I was fired "with cause."

9. ____ The best candidate is the one that can do the job the best.

10. ____ Salary negotiations typically begin at the time of the job offer.

Chapter 6: Answer Key (T/F)

1) True: The more you say "yes" the more likely it is to move forward with the process.
2) False: Phone screens are focused on your career goals and salary expectations.
3) False: "Desired Salary" must match the position, not your goals, to move forward.
4) True: Why you left each one, and how it relates to the position in question, is critical.
5) False: Phone screens are used to ruthlessly weed out candidates.
6) True: Behavioral questions require specific problem solving examples for each line item of the job ad.
7) False: "Questions for them" allow a candidate to re-affirm candidacy, decrease hiring uncertainty, demonstrate strong interest, and trigger a "yes" in the recruiter's mind.
8) False: Employers do not hire people who say they were fired "with cause."
9) False: The best candidate can do the job AND will stay on the job and be happy.
10) False: They usually begin in the phone screen.

Chapter 7:
Salary Negotiations and Desired Salary Quoting

This book has covered the many important parts to getting a new job. All these steps set the stage for quoting salary or performing final negotiations. This area is very misunderstood by job candidates and it has a staggering impact on careers.

It is estimated that 85% of employers expect job candidates to negotiate salary. The reality is that only 37% to 44% of candidates enter into some type of negotiation. The lack of salary negotiating in your career can cost an average of $500,000 in lifetime lost earnings. In addition, women are much less likely to negotiate than men. A partial contributor to the female gender pay gap (where women make 77 cents of every dollar a man earns) is a reluctance to negotiate.

The fact that the salary topic comes up so quickly in the job search process, sometimes on the application itself, adds to the complexity of this topic. Salary negotiation fears are not without merit. A bad negotiation can end the job offer.

Let's explore some salary myths and common beliefs.
This lesson will cover:
7.1 – Salary negotiation myths
7.2 – What to quote for desired salary
7.3 – Performing a salary survey
7.4 – New hire salary negotiations

7.5 – Salary adjustment, negotiation, or both

7.1 Salary Negotiation Myths

<u>Myth 1. Salary negotiations begin after interviews when the offer is made.</u>

In the past, salary negotiations were the final step in the hiring process or, for existing employees, a part of the performance review. Now salary negotiations often **begin at the point of application** to a job.

The following list presents the five points where a salary negotiation may occur:
1. At the time of application,
2. During the phone screen,
3. In the first in-person interview,
4. At the point of a job offer, or
5. During a performance review.

When "Desired Salary" is used too early in the process, the question essentially turns into the "Guess What the Job Pays" Game.

Here are the rules of the game:
- The employer uses a field in the Applicant Tracking System or asks a question on the phone screen about salary.
- If you answer wrong, you will not be called for further interviews.
- If you answer correctly, you may continue and might ultimately end with a job offer.

Negotiations don't even begin if you cannot guess what the employer has decided the job is worth.

Below are examples of three different sales positions. The same candidate will apply, and is qualified for, all three jobs.

What answer should the candidate give in the desired salary field on the application or during the first interviews?

3 POSITIONS, 3 SALARIES, 1 APPLICANT			
Job Title	Outside Salesperson	Sales Territory Manager	Sales Manager
Years of Experience Required	1-3 years	3-5 years	3-5 years
Education Level	High School Diploma	Bachelor's Preferred	Bachelor's Required
Salary	??	??	??

These three jobs do not pay the same amount.

If the same figure is quoted, this candidate will not likely advance or get a job offer. If this candidate needs a job, and would consider any of these three, they must figure out what each one pays.

The biggest takeaway is that salary negotiations begin with guessing the value that the employer has placed on the job. If you don't get that right, you won't get an interview or an offer.

193

Myth 2. Salary is not used to screen out a candidate.

When applying for a job, the employers may elect to create pre-programmed fields inside the Applicant Tracking Systems to eliminate candidates that do not meet a certain range of salary amounts. These same questions may also be asked during an initial telephone screen or first in-person interview. If salary is discussed this early, the employer is using this information as a way to screen candidates.

Myth 3. Your desired salary quote is what you want to earn.

No. The desired salary, if you want to get the job offer, is how much the job pays.
The goal of this module is to educate you on determining what an advertised job is worth as indicated by:
1. The value that employer has placed on the position,
2. The prevailing wage information, and
3. How to have a salary conversation with the employer.

Myth 4. You will be told that your stated salary range is acceptable.

The recruiter may tell you that the quoted range is acceptable or they may just continue on with further interviewing. If you are moving along in the process, this is a strong indicator that the stated range is acceptable.

Myth 5. Once the employer makes the offer, the interview process is complete.

No. When the employer is ready to make an offer, the salary negotiation is used as the **final interview** in the process. It is important to know that you are still being evaluated for the job based on how you perform in the salary negotiation.

Myth 6. The candidate will lose if they throw out the first number.

As long as the candidate knows the value of the job, understands the prevailing wages in the professional category, and demonstrates the ability to state their value, a candidate should be in a better position even if they state a range early on.

Myth 7. Once you are hired, it is almost impossible to negotiate salary, so you better get it right first.

This one is partially true. Once you are hired at a job, it is often challenging to get an employer to offer a raise over three percent up to ten percent *without a promotion*. To get paid more money for the same job requires significant evidence, proof of skills, accomplishments, and industry wage information. Section 7.5 on existing employee salary negotiations does discuss this, but it is also important to consider how to get a promotion, which is a more likely method of achieving a large increase.

No matter when the salary negotiation takes place, the formulation of a matching salary requires an understanding of how much the employer and the market values the position. In the following two sections, we will focus on understanding the signals an employer is making about the position's pay rate.

Myth 8: Salary negotiations are always possible and there is always $10,000 or more wiggle room.

If a person has virtually no experience in the field, salary negotiations are almost impossible. For a job candidate that has one or more years of experience, there is usually room for negotiation, but this depends on the salary range of the position according to the following parameters.

- Jobs under $40,000 typically have a $1 to $2 per hour negotiation range.
- Jobs between $40,000 and $65,000 have about a $5,000 per year negotiation range.
- Jobs between $65,000 and $90,000 have about a $10,000 to $15,000 per year negotiation range.
- Jobs above $90,000 will have a $20,000 or higher per year negotiation range.

The following lesson covers how to quote desired salary.

7.2 What to Quote for Desired Salary

Every profession has a huge range of salaries from the entry point to leadership roles. To perform a salary negotiation, the candidate must know two pieces of information:

1. The value the employer has placed on the job - low, mid, or high.
2. The prevailing wage information about salaries for the professional category.

If we assume that every profession can range from $30,000 to $150,000, we need to become masters at reading employer signals of job value.

Indications of Job Value

To state a desired salary that matches the value the employer has placed on the position, a core skill for a successful job hunt requires an analysis of the job advertisement. This value does not have to be a mystery. There is a push for legislation to force employers to state the salary range on job advertisements to eliminate the gender pay gap, however that has not happened on a national level yet.

Employers offer three primary signals in a job advertisement that indicate whether a job pays a low or high salary:
1. The level of education,
2. Job title additions, and
3. The years of experience.

Some areas of the country and some industries will pay at different rates, but these averages offer an excellent gauge of the employer's pay rate perspective on the position. There are exceptions to every rule, however I use these methods every day with accuracy.

1. Level of Education

The level of education required by the job advertisement is a great first indicator of pay levels. The national average for earnings by degree is a consistent indicator of the likely pay within about five dollars per hour, higher or lower, than the average. The following table presents the national average pay rates based on degree level.

Average U.S. Earnings by Degree Level (Source: BLS 2010 Census)
- High School: Average Hourly Wage-$15, Annual Wage-$30,000
- Bachelor's: Average Hourly Wage-$27, Annual Wage-$52,500
- Master's: Average Hourly Wage-$31, Annual Wage-$62,500

High School/Associate's Degree Level

A position that does not require a Bachelor's degree is typically going to be in a range of pay between $10 and $15 per hour unless the job is seeking specialized knowledge, is in a known well-paying industry, or requires many years of experience. If you do not have a Bachelor's degree and make over $15 per hour, then you are outperforming the national average and would be considered to be doing well for your education level.

If you make an income close to or above the Bachelor's or Master's degree level of pay, you will likely need to consider additional education or targeted technical experience to obtain a salary increase, since the current pay rate significantly outpaces the national average. A person who is overpriced in the job market can face a challenging situation. It is better to be proactive if you find yourself in this position in order to maintain income or a job, or to experience continued growth.

When a client has a Bachelor's degree and is making over $40,000 per year, and sees a position that does not require a degree, I know that the employer is not willing to pay the best rate for the job. There are some exceptions in certain fields, particularly manufacturing and industrial, where an employee can make above $65,000 per year with no degree, but these positions are becoming fewer by the day.

No matter what the job pays, if the job advertisement states that it requires a High School graduate, it is a signal that the job is on the lower level of the pay scale. If you have a Bachelor's degree, this should be a flag that this job will probably not pay over $20 per hour.

Bachelor's Degree Level

A position requiring a Bachelor's degree will typically start at no lower than $15 per hour and will likely grow to $20 per hour rather quickly with one to three years of experience. To obtain $27 per hour, or $52,500 annually, a job candidate or employee will usually need to obtain specialized knowledge or have over five years of experience. To obtain $60,000 and above usually requires highly specialized knowledge in the field or having obtained a management position. If you have a Bachelor's degree and are not making $27 per hour or $52,500 annually, then additional years of experience, specialized knowledge, a different career path, or a management position is necessary to push to the higher salary. Salaries of $50,000 to $70,000 for a candidate with a Bachelor's degree between the ages of 30 and 50 are fairly common. Earning over $70,000 requires having higher technical knowledge, holding certifications, being politically savvy, hitting a high growth company, starting with a professional category that tends to pay better, or obtaining a management position.

There are industry considerations as well. For instance, social services and nonprofits tend to pay less than banking or manufacturing.

Since these are averages, there are people making less and more than this amount, however this is a beginning indicator of the value the employer is putting on the advertised job.

Master's Degree Level

A position that mandates, or even prefers, a Master's degree, is indicating a pay rate over $30 per hour and potentially much more. However, job candidates who have a Master's degree but limited related work experience face the same entry-level career path as a Bachelor-degree holder. Experience is the key to obtaining the higher salary ranges. In some industries a Master's degree or higher is the threshold education level even if the pay is low. A Licensed Social Worker is an example of a position that may require a Master's degree but is not in a high-paying field.

In general, if the position is looking for a Master's degree, the candidate should be making over $60,000 per year. In some business fields like finance, a job ad that asks for many years of experience and a Master's degree indicates a position over $90,000.

Tip: If you have a degree that is higher than the job is requesting, then the pay rate will be reflective of what the employer is asking for, not the education level you have obtained.

For instance, if you have a Master's degree and the job is asking for a Bachelor's degree, the employer has determined the pay rate for the position of a person holding a Bachelor's degree. Your higher-level degree will be considered as a Bachelor's degree pay rate. If a job is asking for an Associate's degree and you have a Bachelor's degree, the pay rate will be closer to the Associate's degree level averages than the Bachelor's degree level.

What if you are making a different pay rate than indicated by the national averages for your degree level? Other than looking for different job advertisements that are more closely related to your experience and degree-level, consider the following long-term strategies.

If you are being paid less than your degree level, additional experience or a job change can assist in bumping you to the higher level. Take a lower-level job and treat it like a one- to two-year school program.

If you are at the average pay level for your education, additional experience, education, a job change, or a promotion is necessary to bump you to the next level.

If you are higher than the national average for your education, examine promotion possibilities, seek out management roles, and find ways to get more specialized technical experience or industry certifications to ensure continued increases.

If you make exceptionally more than the average pay rate for your education level, examine the market to gain experience in changing trends in the field, or consider moving geographical markets to maintain income stability.

The next indication of pay level is additions to the job title. Job titles often indicate what the employer is looking for in the level of responsibility and years of experience, which impact the pay rate.

2. Level of Responsibility: Additions to Job Title

The job advertisement will of course list a job title. The title typically holds two pieces of information: 1) the professional category and 2) the level of responsibility, which directly impacts the pay rate.

The following demonstrates the correlation between the job title additions to lower and higher level pay rates.

Low-Level Pay Rates
Coordinator, Specialist, Associate, "Levels" like I or 1, Representative, Clerk, Assistant, Supervisor, Entry-Level

Mid to Higher Level
Consultant, Manager, Director, "Levels" II-III or 2 to 3, Analyst, Compliance, Development

The lower-level title additions may offer below $20 per hour while the mid- to higher-level can reach well beyond $20 per hour. Unlike degree level, there is no national data for pay rate averages based on job title additions. Use the title additions in combination with the desired education level and years of experience to complete the picture of the employer's pay rate perspective.

3. Desired Years of Experience

The requested years of experience will also indicate if the position is valued at a higher or lower level. The following correlates the desired years of experience to lower and higher-level pay rates.

Low-Level Salary Ranges: 0-3 years of experience expected

Mid- to Higher-Level Salary Ranges: 3+ years of experience expected
The requested years of experience, used in conjunction with the degree level and job title additions, can offer the final piece of information on what the employer is willing to pay.

Industry, the life cycle of the organization, demand for workers, supply of workers, and geographic location all play into salary levels. However, degree requirements, the additions to the job title, and the requested years of experience, are good indicators of the potential pay level.

The next step in the process is using your personal knowledge through you or your network to conduct a salary survey. Use the following exercise to determine the likely value the employer is placing on the advertised job.

Exercise 7.2: Value of the Job Evaluation
Look at the job ad and evaluate the position using this guide.

Evaluation 7.2a: Salary below $20 per hour on average
Assessment – check all that apply:
1. ___ Not asking for a Bachelor's degree
2. ___ Uses low-level job title additions.
3. ___ Asking for 0-3 years of experience

If you selected any option from the above list, it may indicate that the position will offer less than $20 per hour. Certain industries and professional categories may pay more.

Evaluation 7.2b: Salary at or above $20 per hour.
Assessment – check all that apply:
1. ___ Asking for a Bachelor's degree
2. ___ Uses higher-level title additions
3. ___ Asking for 3+ years of experience

If you selected any option from the above list, it may indicate that the position will offer at or above $20 per hour.

Evaluation 7.2c: Salary at or above $30 per hour.
Assessment – check all that apply:
1. ___ Asking for a Master's degree or professional certification as mandatory or preferred
2. ___ Uses higher-level title additions
3. ___ Asking for 3+ years of experience

If you selected any option from the above list, it may indicate that the position will offer at or above $30 per hour.

7.3 Performing a Salary Survey Lesson

The previous section explored the value an employer may be placing on the position. This section focuses on the prevailing market wage for similar jobs in the same industry.

There are three ways to gather salary information:
- Your own personal knowledge of the field,
- The knowledge of friends/family/colleagues/professors/mentors, and
- Performing a salary survey of related professional titles or skills.

In some cases, when changing careers, a job candidate has limited personal knowledge of possible salaries, therefore it is important to talk with other people who may be aware of the salary range. Beyond asking other people about the likely pay ranges, learning how to perform a salary survey is the next most important skill. Although there are industry averages, it is better to actually search for similar titles and use the job advertisements that list jobs, speak with recruiting agencies to get an idea of pay rates, and use the salary survey tool built into Indeed.com.

Indeed.com has a salary survey tool built directly into the system. Within the search function there is a "more" option that contains salary survey information. A rule of thumb is to quote an income range for the targeted position. If the candidate, recruiter, and hiring manager have different concepts of a pay rate, a salary range may save the interview and continue the process.

Quoting a single salary number that is much higher than what the recruiter is going to offer can immediately shut down the process. Quoting a range that is too wide may indicate a candidate that does not know the industry or what they want. A quote that follows typical ranges maintains a conversation. If the recruiter indicates that the range is acceptable, you will likely obtain the middle number of the range. The exercise below demonstrates how to perform a salary survey.

Exercise 7.3: Performing a Salary Survey

Follow the steps to obtain the best salary range possible.

Step 1: Who do you know that might have knowledge of income ranges for the job?

Speak to people who you know can be trusted to remain discreet with your career goals and information. Some of the most knowledgeable people about prospective salaries really should not know about your pending career transition.

Step 2: Mine third party recruiters or staffing agencies for information.

Third Party Recruiters and staffing agencies place candidates in positions every single day. They are the single best source of pay rates in your locale. If you do not know someone working in this field, look for a job being staffed by a recruiting/staffing agency and apply for it. If you get a call, you can ask the recruiter what the job pays or what they are seeing in the field. In many cases, a recruiting firm will list the hourly wage right in the job advertisement.

Step 3: Perform a salary survey

Go to Indeed.com and...

- Search by title or keyword combinations.
- Leave the city blank to get a nationwide range for the salary and the best close hits.
- Add the city to get an idea of averages in your local market.
- Keep combining keywords or title until you get job matches that are as close to the same.
- Do not rely on the title alone unless it is very standard like "accountant." Even in this case there are many job levels within a title.
- Click on "More" under the job titles that look closely related.
- Under "More" below the job advertisement there is a Salary Search option. Click on the Salary Search and a window will pop up with salary information.

One result is not enough. Try many combinations of title, keywords, and responsibility level of the roles to get different salary ranges across the country. These ranges will offer a basis for discussion.

7.4 New Hire Salary Negotiations

Salary negotiations ideally begin once a job offer has been made. Even if a dollar amount has been discussed during the screening process, a candidate can still attempt to negotiate. At this point, the candidate, recruiters, and hiring managers have invested a large amount of time and energy into locating the right job candidate. Everyone wants to close the process as quickly as possible. Although there is usually room in a company's pay scale to offer additional income, the employer does not always consider every candidate eligible to negotiate.

Take this self-evaluation to determine if salary negotiations are likely to result in a positive discussion in your next interview.

New Hire Salary Eligibility Assessment

"Am I eligible to negotiate more money in my new hire salary?" Check all that apply:

1. ___ I have at least one year of practical work experience in this field.
2. ___ I have held this title or a similar title.
3. ___ This is not a low-level or entry-level position.
4. ___ There is no pre-stated salary placed on the job.
5. ___ I have not already strongly committed to a salary amount with the employer.
6. ___ I have relevant accomplishments.
7. ___ This is a high-demand field with few qualified applicants.
8. ___ I have knowledge that the employer pays a wide range of salary amounts.

If you selected any option from the above list, you may see positive results from a salary negotiation. If you were not able to select some of the options above, you may experience difficulties in negotiating a salary.

Negotiating a salary may be difficult at the time of hire if a candidate has no relevant experience or accomplishments, the position is entry or low-level, or when the field has many qualified applicants. An employer that lists the pay in the job advertisement will often not be open to negotiation. If a candidate was forced to state a salary history or their desired salary, negotiations may be challenging.

Typically, it is easier to negotiate if the candidate has unique matching skills that are hard to find in the labor market.

New Hire Salary Negotiations: A Balance Between Three People

A salary negotiation in a larger organization balances the wants, needs, and realities of three people:
1. The candidate,
2. The recruiter, and
3. The hiring manager.

The exception is in a smaller organization where there may not be a formal Human Resource department, in which case the negotiation is between the hiring manager and the applicant.

A job candidate theoretically wants the highest salary possible. Recruiters want a salary amount that is within the industry prevailing wage to recruit and retain the right employee. The hiring manager wants to maintain equity of pay in the department and remain within their annual budget.

Sometimes the salary figures of these three people are not in agreement with each other.

The recruiter does not want to lose a candidate during a salary negotiation because it would mean starting again in the process. At the same time, recruiters and hiring managers watch negotiations closely because the candidate is demonstrating how they will behave on the job. A job candidate is still interviewing during the negotiations.

A candidate who meets the basic eligibility to negotiate has an increased potential to maintain their job offer and obtain additional benefits in this final process if they do the following:
1. Express gratitude,
2. Act decisively,
3. Properly calculate value,
4. Provide proof,
5. Be flexible, and
6. Create a positive conversation.

Express Gratitude, Even With an Insulting Job Offer

In a survey of recruiters, the most appreciated job candidates were those who thanked them for the offer. Thanking the recruiter, and even respectfully declining an insultingly low job offer, can result In contlnued negotlations later on for higher value positions. Some candidates have negotiated and turned around job offers that were originally significantly less than the candidate's acceptable range, if they were gracious in their reply. An employer may come back to the candidate and make a new job offer when their budget allows for more money or a higher paying position opens up. On the other hand, an employer will not call a candidate back if a previous job offer was ignored or if the negotiation was unprofessional.

Act Decisively: Timeframes of Negotiations

Recruiters like decisive candidates who know what they want. When you enter into a negotiation, you need to know what your primary points of negotiation are and maintain them. The negotiation typically only goes back and forth one time, rarely two times, for additional well-defined terms.

If the candidate adds or changes their stated desires in this process, the recruiter may determine that the candidate is an indecisive person and rescind the offer.

This decisiveness also pertains to the time needed to accept an offer. Despite the lengthy amount of time candidates have to wait during a job interview process, once the final offer has been made the candidate only has 48 hours to make a decision.

Calculate Total Value

Recruiters like candidates who can calculate the full value of all parts of the offer, not just salary. If you enter into a negotiation, it is probably for a job that requires some level of education and skills. If you are stuck on one aspect of the negotiation and cannot assess everything being offered, then the recruiter may determine that you are not as intelligent as they thought and rescind the offer. This is especially true for managerial or number-driven positions.

Proof of Accomplishments

Recruiters like a candidate who can offer proof of their value in accomplishments. A hiring decision is often made by multiple people, and so a candidate who can succinctly present their competitive advantage makes it easier for the recruiter to support their salary negotiation with the other hiring decision-makers.

Be Flexible

Recruiters like flexibility. A candidate who is flexible in alternative arrangements indicates a team player. Examples of these alternatives are a sign-on bonus, a salary adjustment later in the fiscal year, a better title, the potential for growth, stock sharing, pay for performance arrangements, or additional vacation time.

Create a Positive Conversation

The most common advice you may hear on negotiating new hire salaries is that you should force the employer to tell you a salary amount first. The thought is that whoever states the amount first is the "loser." Not only is this advice unhelpful, but it also sets up a negative interaction with the employer. For instance, if the employer asks, "What are your salary expectations?" and your response is "I am willing to review any acceptable offer," then the conversation could go back and forth and create a negative situation.

A candidate who states, "I feel I should make more" is not likely to be successful. The best way to manage the new hire salary negotiation is to be proactive and have all of the necessary facts to state the position's range and to justify why you, as a candidate, qualify for the upper part of the range. If you have adequately detailed your qualifications with references or supporting documentation, there is a strong basis for your salary negotiation. Evidence-based negotiations yield better results for both parties because the conversation is based on data.

How the candidate handles salary negotiations reflects how the candidate will behave at work. The next section presents scripts for beginning a new hire salary negotiation, what to say during the process, and what to do if the answer is no.

Exercise 7.4: New Hire Salary Negotiations

The New Hire Salary Negotiation Commitment
Answer the following with a "yes" or "no."
_____ I know that by engaging in a new hire salary negotiation I am indicating to the employer that I am unhappy with the offered pay. I have used the evaluation to determine how likely it is for this discussion to be successful or at least well received. I know that basing the negotiation on facts and information is more likely to produce a data-driven unemotional discussion that should maintain positive relations whether an increase occurs or not. If, by some chance, the employer responds negatively, I will use the Exercise 7.4C script and decision process to determine my next moves.

Exercise 7.4a: The Script

"Based on my knowledge of this field, my current salary, and a salary survey of similar titles for this type of work, I have identified that the current salary range for this position is between _____ and _____." (State a $10,000 range based on your salary survey.)

Exercise 7.4b: Scripts for When They Say Yes

If they accept the range continue with the following:
"I feel that I am qualified for the upper range of this position because I have specific accomplishments and experience in the following skills highlighted in the job ad and the interview process _____, _____, and _____." (State skills and past experience in saving money or generating revenue.)

Exercise 7.4c: Scripts for When They Say No

If the recruiter states a lower range, or directly says "no", then there are a few options which depend on the comfort level of the candidate to walk away from the table.

Willing to walk away:

"Thank you for the offer. I am still very interested in this position, however, based on my current salary and a survey of the field, I cannot go below $_____ (State the "drop dead" desired salary amount). *I might consider $_____ with a performance-based bonus and combined benefits package that offers the potential to reach $_____."*

Willing to accept a lower salary offer:

If you are willing, or need, to accept the lower offer, but feel you may be able to negotiate on different terms, use the following script:

"Thank you for the offer. I am very interested in this position. I can understand you wanting to see evidence of my ability to perform. I would like to negotiate a salary adjustment review based on performance in a 6-month timeframe."

Or …

"Thank you for the offer. I am still interested in this position. I would like to negotiate _____. (State one or more of the following.)"

- A sign on bonus,
- A salary bump in the new fiscal year,
- A performance-based bonus structure,
- Additional vacation time,
- A better job title, and/or
- Pay for education and certification.

Willing to accept the lower salary offer:

If you need to take the job but have no intention on working at that rate for a long period of time, consider the following strategy:

- View this position as a way to be paid to "go to school." If you are not getting the pay that you want, then it may be that you need experience. Many positions are worth an increase of $10,000 or more with one year of experience.

- Seek a salary adjustment to the prevailing industry wage at the next performance review. (The next section covers this strategy.) It may take a full year to obtain this increase.
- If you cannot obtain an adjustment, seek a new position within one to two years.
- It may be necessary to re-evaluate the value of the position in the market. Maybe this career path is not worth as much as you thought.

Scripts for a rescinded offer in which the employer walks away:

If the employer terminates the job offer during the negotiation process, or you walk away from the job offer, use the following script:

"I very much appreciate being considered for this position and salary negotiation. Although it did not work out this time due to _____, I hope that we can keep in touch about future possibilities."

7.5 Existing Employee Salary Negotiations Lesson

Salary negotiations for existing employees are different from those for new hires. Employers generally will not exceed a ten percent increase in salary. To achieve higher salaries, you may need to seek a promotion to a higher pay rank. Promotions typically include a different title and higher level of responsibility, while salary negotiations can be for a current position. This section is dedicated to salary negotiations for the position an employee currently holds.

There are two types of salary negotiations for an existing employee: a salary adjustment or a raise. There is one universal HR tip for existing employee negotiations: if you are not meeting or exceeding expectations, do not expect an increase in salary.

Other than performance, there are additional instances where an increase in salary is not likely. Use the evaluation below to determine if your situation fits into this scenario.

Evaluation 7.5a: Existing Employee Salary Negotiation: Less Likely

Assessment: Will your employer be open to a salary negotiation? Check all that apply:

1. ___ Other employees hold the same position and likely same pay for years.
2. ___ People leave the company all the time when they get experience.
3. ___ The employer does not seem to care about employees quitting.
4. ___ The position is designed to be an entry point into the organization.
5. ___ The position is designed as a stepped-development role.
6. ___ The organization or industry is in decline locally or in general.
7. ___ I am a low performer.

If you selected any option from the above list, it may indicate a challenge ahead in having a salary adjustment or raise discussion. If many employees hold the same role at the same pay rate, or if an employee at a low pay-rate has been willing to remain in the position for years, the employer may believe that the job is paying well enough. If people leave the company all the time and the employer does not seem to care about them going, then it is an indicator that this is an "entry-level" organization with no plans to increase wages.

If the company is known for hiring people into "entry" positions, then the person must seek work in other departments or a promotion in the same department for a wage increase. If the position was designed as a development role from the start, then obtaining a higher wage based on the market rate is unlikely.

Some organizations or industries are shrinking in the local or greater economy, which can create salary increase issues or the proverbial "can't get blood from a turnip" situation. Even though salary adjustments are based on the prevailing wage, if an employee is a low performer they will not likely get a raise.

Although there are cases where a salary negotiation is not possible, there are equally as many instances where an employee can obtain a raise. The following sections discuss the difference between the salary adjustment and a raise discussion with corresponding assessments and scripts for a positive outcome.

Salary Adjustments

A salary adjustment typically applies to a job candidate that was hired at an entry-level and has now gained one to two years of experience. It is not uncommon for an entry-level job candidate to be worth $10,000 or more in a short period of time. The challenge is that employers do not typically like to make large jumps in salary. Salary adjustment conversations are a way to get the employer to make a bigger leap in income than they normally would consider by proving the job pays more.

Salary adjustments are an easier discussion to have than merit-based raise conversations.

Why would an employer pay less for a job than the prevailing market wage?

The reasons can include:
1. Income equity amongst workers,
2. A high tolerance for employee turnover,
3. A sign of an "entry-level employer," or
4. A lack of knowledge about prevailing wages.

The first three employer types may not be open to a salary adjustment discussion, but the fourth situation may be open to discussion if the employee can demonstrate proof of a higher prevailing wage in the market.

Income Equity

Some employers and professions require income equity, a standard income rate across employees performing similar duties. This is common in large call centers or any type of profession that has many people working the same job. In this case, the employer reduces the complexity of their pay structure by creating a uniform salary system. This method also reduces potential issues with employees talking to each other about pay and reduces the possibility of a salary adjustment.

"Don't Let the Door Hit You on the Way Out" Employers

There are employers that can be classified as the "if you do not like it, quit" type. In this case, the organization is willing to exchange the threat or reality of people quitting in exchange for low pay rates. An employer with high attrition or many people quitting is not likely to change their ways.

"Entry-level" Employers

There are employers that tend to hire at the entry level. A small business may offer a dynamic, rich experience but is not be able to pay much. For instance, a start-up or a nonprofit that is not well funded can often offer an exceptional work experience. These employers may not want to lose great employees, but there is little room in the budget to prevent employees from leaving once they have gained experience.

Other types of employers have entry-level positions that they deliberately use to develop new employees. These can be formal development positions or the general way the company hires new employees. These types of employers use the entry-level experience to separate the low-performers from the high-performers for future promotion. In this case, a salary adjustment is not possible and the only way to grow is to perform well and seek a promotion.

Overall, entry-level employers are critical in the job market because they tend to have lower requirements for their new hires and allow entry-level or career changers to gain experience. However, if an employee obtains one to two years of experience, and there is no promotion pending, they will have to move on to another employer to get an increase.

<u>Lack of Knowledge about Prevailing Wage</u>

This is the most likely employer type to offer a salary adjustment. Some employers or managers literally have no idea what the market rate is for certain jobs. In this case, the employee needs to educate the employer. This may occur when it is a small organization or a business startup, when you would report to a boss whose professional background is different from yours, or in a business where you are the only professional in a certain category. Gathering market information and presenting it to the employer for a salary adjustment discussion may result in a positive discussion.

The following evaluation demonstrates a likely scenario for success in a salary adjustment discussion.

Evaluation 7.5b: Salary Adjustment Evaluation – More Likely

Assessment: Check all that apply:
1. ___ There are no or few employees with your title or professional background.
2. ___ There is a small or ineffective HR department with no wage analysis experience.

3. ___ The organization is young and inexperienced in wage issues.
4. ___ The last person that held the role was hired many years ago.
5. ___ I have upgraded my skills justifying more money in the market.
6. ___ I can provide evidence of prevailing wage information.
7. ___ This organization or the industry is in a growth or mature phase.
8. ___ I am a high performer that has met or exceeded expectations.

If you selected any option from the above list, it may indicate an easier salary adjustment discussion. If someone is the only person in a professional category, the employer may be unfamiliar with the prevailing wage for an experienced person. For instance, a manufacturer may have one or two I.T. employees. The employer is accustomed to wage discussions in manufacturing, not I.T. If the previous person held the role for many years, they may have been happy with a lower pay and the employer may think that is normal. It is possible to educate the employer with the facts. The same can also be said for organizations that do not have a formal or large Human Resource department.

Lastly, the organization or industry may be on the rise or at its peak, offering additional increase opportunities. In this case, educating the employer on prevailing wages may be possible.

Salary Adjustments and Performance

Even though a salary adjustment is based on the market rate for the position, an under-performing employee will not likely receive a raise. Therefore, a salary adjustment conversation must also include some level of merit-based performance evidence by the employee. The following section discusses raise discussions followed by scripts for each type of salary negotiation.

Raise Negotiations

Both raise discussions and salary adjustments require an employee who is meeting or exceeding expectations. Salary adjustments typically apply to the transition from an entry-level candidate to an experienced candidate, while raise negotiations are for the life of your career and are merit-based or pay for performance.

As with new hire salary negotiations, a salary adjustment discussion requires diplomacy and awareness. Once you enter into this discussion you are essentially saying, "I am not happy with my pay." Sometimes employers do not react well to this information which can be career-limiting. It is important to use the evaluations in this section to determine the perspective of the employer on pay rates so that a salary discussion does not threaten your ability to keep your job or limit your career movement in the company. The next assessment evaluates the likelihood of a positive discussion.

For raise negotiations, use the following evaluation to determine how like it is to obtain a merit-based increase.

Evaluation 7.5c: Raise Negotiations – More Likely

Assessment: Can I get a raise? Check all that apply:

1. ___ The organization has a hard time finding qualified employees.
2. ___ I consistently outperform my co-workers.
3. ___ I can provide evidence that my actions generated revenue.
4. ___ I can provide evidence that my actions saved the company money.
5. ___ My previous performance reviews have been good or great.
6. ___ My previous performance reviews properly document my accomplishments.
7. ___ I have upgraded my skills in some way that justifies more money.
8. ___ The company is in good financial condition.
9. ___ The organization or industry is in growth or mature phase.

If you selected any option from the above list, it may indicate an easier, more successful raise negotiation. If the company cannot find qualified workers, you consistently outperform other colleagues, there is evidence of making or saving the company money, performance reviews are consistently high and all accomplishments are documented, there has been an upgrade in skills, and the company is in a financial position to offer a raise, then it should be possible to have this discussion.

There is an important point to learn as early in your career as possible: Is the organization or industry on the rise, at its peak, or in decline? The answer may influence salary increase and promotion opportunities. The organization's financial health and industry trends are governed by a growth curve.

Increases in salary or promotions are largely dependent on what stage the company or industry is in. The introductory, or startup, periods usually have lower pay scales with the possibility of performance incentives. The growth stage offers a wave of progressive promotions and increases. The maturity stage includes high wages but much fewer promotions. The decline stage often offers exceptionally high wages, called legacy expenses, but there is also little movement and a high potential for layoffs.

Observe your organization and industry to evaluate what movement is possible. It may be worthwhile to attempt to switch companies or industries to ensure continued progression. Identify a start-up company by observing if there are few employees and if the company is being funded by investors until a customer base is achieved. A growth company will be investing in new buildings for expansion. For younger employees, this is a good option to ride a wave of growth. Mature companies have typically been in the same building with limited growth or the growth is from international market penetration. The decline stage typically looks like an aging infrastructure and a reduction in workforce from its peak operating period.

The following section includes exercises for salary adjustment and raise negotiations.

Existing Employee Salary Negotiations

Exercise 7.5a: Salary Adjustment or Raise Negotiations Commitment

Answer the following with a "yes" or "no."

_____I know that by engaging in a salary adjustment or raise negotiation discussion that I am indicating to my employer that I am unhappy with my pay. The employer may not react well to this discussion creating an adverse relationship. I have used the evaluations to determine how likely it is for this discussion to be successful, or at least well received. I know that the more information and evidence I produce, the more likely I am to have a data-driven, unemotional discussion that should maintain positive relations whether an increase occurs or not. If, by some chance, my employer responds very negatively, I am ready to leave them and move on to another position with a company that will pay my worth or the worth of the position in the market. If they say no, then I will use Lesson 7.5D to make my decision on my next moves.

Exercise 7.5b: Salary Adjustment

Fill in the salary adjustment script:

"When I came on board, I was excited for the opportunity to contribute to the organization. I am still completely dedicated to _____ (name of employer). *However, with* ____ (years of experience) *in the field, I have performed a salary survey and have found that the prevailing wage for this position is in the range of* _____ *to* _____ (be prepared to provide evidence). *I know that I came on with limited experience, but that has changed. I would like to discuss a salary adjustment to the prevailing market wages for someone in this position with this*

many years of experience. What are your initial reactions or feelings to what I am proposing? Were you aware of these differences in pay that existed in the market? What is the _____ (employer name) *view on market-wage salary adjustments?"*

Exercise 7.5c: Salary Negotiation

Include any of the phrases that apply.

Hard to Locate Employees Script

"I really enjoy working here and, as we know, the company has had a hard time finding qualified employees with the following skills _____, _____, _____. *With* ___ *year(s) of experience, I have gained this technical ability. I have performed a salary survey and have found that the prevailing wage for this position is in the range of* _____ *to* _____ *(be prepared to provide evidence). What is your perception on my value to the team? Have you been aware of my increase in technical skills?"*

Outperformed Colleagues

"I really enjoy working here and, over the past _____ *year(s), I have outperformed my co-workers on a number of metrics* _____, _____, _____, *yet I am making the same amount of money or have only seen an increase of* _____ *(salary increases). Based on my contribution I believe my value is* ____ *to* _____ *(the goal should be the mid-range number). What is your perception on my value to your team? Have you been aware of these differences in performance? What is the* _____ (employer name) *view on pay for performance?"*

Generated Revenue

"I really enjoy working here and over the past _____ *year(s), I have generated* _____ *in additional revenue for the company, yet I am making the same amount of money or have only seen an increase of* _____ (salary increases). *Based on my contribution, I believe my value is* ____ *to* _____ (the goal should be the mid-range number). *What is your perception on my value to your team? Have you been aware of these differences in performance? What is the* _____ (employer name) *view on pay for performance?"*

Saved Money
"I really enjoy working here and, over the past _____ *year(s), I have saved* _____ (amount saved) *for the company, yet I am making the same amount of money or have only seen an increase of* _____ (salary increases). *Based on my contribution I believe my value is* ____ *to* _____ (the goal should be the mid-range number). *What is your perception on my value to your team? Have you been aware of these differences in performance? What is the* _____ (employer name) *view on pay for performance?"*

Great and Well-Documented Performance Reviews
"I really enjoy working here and, over the past _____ *year(s), I have had excellent performance reviews with documented accomplishments in the following metric areas* (provide a list), *and yet I have only seen an increase of* _____ (salary increases). *Based on my contribution I believe my value is* ____ *to* _____ (the goal should be the mid-range number). *What is your perception on my value to your team? Have you been aware of these differences in performance? What is the* _____ (employer name) *view on pay for performance?"*

Upgrade in Skills

"I really enjoy working here and, over the past _____ *year(s), I have acquired the following* _____ (new technical skills, certifications, and education), *yet I have only seen an increase of* _____ (salary increases). *Based on these additional skills I believe my value is* _____ *to* _____ (the goal should be the mid-range number). *What is your perception on my value to your team? Have you been aware of these differences in performance? What is the* _____ (employer name) *view on pay for performance?"*

Salary Adjustment & Raise Negotiation Combined

"When I came on board I was excited to get the opportunity to contribute to the organization. I am still am completely dedicated to _____ (employer name). *However, with* _____ (years of experience) *in the field, I have performed a salary survey and have found that the prevailing wage for this position is in the range of* _____ *to* _____ (be prepared to provide evidence).

Over the past year(s) I have done the following (list and provide evidence of skills, accomplishments, and accolades).

Based on these additional skills and the prevailing wage for these skills in the market, I believe my value is _____ *to* _____ (the goal should be the mid-range number).

What are your initial reactions or feelings to what I am proposing? Were you aware of these differences in pay that existed in the market? What is the _____ (employer name) *view on market-wage salary adjustments especially in light of my accomplishments?"*

Exercise 7.5d: "What to Say When They Say No" Script

"I really enjoy working here and want to continue to grow. What would I need to do in the next year to reach the income range of ____ to ____?"

- Have the feedback formalized into your review process if possible.
- Give the employer time to make the adjustment. This lets them know you are serious about staying and it buys them time to get it in the budget and speak to upper level decision-makers if necessary.

What to Expect When Implementing This Lesson

- For career changers who are taking a job at an entry-level company or breaking into a new field, remember you have to get experience first. In a very short period of time (one to two years) you may be able to increase to a much higher salary level quickly.
- For experienced new hires, gather the facts, maintain gratitude, and you can be well on your way to more money.
- For existing employees, do not get discouraged. Your manager does not know what you do all day or what you have accomplished. It is your job to protect your salary and position advancement by maintaining a portfolio of accomplishments to make it easy for your boss to see your value.

- Be sure to create a conversation with the employer to avoid a negative backlash. The goal is to keep building evidence to support your claim for more money.
- Keep it positive. Continue to thank the employer for their offers and consideration.
- If salary negotiations do not garner higher pay, seek a promotion or prepare to move to another company to earn more money.

7.6 Alternative Negotiation Item Quick Reference Sheet

In general, you only want to negotiate on no more than one to three items. Most candidates focus on salary but there are alternatives. Refer to the list below for the three types of compensation that can be up for negotiation: Direct, Indirect, and Expense Allowance.

Pick the items based on:

1. Likelihood of success,
2. Whether you were recruited or courted for the job,
3. The items that makes sense due to the dynamics of the position, and
4. The most important items to you.

Tip: Remember to thank the employer for the job offer, express excitement, and use your scripts before negotiating!

Direct (Monetary)

- A sign on bonus (does not accrue for the employer or you—very popular way to make up a difference)

- A salary bump in the new fiscal year (gives time for the organization to budget in increases)
- A performance based salary bump in the new fiscal year (same as above but based on defined performance metrics)
- A performance-based bonus structure or increase in the existing percentage

Indirect (Non-Monetary)

- Additional vacation time
- A better job title (most future job transitions are based on the title you currently hold)
- Guaranteed Severance Package (if company might become insolvent, bankrupt or lays you off due to no fault of your own - more likely in startup or "turnaround" situations)
- An office or better office space
- Flexible scheduling (like four 10-hour shifts)
- Telecommute/remote work
- New laptop, computer, tablet, software, tools
- More or different duties and projects to ensure your continued professional development
- An earlier salary review than the typical 6 months or a year

Expense Allowance Items (depending on job):

- Phone bill subsidy (more likely when a person has to be on call, better than getting a company phone because they do not see calls)
- Transportation (especially if directly recruiting you and the new job is far from home - this may be temporary until a promised move)
- Housing costs (especially if directly recruiting you to a different city)
- Daycare reimbursement (especially if they are directly courting you out of "stay-at-home" status or if the job requires a move and loss of family support

- Wardrobe allowance (if meeting with high-powered clients in a forward-facing position)
- Moving expenses (warning- this is considered income and will be taxable)
- Pay for education and certification (need masters or specialized certification)
- A coach or consultant (speaking, selling, media, executive leadership, management, language...)
- Professional development (work-related conferences, workshops, classes, or membership in a professional association)

>Homework

The key to successful negotiations is to understand what value the employer has placed on the job and to use this information in salary quoting. Successfully getting to a job offer means being able to predict and quote this value. The amount has less to do with the highest earning possible in your field and more to do with the highest value of the range that the employer has placed on the position. The key to more money is to express gratitude, to state the value of the job, to state the value of your skills, and to be able to evaluate the whole compensation package.

Quiz 7: Salary Negotiations (T/F)

1. ___ Desired Salary is how much you want to make.
2. ___ Desired Salary is how much you are worth.
3. ___ If the job asks for a Bachelor's Degree but you have a Master's Degree, the job will pay more due to your degree.
4. ___ If you have a Bachelor's and the job only requires a High School diploma, it will pay more.
5. ___ Salary negotiations are only about the base salary amount.
6. ___ There are good ways to get more money that do not include a bump in salary.
7. ___ There are two types of internal salary negotiations.
8. ___ Salary negotiations are only based on the capabilities you bring to the job.
9. ___ You can negotiate based on increased expenses.
10. ___ A poorly done salary negotiation can end the job offer, and ability to negotiate is a final evaluation method.

Chapter 7: Answer Key (T/F)

1) False: If you want the interview and offer, desired salary is what the job is worth.
2) False: If you want the interview and offer, desired salary is what the job is worth.
3) False: The Master's is valued as a Bachelor's unless the job specifically asks for the higher level degree.
4) False: A job requiring a High School diploma will pay less no matter your degree level.
5) False: There are over 20 monetary and non-monetary items that can be negotiable.
6) True: There are many alternative salary negotiation items.
7) True: Salary adjustment (prevailing wage proof) and raise negotiations (merit-based)
8) False: Salary Negotiations are based on the person's skill value and experience, outside prevailing wage, the internal budget of the department, equity issues in the department, and the ability to find those skills.
9) False: Negotiate on strengths and prevailing wage. In general, the only time expense can be negotiated is with existing employee situations where the employer is dictating job changes that will incur expenses.
10) True: Yes, employers especially expect senior staff to be able to evaluate the entire value or a position as an indication of their ability to evaluate anything. If done poorly, an offer will be rescinded.

Chapter 8:
In-Person Networking to Get a Job
Complete Career Change
Alternative Strategies

Once you have done the "Campaign Kickoff" and start getting interviews, there are additional steps to consider that will increase the number of interviews you get. Many candidates want to start with the methods presented in this chapter but the latest research suggests that in-person "networking to get a job" is not the most prevalent method of getting hired. If you are leveraging your experience and degrees to make a step up, down, or laterally into a different industry, the campaign kickoff and advanced Linkedin search are the most reliable methods to get great results. However, some candidates want to change their profession and industry into something completely different from their existing skills and education. This is referred to as a 'complete career change.' In that case, the strategies discussed in this section are especially important, because a resume alone is not going to achieve your goals. If you are not making a complete career change, I have good news for you, advanced Linkedin search is a much easier form of networking! For now, we will talk about the in-person forms of networking before delving into the exciting world of Linkedin advanced search.

Many of us have heard two common phrases about hiring: 1) it's all who you know and 2) you have to network to get a job. A third common belief is that the Human Resource department is a gatekeeper that blocks great hires. This section explores the common myths and beliefs about networking to get a job and some of the newer methods to accomplish your career goals.

This chapter includes the following lessons:
8.1 – Networking Myths
8.2 – Making a List of Champions & Informational Interviews
8.3 – Volunteering
8.4 – Staffing Agencies, Freelance/Gigs, and Title & Reference Swap

8.1 Networking Myths

Myth 1: Hiring is all who you know.

This can sometimes be true depending on your age. LinkedIn recently performed a survey to report on "job seeker trends: why and how people change jobs." The results of the survey by generation is below.

Top Places People First Hear About Their New Job by Generation
- Millennials (18-35): Job Boards
- Gen X (36-50): Third Party Recruiter
- Baby Boomers (51+): Someone I know

This will not surprise most Millennials - you have to go out and look for a job. Since newspapers are not used much anymore, it is also not a surprise this generation sources their positions via online job boards. Third party recruiters, in general, are not targeting millennials due to lower income and lower commission on placement but the in-house recruiters are on the hunt for this talent pool.

For the Gen X group, the Third Party Recruiting industry is a critical tool in career progression. This is the largest labor pool for leadership positions due to age and experience. Recruiters tend to seek out candidates with the income earning power of $65,000, in part because their earnings are based on a percentage of the new hire's annual salary. The entire campaign kickoff is dedicated to tapping the recruiter's search for talent. They do search for Millennials and Boomers, but their largest percentage of placement at this time are Gen-Xers.

The Baby Boomers are the only generation to report that they are primarily identifying their most recent position through "who they know." The success of this strategy for Boomers may be more indicative of the length of time it takes to build a strong network capable of helping someone get a job, rather than indicating this is a superior way to find a position. Boomers need more personal referrals to get work due to age and income issues, and are less inclined towards technology compared to previous generations.

For Millennials and Gen X, the methods taught in the preceding chapters directly match the primary ways that talent is being sourced for new positions. Boomers, the campaign kickoff can assist your professional contacts ability to help you by presenting a job-market matched profile.

Myth 2: Networking to get a job is easier.

Generally speaking, this is not true. For someone to want to help you, either 1) you are qualified for a position that they have influence over, 2) they have influence over any type of hiring, 3) they care and trust you will deliver if they refer you, and/or 4) they naturally like to develop and help people.

Myth 3: Networking to get a job is faster.

No, this is definitely not true. Networking to get a job can significantly extend your job search compared to the methods used in this book, in which a candidate's background is matched to open positions.

Myth 4: Networking can result in complete career changes.

This can be true. If a candidate wants or needs to change professions and industries, then this is not a "resume-fix." Even if you can technically do a job, that does not mean the market considers you qualified. In the situation where a job candidate does not have specific experience or does not want the open position that matches their experience and education, an employer will not view them as qualified. For instance, a candidate who has worked in journalism writing for a newspaper is not necessarily qualified for a social media marketing specialist, even though those two fields are related to each other. In certain circumstances, leveraging the people you know may be the only way to get a job.

Myth 5: If you have no experience to put on the resume, alternative methods are the only way.

This one is true. A resume cannot fix everything. Some career change candidates want to make total and complete career changes. For instance, I had a tenured Professor in Health Sciences that wanted to do water stream cleanups. There is not much you can do to a resume that is going to help with that career change. Volunteering and working a network can play a large part in these job moves.

Myth 6: Bypassing the gatekeeper is a great strategy.

Sometimes this is true, but there are complexities to this strategy. Bypassing the gatekeeper assumes that HR is blocking great candidates from the hiring manager. Remember that HR is supposed to be doing their job. Perhaps their reason for blocking a candidate is completely valid. However, most candidates have at least one experience where their resume was "quarterbacked" or taken directly to the hiring manager with great results.

LinkedIn offers a modern way to bypass the gatekeeper. Even if this seems desirable, the HR department does not take kindly to being subverted by a job candidate. A hiring manager has primary job duties that do not include hiring and may not want these types of interruptions to their day from a stranger. We will cover this more in the next section.

First, we will explore working a list of champions.

8.2 Making a List of Champions and Informational Interviews

When clients are asked to make a list of people who can help them with their job search, the response over 85% of the time is "I do not know anyone." However, the majority of the time, the candidate does in fact have valuable contacts. Often, the person who will ultimately help you is someone completely unexpected, not necessarily someone who is close to you. The person who helps generally fits one of three categories.

1. They are natural people developers.
2. They care about you personally.
3. They know about a job that fits your background and may even get extra pay for referring a qualified candidate.

The problem is there is no way to pre-identify those people easily. Do not discount anyone in your network and extended network, or even people that are not in your network yet.

This list below presents ideas about the type of people to put on your networking list:

- **People working in organizations that can really use your skill set:** These champions work somewhere that may really need your skills. So, in this case, think of employers and positions and work backwards to identify people you know.
- **People in Professional Organizations or Meetup.com Groups:** There are people meeting every day who you do not know with whom you can network to get valuable industry information and contacts. Look for these groups and start attending meetings.
- **People who are in a hiring capacity:** Do you know people who can make direct hiring decisions? The type of work they hire for may be completely unrelated to

your skills and you will need to convince them of your fit or willingness to try something new.

- **People developers:** Do you know someone who has helped someone else get a job? Reach out to anyone you know who has the personality and who really enjoys this.
- **Mentors for informational interviews:** There may be people working in certain fields who you suspect might be a fit for your background. A great way to get feedback and also present yourself as a possible candidate without asking for their help to get a job is to alter your resume and set up a discussion to see if the resume fits the role.
- **People in your telephone, email, and LinkedIn list of contacts and their contacts:** Anyone in your contact lists and people they know may be an asset in your job search.

In the following exercise, a list of contacts will be made. You will then create a strategy on how to build a list and talk to the people you identify in your network. It is important to note again that expecting a job lead should be secondary in this approach. The goal is to send out signals of your skills and candidacy and to receive educational information about careers you may not have known about. It may result in a job lead later on.

Exercise 8.2a: Make a List of Champions

Start creating a list of people and where they work. Reach out via email, telephone, and LinkedIn emails. Use these ideas to start creating a list.

- People working at organizations that can use your skills.
- Professional organizations or meetup.com meetings you can attend.
- People that work in a hiring capacity no matter what the type of job.
- People that like to help people get jobs.
- People who can perform a resume review and provide an informational interview about a certain field.

Exercise 8.2b: Talk to Your Network

Before you make contact, find out the person's title, industry, and type of work. Be prepared to interview them with the following ideas in mind:

- If possible, locate a job in which you are qualified for positions or organizations that person can influence. Prepare your matching resume. Do normal interview preparation.
- People can support passion and concepts. If you have great soft skills, even if you are missing the "hard-skill" work experience, a good dose of reasonable passion can overcome missing technical abilities.

If this is more of a true "informational" interview, use the questions below to generate a conversation. Most likely this will not result in a job, but you can obtain career guidance.

- What does a day in your work life look like?
- What educational program or certification is typical for this field?

- What is a typical career path for this field?
- Are there nontraditional ways to obtain work experience in this field?
- What are the important keywords and skills to highlight on a resume?
- What are areas of job opportunities that are in demand that I might be able to fit into?

Based on their answers, say the following:

"I have done some of the work you are describing. For instance, I did _____, _____, _____." (List relevant experiences matching what they described). *Do you think an employer would be interested in my experiences as it applies to this position? If so, how do you recommend I highlight it?"*

8.3 Volunteering

If a job candidate has a goal to work in one type of position that is completely unrelated to their background, volunteering can be helpful in the following unexpected ways:

- Volunteer in exchange for a title and recommendation.
- Fill in gaps on the resume.
- Send the message that you are seeking work.
- If the volunteering is professional, and potentially for the desired organization, it offers a sample of your work.
- If you want to enter into the nonprofit field and can identify a professional level experience, volunteering can demonstrate your skills.

- Volunteering can make networking easier because you are actually doing something, versus cold-networking which is difficult for most people.
- This can be in the form of a leadership opportunity which looks good on the resume.

Here are a few examples of volunteer opportunities that ultimately resulted in job interviews or offers.

- A candidate with no formal work experience talked to friends who owned their own business, needed help, but could not afford to pay. The candidate worked for no money in exchange for a title, work experience, and a recommendation. This filled in a gap on the candidate's resume and taught him new skills.
- Another person volunteered to help at industry conferences. This was much easier than trying to network and she got to know the people who were active in the field, which resulted in a job.
- The candidate who wanted to leave her professor job to do stream clean up worked for a local environmental nonprofit. She volunteered doing grant-writing, fundraising, developing plans, and volunteer coordination, and was offered a position after about six months of volunteering.
- Sometimes a variety of candidates will get leads from volunteering with their hobbies, which makes them happy and promotes networking. Their happiness is infectious and it can open the door to people helping them with job leads.

Note: Organizations may use and abuse volunteers. It can be a real waste of time and very frustrating to spend too much effort in this area. One way to protect yourself is to focus on opportunities which demonstrate your level of professional abilities. Locate professional project opportunities to "try on" a new position with no expense to the employer. Set boundaries and well-defined limits to your contribution. Remember, the happier you are doing it, the more likely it is to result in an opportunity.

In the following exercise, you will brainstorm about different possible volunteer opportunities that can leverage your career change.

Exercise 8.3 Make a list of possible volunteer opportunities.

Exchange volunteer work for job title and a recommendation. Identify businesses needing free help that can offer you valuable experience, a title, and a reference to help get your career change moving.

If you desire to work in the nonprofit industry, seek out targeted volunteer experiences that demonstrate your abilities to the organization. (Be careful to not let the organization take advantage of you.)

Find professional conferences that allow you to attend for free in exchange for networking.

8.4 Staffing Agencies, Freelance/Gigs, and Title and Reference Swap

There are many opportunities for employers and candidates to work with each other first before making a long-term commitment. These short-term contract employment opportunities can facilitate powerful life-altering career changes.

Staffing Agencies

If someone is currently employed, it may not make sense to leave a full-time job for a contract position. However, when someone is really ready to move on, or is unemployed, it is worth exploring these options. In this section, there is a differentiation between a staffing agency and a Third Party Recruiter.
One of the primary benefits of this method is that the interview process can be very short or nonexistent because the focus is on skill based questions. Because this may not be a "marriage for life" there is less interest in the long-term motivations of the candidate. Also, a staffing agency is more likely to consider a functional style resume and may use assessments to verify candidate requirements.

A staffing agency usually places for positions in office administration, accounting, and manufacturing opportunities. Not only can these opportunities be beneficial in making a career change but these staffing agencies are often used by employers for other opportunities that come up because they already have a recruiting agreement with the organization. Adecco and Kelly Services are well-known names in the staffing world for professional office work. These two organizations also have divisions that place science and engineering opportunities.

Positions with staffing agencies often have lower expectations of their placements, which allows candidates with large gaps in their resume to obtain work. These contract opportunities allow for job changes that would not otherwise be possible. Do not ignore the possibilities of obtaining work through these agencies.

In addition to staffing agencies, some industries like publishing have had freelance opportunities for decades. The freelance concept has become even more popular now, to the point that newspapers write about how our economy is changing into a "gig economy." Obtaining short term or one-project-at-a-time opportunities can build a portfolio of work and referrals that allow for a permanent career change. Gigs are typically found through a person's network of family, friends, colleagues or websites like Craigslist.com, Elance.com and Odesk.com. Like staffing agency contracts, this can be a powerful way to move careers.

Freelance/Gigs: Create Your Own Business and Select the Right Title

Freelancing or gigs is not just about seeking work experience. It is also about creating your own business. This can be a primary method of covering large employment gaps or of facilitating a complete career change by presenting recent history that matches your goal position. There are many professionals who freelance alongside their regular job. They may wish to create a business that will replace their income, make a side income, or they are dynamic individuals with many interests. It is possible to present your freelance and side gigs in a way that facilitates job acquisition.

With this strategy, candidates create a business name (one that does not currently exist) and creates a title for themselves as if they were working for someone else. It is important to title yourself with the likely title of your next position. For instance, don't say you are CEO of a marketing agency when the likely job for your skill level is Marketing Coordinator. Instead, make a business, title yourself Marketing Coordinator, and present yourself as an employee working for the self-owned company.

Title and Reference Swap: Work in Exchange for Learning, Title, and Reference (Internship Strategy)

This strategy is recommended when someone is really stuck or absolutely committed to heading in a new career direction. Find a small business in need of assistance related to what you want to do. Ask the business owner to exchange work, paid or not, for the ability to gain experience, receive a title, and have a strong reference. This is similar to an internship. For the older experienced candidate, it is better to call it a short-term contract than an internship.

This works for some fields better than for others. For instance, social media marketing has a large growth trajectory right now and there is a low supply of experienced workers. Someone interested in this work could do use this method to implement digital campaigns in exchange for a title and reference on their resume.

Creative temporary work arrangements from staffing agencies, freelance opportunities, and gigs are an additional angle in an overall strategy. They are not better or worse than full-time opportunities; they are different, and can be used to your advantage. If you have no experience in a certain field, this is sometimes the only way to make a move in a new direction because it provides proof of your ability to handle the new job duties. This can really work well for step downs or for a return to work after an extensive period of unemployment.

Exercise 8.4 Short-Term or Temporary Contracts Checklist

Use the checklist to become aware of and use short-term contract opportunities to earn money and change careers.

_____ **Staffing Agencies:** Look for contract or permanent-to-hire positions with staffing agencies in your field of interest. You can search on Indeed.com for this using the appropriate filter. It may be better to go straight to the agency's website to look for jobs or walk into a local office and talk to a staffing person.

____ **Freelance Gigs:** Look for freelance work within your network to help fill in the gaps, get new types of work experience, and keep yourself busy and making money while you continue your search.

____ **Title and Reference Swap:** Exchange work, paid or not, for the ability to gain experience, receive a title, and have a strong reference.

>Homework
If you are trying to go for a job for which you have absolutely no recent paid work experience, you will likely need to leverage

your network, a staffing agency, or volunteering to make a shift. It is not a resume "fix" because a resume presents what you have done. You can search for roles that are different but will still need some background for the resume to do its job.

Quiz 8: Networking (T/F)

1. ___ Hiring is "all who you know."
2. ___ Alternative strategies are needed if work background is missing for the job.
3. ___ People in hiring manager capacity make the most effective champions.
4. ___ People of different ages get jobs in different ways.
5. ___ HR acts as a Gatekeeper and blocks candidates the Hiring Manager would consider.
6. ___ Volunteering can open doors.
7. ___ Finding freelance gigs or short-term contracts can cover gaps and direct your search.
8. ___ Staffing firms can overcome large gaps in work.
9. ___ You can exchange work for title to assist in getting a job.
10. ___ All gigs and volunteer opportunities offer the same level of opportunity.

Chapter 8: Answer Key (T/F)

1) False: Recruiters search and hire complete "unknowns" every day.

2) True: This may be the only way to get a job if the candidate has no matching experience.

3) False: People who are people developers or that care about you tend to be more effective.

4) True: Millennial=Job Boards, GenXers=Recruiters, Baby Boomers=Network.

5) True: HR does act as a "Gatekeeper" and blocks for many reasons.

6) True: Volunteering can help but, when used for career be strategic about it.

7) True: Freelance gigs and short-term contracts can overcome gaps and shift careers.

8) True: Staffing firms' temp and temp-to-hire jobs can overcome gaps in work.

9) True: There are some fields that may permit work in exchange for title and reference.

10) False: The more targeted to your goal position, the better the opportunity.

Chapter 9:
Advanced
LinkedIn Strategies

Once you have done the "Campaign Kickoff" and have keyword-stacked your profile for your target position, there are advanced opportunities via LinkedIn to reach straight into an organization. If you recall the beginning of the book, I told you about a client that went from 24 connections to over 500 in a week's time and he received four job interview requests. This lesson is the final piece on how I achieved those results.

Advanced Linkedin search is a unique networking strategy that is ideal for job candidates who meet the following criteria:
- Every working professional between 18-65 years of age,
- A one-company hyper-targeted focus,
- Highly-specialized professional field, and
- Low job supply.

Every working professional
Any professional that is 18-65 years old needs to be networking. In this section, we will learn that Linkedin is programmed to function better for professionals with a high number of connections. This means that connecting with many people is not an exercise in popularity, it is maximizing the functionality of the system. At the time of this publication, this networking hack also means you can unlock the benefits of Linkedin without paying for a costly Linkedin Premium account.

This is also the easiest form of networking you will ever do in your lifetime. My introverted candidates will LOVE this form of connecting. With a few clicks you can offer a virtual handshake and send your electronic business card to thousands of targeted people. It is much quicker and effective than going to a cold in-person networking event.

When is it a good time to start networking? You intuitively know that it is better to have a network built BEFORE you need it. However, if you have not built it yet, and you need a job right now, you can still quickly leverage the benefits of Linkedin advanced search to build and communicate with your network.

One-company hyper-targeted focus
There is a growing trend, particularly with job candidates under the age of 30, to become hyper-focused on working for one specific company like Google, Facebook, or other unique players. Highly desirable companies sometimes have a very long hire cycle and the entry-role is lower than what the professional could obtain with another company. There have been cases where a candidate was sourced and qualified for employment but had to wait a year or more for a position to open. That candidate may have been able to obtain a position with greater breadth, depth, and income with another organization. I advise you to run a general campaign and a hyper-targeted method at the same time to ensure the most job interviews. You need both quantity and quality to succeed.

Highly-specialized professional field
Some candidates work in very specialized fields and, over time, they will work with many of the same colleagues, creating a

"very small world." This can be common in the science, research, and creative fields. In this instance, it is a good idea to constantly expand and maintain a wide network of contacts through these advanced methods. This can offer protection from unemployment and stimulate advancement opportunities over time.

Low job supply

As in highly-specialized fields, there are certain professionals that either work in fields or locations with a low supply of jobs, or they have reached an executive level which automatically reduces the supply of positions. These methods may be necessary to maintain continued employment over the long-term.

Most candidates that are interested in an advanced LinkedIn strategy ask themselves one question: Should I pay for a LinkedIn Premium account? The following section offers advice and recommendations to that question along with advanced strategies that work.

* Note: The optimized LinkedIn profile taught in the Campaign Kickoff section is critical for success with this method because the first information a contact will see is your profile headline, location, and picture, not your resume. The profile has to be 100% direct-hit match to your goal to get results.

This chapter includes the following lessons:
9.1 – Advanced LinkedIn Strategy Myths
9.2 – LinkedIn Premium – To Buy or Not to Buy
9.3 – Networking 2.0 via a Linkedin Connection Campaign

9.1 Advanced LinkedIn Strategy Myths

Myth 1: A LinkedIn Premium account is required to use advanced strategies.

No! At this moment, LinkedIn Premium is not required for the advanced strategies, which require search abilities which are available for free. The benefit structure of a Premium account is not well-designed to help someone "get a job" at this time. The following lesson will discuss the attributes of a Premium membership to assist in purchase decisions.

Myth 2: An advanced strategy requires specialized research skills.

No! I will teach you how to search for and communicate with the right individuals.

Myth 3: Advanced LinkedIn strategies are the best way to get a job.

No! The "Campaign Kickoff" taught in this book is the best way to get a job. However, once that method has been implemented, a job candidate will want to use advanced strategies to increase their interviews.

Myth 4: Advanced LinkedIn strategies are only for Executive-level positions.

No! This method can be used for any level of employment.

Myth 5: I have to know which company I want to work for to perform an Advanced LinkedIn strategy.

No! There are a multiple search parameters available including industry, location, and professional title.

Myth 6: The primary use of an advanced Linked strategy is to bypass the gatekeeper.

Yes and no. One goal is to use LinkedIn to network and bypass formal hiring procedures and the Human Resource department. However, in some cases it may be used to reach out and network with recruiters, hiring managers, and employees to "get on their radar."

Myth 7: Inmail and email are the same thing.

No. Linkedin has an internal email system called Inmail. You can only Inmail 1st connections.

Let's dig in and explore the advanced strategies that can be used with LinkedIn. I cannot stress enough that you absolutely must have a keyword-stacked optimized profile for your goal position for these methods to work. Perform the Campaign Kickoff first.

9.2 LinkedIn Premium – To Buy or Not to Buy?

The following lesson is used to help a candidate make a purchase decision in regards to LinkedIn Premium. At this time, purchase is not recommended or needed for an advanced LinkedIn strategy. However, this is a hot topic for job candidates right now which requires further explanation.

LinkedIn Premium is a paid account which professionals can use to access more features of the website. From a "double the interviews and leverage recruiters" perspective, the concept is to use LinkedIn to directly communicate with recruiters, or bypass the gatekeeper completely by contacting hiring managers or other employees personally. For this to work well, everything else taught in this book about matching your profile to job opportunities must be complete because the contact will primarily understand who you are through your LinkedIn profile.

With LinkedIn Premium, a professional can pay $30 a month or more for a LinkedIn Premium account. Below is a list of the attributes of the paid account.

LinkedIn Premium Attributes

1. LinkedIn Premium Badge
2. You surface higher in recruiter search
3. You can see who viewed your profile
4. Larger search parameters
5. At least three 'free' Inmails (LinkedIn's internal messaging system) per month

Let's review each benefit.
1. LinkedIn Premium Badge

There are some theories on the value of the LinkedIn Premium Badge. It can make a professional look more elite and established in their career but this is largely a perception. For someone seeking a job, it has a very limited impact because we know that the employer is looking for a direct-hit match to their needs, not someone who looks elite.

2. Surface higher in recruiter search

This is the only true "job getting" benefit of a Premium membership. Job candidates may be willing to pay for a Premium account if it will boost their chances of being found. The idea is that, if a recruiter is looking for a candidate with your qualifications, your Premium profile should surface higher in the rankings for their search terms. For instance, if there are 50 candidates, instead of being #45 perhaps you will be listed as #10. On paper this sounds good, but there is no way to verify if this works. To test the benefit, try one month of Linkedin Premium. If there is an uptick in recruiter contacts, then this method is working for your background. If you receive no new reach outs, then this method will not be a good reason to maintain a paid LinkedIn Premium account.

3. See who looked at your profile

Some people want to know who is looking at them on LinkedIn. In hiring, this will have limited value. If a recruiter looks at your profile but does not reach out to you, contacting them is not going to help much. It might be deemed inappropriate to contact someone who viewed your profile but did not reach out (like calling an unidentified telephone number back after they called you but did not leave a message).

4. Larger search parameters

As reviewed in the beginning of this book, a recruiter can search for a job candidate among a variety of parameters; keyword, location, industry, and job title. Technically everyone can do this through the free advanced search option on LinkedIn, however when a recruiter or a job candidate pays more, they can search by a greater number of parameters. The parameter of interest to most recruiters is "rank" like Director, Manager, or Vice President. This has limited value to the job candidate. At this moment, the parameters needed by a job candidate are available for free.

5. "Free Inmails"

This is pitched as the biggest "job-getting" benefit for a Premium account. A Premium member can contact at least five non-connections per month and pay for at least ten more Inmails. These numbers can increase based on more expensive LinkedIn packages. There is a popular "free" way of doing the same thing so this has very limited value to a candidate.

The key to LinkedIn for most users is not a paid Premium membership. This will come as a relief for some job seekers who want to leverage LinkedIn to get more interviews, bypass the gatekeeper, or extend their professional network but do not want to pay $30 a month for questionable value. Refer back to chapter 4 which discusses online optimization and the free "Recruiter Push" function to get the maximum benefit from a LinkedIn.com account.

As we know, social media changes quickly and I will not be surprised if my recommendations about LinkedIn Premium change as the website develops. For now, LinkedIn Premium is not necessary. Let's review how to perform the advanced job search strategies that are available at no charge to the candidate.

9.3 Networking 2.0 via a Linkedin Connection Campaign

The purpose of doing a Linkedin advanced search connection campaign is to 1) capture low-hanging fruit, 2) offer another point of connection, and 3) become a 1st Degree Connection.

Low hanging fruit
A new connection may say *'oh, look at this person. They are perfect for that position I have coming open soon. I should talk to them.'* Yes, this does happen.

Offer another point of connection
Many large companies complain that they receive over 500 resumes for one position. An advanced Linkedin campaign offers another point of introduction to the employer. It is a virtual handshake that passes them your electronic business card. An overwhelmed hiring manager may say *'this person is obviously interested in the role. I should consider them for my pool of candidates.'* Yes, this does happen.

Become a 1st Degree Connection
The hack I am about to teach you is far more effective than the paltry amount of inmails you get with a Linkedin Premium account. The reason you want to get connected is that you can Inmail a 1st degree connection for free as often as you like (within the confines of professionalism). If they are not a 1st degree connection, you have to pay to contact them.

As a professional that needs a job, you want to bypa
barriers placed in your way by connecting, networking, and
contacting potential hiring managers in a friendly way. The
following are the steps you need to take to maximize Linkedin.

Exercise 9.3a 2nd Degree 'Quick Connect' Campaign

Initial Connections

If you have not connected with many Linkedin members yet, it
will be necessary to go to 'my network' and load up your email
accounts and also seek out people that you know that may
already be highly connected. For instance, a pastor of a large
church, a friend that works in Human Resources, or an
entrepreneur that is very networked in the community. Tapping
your existing network opens up many initial 2nd degree 'quick
connect' options.

2nd Degree 'Quick Connect' Steps

Click on the Advanced Search Feature on your Linkedin profile
which is the magnifying glass at the top of your home page.

The First Pass

Do a job search on LinkedIn and Indeed to see companies hiring
for your various keywords and start making a list of the
company names. Then take the company name that was hiring
and do a general search and seek out 2nd level connections
which allow the 'quick connect' feature. Send a 'quick connect.'
A first pass can also be targeted by potential locations in a

targeted industry and city.

The goal of the first pass is to connect with at least one person, literally any person, at each company. This connection can open up 'a universe' of 2nd connections at that company.

Second Pass

Now that you have gained one connection you will have the option for many more 2nd degree 'quick connects.' Sometimes this can be overwhelming. Just one new highly networked 1st degree connection can open up thousands of 2nd degree connections you did not have prior to the 'first pass.' Therefore, this may require a more targeted search for keywords or titles that are related to your professional skills. For instance, recruiter, human resource, VP of Marketing, Director of I.T, Help Desk Manager…etc.. You can also narrow down the target location, or remain open and do a broad 2nd degree 'quick connect' campaign with all your options at that company.

Select combinations of the following:
- Current company - enter the goal company name
- Title - enter job title
  - ➤ Title of peers (your title or titles from the Core-3$^{©}$)
  - ➤ Recruiter or human resources
  - ➤ Hiring manager title (your boss's title or similar)
- Location - leave blank or enter specific city
- Review results and click the "connect" button

Remember, this is softly handing out your virtual business card to more people at the company which will start raising awareness about you as a candidate and potentially capture low-hanging fruit. You are not necessarily saying anything – just clicking connect.

Repeat the first and second pass as often as necessary to target new companies, locations, industries, or professionals holding a certain title.

Exercise 9.3b Networking with your 1st Degree Connections

You now have many 1st degree connections that you can Inmail for free. This final step is optional in most cases. For instance, if your profile is optimized, online, and you are now well connected, you should already be the recipient of many job interviews. However, if you need or want to start reaching out on a more personal level to your 1st degree connections, use the following Inmail scripts.

Inmail Content to Peers

• *(Name), thanks for the connection. I have been interested in working for (company name) and would like to network with you to see what the job requirements are and if any openings may be coming up.*

Inmail to Recruiters

• Recruiter Email Content (No Advertisement):
(Name), thanks for the connection. I have been interested in working for (company name) and would like to network with you to see what the job requirements are and if any openings may be coming up.

• Recruiter Email Content (Advertised Job):

(Name), thanks for the connection. I have applied for (position title) and would like to network with you about the job. Based on my background in (previous titles, education, professional experience), I feel I would be a unique fit for the role.

Likely Hiring Manager Inmail Content

• Hiring Manager Inmail Content (No Advertised Job):

(Name), thanks for the connection. I am interested in working on your team and would like to network with you see if any openings may be coming up. Based on my background in (previous titles, education, professional experience), I feel I would be a unique fit for the team. Please review my profile and consider my background for your open role.

• Hiring Manager Inmail Content (Advertised Job):

(Name), thanks for the connection. I am interested in your team's (position title) position. I have applied for the position but have not heard back. Based on my background in (previous titles, education, professional experience), I feel I would be a unique fit for the role. Please review my profile and consider my background for your open role.

In recap, this final goal of the advanced connection campaign allows you to Inmail for free. You may never really have to use this stage but the option will be there for you which, if you had not done the connection campaign, would not exist without paying for LinkedIn Premium and, even with that, you get 10 Inmails per month. This is a much more elegant method of doing it for free and capturing low-hanging fruit in a 'nice' collegial way. Most LinkedIn members are still very click happy and non-protectionist towards connecting.

>Homework
It is much easier to learn how to do these campaigns via the online class. In addition, Linkedin is always changing. Join the class to remain current on new campaigns and strategies. I use these methods every day for my clients. When I see a change or develop a winning campaign, I record a new video module and update the class.

Get the class at www.karengurney.com/stacked.

Quiz 9: Advanced Linked Strategies (T/F)

1. ___ A paid LinkedIn Premium membership is helpful in getting a job.
2. ___ The advanced strategy is really a free LinkedIn search function.
3. ___ Advanced LinkedIn strategies are the best way to get a job.
4. ___ All professional levels can use free advanced LinkedIn strategies.
5. ___ LinkedIn search can be by title, profession, or company.
6. ___ A popular use for advanced search is to bypass the HR gatekeeper.
7. ___ Just connecting can result in job interviews.
8. ___ A paid Premium membership is necessary to communicate with non-connections.
9. ___ A 2nd Degree connection can be personalized or just a quick handshake and electronic business card pass.
10. ___ The only way networking with Linkedin can be productive is if I personally reach out to all connections.

Chapter 9: Answer Key (T/F)

1) False: Premium offers little or no help in getting a job (right now).
2) True: The advanced method is a free search function.
3) False: This is one step following the Campaign Kickoff.
4) True: Any professional level can use and benefit from these free techniques.
5) True: LinkedIn search allows a number of search parameters.
6) True: Getting around HR is a popular reason to use advanced search.
7) True: The act of connecting itself can result in 'low hanging fruit.'
8) False: The 2nd Degree 'quick connect' allows you the potential to communicate for free.
9) True: Yes- you can write a personalized note on your 'quick connect' or perform a quantity campaign.
10) False: The act of connecting, when your profile is optimized, can result in job interviews. The option will be there later to do personalized networking.

Chapter 10:
Unique Career Change
Types and Strategies

The beginning of the Stacked Strategy is a campaign kickoff that teaches you how to keyword-stack your resume and online job board profiles to leverage recruiters. This section is dedicated to special issues that do not apply to every single candidate and therefore have been divided into different lessons. There are about 10 unique career changes you could make in a lifetime. Let's take a look at some myths and common beliefs about career changes and then dive into job search, resume, and interview strategies that are common with each unique type.

This chapter includes the following lessons:

10.1 – Career change common myths

10.2 – Lateral career moves

10.3 – Overqualified-step down

10.4 – Move for promotion

10.5 – Return to a prior profession

10.6 – New graduate or entry-level

10.7 – New industry

10.8 – New profession (complete career change)

10.9 – Gaps on resume

10.10 – Geographic relocations

10.1 Career Change Common Myths

Myth 1. There are no resume or interview challenges when making a lateral move.

A lateral move typically is a job change into a position that is virtually the same title and industry. However, at this point in the course you know that candidates can reposition themselves for market opportunities by highlighting skills that match the job advertisement so that recruiters can identify you as qualified for the role. Whether the most recent title matches the future position or not, this process essentially mimics the look and feel of a lateral move.

Even though the lateral move is the easiest career change to make, it can still be difficult to explain your job transition goals. An employer will wonder why you would want to leave one job for the next if the work is that similar, and this is a key reason candidates often get overlooked for positions even when they are a "shoe-in." Lesson 10.2 discusses strategies for "lateral moves."

Myth 2: Being over-qualified is a good thing in the job market.

It would seem that in a market hungry for skills, no candidate can be too "over-qualified." This unfortunately is not the case. When a candidate hears that they are over-qualified, the employer is essentially saying "I do not think you will be happy or that you will stay in this job." The hiring manager may also feel threatened if they hire someone with the same or higher level of experience. The goal is to make the resume and interview look like a lateral move but this can be especially difficult when a candidate has had upper-level titles. Because there are so many reasons a candidate could be tagged as overqualified, this will receive special treatment in lesson 10.3.

Myth 3. You can't achieve a promotion through a new position.

Actually, this is sometimes the *only* way to get a promotion because employees tend to be pigeon-holed by their employers. The key to achieving a promotion through a new job is to capture and communicate upper-level accomplishments for targeted skills required by the new job. This creates a lateral move even if your most recent title is at a lower or different level. Move-for-Promotion strategies are discussed in lesson 10.4.

Myth 4. You can't move back to a prior profession.

This is one of the most popular job moves to make and it is even easier if skills from the current position can be mixed with previous positions and industries. The challenge with this move is that the employer may perceive skills as stale if the candidate held the previous role a long time ago. In addition, explaining job transitions in a way that makes sense to the interviewer can take persistence. However, many incredible career changes can be made by leveraging previous roles. These strategies are covered in Lesson 10.5.

Myth 5. New graduates have no skills to leverage in the job market.

It is actually very rare for a new graduate to have no skills. There are ways to use classwork and even side jobs to locate new work. New graduates can also be attentive to ways to take on management roles in their pre-professional jobs or to seek temporary or contract work that can be leveraged later. New graduate strategies are covered in Lesson 10.6.

Myth 6. Switching industries is not possible.

This is often one of the easier career changes to make for a professional. A job candidate can neutralize or remove industry information and focus on professional category information to help make moves between industries. For instance, if an accountant is working in manufacturing and is seeking to move into a bank, the resume can remove all of the targeted manufacturing industry information and leave just accounting details. This strategy is covered in Lesson 10.7.

Myth 7. Switching both industries and professional categories is not possible.

This is where things can get tricky; next to being "overqualified" this is the most difficult career change. It is possible if you have an unusual mix of transferable skills, however these can often be lengthy career transitions, or, require a job candidate to angle in through alternative methods like a volunteer opportunity or short-term contract. Lesson 10.8 covers special strategies.

Myth 8. Years of experience, education, and level of responsibility are not that important.

The very first lesson in this book on how a recruiter uses LinkedIn should convince you that managing this information is a critical component of career change. A matching education is more important in quantitative fields like science, technology, engineering, accounting, finance, and math. Many other professional categories are tolerant of different educational backgrounds if the same level of education is present. Specific strategies on how to manage these issues are covered in lesson 10.9.

Myth 9. A history of many different types of jobs shows how flexible and adaptive I am.

That is not what the employer values. An employer wants to see a strong commitment to one path by the candidate. A candidate who changes professions, industries, and jobs often is usually perceived by the employer as someone who does not know what they want, is wishy-washy, lost, and (if the jobs were short-term) unreliable. Lesson 10.10 covers the creation of a cohesive storyline of a stable and happy employee.

Myth 10. Gaps between employment periods are the worst thing on the resume.

If a gap in employment is in the past and there is a more recent stable work history, the gap is practically irrelevant. The job market is accustomed to people losing jobs due to reorganizations, closures, and relocations, therefore a gap on the resume for those reasons is almost expected. If the gaps are current, you have to be very thoughtful in how you present your reason for leaving the last position. Lesson 10.11 presents a special section for assisting on this matter.

Myth 11. Relocating to a new city is no problem.

Actually, this can be a big problem. The employers know there is a large statistical link between how close a person lives to their job and the likelihood that they will stay. Applicant tracking systems are pre-programmed to search for distance to your zip code. If it is too far, you will be eliminated. Also, job candidates who relocate tend to have no support system and are very likely to return back to their home town or move somewhere else.

There is an exception to this rule. Some professions have relocation built right into the work. Executives, professors, new doctors, and certain professionals virtually require a geographic relocation at some point in their career. For everyone else, lesson 10.12 offers different strategies.

Move to the lesson that most closely matches your job search goal at this point in your career.

10.2 Lateral Move Lesson

When a candidate is making a lateral career move, it typically means they are applying for positions that have the same title, and often with the same years of experience, level of responsibility, and industry experience. Let's explore some myths and beliefs about this type of career change.

10.2.1 Lateral Change Common Myths

Myth 1: There is only **one** basic lateral move for each person at any given time.

This is not true. Most candidates have at least three lateral moves possible at any given time in their career because jobs are multifaceted. Even if you feel that you do not want to be in the same field, there is a high degree of likelihood that one of your available lateral moves would match your career goals. The Core-3© helps identify these moves.

Myth 2: A candidate who is making a lateral move tends to have a higher degree of success in receiving calls on their resume because the profile has the keywords and stylistic appearance that recruiters identify as a good match for the position.

Yes, this statement is true. Lateral moves tend to be successful because the job candidate naturally understands how to present their background to match a direct market need. The job market can provide the profile information necessary for a candidate to build a lateral shift profile that represents a different work or lifestyle even though the market perceives the move as lateral. There are other types of career changes but this method produces the fastest and most profitable results.

Myth 3: Lateral career changers face no challenges on their resume or in the interview.

Even though this is the easiest career change to make there are still challenges. The Market-Based Resume Profile© recommendations are all designed to facilitate this career change, however there are more tips for aligning directly for a lateral move, which we will cover below.

Candidates making lateral moves often face unique challenges during the interview. If the person is currently employed and applying for the same position that they currently hold, the big question in the mind in the recruiter is, "Why would this candidate want to move into the same basic position that they currently have?" If the job candidate is currently unemployed, the recruiter may also ask themselves, "Is this a problem employee that created a bad situation at their previous employer and got fired or quit?"

Myth 4: A Lateral Move cannot be a "Move for Promotion."

A lateral move can also be a promotion if the candidate can verify that they have been performing work at a higher level than their title.

Myth 5: Moving for money or anger is a successful "reason for leaving" answer.

Another common issue with "lateral move" job candidates is that they are angry or extremely frustrated by their current career situation. Common sources of anger are pay, job conditions, or lack of promotions. Employers do not like to hire people that state these answers. Job candidates may feel frustrated because they feel they are being asked to lie in order to get a job offer and improve their life. The recommendation in both cases is to restate and find another truth that is more attractive to the employer.

The following exercises assist in lateral move resume changes and interview answers specific to a lateral move.

Exercise 10.2a: General "Lateral Move" Resume Tips

The following resume tips will help with lateral moves. Check them off to make sure you have done them.

1. ____ Follow the Market-Based Resume Profile© techniques.
2. ____ Match the skill need of the job advertisement -- line item by line item.
3. ____ Do not oversell experiences.
4. ____ Prepare accomplishments at the level of the new job - not over and not under.

Exercise 10.2b: Scripts and Explanations for Making a Lateral Move

The most important question that an interviewer has for a candidate making a lateral move is, "Why are you leaving your current position?" This information is sometimes asked on the job application under the section "reason for leaving" but it is most common during a phone screen and later while performing the in-person interviews. A candidate must select the answer that fits the new job they are applying for. Answers can be combined if there is more than one that applies. Money can be mentioned but typically not as the only answer.

Scripts and Explanations Based on Scenario

Situation 1: If the new job is closer to your house than the old job:
"This position is closer to home which will allow me to dedicate more time to work and less to commuting."

Situation 2: If the organization is dramatically smaller than the current organization:
"I prefer a smaller organization that is more personable than the large company I currently work for."

Situation 3: If the organization is dramatically larger than the current organization:
"I prefer a larger organization that offers growth opportunities."

Situation 4: If the organization offers a better schedule than the current position:
"This company offers a better schedule."

Situation 5: If the new organization pays better:
"This organization offers a better combined compensation package."

Situation 6: If your previous organization is closing or relocating:

"The organization I work for is _____ (closing, relocating, or there are funding changes)"

Situation 7: If your previous/current work environment is terrible for whatever reason and the above previous answers do not fit:

"The business I work for has re-organized and my work has dramatically changed. I enjoy doing the work that I have been doing _____ (state the skills the new job has)."

Situation 8: If there is growth or a better use of skills at the new organization.

"The business I work for has re-organized and my work has dramatically changed. I enjoy doing the work that I have been doing _____ (state the skills the new job has)."

Situation 9: If you are losing your job and the previous answers do not fit:

"Due to industry changes, the organization I work for has re-organized and my position is being eliminated."

10.3 Overqualified - Step Down Lesson

Many candidates in today's market are hearing that they are overqualified. This section explores myths and beliefs related to this career change.

10.3.1 Overqualified Common Myths

Myth 1: The only people that seek to take a "step down" are desperate unemployed people.

This is not true. There are five common reasons that candidates move on to positions that are technically a lower level of responsibility, title, or pay than their most recent position.

Step Down Assessment

Select any option that applies:

_____ You are unemployed and need to find a job, any job, regardless of title or pay level.

_____ You are tired of supervising people and want a non-supervisory role.

_____ You have many skills and want to work in one functional area.

_____ You are burned out from your current level of responsibility.

_____ You are primarily motivated by priorities other than money.

Myth 2: The candidate determines if they are taking a "step-back" or "step down."

Sometimes a candidate will understand that the role is a step back; in other cases, the employer will surprise a candidate by telling them that the role is a "step down." Even when the job candidate feels the move is acceptable or desirable, the employer may fear the prospective employee will not be happy or will not stay in the position. Therefore, this can both be a conscious decision by the candidate or an unexpected, and unwelcome, employer announcement.

Myth 3: Candidates always know that they are applying for jobs that they are overqualified for.

As we just discussed, no, this is not true. There are instances where being "overqualified" comes as a surprise when the candidate feels they are perfectly suited for the position. Hearing the proclamation of "overqualified" is an indicator that the job is either below your skill level, below your expected pay level, or the new boss feels threatened by you. The resume either needs to be re-aligned more or you need to apply for positions that are at a higher level.

Myth 4: Having more skills should make it easier to move jobs.

That is not always true. Remember, making an exact match on many different factors, including skill and level of responsibility, is critical to avoid this issue. Of all the career changes, this is one of the most difficult to perform because employers do not trust that the candidate will be happy or that they will stay in a position that makes significantly less, or that has less responsibilities, than their most recent position.

<u>Myth 5: When the employer says overqualified it means just that - overqualified.</u>

This is not necessarily true. What the recruiter is really trying to tell the job candidate is the following:

"Although you may be qualified, I do not think you will be happy or stay in the position. I would rather seek someone with lesser skills than take the chance you will destabilize the team or force me into the hiring process again in a few months because you quit when you find something better."

Or ...

"You could easily do my job or my boss's job. I am not going to hire someone with the same level of skills or greater than mine and face competition or confrontation."

<u>Myth 6: I will get hired in a step-down position if I just tell the employer I need the job because of unemployment, burnout, personal preference, or passion.</u>

Although passionate commitment can sometimes get you a job, it typically does not work if your work experience is not there to back it up. These answers do not tell the recruiter that you will be a capable, happy, and stable employee. To manage this issue, you must re-position your image to match the level of responsibility of the position that you are applying for and tell the recruiter "I want this job." In addition, you must convince yourself that you want to make a step down. This is important because most people are not great actors. The recruiter can usually feel if a candidate is planning on quitting quickly. The most powerful statement a job candidate can tell a recruiter, both on the resume and in the interview, is that "this is the exact work I have done and I want this job." Saying it is not enough. You have to feel it too.

<u>Myth 7: I can get a management position or lower once I have been a Director, Vice President, or some upper-level title</u>.

Unfortunately, if you have upper level titles on your resume, it will be very challenging to take a step down. The advice throughout this program and in this section should be sufficient for a candidate who has not reached an executive level of employment. Most candidates can tailor their resume and their answers to present a customized "lateral" fit image for the position, even for a step-down.

If you have reached a title of Director or higher, you may need to consider moving for a new job, traveling for work, consulting, or becoming entrepreneurial to maintain employment. Unless you lie, your title is a giveaway of your level of responsibility. This is one of the reasons that candidates over fifty years of age can face challenges in the job market. Once an applicant has reached a high-level of employment, there simply may not be many jobs in one geographic location at that title.

<u>Myth 8. Only older "upper-level" candidates are told they are overqualified</u>.

This is absolutely not true. A candidate can be between ages 20 and 80 and still hear they are overqualified if the employer feels that the applicant has more skills than the job requires.

<u>Myth 9. I can get the same pay rate as my highest responsibility position at a lower level job.</u>

If you have reviewed the salary negotiations lessons, you will now know that every job has a pay range assigned to it by the employer. No matter how much you have made in previous positions, the assigned rate for that role will not change. Your skills will determine where you fall within the range of pay or if you even qualify for the range. The average

Bachelor-degreed American makes $65,000 per year. If you have worked above that pay rate, you may be surprised that a large amount of available jobs you will be interested in, with some exceptions, sit between $65,000 and $75,000. The pay rate is based on the value the employer has placed on the job, not necessarily on your highest salary.

The next exercise offers specific resume changes that can set the stage to get calls and to perform a successful "step down" interview.

Exercise 10.3a: Resume Tips for Step-Down Career Transitions

The following resume tips will help with a step down. Mark the checklist to refine this resume type:

1. _____ Follow the Market-Based Resume Profile© techniques.
2. _____ Create simple statements and use the skills and abilities at the same level of responsibility as the new job.
3. _____ Look more like a new graduate. If you are unemployed and in an education program related to the

job, list education first with no date unless recent. Remove any work experience over ten years old.

4. ____ Remove all upper-level unrelated accomplishments.

5. ____ Remove any educational degrees above a Bachelor's degree unless the Master's degree is directly related to the job.

6. ____ Minimize the impact of a higher level title by putting the employer and job title on the same line which reduces the visual impact of the title and keep the job title un-bolded.

7. ____ Use bolding of the skill keywords to emphasize matching qualifications.

8. ____ When creating a LinkedIn profile, make the most recent job title be a skill highlight, instead of a title, and make sure the rest of the profile matches your step down goals.

The next step is to create explanations that can ease the recruiter's concerns.

Exercise 10.3b: Interview Scripts and Explanations for Making a Step Down

If the resume is done well and sufficiently minimizes the impact of previous upper level titles, the conversation about having had a higher level of responsibility may be entirely avoided. However, assuming the recruiter sees the upper level titles and still calls on the resume, the following scripts are offered in order of preference when answering the interview question "Why are you seeking to take a step down in your career?"

Situation 1: The job candidate may need to find a job, any job, regardless of title or pay level, due to a period of unemployment.

"This work is the exact work I have done every day. Regardless of title, my daily duties were _____, _____, _____ (name the skills from the job ad). This is the type of work I want to be doing."

Situation 2: The job candidate finds themselves "burned out" or stressed out at their current title or industry.

"This is the exact type of work that I have done even though my title and industry says that it is different. Regardless of title, my daily duties were _____, _____, _____ (name the skills from the job ad). This is the type of work I want to be doing."

Situation 3: The job candidate prefers to do one aspect of a job that happens to be a lower title or pay level.

"I know that my previous title suggests that I am overqualified for this position. Regardless of title, this is the exact type of work I have done and prefer to do. My daily duties in my previous position include _____, _____, _____ (name the skills from the job ad). This is the type of work I want to be doing."

Situation 4: Some candidates want to change into a new industry and are willing to accept a lesser position to make the move.

"This is the exact type of work I have done even though it is not reflected in my previous titles. Regardless of title, I have experience in the following _____, _____, _____ (name the skills from the job ad) while working at _____ (name the employer from the resume) or volunteering with _____ (name

the organization). This is the type of work I want to be doing for this organization and in this industry."

10.4 Move for Promotion Lesson

This career change is for candidates who have the skills necessary to perform at a higher level title or for more money.

10.4.1 Move for Promotion Myths

Myth 1: Getting a job at a higher level than the title I currently hold is difficult.

Strategically, seeking a promotion in a career change is often the only way you can grow quickly in your field. Most employers do not have the level of organizational growth possible to move an employee quickly up through the ranks, nor do they like to give large salary increases and promotions. Therefore, a move for promotion will be necessary if you are seeking growth in responsibility or income.

Myth 2: I can only move up in the same industry.

These jobs are usually in the same professional category and sometimes in the same industry. A job move for promotion may include an increase in pay or it may be a step to gain additional experience and a better title that can be leveraged later in the career for salary increase. If the candidate has a mix of desirable skills, a move for promotion may include a change in professional category and industry.

Myth 3: Employers fear overly-ambitious candidates.

Sometimes this is true. The unique challenge with this career change is that recruiters may fear that ambitious candidates will take the job and leave quickly when another higher-level position or more money presents itself. In addition, a frequent job jumper may appear unstable if they are not maintaining a certain amount of time at each employer. A job candidate can pull off frequent moves for promotion if the career changes add skill mixes that are in hot demand. However, in many fields, a job candidate has about a 10-year window of time when they can jump about once every two years. Remember, your previous history allows the employer to predict your behavior. If you jump at regular intervals, there will be a point where an employer is concerned about hiring you.

Myth 4: The recruiter may be concerned that a job candidate with a lower level title does not have the skills and abilities for the higher level position.

An applicant can use skills and accomplishment statements to combat the lack of job title for the upper level positions the candidate is seeking to grow into.

Myth 5: Anyone can make a move for promotion.

Technically, anyone can attempt to make a move for promotion but it is easier if the candidate meets these basic characteristics.

Select one or more of the following:
1. _____ I have been doing the job of a higher-level title but I have not been given the money or title that match my unique skills and accomplishments.
2. _____ I have gained unique skills and accomplishments from a large organization that are the equivalent to a

higher-titled or higher-paying position at a small organization.

3. _____ I have gained unique skills and accomplishments from a small organization that I can use to enter into a large organization that has more growth opportunities and money.

4. _____ I have a combination of unique hard-to-find skills that employers need.

Job candidates who meet the qualities listed in the assessment tend to be more successful in making a "move for promotion."

A candidate can make a move for promotion by taking experience gained in a large organization and applying it to a smaller one with the goal of obtaining a better title and potentially more money. An example of this might be an accountant for a larger manufacturer seeking to become the controller for a small manufacturer. Even though the candidate held a much lower title at the larger organization, the breadth and depth of skills gained at the large manufacturer may qualify the candidate for a controller-level position within a smaller company.

Smaller organizations sometimes offer deep, rich experiences that do not pay well or have the high-growth path desired by the job candidate. However, these rich experiences may be used to enter into a larger organization offering the potential for growth, higher income, or performance incentives.

It may become evident to the job candidate that they are doing the work of a higher-level title or pay rank. In addition, the candidate may find a skill mix that can create a unique advantage that leads to a higher-level title or income. For instance, an accountant who is moving to a controller-level position may be able to leverage the employer's need for an industry-specific skill, a second language, or knowledge of articular software.

Myth 6: I can make a move for promotion without capturing, quantifying, and communicating my accomplishments.

A job candidate who wants to climb quickly will have to learn how to capture, quantify, and communicate accomplishments as soon as possible. This job candidate needs to make an extensive effort to move away from a duty-based resume and into an accomplishment-based profile.

Myth 7: The recruiter will wonder why an exceptional candidate has not been promoted by the current employer.

This can be an issue for this career change type. The recruiter may wonder why an accomplished candidate has not been previously promoted or, if the applicant is unemployed, why they were let go if they were skilled. The solution is to create an irresistible "exact fit" resume profile and interview answers.

Myth 8: Telling the employer that I want to move for more money is appropriate in this case.

An explanation for a move for promotion should not only be about better compensation or benefits because the employer may be concerned that you will quit your job later for more pay.

The next exercise offers specific resume tips and interview scripts to help the process flow smoothly.

Exercise 10.4a: Resume Tips for Promotion Career Transitions

The following resume tips will help with a job transition for promotion.

Mark the checklist to refine this resume type:

1. _____ Follow the Market-Based Resume Profile© techniques.
2. _____ Upsell experience with accomplishments at the level of the next job.
3. _____ Quantify accomplishments that match the job level.
4. _____ Move from a duty-based resume.

Exercise 10.4b: Interview Scripts and Explanations for a Move for Promotion

If the resume is done well, it will sufficiently demonstrate that the candidate has the skills to do the position. The following scripts help you explain to the employer that you want "this job" and that you will not leave quickly to move on for more growth and additional money. Combine this with the answers that describe the reason for leaving a job (listed below) for a powerful explanation.

Situation 1: The job candidate is seeking to take experiences gained in a larger organization to a smaller organization with a higher level of title and responsibility.

"While working at _____ (state the name of the larger organization), I gained upper level experiences in _____, _____, _____ (state the desired accomplishments). But, I

am just a cog in a machine. I prefer a smaller organization that can really use these skills to make a difference."

Situation 2: A job candidate who worked in a smaller organization and gained many skills but no title is now seeking growth with a larger organization.
"At my current smaller employer, I am required to be a "jack of all trades" without being given the title. On the positive side, I have developed a wide breadth of skills that you can use. I feel the larger organization is a better fit for me."

Situation 3: The job candidate has performed the work but has not been given the title.
"I have done this exact work and gained many skills and experiences as evidenced by my accomplishments, but my current employer is not in a position to offer me the next step due to business or industry conditions. For this reason, I am seeking a role that can use these skills and offer me the title that goes with them."

Situation 4: The job candidate has a number of key skills for this position which
are difficult to locate in the job market right now.
"I have done this exact work and I am seeking a position that can use the following skills _____, _____, _____ (state at least two to three hard-to-locate skills), and accomplishments _____, _____, _____ (state one to three desirable accomplishments).

Combine the responses above with answers to "Common Interview Question #2": Why did you transition from one job

to another? and/or Why are you looking to leave where you are?

Use the following script to answer the question:

- *"I moved from my employer because _____ (select one or a combination of the following options)."*
- *the next position was the next step in my career path of _____ (a skill that the next job has) or,*
- *I enjoy doing _____ (a skill that the next job has) or*
- *this is a better use of _____ (a skill that the next job has) or,*
- *this is a return to an industry or,*
- *this is closer to home or,*
- *this has better hours or,*
- *_____. (some unique aspect that I like that the old place did not have.)*

10.5 Return to Prior Profession Lesson

Most people have worked in multiple professional categories or industries. Any time the most recent work experience is different than the job you are applying for, yet matches a previous work experience, it falls within the category of retuning to an old profession.

10.5.1 Return to Prior Profession Myths

Myth 1: This is one of the hardest job moves to make especially with modern hiring systems.

This answer is both true and not true. In one way, this is not difficult because the resume's Title Bar, Summary of Skills, and Skill Highlights can all point towards the old professional accomplishments. However, recruiters and ATS programs stress the use of the reverse chronology resume which focuses on the most recent work experience first. Even with LinkedIn, the recruiters focus on searching the most recent job title to identify candidates. However, these job moves can be very successful if the skills gained from the most recent position can complement the previous profession.

Myth 2: Employers will not be concerned about when I did the work.

This is not true. If the resume makes it through the software or online search, the recruiter will have a variety of red flags: "Why did you move from this type of work in the first place? Why do you want to return to this type of work? If you have not been doing this work lately maybe you are rusty."

In the past, the solution to this resume problem was to use the functional style that stresses skills over title, employers, and dates of employment. However, the ATS program is diminishing the use of the functional resume. The best solution is to create a combination of the reverse chronology and the functional resume using the Market-Based Resume Profile© techniques.

Myth 3: The biggest issue I will face is proving I can still do the work.

Actually, the biggest issue is explaining your job transitions in a way that makes the employer believe that this is something you really want to do. An employer may not be excited about hiring an employee that abandoned the profession. The interviewer will dig deep to uncover what happened until they are satisfied with the response. This can be a challenging process that requires repeating the same answer over and over again.
The next exercise offers specific resume, applicant tracking and online profile tips, and interview scripts to help the process flow smoothly.

Exercise 10.5a: Resume Tips for Career Change Back to Recent Prior Profession -Recent Job Has Some Matching Skills

The following resume tips will help with a job transition back to a prior profession.
Mark the checklist to refine this resume type in the order presented:

1. _____ Follow the Market-Based Resume Profile© techniques.

2. _____ Create a larger Skill Summary area at the top of the page.

3. _____ Highlight related skills at the current employer and leave unrelated skills off.

4. _____ Put the employer, title, and years of employment on the same line to minimize the impact of an unrelated title. Do not bold the employer/title/dates of the employment line.

5. _____ Create a skill statement that directly matches the job. Bold the statement to take the eye away from the employer and on to the skill statement.

6. _____ Make sure the previous matching job title is on the first page.

7. _____ In the ATS, use the correct title but paste in all the functional related skills into the job description box.

8. _____ In LinkedIn, use a summary and headline that focuses on the previous profession.

Exercise 10.5b: Interview Scripts and Explanations for a Career Transition Back to a Prior Profession

If the resume is done well and sufficiently presents accomplishments at the level of responsibility of the next position the conversation regarding any concerns about returning to a prior profession should be easier, but will not be avoided. The following script assists in the conversation.

"While I was working in my most recent profession, I really came to realize how much I missed _____, _____, _____ (fill in the blanks with skills or experiences that match the prior

301

profession that are not a part of the most recent profession). Now I am seeking to return to my prior profession because that is the work I prefer to do. I particularly miss _____, _____, _____ *(state skills and work environment descriptions that match the job)."*

10.6 New Graduate or Entry-level Lesson

A new graduate resume puts the job candidate's education before the work experience section. The next section reviews common myths and beliefs about this resume style.

10.6.1 New Graduate Common Myths

<u>Myth 1: If I am a new graduate I should put my education first.</u>

No, not always. This strategy should be used only in certain circumstances because relevant practical current work experience is always more important than education. Although new graduates feel that they do not have professional experience, in most cases they do and it should be presented first when it relates to the job application.

The following examples present the common scenarios in which the new graduate resume is the expected and necessary choice.

Select one or more of the following:
1. _____ I am applying for internships.
2. _____ I am a new graduate with no internship, work study, or professional work experience.
3. _____ I am applying for a job in which the degree is a prerequisite to work in the field.

If you selected any of the options above, then you should put education first on your resume. Internships are usually for younger new graduates or those still in school. It is less common for an older and more experienced job candidate to obtain an internship. An older candidate (over 40 years of age) will need to highlight academic accomplishments and recent matching professional work experience. New graduates who have absolutely no internships, work-study jobs, or professional work experience should use this format. There are certain scientific, medical, and quantitative fields that require a specific education; it often makes sense to state that information at the top of the resume.

<u>Myth 2: If I have many years of work experience, I should not use this resume style.</u>

There are a few instances when a candidate may want to use a New Graduate or Entry-level resume as a strategic choice.

New Graduate Resume Style Selection

____I need to make a "step down" so I want to appear younger and less experienced.

____I have been unemployed for over a year and I am currently in school or have recently graduated.

____I have had many jobs with less than a year or two of experience.

This type of resume helps "step downs" by presenting an image of a candidate with less skills, accomplishments, and work history; it can assist someone who is "overqualified" to make a career change in a new direction. In addition, going back to school can be used strategically to help a candidate cover a period of unemployment or to change professional categories. School can be used as a "reset" button for applicants who are having trouble getting a job due to many periods of unemployment, job jumping, or erratic employment.

If a job candidate is unemployed and in school, this is an excellent opportunity to cover an employment gap. Putting education first is useful if the candidate is in school and seeking to return to an earlier profession, particularly a job related to the education. There are some academic, science, and math degrees where the proper education and licensure are mandatory prerequisites to employment.

Some candidates just cannot or do not remain in a job for very long, which tells the employer two things: the job candidate will not be happy and will not stay in the new job. Since these are the two qualities that employers value the most, even above skills, it may be important to use school as a "reset button." Use the following assessment to determine if you have a job transition history that allows employers to predict if you will leave quickly.

Job Jumper Identification: Check the items that apply.
____ I have had a different job every year for the past five years.
____ I have had a job every two years for the past ten years.
____ I held a job for over three years in my past but recently, I have had two jobs that lasted no more
than two years each.

If you were able to check any of the above, consider going back to school and presenting your education first on your resume. After education, present those different jobs as "school-time" or "pre-professional" employment. If you are under 40 years of age, consider shaving off a tremendous amount of past history to present that new-graduate image. There is one more thing to note here: employers do not value a person's ability to job jump. Job jumpers sometimes feel that their ability to do many different things (as reflected by many different jobs) demonstrates their flexibility, adaptability, and teach-ability. Although this may be true, it also tells the employer you will not stay and be happy.

Some job jumping at the beginning of your career or after a period of unexpected unemployment is acceptable to the job market. Beyond that, from a job market perspective you are expected to "find yourself" and commit to an employer and a career.

The biggest challenge with a new graduate or entry-level professional is whether you have the skills to do the job, if it is what you really want to be doing, and if you will stay with the organization once you have the work experience. The next exercise offers specific resume tips and interview scripts to help the process flow smoothly.

Exercise 10.6a: Resume Tips for New Graduate and Entry-Level Career Transitions

The following resume tips will help with new graduate and entry-level career transitions. The items in CAPS denote a written resume header section.

I am applying for internships.

Resume Tip Checklist: Internship Application
Mark the checklist to refine this resume type:

1. ___ Appear like a younger person with no more than 10 years of experience, if any.
2. ___ Follow the Market-Based Resume Profile© techniques but do not use the classic reverse chronology format; instead use the recommendations below:
3. ___ Place the current EDUCATION section at the top.
4. ___ Detail classroom projects as if they were work experiences.
5. ___ List other internship experience if available.
6. ___ Follow with WORK EXPERIENCE.
7. ___ Present unrelated education at the bottom ADDITIONAL EDUCATION.
8. ___ Add SCHOLARSHIPS AND ACADEMIC AWARDS.
9. ___ Add a section for VOLUNTEER AND LEADERSHIP EXPERIENCE.
10. ___ Professionalize work experience by speaking about the volume of customers, special projects, and working extra shifts.

I am a new graduate with no internship, work study, or professional work experience.

Resume Tip Checklist: New Graduate - Absolutely No Work Experience
Mark the checklist to refine this resume type:
1. ___ Follow the Market-Based Resume Profile© techniques but do not use classic reverse chronology format using the recommendations below.
2. ___ Place the current EDUCATION section at the top.

3. ___ Detail classroom projects as if they were work experiences.
4. ___ List other internship experience if available.
5. ___ Follow with WORK EXPERIENCE.
6. ___ Present unrelated education at the bottom as ADDITIONAL EDUCATION.
7. ___ Add SCHOLARSHIPS AND ACADEMIC AWARDS.
8. ___ VOLUNTEER AND LEADERSHIP EXPERIENCE.
9. ___ Professionalize work experience by speaking about the volume of customers, special projects, and working extra shifts.

I have been unemployed for over a year and I am currently in school or have recently graduated.

Resume Tip Checklist: New Graduate - Unemployed
Mark the checklist to refine this resume type:
1. ___ Follow the Market-Based Resume Profile© techniques but do not use classic reverse chronology format. Use the recommendations below:
2. ___ Put EDUCATION first after the summary of skills and list the dates as if it were a job to visually cover the gap.
3. ___ Match previous work experience to the job and present no more than 10 years of experience, preferably much less.
4. ___ List other internship experience if available.
5. ___ Follow with WORK EXPERIENCE.
6. ___ Present unrelated at the bottom as ADDITIONAL EDUCATION.
7. ___ Add SCHOLARSHIPS AND ACADEMIC AWARDS.
8. ___ Add VOLUNTEER AND LEADERSHIP EXPERIENCE.

I need to make a "step down" so I want to appear younger and less experienced.

Resume Tip Checklist: Step-Down/Appear Younger
Mark the checklist to refine this resume type:

1. ___ Appear like a younger person with no more than 10 years of experience if any.
2. ___ Follow the Market-Based Resume Profile© techniques but do not use the classic reverse chronology format. Use the recommendations below:
3. ___ Place the current EDUCATION section at the top.
4. ___ Detail classroom projects as if they were work experiences.
5. ___ List other internship experience if available.
6. ___ Follow with WORK EXPERIENCE but shave off years of work and upper level titles.
7. ___ Present unrelated education at the bottom as ADDITIONAL EDUCATION.
8. ___ Add SCHOLARSHIPS AND ACADEMIC AWARDS.
9. ___ Add a section for VOLUNTEER AND LEADERSHIP EXPERIENCE.
10. ___ Professionalize work experience by speaking about the volume of customers, special projects, and working extra shifts.

I have had many jobs with less than a year or two years of experience.

Resume Tip Checklist: Job Jumper Using Education as Reset
Mark the checklist to refine this resume type:

309

1. ___ Follow the Market-Based Resume Profile© techniques but do not use classic reverse chronology format. Use the recommendations below:
2. ____ Put EDUCATION first after the summary of skill and list the dates as if it were a job to visually cover the gap.
3. ___ Match previous work experience to the job.
4. ___ List WORK EXPERIENCE that was during school or five years before school, for a total of about ten years of work history.
5. ___ Present unrelated education at the bottom as ADDITIONAL EDUCATION.
6. ___ Add SCHOLARSHIPS AND ACADEMIC AWARDS.
7. ___ Add VOLUNTEER AND LEADERSHIP EXPERIENCE.

Exercise 10.6b: Interview Scripts and Explanations for a New Graduate and Entry-Level Career Transitions with Little Professional Experience

The following scripts help to answer recruiters' concerns when they ask themselves, "Does this person have the abilities to do the job? Is this really the job the candidate wants to be doing? Will they stay after the organization invests in their development?"

The Script:
"As a new graduate or entry-level candidate in this field I bring with me a host of experience that demonstrates my interest and dedication to my growth in this field. These include_____ (a list of school, leadership, or volunteer activities that match the job). This is the position I want and this is the organization I

want to grow with because _____ (fill in the blank with a background research about the organization or job).

10.7 New Industry But Same Profession Lesson

A career change into a new industry but same profession means that the job candidate is doing the same type of work but in a different type of business.

10.7.1 Changing to New Industry Myths

<u>Myth1: Industry should not matter if you know how to do the work.</u>

The biggest challenge with this transition is that industries use different systems, methods, rules, and regulations, and have different environments. An employer may ask why a candidate would want to change industries, or may have concerns about their adjusting to differences. Changing industry is one of the easier career changes to make but it is important to present an industry neutral profile.

The next exercise offers specific resume tips and interview scripts to help the process flow more smoothly.

Exercise 10.7a: Resume Tips for a Career Change into a New Industry

The following resume tips will help with a new industry job transition.

Resume Tip Checklist: New Industry

Mark the checklist to refine this resume type:

1. ____ Follow the Market-Based Resume Profile© techniques.

2. ____ Only present industry neutral information that applies to the professional category.
3. ____ Present the professional title before the employer.
4. ____ Bold the professional title and related skills and un-bold the employer to keep the focus on the matching professional category.

Exercise 10.7b: Interview Scripts and Explanations for a Career Change into a New Industry

The following scripts help to answer an employer's concerns when they ask themselves or the candidate, "Why are you interested in changing industries?" and "How do you think you will adjust to this new industry?"

The Script:
"This is the exact work that I have done. Although I have been working in _____ (fill in the blank by naming the most current industry) the work is the same or similar. I may need to learn some new systems but from starting and learning the previous system from scratch, I do not foresee a problem. In addition, any rules or regulations will take limited time to learn. I believe my previous work environment and this work environment and job have the following in common _____ (list the items that they might have in common). I believe this business can gain from what I learned in the last one. For instance, in the areas of ____, _____, and ____ (state the possible areas that will could be positive).

10.8 Complete Career Change into a New Profession and Industry Lesson

A complete career change into a new industry and professional category suggests that the desired job move has absolutely nothing to do with the most recent or previous work experience. In other words, the professional is seeking a new experience that does not leverage their background. It is important to examine motivations behind these changes because the Core-3© exercise and job search will often identify new career trajectories, work environments, and lifestyle opportunities (new city, part-time, work-from-home, contractor) for existing skill sets. Lets explore myths related to a complete career change.

10.8.1 Changing Profession and Industry 'Complete Career Change' Myths

Myth 1: Getting into a new profession and industry is the hardest career change to make.

Believe it or not, taking a step-down can be more difficult than a complete career change but yes, this is a difficult move. The primary issue in this situation is that there is no pattern recognition basis for the recruiter to call the job candidate based on resume alone. The candidate cannot produce a 'direct-hit' match. You can achieve the career you want, in most cases, without making such a drastic move, but if your heart is set on this path, there are options.

Myth 2: A resume will help me make this transition.

A resume will probably not help unless you can figure out a way to leverage your previous work experience and education to the benefit of the new industry and profession. For this reason, these types of career changes are often facilitated by volunteer experience, informational interviews, referrals, or returning to school to obtain an education that moves a career in a completely new direction.

Myth 3: I can make this move in a few months.

Be prepared for this career change to take well over six months to a year unless you have a strong personal network that can communicate your abilities to the employer, since there will be no matching education and work experience. These career changes do happen every day with the help of an applicant's personal network, with luck, or through experiences gained outside of the work environment.

The next exercise offers specific resume tips and interview scripts to help the process flow more smoothly.

Exercise 10.8a: Resume Tips for a Complete Career Change into a New Industry and Professional Category

The following resume tips will help with a career change into a new industry and professional category.

Resume Tip Checklist: Complete Career Change New Industry & Profession

Mark the checklist to refine this resume type:

1. ____ Follow the Market-Based Resume Profile© techniques.
2. ____ Remove or minimize information that does not apply to the new industry and professional category, and replace with a heavy focus on general skills that can be used across different industries and professional categories.
3. ____ Attempt to describe experience in a way that the new job can use. This may require the help of someone working in that industry who also knows your background.
4. ____ Use volunteer and leadership experience if it applies.

Exercise 10.8b: Interview Scripts and Explanations for a Complete Career Change into a New Industry and Professional Category

The following script helps to answer employers' concerns when they ask themselves or the candidate, "Is this person qualified to do or even learn this job?"

The Script:

"Although I have been working in _____ (name the various professional categories) I have been interested in this work for a long time. I believe my background in ____ (list any experiences or skills that may apply) can make up for my lack of experience in the following areas ____ (name the skills they are seeking). I may need to learn some new systems but from starting and learning the previous systems from scratch, I do not foresee a problem. I believe my previous work environment and this work environment and job have the following in common _____ (list the items that they might have in common). I also have previous

316

volunteer and leadership background that applies to this position."

10.9 Gaps in Employment Lesson

A gap in employment could be due to a termination or quitting a job.

10.9.1 Gaps in Employment Myths

Myth 1: Gaps in employment are the worst red flag on the resume.

Gaps on a resume differ in the severity of their impact depending on the length of time and when they happened in a job candidate's work history. Some gaps are more severe than others. Use the following assessment to determine how challenging your gaps are to your career change.

Gaps in Employment Assessment
Select which option applies to your situation:
Less Severe:
_____ I am currently employed but have had one or two gaps under a year in length in the past.
_____ I am currently employed and had one large gap over two years long.

More Severe:
_____ I am currently employed but have had more than two gaps in the past.
_____ I am currently unemployed for over a year.
_____ I am current unemployed and I have gaps in the past.

In the past, gaps in employment were the worst red flag. The recruiter used to have immediate concerns about the candidate being an unmotivated low-producing employee that either could not do the job or created problems for the organization resulting in their termination. With today's economy, it is much more common to see job gaps on the resume and they no longer hold the immediate stigma that they did in previous years.

Myth 2: The employer only cares whether I was terminated or quit - not why it happened.

Why a person left a job, or the "reason for leaving," is one of the most important indicators of a job candidate's ability to stay on the job and be happy with their work. The recruiter will continue asking about this until they are satisfied that the employee truly wants the job, that they will stay, and that they will be happy.

Myth 3: I should cover my gaps in employment, no matter how short-term the work experience was that filled the gap.

In some cases, it is better to have a gap on the resume than many brief work engagements or a recent short-term job that did not work out. A job candidate does not want to explain many job transitions. It may be better to say "I was looking for work" than to say "This job did not work out because of ___."

Because job transitions are so important in determining your future success, you want to explain as few of them as possible. Do not create more problems for yourself by explaining additional career changes if you do not have to. A gap, especially one under a year long, may be better than having to tell the employer why you moved from job to job over short periods of time.

The next exercise offers specific resume tips and interview scripts to help the process flow more smoothly.

Exercise 10.9a: Resume Tips for Career Changes with Gaps in Employment

The following resume tips will help with a career change when there are gaps in employment. The options depend upon the scenario.

Resume Tip Checklist: Gaps in Employment
Mark the checklist to refine this resume type depending on scenarios.

Scenario 1 & 2: Currently employed, one or two gaps under a year in length in the past, or currently employed and had one large gap over two years long.

1. _____ Follow the Market-Based Resume Profile© techniques.
2. _____ Use year-to-year dates on the resume to minimize the impact of gaps under a year in duration. For instance, 2013-2014 or 2013 to 2014.

Scenario 3: Currently employed but with a gap over two years in the past.

1. _____ Follow the Market-Based Resume Profile© techniques.

2. _____ Use year-to-year dates on the resume to minimize the impact of gaps under a year in duration. For instance, 2013-2014 or 2013 to 2014.

3. _____ Take up the entire first page with the summary of skill, skill highlights, and the current position accomplishments if there is enough material.

4. _____ Move the employment gap to the second page.

5. _____ On the second page, list each employer in a single line in the following order: employer name, title, and then years of employment. Leave un-bolded. Bold the skill highlights or;

6. _____ If the current job is highly related, create a section called TITLES AND POSITIONS and list employer, title, and years in one line with no detail, un-bolded.

Scenario 4: Currently unemployed, or currently unemployed with previous gaps.

1. _____ Follow the Market-Based Resume Profile© techniques.

2. _____ Use year-to-year dates on the resume to minimize the impact of gaps under a year in duration. For instance, 2013-2014 or 2013 to 2014.

3. _____ If in school, do a new graduate resume to cover the gap.

4. _____ If working on the side or freelancing, create a business name and have the information as your current employment.

5. _____ Seek out unpaid work experiences in exchange for a title and reference and put the information in the current employment section.

6. ____ Move previous employment gaps to the second page. If during an educational period, consider removing and letting school take up the time period.

Exercise 10.9b: Interview Scripts for Career Changes with Gaps in Employment

If the resume has properly managed a gap, this issue should be minimized. In the interview, this commonly appears as two questions: 1) "Why did you leave each job?" and 2) "Were you ever terminated from a position?" The following interview scripts will help with a career change where there are gaps in employment. Select the response based on the different scenarios.

Choose from the list of answers which are ordered from the most preferable to the least.

Script 1: "I left each position before having a new job for the following reason ___ (choose from the following options but not use the same one twice)."
- I decided to go back to school.
- I moved cities.
- The employer closed.
- The job, department, or business was moved to another location..
- The market and industry for this position fell apart.
- There was not enough work.
- I left this position to take another one but it did not work out leaving me unemployed for a period of time.
- There were changes in management and they restructured the department.

10.10 Geographic Relocation Lesson

Many candidates seek to move geographic regions for personal reasons or for new career opportunities.

10.10.1 Geographic Relocation Myths

Myth 1: People move to different cities for work all the time.

Although the United States has one of the most geographically mobile labor forces in the world, only about two percent of people actually move out of their town or state for a job each year.

Myth 2: An employer should not be worried that I will stay on the job.

Employers report that 60% to 80% of their relocating new hires quit within two years. This strong statistical correlation between relocation and attrition cause employers to program their Applicant Tracking Systems (ATS) to look for only local job candidates in a certain set of local zip codes. A relocating candidate may be skilled enough to do the job but they may not be happy or stable enough to remain in the position. One reason this occurs is that it can be quite difficult for a job candidate to focus on work when their entire support system is in another location. This is especially true as the job candidates gets older.

Myth 3: All professions are the same when it comes to problems with changing cities.

Some positions have relocation built in to the professional category, such as in construction, professors, and executives. There is an expectation that these employees will relocate for work one to three times (or more) in their career. However, the vast majority of job types and people will remain in one area for their whole life.

The following exercise presents a checklist to help with the relocation resume and interview.

Exercise 10.10a: Relocation Resume Tips

Use the following resume tip checklist to assist with the visual impact of relocations.

Resume Tip Checklist: Relocations
Mark the checklist to refine this resume type:

1. ____ Follow the Market-Based Resume Profile© techniques.
2. ____ Use a local address and zip code on the resume even if you are not there yet.
3. ____ Consider a local telephone number through google voice and list it on your resume.
4. ____ Remove employer locations from the resume.

Exercise 10.10b: Relocation Interview Scripts

If you have stated a local address and telephone number, the issues about relocation should be minimized from the perspective of the recruiter. However, assuming they know that you are a relocation candidate, or if you do not have an address to use, the following scripts will help to answer the recruiters' concerns when they ask themselves "Will this person stay in this job?" A job candidate wants to express stability by saying there is a friend or family support system in the area.

Scenario 1: Moving Away from Hometown or Long-term Location

- *"I moved to this location because my spouse found (or was relocated) for a job here."*
- *"I moved to this location for better opportunities, and I have always wanted to live here because I have family or friends that live here."*

Scenario 2: Moving Back to Hometown or Long-term Location

- *"I had wanted to move back home to be near my family, so I did it."*

>Homework

Keep in mind that every recruiter is seeking someone who can do the job and will stay with the organization. When presenting your resume and speaking in an interview, build a cohesive story that shows you are a stable, happy, non-disruptive team member.

Quiz 10: Career & Job Change Types (T/F)

1. ___ There are no resume or interview challenges when making a lateral move.
2. ___ Being over-qualified is a good thing in the job market.
3. ___ You can achieve a promotion through a new position.
4. ___ You can move back to an old profession.
5. ___ New graduates have no job skills.
6. ___ Switching both industries and professional categories is difficult.
7. ___ The years of experience, education, and level of responsibility are not that important.
8. ___ A history of many different types of jobs shows how flexible and adaptive I am.
9. ___ Gaps between employment are the worst thing on the resume.
10. ___ Relocating to a new city is no problem.

Chapter 10: Answer Key (T/F)

1) False: Lateral career moves face unique resume and interview issues.
2) False: The employer fears an over-qualified candidate.
3) True: It is easier to get promoted through a new job than your current employer.
4) True: A return to a previous profession is one of the easier career changes.
5) False: Most new graduates have job skills to leverage.
6) True: Switching both industries and professions is one of the most difficult moves.
7) False: Matching years of experience, education, and level of responsibility are critical.
8) True: A history of many different types of jobs shows how flexible and adaptive I am.
9) False: Gaps between employment are almost expected and old ones are barely relevant.
10) False: This is truly becoming a chronic issue requiring an advanced strategy.

Chapter 11:
Timing and Troubleshooting the Job Search Campaign

The first part of this section includes my nitty-gritty comprehensive Stacked strategy for doubling your interviews, leveraging recruiters, and unlocking Linkedin. If you have read the previous chapters and passed the quizzes, you can skip the recap and jump straight to the checklists that offer a quick strategy recap, troubleshooting issues that may arise, and common questions about 'how long things take' in hiring.

Campaign Kickoff Steps Recap

Step 1: Use the Market: Identify Skills and Search for Demand – The Core-3©

The **Stacked Strategy** is built on the concept that writing your resume and online profiles using keywords sourced from job advertisements allows recruiters to find and identify you as a qualified professional. This begins with an inventory of skills, a gathering of keywords, and then using the market to tell you where those skills are needed. This method doubles interviews, reduces transition time, and can often result in a higher income and more career growth by matching your abilities with demand in the market.

Step 2: Perform a Search on Indeed.com

When searching for jobs based on key skills, titles will come up that you may never have considered. Use the market at all times in building your career. Indeed.com aggregates from multiple job boards, making it one of the best sources for identifying jobs.

Step 3: Refine Search Based on Additional Information Derived from Job Ads

The job advertisements will offer a wealth of information on additional keywords, titles, and industry players that you may not have considered. Add those qualifying skills to refine the search.

Step 4: Create Job Alerts on Indeed.com to Receive Daily Pre-Qualified Job Ads

Job alerts can assist in your job hunt by dropping pre-qualified job ads into your email inbox on a daily basis.

Step 5: Create Resume Profiles that Match the Job Ads

Most candidates have three potential lateral moves matching a certain profession, in addition to multiple non-lateral career changes. Use the keywords and duties listed in job ads to help build a Market-Based Resume Profile© so that the resume looks like the job listed.

Step 6: Create a Line-item Accomplishment Inventory

Accomplishments increase the chances of getting a call for a job, getting a job offer from an interview, and getting more money from salary negotiations.

Step 7: Post Resume to Job Boards

Use the resume to build a robust online presence that will bring recruiters straight to you for the jobs you want. The job boards include Indeed.com, Monster.com, niche professional or recruiter websites, and for leadership roles, theladders.com.

Step 8: Adjust the LinkedIn Profile

Ensure that LinkedIn is also keyword-stacked and matches the likely recruiter search for your background based on the job ads and new resume built for those positions.

Step 9: Submit 10 Applications Matching the First Goal Campaign.

Recruiters search online resumes to hunt down qualified applicants. Since this requires little effort, a passive search is an important additional component of a job search. Use multiple websites like Monster.com, Indeed.com, and local job websites because a recruiter may only search one. In addition, many job boards offer "quick apply" options that can allow a professional to do a large quantity of applications quickly.

Step 10: Receive Unexpected Phone Screens from Recruiters Who Find You

With this method you will receive calls for jobs that you both applied for and did not apply for. Sometimes candidates are upset that they get unsolicited calls, but these calls indicate that the campaign is working efficiently. You need to be proactive and take control of these interviews. To manage the phone screen for a job you did not apply for, take a message, ask for the job ad, and set a time to interview in a way that gives you time to prepare. These phone screens can come as a surprise and you cannot interview well in a caught-off-guard position, so control the engagement.

Step 11: Receive Phone Screens for Direct Applications

Phone screens will also come in for jobs that you applied for. In this case, you still need to manage the call by taking a message or letting the call go to voicemail. Find the job advertisement and resume you sent. Prepare the phone screen questions. An alternative strategy is to say "yes" to everything and keep the "ball in the air" as long as possible, resulting in better overall decision-making about new possibilities.

Step 12: Do Not Do On-the-Spot Phone Screens

Can I say much more about this? It is that important that you not treat these calls casually - learn how to answer the questions that come with the phone screen. However, at some point you will become a pro at saying "yes" and getting the recruiter excited about your potential. You can always decline a future interview later.

The campaign kickoff is the heartbeat of the "Double Your Interviews" strategy. If these actions do not double your interviews, use the troubleshooting checklist (Section 11.2) to get your job search moving.

11.1 The 3-Month Stacked Job Search Checklist

Post this schedule to stay on track with your job search.

FIRST TWO WEEKS

_____ *Identify keywords, core skills, and skill mixes using the Core-3© exercise.*

_____ *Perform a search on Indeed.com.*

_____ *Refine your search based on additional information derived from job ads.*

_____ *Create job alerts on Indeed.com to receive daily pre-qualified job ads.*

_____ *Create* Market-Based Resume Profile© *that matches the job ads.*

_____ *Create a line-item accomplishment inventory that matches the job ads.*

_____ *Post resume on the job boards.*

_____ *Revise your LinkedIn.com account.*

_____ *Submit at least 10 applications matching to first goal campaign.*

_____ *Receive unexpected phone screens from recruiters who find you.*

_____ *Receive phone screens for direct applications.*

_____ *Do not do "on-the-spot" phone screens! Prepare for each one before answering.*

If there are no calls on the resume within two weeks, proceed to the next strategy.

THIRD WEEK

_____ Perform a campaign kickoff on the second set of jobs identified in the Core-3© exercise.

_____ Rotate the resume on the job boards.

_____ Revise LinkedIn.com account for current strategy.

_____ Submit 10 resumes.

_____ Receive unexpected phone screens from recruiters who find you.

_____ Receive phone screens for direct applications.

_____ Careful with phone screens! Multiple campaigns = different conversations. Be ready!

If there are no calls on the resume in three weeks, proceed to the next strategy

FOURTH WEEK

_____ Perform a campaign kickoff on the third set of jobs identified in the Core-3© exercise.

_____ Rotate the resume on the job boards.

_____ Revise your LinkedIn.com account for current strategy.

_____ Submit 10 resumes.

_____ Receive unexpected phone screens from recruiters who find you.

_____ Receive phone screens for direct applications.

_____ Careful with phone screens! Multiple campaigns = different conversations. Be ready!

If there are no calls on the resume in four weeks, proceed to the next strategy. Perform some troubleshooting using the following section.

11.2 Troubleshooting Checklists

Sometimes a job candidate will think their entire search is ineffective when actually only a specific area needs their attention. There are four main areas to focus on:

1. *No Calls*
2. *No in-person interview invites*
3. *No offers*
4. *Dreamy change*

1. RESUME & APPLICATION TROUBLESHOOTING: NO CALLS

You are submitting your resume but not getting calls for interviews.

____ I have created a keyword-optimized resume matching a stream of jobs.

____ I periodically change the top third of the resume to match jobs.

____ I have my online profiles optimized and running.

____ I do not talk myself out of applying for jobs.

____ I have done "quick applies" and direct applications.

____ I have submitted at least 10 resumes per job stream in the first month.

____ I am focused on getting calls, not on a "dream-employer/dreamy-job" scenario.

____ I have at least 75% of the requested qualifications on jobs I apply for.

____ I say "yes" to skill based questions so that I get through the ATS.

____ I did not start my search during the "slow hiring season" November 15th through January 15th.

____ If I want a job I have never done before, I know my search is not a "resume" solution.

2. PHONE SCREEN TROUBLESHOOTING: NO IN-PERSON INTERVIEWS

You are getting phone screens but are not invited for an in-person interview.

_____ I let unidentified calls go to voicemail or take a message.

_____ I use the job advertisement to prepare for phone screens.

_____ I have learned how to quote different desired salary expectations per job.

_____ I know how to explain my job transitions and goals to match the job.

_____ If no job ad, I ask questions to uncover the requirements and say "I have done it."

_____ I treat every job as my dream job until I get an offer.

_____ I respond to emails and phone calls within 24 hours.

_____ I love unexpected calls by recruiters and know how to manage these calls.

_____ I know that third party recruiters are sales people and I manage these relationships.

_____ I do not show I am upset when HR departments miss phone screens.

_____ I know the only time I am in a power position is once I receive an offer.

_____ I know my whole job during a job search is to get job offers.

_____ I adjust my answers for each job, including desired salary so that I get job offers.

3. INTERVIEWING TROUBLESHOOTING: NO OFFERS

You have been through the full interview process multiple times but did not get an offer.

____ I send thank-you emails every week until I receive a final determination.

____ I know that it can take weeks to get a final offer or next call after my last interview.

____ I have updated my clothes, hair, and shoes for interviewing.

____ I have developed solid behavioral interview examples for each job.

____ I prepare for every single interview even if it is the fifth one.

____ I use the "Questions for Them" strategy.

____ I have performed a mock interview and received constructive feedback.

4. "DREAMY JOB" TROUBLESHOOTING

You are not getting calls, interviews, or offers, which significantly delays transition time:

____ I only pursue dream scenarios.

____ I only apply for jobs for which I am missing over 25% of the qualifications.

____ I apply for only one job a month.

Strategies for "Dreamy Job" goals:

____ Consult with a career strategist to find the right method.

____ Seek jobs across the nation (geographic move) which takes longer.

____ Create a list of champions for informational interviews (leveraging who you know).

____ Locate and perform the right volunteer opportunity (creating more connections).

_____ Target staffing agencies and freelance/gig opportunities (get experience).

_____ Identify hot degrees or certifications that the market wants (re-education).

11.3 Job Search Timing Checklist

Use the checklist to maintain awareness of the different timing that can occur in career changes:

Milestone 1: Campaign Kickoff (5-10 hours)
- Identify jobs, write matching resume, align online profiles, and 10 combined quick-apply and direct applications.

Milestone 2: Phone Screens - Calls on Resume (2 weeks)
- Following a Campaign Kickoff, first phone screens come in between 3 days and 2 weeks. A fast result indicates a well-optimized campaign and/or a hot area for hiring.
- No phone screens indicate a campaign poorly aligned to job market need.
- Attempt alternative campaigns to get calls if there is nothing in 2 weeks.

Milestone 3: Phone Screen to In-Person Interview Request (3 weeks from call)
- If the phone screen is a Third Party Recruiter you can communicate regularly, but they have limited control over the employer. This can take one to three weeks on average and you can call the recruiter weekly to get status reports.

- If the phone screen was an internal HR recruiter or hiring manager, they will do one of the following:
  - ➢ If they are interested in proceeding they typically schedule an in-person interview within two weeks of your phone screen,
  - ➢ if they are not interested, they will send an email or, unfortunately, they may say nothing and just avoid the issue, and
  - ➢ if something happens to the position that delays the process, they may say nothing.

The HR department often have their hands tied by the hiring managers and they typically have multiple duties. Communicating with job candidates is often the bottom of their list. In the best scenarios, they will proceed with in-person interviews within two weeks of the phone screen or indicate if they are not moving forward. If there is no response that does not mean much except to proceed with your job search until you hear a yes or a no about your candidacy.

Milestone 4: 2nd, 3rd, 4th, and 5th Interviews (3 to 6 months from phone screen)

After the phone screen, it may take two to three weeks to hear back about scheduling another interview. On average it takes 3 to 6 months for non-executive roles and 6 months to 2 years for executive roles.

_____ There may be three weeks between the first in-person interview and the next round.

_____ It is common for there to be up to four rounds of interviews.

_____ It is common to wait months before receiving a rejection on a job (if ever).

_____ By the third or fourth interview you should be close to a job offer or rejection.

Milestone 5: Negotiation (48-Hours from offer)

_____ Once a job offer is made you have no more than 48 hours to make a decision on the final negotiated offer. At this time, you are still interviewing. How you handle this time period is critical to maintaining a job offer.

>Homework

Getting the job offer, especially under three months, is like training for a marathon. To win the big cash prize takes practice, apply for a variety of jobs, even ones you are not sure about, to get practice at getting interviews and job offers. You may just uncover an amazing opportunity that you would have talked yourself out of if you did not take this approach.

Quiz 11: Job Search Strategy (T/F)

1. ____ If I talk myself out of applying for jobs, I will not get as many calls.
2. ____ There is both a quality and a quantity approach to applying.
3. ____ Phone screens are ultra-serious and not casual.
4. ____ Every job is my dream job until I get the offer!
5. ____ The only time I am in a power position is once I get a job offer.
6. ____ My whole job in my job search is getting offers.
7. ____ If I have no experience with the job I want, I need to take alternative steps.
8. ____ Getting unexpected calls is a good thing.
9. ____ There are multiple jobs I am qualified for, requiring a rotation of different resumes.
10. ____ Most active job hunts take 3 to 6 months.

Chapter 11: Answer Key (T/F)

1) True: The first step to a great strategy is to actually apply for jobs!!

2) True: Once the resume is keyword-optimized for a general profile a large quantity of submissions is required as well as tweaking the top for special interest positions.

3) True: The phone screen questions address all the reasons they are concerned about your candidacy.

4) True: Employers want to hire people that want the actual job they are hiring for! Therefore, every respective job you interview for has to be your "dream job" to get an offer.

5) True: Once the employer commits to you, you are in power; until then, they are in control. Your power is only subtle in that you understand how to respond and what to present.

6) True: Yes, Yes, Yes. This program teaches you how to get to the offer.

7) True: Resumes present matching experience. If you have none, alternative measures are required.

8) True: Getting unexpected calls means your campaign is optimized for the in-demand jobs you are qualified for.

9) True: Try different campaigns based on profiles that surfaced in the 'Core 3' exercise.

10) True: Yes, in most cases it takes about 3 months of interviewing alone from first contact to transition.

~•~

You have reached the end of the strategy I use for every candidate I work with to double their interviews. This strategy:

- brings recruiters to you for the jobs you want,
- allows you to perform a passive and active job search,
- perform cutting-edge interviews,
- achieve salary increases,
- decrease unemployment time, and
- plan your career.

This book also came with a bonus link to the online video class with downloads and the ability to ask me specific questions (www.karengurney.com/stacked) . I look forward to helping you achieve your career goals!

About the Author

Dr. Karen Gurney was born, raised, and lives in Cleveland Ohio with her husband, two Goldendoodles, and a Papillon. As a Clevelander, she grew up living 'the death of a city.' This fostered her interest in urban economic development and why places grow, die, and are re-born and what the people that live there can do about it.

Your author loves economies. One of the greatest joys of coaching across the nation (and even the world) is to understand the job market that creates the demand for her clients' background. For instance, there has been a huge outmigration of jobs from the expensive Northern California market to places like Chicago or Houston where the labor pool is highly trained, less expensive, and more central to serving the country. This background has created her unique market-based strategy for career coaching.

Karen has 20 years of combined experience in executive search consulting, career coaching, and human resources. As the Director of Strategic Development of Career IQ, she leverages a Doctorate in Economic and Workforce Development and a Masters in Business Administration. Dr. Gurney's work has been featured on major U.S. news networks and she currently has eight online classes that teach career and business strategies in over 100 countries assisting over 8,000 students in their career pursuits. To learn about Karen's workshops, keynotes, and consulting email the author at karen@karengurney.com.

Hiring, Linkedin, and the job boards are always changing so I update my class frequently. In addition, I have a variety of specialized career books and classes in the works so do not miss out! Join my class to stay current with releases at www.karengurney.com/stacked.

One Last Thing

If you liked this book and found it useful I would be very grateful if you would post a short review on Amazon. Your support really does make a difference to me and other readers that need this information. Go to this link to for the review section of the book http://geni.us/StackedReview.

If you have other feedback or requests for me please connect on www.linkedin.com/in/karengurney. I respond to each and every comment personally. Thanks again for your support.

Dr. Karen Gurney

Made in the USA
Middletown, DE
20 September 2017

P9-DHN-175

Popular Mechanics

THE BOY SCIENTIST

Popular Mechanics

THE BOY SCIENTIST

160 Extraordinary
Experiments *and* Adventures

HEARST BOOKS
A division of Sterling Publishing Co., Inc.

New York / London
www.sterlingpublishing.com

Library of Congress Cataloging-in-Publication Data
The boy scientist : 160 extraordinary experiments & adventures / the editors of Popular mechanics.
    p. cm.
  Includes index.
  ISBN 978-1-58816-771-2
  1. Science--Experiments--Popular works. I. Popular mechanics.
  Q164.B69 2009
  507.8—dc22

                         2009011419

10 9 8 7 6 5 4 3 2

Book design by Barbara Balch

Published by Hearst Books
A Division of Sterling Publishing Co., Inc.
387 Park Avenue South, New York, NY 10016

Popular Mechanics is a registered trademark of Hearst Communications, Inc.

www.popularmechanics.com

For information about custom editions, special sales, premium and corporate purchases, please contact Sterling Special Sales Department at 800-805-5489 or specialsales@sterlingpublishing.com.

Distributed in Canada by Sterling Publishing
c/o Canadian Manda Group, 165 Dufferin Street
Toronto, Ontario, Canada M6K 3H6

Distributed in Australia by Capricorn Link (Australia) Pty. Ltd.
P.O. Box 704, Windsor, NSW 2756 Australia

Manufactured in China

Sterling ISBN 978-1-58816-771-2

Contents

FOREWORD

Do you remember building a volcano out of paper-mâché? That simple middle-school science project, with its tablespoon of baking soda and cup of vinegar, turns out to be responsible for launching many careers in the sciences. Few subjects are as captivating. In the last century alone we've seen astonishing advances, from landing a man on the moon to finding cures for diseases to the invention of television. Science has changed all our lives in profound and magical ways.

Much of that innovation started in a laboratory. That's why we've spent many happy hours in the *Popular Mechanics* archives to uncover some of the most interesting experiments performed by the "junior scientists" of yesterday. Even if you don't see yourself constructing a supercollider in your basement, perhaps these projects will transport you back to that magical time when all you needed was a beaker and a Bunsen burner or even just the powers of observation.

It's important to note that some of these projects and experiments were created nearly 100 years ago when safety standards were more relaxed than they are today. We present the topics in their original form because the procedures and ideas outlined are both informative and entertaining, but please do follow safety precautions when duplicating them.

With that said, there are plenty of great experiments to do and devices to make in these pages. Whether you're exploring the properties of sound waves through a basic experiment using only a stick and a table, or you're building a simple device for detecting electrical currents, you'll rediscover essential scientific principles that govern all our lives.

Dive right in and discover what a galvanometer does, how to measure voltage in an alternating-current circuit, and the best way to determine whether rain is in the forecast (using your very own barometer!). Investigate the fascinating science behind sundials, learn how to build a voltammeter from a discarded pocket watch, use the amazing diving bottle and experiment with water pressure, and design and construct your own homemade mariner's compass using the science of magnetism.

So turn the page and begin your experimenting here with the fantastic projects and exciting, new discoveries every boy scientist should know.

The Editors
Popular Mechanics

{ CHAPTER 1 }

LAB TOOLS
and TECHNIQUES

HELPFUL DEVICES

— A MICROSCOPE WITHOUT A LENS —

Nearly everyone has heard of the pinhole camera, but the fact that the same principle can be used to make a microscope, having a magnifying power of 64X, will perhaps be new to some readers.

To make this lensless microscope, procure a wooden spool, *A* (a short spool, say ½ or ¾ in. long, produces a higher magnifying power), and enlarge the bore a little at one end. Then blacken the inside with India ink and allow it to dry. Cut out a small disk, *B*, from a piece of thin

transparent celluloid or mica. Fasten it to the end with the enlarged bore by means of brads. On the other end, glue a piece of thin, black cardboard, *C*, and at the center, *D*, make a small hole with the point of a fine needle. It is very important that the hole be very small, otherwise the image will be blurred.

To use this microscope, place a small object on the transparent disk which may be moistened to make the object adhere. Look through the hole. It is necessary to have a strong

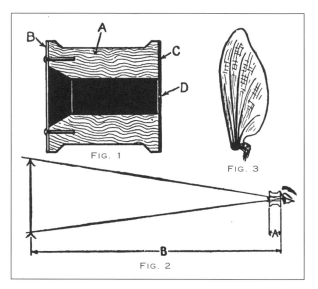

DETAIL OF LENSLESS MICROSCOPE.

light to get excellent results and, as with all microscopes of any power, the object should be of a transparent nature.

The principle on which this instrument works is illustrated in *Figure 2*. The apparent diameter of an object is inversely proportional to its distance from the eye, i.e. if the distance is reduced to one-half, the diameter will appear twice as large; if the distance is reduced to one-third, the diameter will appear three times as large, and so on. Because the nearest distance at which the average person can see an object clearly is about 6 in., it follows that the diameter of an object ¾ in. from the eye would appear 8 times the normal size. The object would then be magnified "8 diameters," or 64 times. (The area would appear 64 times as large.) But an object ¾-in. from the eye appears so blurred that none of the details are discernible, and it is for this reason that the pinhole is employed.

Viewed through this microscope, a fly's wing appears as large as a person's hand held at arm's length and has the general appearance shown in *Figure 3*. Mother of vinegar examined in the same way, is seen to be swarming with a mass of wriggling little worms, and may possibly cause the observer to abstain from all salads forever after. An innocent-looking drop of water, in which hay has been soaking for several days, reveals hundreds of little infusoria darting across the field in every direction. These and hundreds of other interesting objects may be observed in this little instrument which costs little or nothing to make.

— COLOR FILTER FOR MICROSCOPE IS ADJUSTABLE —

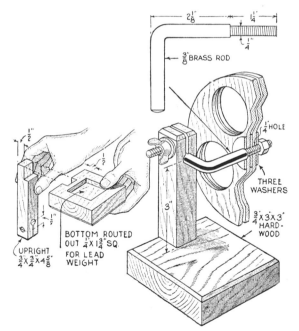

A ny one of four colors, or combinations of the four, for use with a microscope, is available with this filter. It consists of two ⅛-in. plywood disks which have four corresponding openings over which pieces of colored plastic are glued. The disks are pivoted to a suitable support by means of a brass rod and are separated by a thin washer as indicated.

— A Small Bunsen Burner —

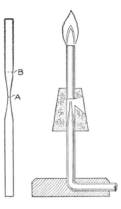

An excellent Bunsen burner for small work can be made as follows: Draw a glass tube to the shape shown, to produce a fine hollow point. Mark carefully with a file and break at *A* and then at *B*. Bore or burn a hole in a cork to fit the tube. Cut a V-shaped notch in the side of the cork extending to the hole. Bend the lower tube at right angles and insert it in a wood block previously slotted with a saw to make a snug fit. A little glue will hold the glass tubes, cork, and base together. The air mixture can be adjusted by sliding the upper tube before the glue sets.

The burner is especially adapted to work continuously, such as sealing packages, etc. The flame will not discolor the wax.

— How to Make an Experimental Lead Screw —

A COPPER WIRE WRAPPED AROUND AND SOLDERED TO A STRAIGHT ROD FOR A LEAD SCREW.

Often in experimental work a long, narrow, parallel screw is desired for regulating or moving some part of the apparatus in a straight line. A simple way of making such a screw is to tin thoroughly a small straight rod of the required length and diameter. After wiping off all the surplus solder while it is yet hot, wrap it with a sufficient length of bright copper wire and fasten the ends. This wire is then securely soldered in place by running the solder on while holding the screw over a blue gas flame. To make the solder run freely, brush frequently during the heating with a small mucilage brush dipped into the soldering flux. An even pitch can be secured by winding on two wires side by side at the same time, the second one being unwound before soldering.

— MICRO-REFLECTOR AIDS IN SKETCHING SPECIMENS UNDER MICROSCOPE —

Biology students and microscope fans will find that this reflector eases eyestrain while sketching a magnified specimen because the image of the latter is reflected on ground glass, making it unnecessary to look into the eyepiece of the microscope. The reflector is a light-tight box, about 3 x 4 in., containing a mirror inside as shown. An opening in the bottom of the box fits snugly over the microscope eyepiece and has a camera lens at the upper end to direct the image onto the mirror.

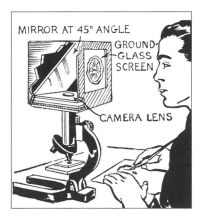

MIRROR AT 45° ANGLE
GROUND-GLASS SCREEN
CAMERA LENS

— MINIATURE PUSHBUTTON —

A very neat and workmanlike pushbutton may be made in the follow-

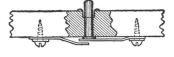

ing manner: Procure an unused tan-shoe eyelet with an opening about $3/16$ in. in diameter. At the proper point, drill a hole into the board in which the button is to be set. Force the eyelet in flush, using a little shellac to hold it in tightly. For the button proper, polish off and round one end of a piece of brass rod of a diameter that will move freely up and down in the eyelet. Solder a small piece of sheet brass across the lower end to keep it from coming out, then adjust and fasten on the two contact pieces, all as indicated in the sketch. The larger piece should be quite springy so as to bring the button back each time. The connections may be made by slipping the wires under the heads of the two wood screws that hold the contact pieces in place.

As every experimenter knows, it is almost impossible to drill a hole in the varnished base of an instrument without leaving a raw edge. Under such circumstances, when it is desired to make an opening for conducting cords and the like, simply drill a hole with an ordinary drill and then set in a small shoe eyelet which immediately presents a very finished appearance.

— HOMEMADE MICROMETER —

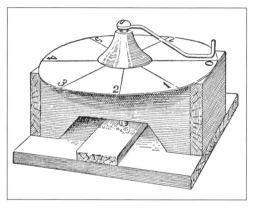

It is often necessary to find the thickness of material so thin, or inconvenient to measure, that a rule or other measuring device will not serve the purpose. A simple, fairly accurate, and easily made apparatus may be constructed as shown by the accompanying sketch. Secure a common iron or brass bolt about ¼-in. in diameter and about 2½ in. long with as fine a thread as possible (the thread should be cut to within a short distance of the head of the bolt). The head of the bolts should have a slot cut for the use of a screwdriver. Clamp together two blocks of wood with square corners that are about 1 in. wide, ¾ in. thick, and 2½ in. long, and fasten them together with small pieces nailed across the ends.

The width of the blocks will then be about 2 in. Bore a ¼-in. hole through the center of the blocks in the 2 in. direction. Remove the clamp and set the nut into one of the blocks so the hole will be continuous with the hole in the wood. Cut out a piece from the block combination, leaving it shaped like a bench, and glue the bottoms of the legs to a piece of thin board about 2½ in. square for a support.

Solder one end of a stiff wire that is about 2 in. long to the head of the bolt at right angles to the shaft. Fix a disc of heavy pasteboard to the top of the bench. The disc should have a radius equal to the length of the wire and its circumference graduated into equal spaces to serve in measuring revolutions of the end of the wire. Put the bolt in the hole, screwing it through the nut, and the construction is complete. The base is improved for the measuring work by fastening a small piece of wood on the board between the legs of the bench. A small piece of metal is glued on this piece of wood at the point where the bolt meets it.

Find the number of threads of the screw to the inch by placing the bolt on a measuring rule and counting the threads in an inch of its length. The bolt will descend a distance equal to the distance between the threads in making one revolution.

To use the device, place the object whose thickness is to be measured on the base under the bolt and screw the bolt down until its end just touches the object. Then remove the object and screw the bolt down until its end just touches the base, carefully noting while doing so the distance that the end of the wire moves over the scale. The part of a rotation of the bolt, or the number of rotations with any additional parts of a rotation added, divided by the number of threads to the inch, will be the thickness of the object. Quite accurate measurements may be made with this instrument, and, in the absence of the expensive micrometer, it serves a very useful purpose.

— CLOTHESPIN SERVES AS CLAMP TO HOLD TEST TUBE —

A spring-type clothespin is just the thing for holding test tubes up to ½ in. in diameter. The curved recess cut in the inner surfaces of the jaws for gripping the clothesline are just right for fitting around the test tube. For tubes larger than 1½ in. in diameter, it may be necessary to enlarge the recesses.

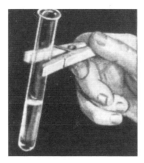

— RENEWING THE MARKINGS ON GRADUATES —

Graduates that have been in use a long time, especially for measuring alkalis, become unreadable. The graduations are easily restored in the following manner. Moisten a small piece of absorbent cotton with a solution of white shellac, cut in alcohol. Rub this well into all the etched parts and allow to dry for about two minutes, then rub in a fine whiting or litharge with an old toothbrush. If red is desired, use rouge; if black is preferred, use lampblack or powdered graphite. When dry, wipe off the excess pigment with a cloth moistened in alcohol.

— LABORATORY FORCE FILTER —

The sketch shows a force filter that is well adapted for use in small laboratories. The water is turned on at the faucet and draws the air through the side tube by suction which in turn draws the air in a steady stream through the Wolff bottles. The tubes may be attached to a filter inserted in a filter bottle and filtering, greatly facilitating the filtering. The connection to the faucet can be made, as shown in the detailed sketch, out of a long cork. A hole is bored large enough to fit the faucet through the cork and another slanting hole,

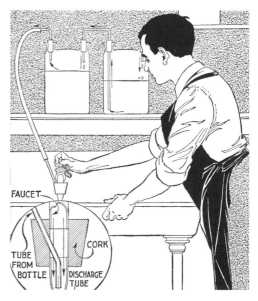

A SLIGHT VACUUM IS FORMED
BY THE WATER FLOWING THROUGH
THE CORK, WHICH FORCES THE FILTER.

joining the central hole, on the side for a pipe or tube. At the lower end of the cork, a tube is also fitted which may be drawn out to increase the suction. The inclined tube should be slightly bent at the lower end.

— Speedy Slotting Tools from Nails and Washers —

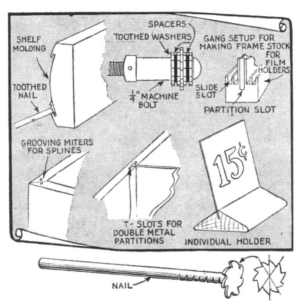

If you've ever encountered the problem of cutting tiny slots or grooves such as those shown above, you will appreciate the possibilities of this simple kink. By filing teeth in the head of a 10d nail as shown and cutting the body to proper length to fit the drill-press chuck with as little overhang as possible, you can do accurate T-slotting, undercutting, and grooving even in medium hardwoods. Multiple slotting can be done with washers, teeth being filed in the edges in the same fashion as described for the nail head. A machine bolt makes a good arbor, spacing collars being used to bring the cutters in the desired position. Only a few minutes are required to make one of these special tools, yet they are quite durable.

— How to Keep a Laboratory Hose from Slipping Off Wall Hook —

The tendency of a length of rubber hose to slide off the wall hook in a laboratory led one instructor to drive a couple of glass picture nails into

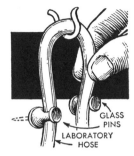

GLASS PINS
LABORATORY HOSE

the wall below the hook as indicated. These held the hose in place on the hook but still did not interfere with its removal when it was needed.

— Wedge Stick for Setting Your Calipers Quickly —

Tapering from 2½ to ½ in. in width, this wedge-shaped stick will save time in setting calipers because all you do is hold the legs at the desired division line and tighten

against the sides of the stick. It is made of hardwood, and the division lines are spaced so that they vary progressively 1/16 in. in length, the lines are drawn with black waterproof ink.

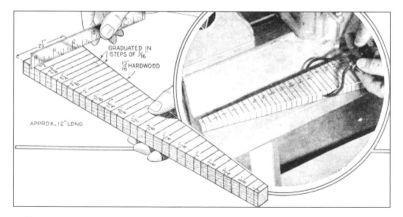

GRADUATED IN STEPS OF 1/16

HARDWOOD

APPROX. 12" LONG

KEPT NEAR THE LATHE, THIS WEDGE STICK WILL SAVE MUCH TIME ON JOBS WHERE IT IS NECESSARY TO SET THE CALIPERS FREQUENTLY.

— What You Can Do with a Ring Stand —

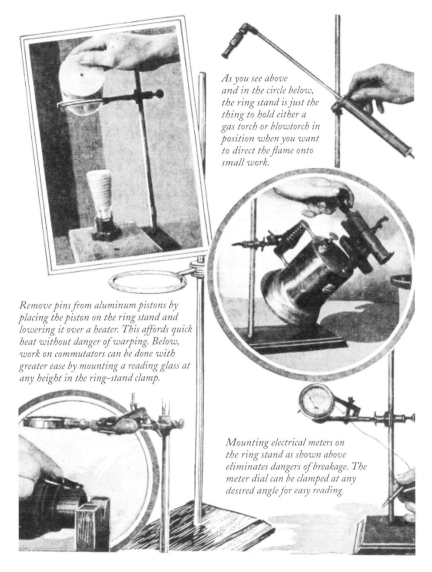

As you see above and in the circle below, the ring stand is just the thing to hold either a gas torch or blowtorch in position when you want to direct the flame onto small work.

Remove pins from aluminum pistons by placing the piston on the ring stand and lowering it over a heater. This affords quick heat without danger of warping. Below, work on commutators can be done with greater ease by mounting a reading glass at any height in the ring-stand clamp.

Mounting electrical meters on the ring stand as shown above eliminates dangers of breakage. The meter dial can be clamped at any desired angle for easy reading.

— COOLING TUBE
FOR A LABORATORY STILL —

A simple and very effective device to replace the cumbersome cooling or condensation coil of a still for the amateur's laboratory can be easily made as follows:

Procure an ordinary straight glass tube of fairly large diameter and heat it in the flame of a Bunsen burner with a very reduced flame so that only a small spot of the tube is brought to a red heat at one time. Then, with a previously pointed and charred stick of wood—a penholder, for instance—produce a small recess in the wall by pushing the charred end gently into the glowing part of the tube. This procedure is repeated until the whole tube is thus provided with small recesses. The indentations should be made in spiral lines around the tube, thus increasing the surface that is in contact with the cooling water. The operation of making the recesses is shown in *Figure 1*. The walls of the recesses should have a regular and uniform slant.

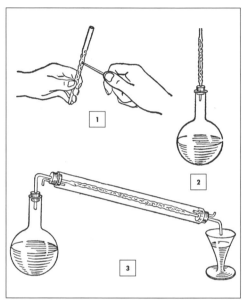

METHOD OF INDENTING THE WALLS OF THE GLASS TUBE AND ITS APPLICATION AS A STILL.

The tube thus produced can either be used as a rectifier (*Figure 2*) above a vessel, for fractional distillation, because it will allow the most volatile parts to pass out first, or as a condenser (*Figure 3*), the arrangement of which needs no explanation. The amateur will find it much easier to make this tube than to coil a very long one.

— How to Make an Aspirator —

A simple aspirator that may be used for a number of different purposes such as accelerating the process of filtering, emptying water from tubs, producing a partial vacuum in vessels in which coils are being boiled in paraffin, etc., may be constructed as follows:

Obtain two pieces of brass tubing of the following dimensions: one 7 in. long with ¾ in. outside diameter, and the other, 3 in. long with ¼ in. outside diameter. Drill a hole in one side of the large tube, about 3 in. from one end, of such a diameter that the small brass tube will fit it very tightly. Use an ordinary hacksaw to cut a slot in the side of the large piece, as shown at *A*. This slot is sawed diagonally across the tube and extends from one side

to the center. Obtain a piece of sheet brass that will fit into this slot tightly, and then solder it and the small tube into the large tube. The slot and hole for the small tube should be so located with respect to each other that the small tube will empty into the larger one directly against the piece of sheet brass soldered in the slot.

The upper end of the large tube should be threaded inside to fit over the threads on the faucet or an attachment soldered to it similar to those on the end of an ordinary garden hose. A rubber hose should be attached to the small tube and connected, as shown, to a piece of glass tubing that is sealed in the cork in the top of the large bottle. The funnel holding the filter paper is also

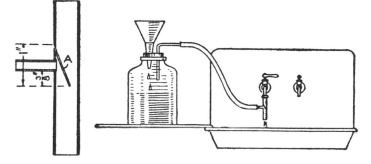

DETAIL OF THE ASPIRATOR AND ITS CONNECTIONS TO A FAUCET, FOR INCREASING THE SPEED OF FILTRATION.

sealed into the cork. Melted paraffin may be used in sealing the glass tube, funnel, and cork in place, the object being to make them airtight. The filter paper should be folded so that it sticks tightly against the sides of the funnel when the liquid is poured in, thus preventing any air from entering the bottle between the paper and the funnel. Turn on the faucet and discover that the time required to filter any liquid will be greatly reduced. Be careful, however, not to turn on too much water, as the suction may then be too strong and the filter paper become punctured.

— MAKE A WONDERGRAPH —

An exceedingly interesting machine is the so-called wondergraph. It is easy and cheap to construct and excellent for entertainment and instruction for young and old alike. It is a drawing machine, and the variety of designs it will produce, all symmetrical and ornamental and some wonderfully complicated, is almost without limit. *Fig. 1* represents diagrammatically the machine shown in the sketch. This is the easiest to make and has as great a variety of results as any other.

To a piece of wide board or a discarded box bottom, three grooved circular disks are fastened with screws so as to revolve freely about the centers. They may be sawed from pieces of thin board or, better still, three of the plaques so generally used in burnt wood work. Use the largest one for the revolving table (*T*). *G* is the guide for the guide wheel and *D* is the driver with the attached handle. Secure a piece of a 36-in. ruler, which can be obtained from any furniture dealer, and nail a small block, about 1 in. thick, to one end. Drill a hole through both the ruler and the block, and pivot them by means of a wooden peg to the face of

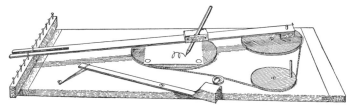

AN EASILY MADE WONDERGRAPH.

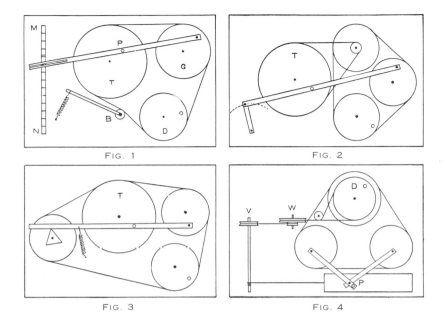

FIG. 1

FIG. 2

FIG. 3

FIG. 4

DIAGRAMS SHOWING CONSTRUCTION OF WONDERGRAPHS.

the guide wheel. A fountain pen or pencil is placed at *P* and held securely by rubber bands in a grooved block attached to the ruler.

A strip of wood (*MN*) is fastened to one end of the board. This strip is made just high enough to keep the ruler parallel with the face of the table, and a row of small nails is driven part way into its upper edge. Any one of these nails may be used to hold the other end of the ruler in position as shown in the sketch. If the wheels are

not true, a belt tightener, *B*, may be attached and held against the belt by a spring or rubber band.

After the apparatus is adjusted so it will run smoothly, fasten a piece of drawing paper to the table with a couple of thumb tacks, adjust the pen so it rests lightly on the paper, and turn the drive wheel. The results will be surprising and delightful. The accompanying designs were made with a very crude combination of pulleys and belts, such as described.

SPECIMEN SCROLLS MADE ON THE WONDERGRAPH.

The machine should have a speed that will cause the pen to move over the paper at the same rate as ordinary writing. The ink should flow freely from the pen as it passes over the paper. A very fine pen may be necessary to prevent the lines from running together.

The dimensions of the wondergraph may vary. The larger designs in the illustration were made on a table, 8 in. in diameter, which was driven by a guide wheel, 6 in. in diameter. The size of the driver has no effect on the form or dimensions of the design, but a change in almost any other part of the machine has a marked effect on the results obtained. If the penholder is made so that it may be fastened at various positions along the ruler, and the guide wheel has holes drilled through it at different distances from the center to hold the peg attaching the ruler, a very great number of combinations will be possible. Even a slight change will greatly modify a figure or give an entirely new one. Designs may be changed by simply twisting the belt, thus reversing the direction of the table.

The number of modifications of this simple contrivance is limited only by the ingenuity of its inventor. *Figures 1* through *4* demonstrate a few of the many adjustments that are possible. The average boy will take delight in making a wondergraph and in inventing the many improvements that are sure to suggest themselves to him. In any event it will not be time thrown away, for, simple as the contrivance is, it will arouse latent energies which may develop along more useful lines in maturer years.

— HOW TO MAKE A SIMPLE STILL —

A still to distill water can be made from a test tube, some heavy rubber hose, and an ordinary bottle. Secure a stopper for the test tube and bore a hole through the center into which will be placed a small piece of tube. The bottle will also be fitted with a stopper containing a piece of tube, and both bottle and test tube connected with a rubber tube.

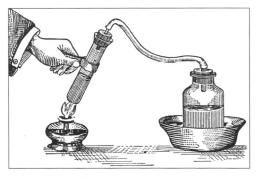

DISTILLING WATER.

The test tube is partly filled with water and supported or held over a Bunsen burner. The bottle should stand in a basin of cold water. When the water in the test tube begins to boil, the steam passes over to the bottle where it condenses. The basin should be supplied with cold water as fast as it begins to get warm. The rubber tube will not stand the heat very long, and if the still is to be used several times, a metal tube should be supplied to connect the test tube and bottle.

— A Laboratory Gas Generator —

The sketch illustrates a gas generator designed for laboratories where gasses are frequently needed in large quantities. The shelf holding the large inverted bottle is of thick wood, and, to reinforce the whole apparatus, a 1-in. copper strip is placed around the bottle tightly and fastened with screws turned into the woodwork. The shelf above is attached last, and upon it rests a bottle full of the liquid required in the gas genera-tion. The pump shown is for use in starting the siphon.

The large bottle used as a generator may be either 3 or 5-gal. size, and, after it is placed in the position shown, a sufficient amount of the solid reagent needed in gas generating is placed in the mouth before the exit tube is fixed into position. Whatever gas is required, a sufficient quantity of the solid material is put in to last for some time in order not to disturb the fastenings.

When all is ready, the pump is used to gently start the liquid over the siphon and into the generator from

GAS GENERATOR OF LARGE CAPACITY THAT WILL WORK AUTOMATICALLY AS THE GAS IS REMOVED.

below. The gas generated by the action of the liquid on the solid soon fills the bottle. The screw clamp on the exit tube is loosened and the gas passes into the bottle of water and charges it, in the case when sulphureted hydrogen is required. In the other cases, when sufficient gas has been generated, the screw clamp is tightened, and the gas soon attains considerable pressure which forces the liquid back out of the generator and into the bottle above. The whole apparatus now comes to an equilibrium, and the gas in the generator is ready for another use.

— A Self-Igniting Gas —

One of the most interesting of simple chemical experiments is the making of gas which ignites spontaneously on exposure to the air. A glass flask is fitted with a cork bored to take two bent pieces of glass tubing, one piece being long enough to reach within a short distance of the bottom of the flask, the other one coming just below the cork. The flask is half filled with a strong solution of sodium or potassium hydroxide, and a piece of yellow phosphorous, about the size of a pea, is added. These materials must be prevented from coming in contact with the skin at all times as they are extremely caustic and will cause burns. The longest glass tube is connected to a small canister of gas like that used for an outdoor grill, and the other is joined to a length of rubber tubing, as indicated; this is submerged in a basin of water. The flask

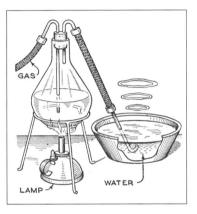

is supported on a stand, and a lit alcohol lamp is placed underneath. The gas is turned on and, as the solution in the flask begins to boil, the resulting mixture of gas and vapor is forced through the tube submerged in the basin. As soon as the bubbles reach the surface of the water, they burst and appear as rings which ignite as they come in contact with the air.

— ❖ ❖ ❖ —

CHAPTER 2

MEASURING OUR WORLD

— MEASURING THE HEIGHT OF A TREE WITHOUT AID —

Near the end of the season, our boy announced the height of our tall maple tree to be "33 ft."

"Why, how do you know?" was the general question.

"Measured it."

"How?"

"Foot rule and yardstick."

"You didn't climb that tall tree?" his mother asked anxiously.

"No ma'am. I found the length of the shadow and measured that."

"But the length of the shadow is constantly changing."

"Yes ma'am. But twice a day the shadows are just as long as the things themselves. I've been trying it all summer. I drove a stick into the ground, and, when its shadow was just as long as the stick, I knew that the shadow of the tree would be just as long as the tree, and that's 33 ft."

The above paragraph appeared in one of the daily papers that comes to our office. The item was headed, "A Clever Boy." Now, we do not know who this advertised boy was, but we know another clever boy who measured the approximate height of the tree without waiting for the sun to shine at a particular angle or to shine at all for that matter. The way boy No. 2 went about the same problem was this: He planted a stick in the ground and then cut it off just at the level of his eyes. Then he went out and took a look at the tree and made a rough estimate of the tree's height in his mind, and, judging the same distance along the ground from the tree trunk, he planted his stick in the ground. Then he lay down on his back with his feet against the standing stick and looked at the top of the tree over the stick.

METHOD OF APPLYING
THE TRIANGLE MEASURE.

If he found that the top of the stick and the tree did not agree, he tried a new position and kept at it until he could just see the tree top over the end of the upright stick. Then all he had to do was to measure along the ground to where his eye had been when lying down, and that gave him the height of the tree.

The point about this method is that the boy and stick made a right-angled triangle with boy for base, stick for perpendicular (both of the same length), and the "line of sight," the hypotenuse or long line of the triangle. When he got into the position that enabled him to just see the tree top over the top of the stick, he again had a right-angled triangle with the tree as perpendicular, his eye's distance away from the trunk as the base, and the line of sight as the hypotenuse. He could measure the base line along the ground and knew it must equal the vertical height, and he could do this without reference to the sun. It was an ingenious application of the well-known properties of a right-angled triangle.

— A Lightning-Calculation Trick —

By simply rearranging numbers, a calculation can be made that will easily puzzle any unsuspecting person. If the two numbers 41,096 and 83 are written out in multiplication form, very few will endeavor to write down the answer directly without first going through the regular work. By placing the 3 in front of the 4 and the 8 in the back of the 6, the answer is obtained at once, thus:

$41,096 \times 83 = 3,410,968$.

A larger number that can be treated in the same way is:

$4,109,589,041,096 \times 83 = 341,095,890,410,968$.

— A Handy Calendar —

"Thirty days hath September, April, June, and November," etc., and many other rhymes and devices are used to aid the memory to decide how many days are in each month of the year. But here is illustrated a very simple method to determine the number of days in any month. Place the first finger of your right hand on the first knuckle of your left hand, calling that knuckle January; then drop your finger into the depression between the first and second knuckles, calling this February. Then the second knuckle will be March, and so on, until you reach July on the knuckle of the little finger. Then begin over again with August on the first knuckle and continue until December is reached. Each month as it falls upon a knuckle will have 31 days, and those down between the knuckles 30 days, with the exception of February, which has only 28 days.

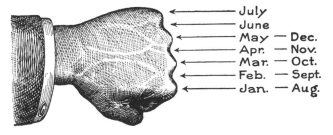

July
June
May — Dec.
Apr. — Nov.
Mar. — Oct.
Feb. — Sept.
Jan. — Aug.

THE KNUCKLES DESIGNATE THE 31-DAY MONTHS.

— What Is a Sea Mile? —

In a circular issued by the Hydrographic Office of the Navy in reply to many inquiries, the following information is given as the official definition of a sea mile: In the United States, the nautical mile, or knot, or sea mile, used for the measurement of distances in ocean navigation, has a length of 6,080.27 ft. In England, the nautical mile, corresponding to the "Admiralty Knot," is 6,080 ft.; in France, Germany, and Austria, the nautical mile or, sea mile, has a length of 6,076.23 ft. The geographic mile, which is the length of one minute of longitude of the equator of the terrestrial spheroid, is 6,087.15 ft. The statute mile, used principally in measurements on land, is 5,280 ft.

— A Homemade Barometer —

A barometer is a handy instrument that measures atmospheric pressure and can thus predict changes in the weather. It's easy for the home scientist to make his own to aid in meteorological research.

Take ¼ oz. of pulverized camphor, 62 grams of pulverized nitrate of potassium, 31 grams nitrate of ammonia, and dissolve in 2 oz. alcohol. Put the solution in a long, slender

bottle, closed at the top with a piece of bladder containing a pinhole to admit air. When rain is coming the solid particles will tend gradually to mount, forming little crystals in the liquid which otherwise remains clear. If high winds are approaching, the liquid will appear as if fermenting, while a film of solid particles forms on the surface. During fair weather, the liquid will remain clear and the solid particles will rest at the bottom.

— A Compass Time Chart —

A very instructive little instrument can easily be made for telling the time of any location on the globe. Its construction is extremely simple. Draw a circle, about 1½ in. in diameter, on a piece of paper and

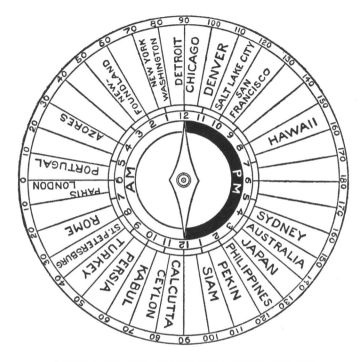

A TIME CHART FOR TELLING THE HOUR OF THE DAY
AT ANY PLACE ON THE GLOBE.

then draw a larger circle, about 4 in. in diameter, around the first one. Divide the circles into 36 equal parts and draw lines from one circle to the other like the spokes in a wheel. These divisions will be 10 degrees, or 40 minutes of time, apart. They should be numbered around the outside, commencing at a point marked 0 and marking the numbers by tens each way until they meet at 180 degrees.

Using a map of the eastern and western hemispheres, write the names of the different cities on the globe in their respective degrees of longitude. The center, or inside, of the smaller circle is divided into 24 sections, representing the hours of the day and night. These are marked from 1 to 12, the left side being morning and the right, afternoon. The noon mark must be set on the line nearest to the location in which the instrument is to be used. In Chicago, it is set as shown in the sketch.

The disk is mounted on a thin piece of board, and a pin is driven through the center from the backside so as to make a projecting point on the upper side on which to place the magnetized needle of a compass. The needle may be taken from any cheap compass.

All that is necessary to tell what time it is in any other city or country is to turn the instrument so that the name of that place points toward the sun. The north end of the compass needle will point to the time it is in that city or locality.

— TIMING THUNDER —

If you are like so many casual observers of inclement weather, you have probably been fascinated by the amazing sight of lightning striking and the subsequent powerful blast of thunder that follows. But as a junior scientist, you may have questioned why the two don't happen at the same time.

In actuality, they do. In the instant lightning strikes, the air is heated to temperatures rivaling the heat of the sun. As it is heated, it expands and then, just as rapidly, contracts, creating an explosion that we call thunder.

But this still doesn't answer the question of why we see lightning and then hear thunder a moment later. The answer is actually quite simple. Light travels much more quickly than sound does. So, the farther away the lightning, the longer the gap between seeing the strike and hearing the thunder. You can actually use this principle to determine how far away lightning is (a handy thing to know if you're near a tall tree or other good conductor!). Count the seconds between the flash of lightning and the burst of thunder, and then divide by five, and you'll have a fairly reliable estimate of the number of miles away the lightning struck.

— INTERESTING RAINFALL GAUGE FROM GLASS GRADUATE —

A 100-cubic centimeter graduate provided with a funnel of correct design is ideally suited for accurate measure of rainfall. With the funnel described, each division on the graduate indicates exactly

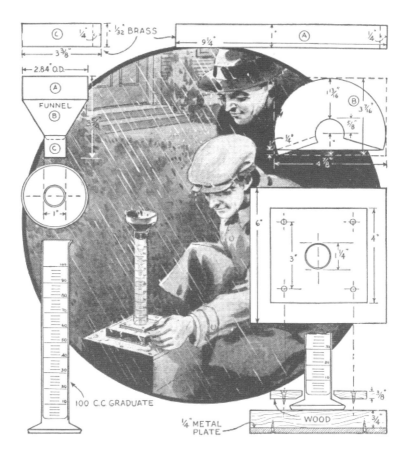

$^1/_{100}$ inch precipitation. The three parts of the funnel are cut to size and shape and assembled with solder. *Part C* is designed for 1-in. inside diameter graduate. The only critical measurement is the inside diameter of part *A*, which should be as close to 2.78 in. as possible. A substantial base is necessary to provide stability in high winds. The gauge should be placed in an open space away from buildings, trees, etc., and raised a foot or so off the ground to produce the most accurate results.

— HOMEMADE WATER METER —

W here it is necessary to measure water in large quantities, the meter illustrated will serve the purpose as well as an expensive one and can be made cheaply. The vessel, or bucket, for measuring the water is made diamond-shaped, as shown in *Fig. 1,* with a partition in the center to make two pockets of a triangular shape, each holding 2 qt., or any amount of sufficient size, to take care of the flow of water.

The part forming the pockets is swung on an axis fastened to the lower part, which engages into bearings fastened to the sides of the casing as shown in *Fig. 2.* Stops, *A,* are placed in the casing at the right places for each pocket to spill when exactly 2 qt.'s of water have run into it. It is obvious that when one pocket is filled, the weight will tip it over and bring the other one up under the flow of water.

The registering device consists of one or more wheels worked with

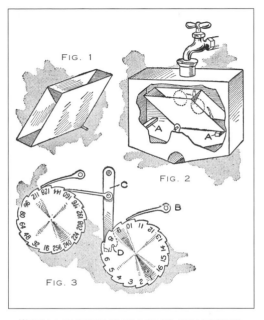

WHEN A BUCKET IS FILLED TO THE PROPER AMOUNT IT IS TURNED OUT BY THE WEIGHT.

pawls and ratchets, the first wheel being turned a notch at a time by the pawl *B, Fig. 3.* If each pocket holds 2 qt.'s, the wheel is marked as shown, as each pocket must discharge to cause the wheel to turn one notch. The second wheel is worked by the lever and pawl *C,* which is driven with a pin, *D,* located in the first wheel. Any number of wheels can be made to turn in a like manner.

— TELESCOPIC RANGEFINDER —

Helpful in both work and play to estimate distances accurately, this simple rangefinder can be made cheaply for the same price as many cheap opera glasses available at toy and novelty stores. More than just a toy, it can be made to work accurately, especially within a distance range of 3 to 50 ft., and thus can be of service to those doing considerable outdoor photography.

In using it, you look through the eyepiece on the back as in *Fig. 1*, focusing in the usual way by sliding the eyepiece in or out. You will see two images *A* and *B*, as in *Fig. 2*. Then, by moving the sliding pointer on the back as in *Fig. 5*, you make image *B* coincide with *A*, after which you merely read the distance on the scale.

The opera glasses used in this particular case magnified 2.5 times and were 4 in. long when fully extended. A longer or shorter pair will also

serve the purpose if the dimensions of the box are changed accordingly. One eyepiece, both objectives (lenses in the front end of the barrels), and two plain mirrors of good quality are used.

The internal arrangement of the rangefinder is show in *Fig's. 3* and *4*, and the diagram of the optical system is shown in *Fig. 6*. You will

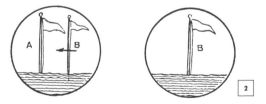

AFTER FOCUSING, TWO IMAGES ARE MADE TO COINCIDE BY MOVING
POINTER AFTER WHICH DISTANCE IS GIVEN ON A SCALE.

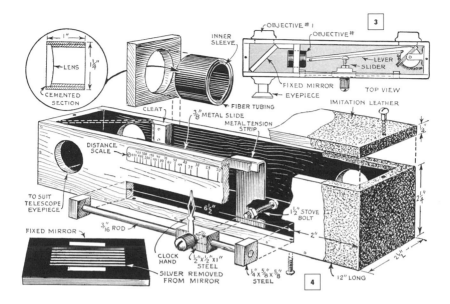

note that the rotating mirror on the right side, *Fig's. 3* and *6*, is placed directly behind the front part of one barrel from which the lens has been removed. The mirror is attached to a moveable lever which is adjusted by means of a slider. The image caught by this mirror is reflected through objective No. 2 which is the lens removed from barrel and cemented in a length of fiber tubing which is held securely in position as indicated.

The image, after passing through objective No. 2, falls on the second mirror which is fixed at a 45-degree angle at the left end of the box. The

fixed mirror is semitransparent so that it will reflect the image coming from the right into the eyepiece at the back. It will also pass the image from objective No. 1 to the eyepiece (objective No. 1 is the front of other barrel with lens intact). This accounts for the double image that you will see before adjusting the slider to merge both into one. Either a partly silvered mirror can be used or a number of thin, parallel lines can be scratched on the silvering, as is shown in the lower left detail of *Fig. 4*, both of which will make the fixed mirror semitransparent.

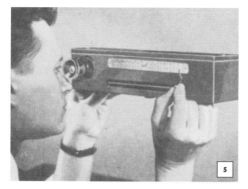

5

as shown, having a strip of brass or iron screwed to the top. A screw attached to the slider runs against the strip. Note that half of the screw head is filed away. A small coil spring on the lever at the large end gives a positive action. The spring is kept in place by a shallow groove in the rounded end of the lever.

The length of the lever attached to the rotating mirror, the straightness of its edge, and the precision of the moving parts determine, to a large extent, the accuracy of the instrument. The lever is detailed in *Fig. 7*. It consists of a piece of hard-pressed wood,

The rotating mirror is locked securely to the lever by means of a small setscrew on the mirror holder. You adjust the mirror to bring the infinity distance to the extreme left of the scale and then lock it. Infinity is determined by sighting on the moon or a large star. Calibration of

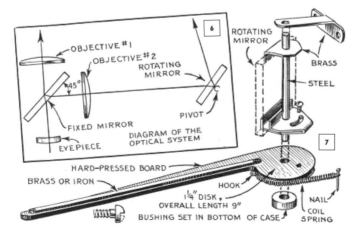

OBJECTIVE #1
OBJECTIVE #2
ROTATING MIRROR
45°
FIXED MIRROR
PIVOT
EYEPIECE
DIAGRAM OF THE OPTICAL SYSTEM

6

ROTATING MIRROR
BRASS
STEEL

7

HARD-PRESSED BOARD
BRASS OR IRON
HOOK
NAIL
COIL SPRING
¼" DISK,
OVERALL LENGTH 9"
BUSHING SET IN BOTTOM OF CASE

the scale is easy if you sight objects at measured distances, and mark these distances on the scale at each location of the pointer. After a paper scale has been made, you can duplicate it on a strip of metal, or you can just cover the paper with a piece of celluloid. A covering of imitation leather will add considerably to the appearance of the case, which should also be provided with a nut in the bottom so you can mount it on a tripod.

HEAVENLY BODIES

— A SIMPLE SEXTANT —

A sextant for measuring the latitude of any place can easily be constructed. A board, 1 in. thick, 6 in. wide, and 12 in. long is recommended for the instrument; however, any dimensions can be used, providing the line *AB* is at perfect right angles to the level of the sights *C* and *D*. The sights are better to use, although the upper edge of the board, if it is perfectly straight, will do as well. If it is desired to use sights, a slight groove is cut in the upper edge. A V-shaped piece, cut from tin, is fastened at one end, and a small pointed nail is driven in at the other. When doing this, be sure to

THE MAIN PART OF THE INSTRUMENT CONSISTS OF A BOARD WITH A PLUMB ATTACHED.

level the bottom of the V-notch and nail point so that in drawing the line *AB* it will be at perfect right angles

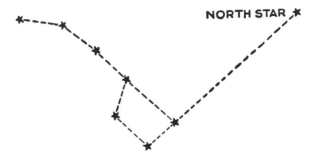

NORTH STAR

THE TWO STARS AT THE END OF THE GREAT DIPPER
ARE POINTERS TO THE NORTH STAR.

to a line between the sights. A tack is driven into the side of the board at the upper edge, a line is fastened to it, and a weight is tied to the lower end, which should swing below the lower edge of the board.

The instrument is placed in such a manner that the North Star is sighted, as shown, and the point on the lower edge of the board is marked where the

Line E comes to rest. A line is then drawn from A to the point marked, and the angle F is measured with a protractor. The number of degrees in this angle will be approximately equal to the number of degrees in the latitude of that place.

The North Star is easily located by reason of its position relative to the Great Dipper, as shown by the diagram.

— HOW TO MAKE AN EQUATORIAL —

This star finder can easily be made by anyone who can use a few tools, as the parts are all wood and the only lathe work necessary is the turned shoulder on the polar axis (this could be dressed and sandpapered true enough for the purpose). The base is a board 5 in. wide and 9 in. long which is fitted

with an ordinary wood screw in each corner for leveling. Two side pieces cut with an angle equal to the colatitude of the place are nailed to the base and on top of them is fastened another board on which is marked the hour circle as shown. The end of the polar axis B, which has the end turned with a shoulder, is fitted in a hole bored in the center of the hour circle. The polar axis *B* is secured to the board with a wooden collar and a pin underneath. The upper end of the polar axis is fitted with a ¼-in. board, *C*, 5½ in. in diameter. A thin compass card divided into degrees is fitted on the edge of this disk for the declination circle.

The hour circle *A* is half of a similar card with the hour marks divided into 20 minutes. An index pointer is fastened to the base of the polar axis. A pointer 12 in. long is fastened with a small bolt to the center of the declination circle. A small opening is made in the pointer into which an ordinary needle is inserted. This needle is adjusted to the degree to set the pointer in declination, and, when set, the pointer is clamped with the bolt at the center. A brass tube having a ¼-in. hole is fastened to the pointer.

The first thing to do is to get a true N and S meridian mark. This can be approximately obtained by a good compass, and allowance made for the magnetic declination at your own place. Secure a slab of stone or some other solid flat surface, level this and have it firmly fixed facing due south with a line drawn through the center

HOMEMADE EQUATORIAL.

```
                                    hr. min. sec.
9 hr. 10 min. shows mean siderial... 1    0    0
   Add 12 hrs....................12       0    0
                                   ___   ___  ___
                                    13    0    0
Right ascension of Venus........... 2    10    0
                                   ___   ___  ___
Set hour circle to before meridian..10  50    0
                Again
                        hr. min. sec.
At 1 hr. 30 min. mean clock
    shows ................. 5   20   0 siderial
Right ascension of Venus.. 2   10   0
                          ___  ___  ___
Set hour circle to........ 3   10   0 afternoon
```

IT'S EASY TO FIND THE PLANETS IN OUR SKIES.

and put the equatorial on the surface with XII on the south end of the line. Then set the pointer *D* to the declination of the object, say Venus at the date of observation. You now want to know if this planet is east or west of your meridian at the time of observation. The following formula will show how this may be found. To find a celestial object by equatorial: Find the planet Venus May 21, 1881, at 9 hr. 10 min. a.m. Subtract right ascension of planet from the time shown by the clock, as shown above.

Books may be found in libraries that will give the right ascension and declination of most of the heavenly bodies. The foregoing tables assume that you have a clock rated to siderial time, but this is not absolutely necessary. If you can obtain the planet's declination on the day of observation and ascertain when it is due south, all you have to do is to set the pointer *D* by the needle point and note whether Venus has passed your meridian or not and set your hour index. There will be no difficulty in picking up Venus even in bright sunlight when the plant is visible to the naked eye.

— THE SCIENCE OF THE SUNDIAL —

Actual construction of a sundial is not complicated and permits the use of almost any material that will withstand exposure to the elements. The dial may be cut from copper or linoleum and mounted on a wooden, steel, or concrete pedestal, or installed vertically on a wall.

If you like, the vertical dial might be painted directly on the wall, or a horizontal dial may be impressed in fresh concrete, laid out in mosaic or when planted in flowers. Thus, you have an almost unlimited range of materials, designs and sizes.

The most important factor in making a sundial that really works is laying out the dial itself. This will vary according to the particular latitude of your home and its longitude in relation to the standard-time meridian. You'll probably want to incorporate the necessary correction in the dial to make its readings agree as nearly as possible with local time.

Before beginning actual selection and layout of a

sundial, it is best to understand the principles on which a sundial functions. These are best explained by the equatorial dials, so named because the dial plate is in the same plane as the earth's equator. This is the simplest type of dial and the one

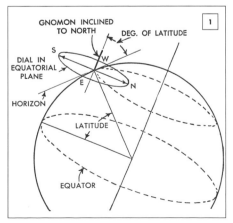

GNOMON INCLINED
TO NORTH   DEG. OF LATITUDE

S
DIAL IN
EQUATORIAL
PLANE

W

E   N

HORIZON

LATITUDE

EQUATOR

1

on which all other dials are based. The gnomon, a thin rod that casts a shadow on the palte of the equatorial dial, works in the same way as a flagstaff at the north pole; that is, as the earth revolves, the summer sun would cast the shadow of the flagstaff through a full circle each 24-hr. period. As the circle is 360 deg., each 15-deg. segment of the circle is equivalent to 1 hour. The equatorial dial is easily made, as shown in the details of *Figure 3*, and will give you an accurate reading. Its one objection, however, is that it will only tell time from March to Sep-

Date		Minutes	Date		Minutes
Jan.	1-6	+ 4	Aug.	1-4	+ 8
	7-16	+ 8		5-25	+ 4
	17-31	+12		26-31	0
Feb.	1-29	+14	Sept.	1-7	0
				8-18	− 4
March	1-11	+12		19-30	− 8
	12-25	+ 8	Oct.	1-14	−12
	26-31	+ 4		15-31	−16
April	1-7	+ 4	Nov.	1-21	−16
	8-25	0		22-30	−12
	26-30	− 4	Dec.	1-3	−12
May	1-31	− 4		4-12	− 8
				13-21	− 4
June	1-3	− 4		22-28	0
	4-23	0		29-31	+ 4
	24-30	+ 4	To obtain civil time, add or subtract the number of minutes shown from the reading on the sundial		
July	1-16	+ 4			
	17-31	+ 8			

DAILY CORRECTION TABLE

tember in the Northern Hemisphere. The horizontal and declining vertical dials are a little more complicated but they will tell time the year round.

There are two corrections necessary for accurate time prediction. One is the daily correction to allow the variation in length of the actual day with that of the 24-hr. day used by civil time. This variation reaches a maximum of 16 min. as indicated by the table, TK. If you desire, a scale for making this correction can be incorporated in the equatorial dial.

The second correction is necessary to make local noon—the time when the sun is due south and at its highest point in the sky—agree with noon according to standard time. The necessity for this becomes obvious when you take into consideration the fact that standard-time zones are based on the sun, or local, time at the nearest meridian. So, unless you live right on a meridian, the sun time shown on the dial will be slow if west of the meridian or fast if east of that line. To compensate for the difference in time, find your locations on a map to the nearest half deg. (30 min.) of longitude. Then determine the difference between your longitude and that of your standard-time meridian. Each deg. of difference equals 4 min. variation in time. Thus, if you are 3 deg. west of the time meridian, 12 min. would be added to the dial time to obtain standard time. If you are the same distance east of the meridian, you would subtract 12 min. This correction remains the same throughout the year and may be incorporated permanently into the sundial.

Your time zone is determined by the following meridians:
Eastern Standard Time, 75 deg. W.;
Central Standard Time, 90 deg. W.;
Mountain Standard Time, 105 deg., W.;
Pacific Standard Time, 120 deg. W.

The easiest method of finding the local noon line, which is the basis of the sundial, is shown in *Figure 2*. First find the standard-time correction, as mentioned in the preceding paragraph, and check with the table to find the daily correction. Then set your watch accurately. The next step is to set up a board and free-hanging plumb line, *Figure 2*, in the location in which you will set up the sundial. The shadow cast on the board by the plumb

line will indicate local noon when the time on your watch reads noon plus or minus the two corrections. Note the example in *Figure 2*.

Layout and construction of an equatorial sundial are detailed in *Figure 3*. As in the upper detail, the noon line is established first and the hour lines are laid out at 15-deg. intervals in both directions from the noon line. Each hour is divided into 15-min. segments that, in turn, are marked off in 5-min. divisions. If the dial plate is mounted on a backboard so that it can be rotated slightly, a daily correction scale may be marked just outside the face of the dial and the dial plate adjusted each day to incorporate the correction. The scale is graduated in 4-min. intervals to indicate a maximum of plus or minus 16 minutes.

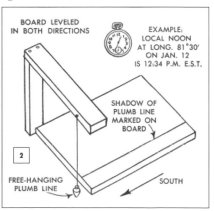

BOARD LEVELED IN BOTH DIRECTIONS

EXAMPLE: LOCAL NOON AT LONG. 81°30' ON JAN. 12 IS 12:34 P.M. E.S.T.

SHADOW OF PLUMB LINE MARKED ON BOARD

2

FREE-HANGING PLUMB LINE

SOUTH

THIS VERTICAL DECLINING SUNDIAL
DECLINES A FEW DEGREES TOWARD
EAST SO BASE OF STYLE FALLS
IN MORNING HOURS.

Although the dial can be any diameter desired, a diameter of 7½ in. is convenient. This makes the hour segments about 1 in. long and facilitates marking the minute divisions. The gnomon should be a straight length of thin rod, preferably brass or aluminum, mounted vertically in the center of the dial.

The leveled board that you used to find the local noon line can be used as base for the dial or a replacement base can be made of more substantial material. This, of course, must be located and marked carefully to be sure that it is level in both directions and that the position of the local noon line is accurate. As shown in the lower detail of *Figure 3,* the noon line on the dial should be aligned with the local noon line, with the gnomon pointing north. The angle of the dial plate to the base, which is horizontal, should be 90 deg. minus the deg. of latitude. This setup thus inclines the gnomon to the north at an angle to the horizon equal to the degree of the latitude. Note that this corresponds with the diagram in *Figure 1.* If carefully installed and properly calibrated, the dial can be expected to tell time within a range of about 2 min., plus or minus.

Of the several types of sundials that will tell time throughout the year, the horizontal dial is the most popular and is frequently seen mounted on top of a concrete column in the center of a formal garden. A somewhat similar dial, designed for installation on outside wall surfaces, is called a declining vertical dial.

The horizontal dial is detailed in *Figure 5,* the same layout being used whether the shape of the dial plate is round, square, hexagonal or any other geometric pattern. The popular round design mounted on a concrete column is shown in the photo to the right of *Figure 3.*

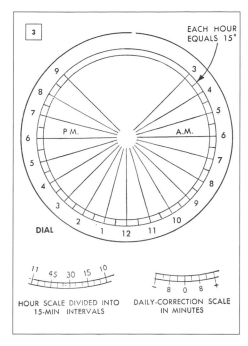

3

EACH HOUR
EQUALS 15°

P M.   A.M.

DIAL

HOUR SCALE DIVIDED INTO
15-MIN INTERVALS

45 30 15

DAILY-CORRECTION SCALE
IN MINUTES

8   0   8

Note in the hour-line layout in *Figure 5* that there are two critical dimensions involved—the lengths of lines *A* and *B*. The first step is to decide on a length for line *A,* determining it by the size of the dial you want to make. Then, as in detail *A,* use line *A* as a diameter and scribe a half circle. From one end of the half circle, lay out a line perpendicular to the base, *A.* Then, using the degree of latitude as the angle, draw in line *B* from the base of the perpendicular. The length of line *B* is determined

by measuring from the base to the point where the line intersects the arc of the half circle.

On the hour-line layout, line *A* becomes a portion of the local noon line. From the upper end of line *A,* line *B* is drawn at right angles on each side. The line *BB* forms the six o'clock line. Using the ends of line *BB* and the lower end of line *A* as reference points, draw three sides of a rectangle perpendicular to the reference lines, as shown. Extend both ends of line *BB* a distance equal to

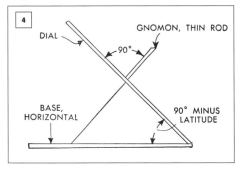

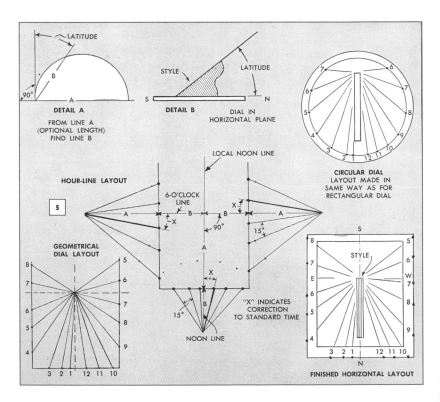

line *A* to establish a point on both sides of the rectangle for laying out the hour lines. Extend the lower end of vertical line *A*, a distance equal to line *B* for laying out the hour lines at the bottom of the rectangle.

The standard-time correction should be incorporated into the horizontal dial at this stage of the layout. Both the noon line and the two six o'clock lines are moved as indicated by *X* in the detail. The angle *X* is equal to the number of deg. necessary to correct for standard time in your area as previously mentioned. In the example in *Figure 5*, the location of the dial is west of the meridian and the time is added. Were the dial east of the meridian, the *X* correction would be made in the opposite direction.

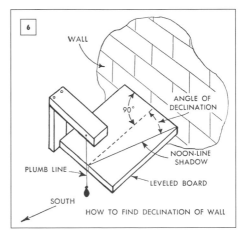

6

WALL

ANGLE OF DECLINATION

90°

NOON-LINE SHADOW

PLUMB LINE

LEVELED BOARD

SOUTH

HOW TO FIND DECLINATION OF WALL

Then, using the relocated noon lines and six o'clock lines as bases, draw in lines at 15-deg. intervals. Mark the sides of the rectangle where the lines intersect them. From the upper end of line *A*, at the point where line *BB* intersects it, draw lines to the marks along the sides of the rectangle. These become the hour lines, as indicated by the geo-metrical dial layout.

The style is cut out as in detail *B*, its angle being equal to the deg of latitude. The apex of the style angle points south, or to the top

of the layouts shown in the details, and is located at the intersection of lines *A* and *BB*. The style should be of thin material or both sides of its

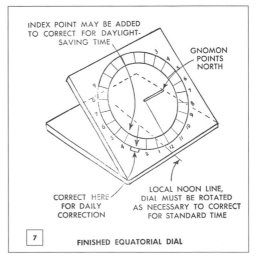

INDEX POINT MAY BE ADDED TO CORRECT FOR DAYLIGHT-SAVING TIME

GNOMON POINTS NORTH

CORRECT HERE FOR DAILY CORRECTION

LOCAL NOON LINE, DIAL MUST BE ROTATED AS NECESSARY TO CORRECT FOR STANDARD TIME

7

FINISHED EQUATORIAL DIAL

top edge should be carefully beveled to cast an accurate shadow. The finished style should be mounted directly over the local noon line.

The declining vertical dial, detailed in *Figures 8* and *9,* is designed for mounting on any wall that faces in a southerly direction. The angle of declination is the angle that the wall deviates from south. If there were no angle of declination; that is, if the wall faced directly to the south, the dial would be laid out in almost the same way as a horizontal dial. The only difference between the horizontal and vertical dials, in this case, would be the use of the degrees of latitude when determining line *B,* as in *Figure 8,* detail *A.*

To make the declining vertical dial, it is first necessary to find the angle of declination. This is done as in *Figure 6,* suing a leveled board and a plumb line to cast a shadow of the noon line. Use the same method for finding the noon line as that referred to in *Figure 2,* except that in this case the board is mounted against the wall instead of being faced due

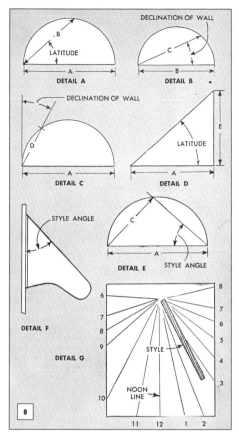

south. When the noon-line shadow is cast on the board, draw in the noon line and draw a line at a right angle to the wall to meet the noon line at the outer edge of the board. The angle which is formed by the noon line and the perpendicular is the angle of declination.

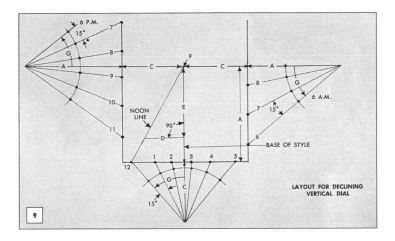

LAYOUT FOR DECLINING VERTICAL DIAL

The lengths of the various lines necessary to lay out the declining vertical dial are figured as in the upper details of *Figure 8.* Following the details *A* to *E* in sequence enables you to determine the line lengths for the layout plus the angle of the style. Here again, the optional length of line *A* controls the size of the sundial. First layout line *A* to the decided length and, using it as a diameter, scribe a half circle. Then draw in line *B*, as indicated in detail *A.* After measuring the length of line *B*, use it as a diameter and scribe another half circle. In this case, use the angle of declination to find the length of line *C*, as in detail *B.* To find the length of line *D*, use the half circle having line *A* as its base, and draw in a perpendicular at one end of the base. Then, using the angle of declination, find the length of line *D*, detail *C.* Detail *D* shows how line *A* becomes the base of a right triangle, having the degree of latitude as the known angle, to determine the length of line *E.*

The style angle is determined from lines *A* and *C*, as in detail *E*, and the style itself is made as in detail *F.* The length of the style is optional. The base of the style will be mounted along line *E* so that the apex of the style angel is at point *F.*

After the lengths of the lines have been determined, the layout is made as in *Figure 9.* Approximately the same procedure is used as that for laying out the horizontal dial.

Note that the noon line is located by drawing line *D* at right angles to the lower end of line *E*. Line *D* is drawn to the left of line *E* for a dial that declines to the west. If the dial declines to the east, as it would if mounted on the wall in *Figure 6*, line *D* would be added to the right of line *E*.

Line *E* is extended below the bottom of the rectangular layout a distance equal to line *C*. Then a line is drawn between the bottom of line *C* and the end of the noon line. The hour lines, from noon to 5 p.m., are laid out at 15-deg. intervals from this line. At this point, the angle *G* is measured as indicated and transposed to both the right and left-hand sides of the layout to determine the 6 a.m. and 6 p.m. lines. The standard-time correction can also be added at this time. This is done in the same way as shown in the hour-line layout in *Figure 5*, angle *X*, adjusting all the hour lines are all drawn to the counterpoint, F, the layout is turned to bring the noon line in the vertical position. The finished layout is shown in *Figure 8*, detail *G*.

When mounting the declining vertical dial on a wall, it is best to use a plumb line to be sure that the noon line is vertical. Be sure, however, that in mounting the dial, you do not change the angle of declination. The style should be vertical to the dial plate.

— HOW TO LAY OUT A SUNDIAL —

The sundial is an instrument for measuring time by using the shadow of the sun. They were quite common in ancient times before clocks and watches were invented. At the present time they are used more as an ornamentation than as a means of measuring time, although they are quite accurate if properly constructed. There are several different designs of sundials, but the most common one described here is the horizontal dial. It consists of a flat

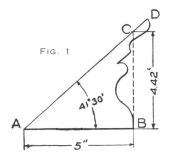

FIG. 1

circular table placed firmly on a solid pedestal on which is attached a triangular plate of metal, *Figure 1*, called

Latitude	Height	Latitude	Height
25°	2.33	42°	4.50
26°	2.44	44°	4.83
27°	2.55	46°	5.18
28°	2.66	48°	5.55
30°	2.89	50°	5.96
32°	3.12	52°	6.40
34°	3.37	54°	6.88
36°	3.63	56°	7.41
38°	3.91	58°	8.00
40°	4.20	60°	8.66

TABLE NO. 1
HEIGHT OF STILE IN INCHES
FOR A 5 IN. BASE, FOR
VARIOUS LATITUDES

the gnomon. The gnomon is inclined toward the meridian line of the dial at an angle equal to the latitude of the place where the dial is to be used. The shadow of the edge of the triangular plate moves around the northern part of the dial from morning to afternoon, and thus supplies a rough guide as to the hour of the day.

The style, or gnomon, as it always equals the latitude of the place, can be laid out as follows: Draw a line *AB, Figure 1,* 5 in. long, and at the one end erect a perpendicular, *BC,* the height of which is taken from Table No. 1. It may be necessary to interpolate for a given latitude, as for example,

lat. 41°-30'. From Table No. 1 lat. 42° is 4.5 in. and for lat. 40°, the next smallest, it is 4.2 in. Their difference is .3 in. for 2°, and for 1° it would be .15 in. For 30' it would be ½ of 1° or .075 in. All added to the lesser or 40°, we have 4.2+.15+.075 in. = 4.42 in. as the height of the line *BC* for lat. 41°-30'. If you have a table of natural functions, the height of the line *BC,* or the style, is the base (5 in. in this case) times the tangent of the degree of latitude. Draw the line *AD,* and the angle *BAD* is the correct angle for the style for the given latitude. Its thickness, if of metal, may be conveniently from ⅛ to ¼ in. Or if of stone, an inch or two, or more, according to the size of the dial. Usually for neatness of appearance the back of the style is hollowed as shown. The upper edges that cast the shadows must be sharp and straight, and for this size dial (10 in. in diameter) they should be about 7½ in. long.

To layout the hour circle, draw two parallel lines *AB* and *CD, Figure 2,* which will represent the base in length and thickness. Draw two semi-circles, using the points *A* and *C* as centers, with a radius of 5 in. The points of intersection with the lines *AB* and *CD* will be the twelve o'clock marks. A line *EF* drawn through the points *A* and *C* and perpendicular

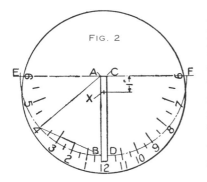

Fig. 2

DETAILS OF THE DIAL.

intermediate hour and half-hour lines can be plotted by using Table No. 2 for given latitudes, placing them to the right or left of the twelve o'clock points. For latitudes not given, interpolate in the same manner as for the height of the style. The ¼-hour and the 5 and 10-minute divisions may be spaced with the eye or they may be computed.

When positioning the dial, care must be taken to get it perfectly level and have the style at right angles to the dial face, with its sloping side pointing to the North Pole. An ordinary compass, after allowing for the declination, will enable one to set the dial, or it may be set by placing

to the base or style and intersecting the semicircles, gives the six o'clock points. The point marked X is to be used as the center of the dial. The

Latitude	HOURS OF DAY										
	12-30	1	1-30	2	2-30	3	3-30	4	4-30	5	5-30
	11-30	11	10-30	10	9-30	9	8-30	8	7-30	7	6-30
25°	.28	.56	.87	1.19	1.57	1.99	2.49	3.11	3.87	4.82	5.93
30°	.33	.66	1.02	1.40	1.82	2.30	2.85	3.49	4.26	5.14	6.10
35°	.38	.76	1.16	1.59	2.06	2.57	3.16	3.81	4.55	5.37	6.23
40°	.42	.85	1.30	1.77	2.27	2.82	3.42	4.07	4.79	5.55	6.32
45°	.46	.94	1.42	1.93	2.46	3.03	3.64	4.29	4.97	5.68	6.39
50°	.50	1.01	1.53	2.06	2.68	3.21	3.82	4.46	5.12	5.79	6.46
55°	.54	1.08	1.63	2.19	2.77	3.37	3.98	4.60	5.24	5.87	6.49
60°	.57	1.14	1.71	2.30	2.89	3.49	4.10	4.72	5.34	5.93	6.52

TABLE No. 2
CHORDS IN INCHES FOR A 10 IN. CIRCLE SUNDIAL

it as near north and south as one may judge and comparing with a watch set at standard time. The dial time and the watch time should agree after the watch has been corrected for the equation of time from Table No. 3, and for the difference between standard and local time, changing the position of the dial until an agreement is reached. Sun time and standard time agree only four times a year, April 16, June 15, Sept. 2 and Dec. 25, and on these dates the dial needs no correction. The corrections for the various days of the month can be taken from Table 3. The + means that the clock is faster, and the - means that the dial is faster than the sun. Another correction must be made which is constant for each given locality. Standard time is the correct time for longitude 750 New York, 900 Chicago, 1050 Denver and 1200 for San Francisco. Ascertain in degrees of longitude how far your dial is east or west of the nearest standard meridian and divide this by 15, reducing the answer to minutes and seconds,

Day of month	1	10	20	30
January	+3	+7	+11	+13
February	+14	+14	+14	
March	+13	+11	+8	+5
April	+4	+2	−1	−3
May	−3	−4	−4	−3
June	−3	−1	+1	+3
July	+3	+5	+6	+6
August	+6	+5	+3	+1
September	+0	−3	−6	−10
October	−10	−13	−15	−16
November	−16	−16	−14	−11
December	−11	−7	−3	+2

TABLE NO. 3
CORRECTIONS IN MINUTES TO CHANGE SUN TIME TO LOCAL MEAN TIME—ADD THOSE MARKED +, SUBTRACT THOSE MARKED -, FROM THE SUNDIAL TIME

which will be the correction in minutes and seconds of time. If the dial is east of the meridian chosen, then the watch is slower; if west, it will be faster. This correction can be added to the values in Table No. 3, making each value slower when it is east of the standard meridian and faster when it is west.

The style, or gnomon, and its base can be made in cement and set on a cement pedestal which has a sufficient base placed in the ground to make it solid. The design of the sundial is left to the ingenuity of the maker.

ELEGANT LOGIC

— FINGER MATHEMATICS —

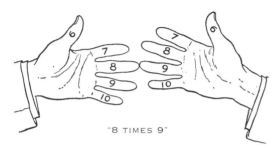

"8 TIMES 9"

All machinists use mathematics. Ask a machinist what would be the product of 9 times 8 and his ready reply would be 72. But change the figures a little and say 49 times 48 and the chances are that instead of replying at once he will have to figure it out with a pencil or calculator. By using the following method it is just as easy to tell at a glance what 99 times 99 is, as 9 times 9. Using this method you will be able to multiply far beyond your most sanguine expectations.

In the first numbering, begin by holding your hands with the palms toward the body and make imaginary numbers on the thumbs and fingers as follows: Thumbs, 6; first fingers, 7; second fingers, 8; third fingers, 9, and fourth fingers, 10. Suppose you desire to multiply 8 by 9, put the 8 finger on one hand against the 9 finger of the other hand as shown.

The two joined fingers and all the fingers above them (calling the thumbs fingers) are called the upper fingers and each has a value of ten; the tens get added together. All the fingers below the joined fingers are termed the lower fingers, and each of the lower fingers represents a unit value of one. The sum of the units on one hand should be multiplied by the sum of the units on the other hand. The total of the tens added to this last named sum will give the product desired. Thus: Referring to the picture or to your hands we find three tens on the left hand and four tens on the right, which would be 70. We also find two units on the left hand

and one on the right. Two times one are two, and 70 plus 2 equals 72, or the product of 8 times 9.

Supposing 6 times 6 were the figures. Put your thumbs together; there are no fingers above, so the two thumbs represent two tens or 20; below the thumbs are four units on each hand, which would be 16, and the 20 plus 16 equals 36, or the product of 6 times 6.

Supposing 10 times 7 is desired. Put the little finger of the left hand against the first finger of the right hand. At a glance you see seven tens or 70. On the right hand you have three units and on the left, nothing. Three times nothing gives you nothing and 70 plus nothing is 70.

In the second numbering, or numbers above 10, renumber your fingers; thumbs, 11; first fingers, 12, etc. Let us multiply 12 by 12.

Put together the tips of the fingers labeled 12. At a glance you see four tens or 40. At this point we leave the method explained in Case 1 and ignore the units (lower fingers) altogether. We go back to the upper fingers again and multiply the number of upper fingers used on the one hand by the number of upper fingers used on the other hand, viz., 2 times 2 equals 4. Adding 4 to 40 gives us 44. We now add 100 (because anything over 10 times 10 would make over 100) and we have 144, the product of 12 times 12.

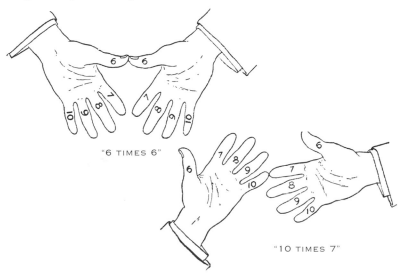

"6 TIMES 6"

"10 TIMES 7"

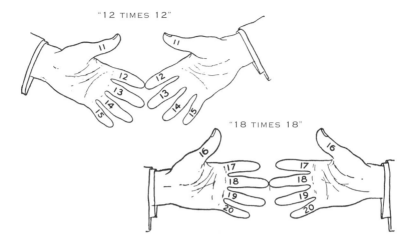

"12 TIMES 12"

"18 TIMES 18"

The addition of 100 is arbitrary, but being simple it saves time and trouble. Still, if we wish, we might regard the four upper fingers in the above example as four twenties, or 80, and the six lower fingers as six tens, or 60; then returning to the upper fingers and multiplying the two on the right hand by the two on the left we would have 4; hence 80 plus 60 plus 4 equals 144; therefore the rule of adding the lump sum is much the quicker and easier method.

In the third numbering, to multiply above 15 renumber your fingers, beginning at the thumbs with 16, first fingers 17, and so on. Oppose the proper fingertips as before, the upper fingers representing a value of 20. Proceed as in the first number-

ing and add 200. Take for example 18 times 18.

At a glance we see 6 twenties plus 2 units on left hand times 2 units on right hand plus 200 equals 324.

In the fourth renumbering, the fingers are marked, thumbs, 21, first fingers, 22, and so on. The value of the upper fingers is 20. Proceed as in the second numbering, adding 400 instead of 100.

Above 25 times 25 the upper fingers represent a value of 30 each and after proceeding as in the third renumbering you add 600 instead of 200.

This system can be carried as high as you want to go, but you must remember that for figures ending in 1, 2, 3, 4, and 5, proceed as in the second numbering. For figures ending in 6, 7, 8, 9, and 10, the third numbering applies.

Determine the value of the upper fingers whether they represent tens, twenties, thirties, forties, or whatever. For example, for any two figures between 45 and 55, the value of the upper fingers would be 50, which is the halfway point between the two fives. In 82 times 84 the value of the

upper fingers would be 80 (the halfway point between the two fives, 75 and 85, being 80), and the lump sum to add.

Just remember which numbering to follow (second or third), the value that the upper fingers have, and, lastly, the lump sum to add, and you will be able to multiply faster and more accurately than you have ever dreamed of before.

— A Puzzle with Figures —

This puzzle is to arrange all the figures or digits, from 1 to 9 inclusively, in two rows. Each should contain all the digits, so that the sum, as well as the remainder (in subtraction), will have nine figures in which all the digits are represented. There are several solutions to the puzzle, and the following is one of them:

3 7 1 2 9 4 5 6 8

2 1 6 3 9 7 8 4 5

The sum of the foregoing numbers and the remainder, when the lower row is subtracted from the upper, will both have nine figures and include all the digits from 1 to 9.

Geometrically Speaking

— Trisecting an Angle —

A perplexing problem for any person interested in geometry is determining the geometrical construction for trisecting any given angle. The solution of this problem has been declared impossible by some of the ablest mathematicians. Of course an

angle may be approximately trisected by making numerous trials, and the results obtained in this way may be sufficiently accurate for all practical purposes, but as yet there is no direct method that can be demonstrated along geometrical lines.

— APPARENTLY INCREASE THE AREA OF A SQUARE —

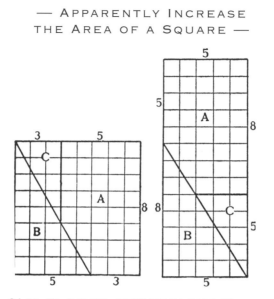

64 SQ. IN. CUT AND ARRANGED TO MAKE 65 SQ. IN.

The sketch here shows how to cut a square of 64 sq. in. to form a rectangle of 65 sq. in. The area of any square may be increased in the same way by dividing it into 64 small squares like a checkerboard and cutting as shown by the heavy lines in the sketch. The result is 65 squares from 64 squares. Where does this extra square come from?

{ CHAPTER 3 }

ELECTRIC EDUCATION

DYNAMIC STATIC

— EXPLORING STATIC ELECTRICITY —

Any boy who has, for purposes of his own amusement, shuffled his feet over a synthetic carpet and then held his fingernail to a companion's skin to transfer a quick and surprising shock, has made use of the principles of static electricity.

In definition, static electricity is basically the "charging" of an insulated or otherwise inert body. We can illustrate this with a simple party trick. You know that a rubber balloon will not conduct electricity—that's why rubber is used as an insulator against electric charges. But if you rub

that same balloon vigorously against a wall, you can "stick" it to the wall with the pull of static electricity. But where did the electricity come from?

That's simple. You know that everything is made up of very small particles called atoms. Atoms have a certain number of electrons circling them. The atoms of insulators such as rubber hold tightly to their electrons . . . that is until you force them off with an action such as rubbing. When there is an imbalance in the number of electrons, the material becomes very slightly "charged." The insulator is then drawn to other inert materials or materials with no charge (a balanced number of positive particles and electrons). This electricity does not flow as an electrical current does. It stays on the charged body, and in that sense, is "static."

Another way to see how a charged material attempts to draw the electrons from an uncharged material is with a wool sweater or pants, and a hairbrush. Rub the bristles of the brush forcefully against the sweater several times. Then hold the brush close to your hair while looking in the mirror. What a sight! Your hair stands on end, following the brush as the hair's electrons are attracted to the imbalanced "charged" surface of the brush bristles.

— MAKE A STATIC MACHINE —

Static electricity is produced by revolving glass plates upon which a number of sectors are cemented; these sectors, passing through neutralizing brushes, distribute electric charges to collecting combs attached to discharging rods. The glass selected for the plates must be clear white glass, free from wrinkles, and of a uniform thickness. Two plates are necessary to make this machine, and the glass should be of sufficient size to cut a circular plate 16 in. in diameter.

A hole must be made exactly in the center of each plate, and this should be done before cutting the circle. One of the best ways to make the hole is to drill the glass with a very hard-tempered drill, the cutting edge of which should be kept moistened with 2 parts turpentine and 1

part sweet oil while drilling. The hole is to be made ¾ in. in diameter. The circle is then marked on each plate and cut with a glass cutter. The plates are trued up, after they are mounted, by holding a piece of emery wheel to the edges while they are turning. Water should be applied to the edges while doing the work.

The sectors are cut from tinfoil, 1½ in. wide at one end, ¾ in. at the

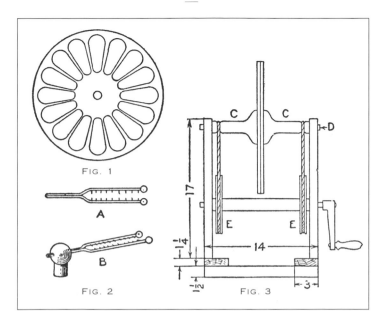

FIG. 1

A

B

FIG. 2

FIG. 3

DETAILS OF A HOMEMADE STATIC MACHINE.

other, and 4 in. long. A thin coat of shellac varnish is applied to both sides of the plates, and 16 sectors put on one side of each plate, as shown in *Fig. 1*. The divisions can be marked on the opposite side of the plate and a circle drawn as a guide to place the sectors at proper intervals.

The sectors should lie flat on the glass with all parts smoothed out so that they will not be torn from their places as the plates revolve. The shellac should be tacky when the pieces of tinfoil are put in place.

The collectors are made, as shown in *Fig. 2*, from about ¼-in. copper wire with two brass balls soldered to the ends. The fork part is 6 in. long and the shank 4 in. Holes are drilled on the inside of the forks, and pins inserted and soldered. These pins, or teeth, should be long enough to be very close to the sectors and yet not close enough to scratch them when the plates are turning.

The frame of the machine is made from any kind of finished wood with dimensions shown in *Fig. 3*, the side pieces being 24 in. long and the standards 3 in. wide. The two pieces, *C C, Fig. 3,* are made from solid, close-grained wood turned in the shape shown, with the face that rests against the plate 4 in. in diameter, and the outer end 1½ in. in diameter, the smaller end being turned with a groove for a round belt. Before turning the pieces a hole is bored through each piece for the center, and this hole must be of such size as to take a brass tube that has an internal diameter of ¾ in.

The turned pieces are glued to the glass plates over the center holes and on the same side on which the sectors are fastened. Several hours' time will be required for the glue to set. A fiber washer is then put between the plates and a brass tube axle placed through the hole. The plates, turned wood pieces, and brass axle turn on a stationary axle, *D.*

The drive wheels, *E E,* are made from ⅞-in. material 7 in. in diameter, and are fastened on a round axle cut from a broom handle. This wood axle is centrally bored to admit a metal rod tightly, and extends through the standards with a crank attached to one end.

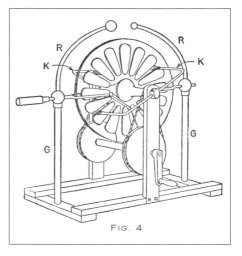

FIG. 4

THE ASSEMBLED MACHINE.

Two solid glass rods, *G G, Fig. 4,* 1 in. in diameter and 15 in. long, are fitted in holes bored into the end pieces of the frame. Two pieces of 1-in. brass tubing and the discharging rods, *R R,* are soldered into two hollow brass balls 2 or 2½ in. in diameter. The shanks of the collectors are fitted in these brass balls with the ends extending, to which insulating handles are attached. Brass balls are soldered to the upper ends of the discharging rods, one having a 2-in. ball and the other one ¾ in. in diameter.

Caps made from brass are fitted tightly on the ends of the stationary shaft, *D,* and drilled through their diameter to admit heavy copper rods, *K K*, which are bent as shown. Tinsel or fine wire such as contained in flexible electric wire are soldered to the ends of these rods, and the brushes thus made must be adjusted so they are fitted with screws for adjusting the brushes. These rods and brushes are called the neutralizers. A little experimenting will enable one to properly locate the position of the neutralizers for best results.

— ELECTROSTATIC ILLUMINATION —

Anyone having the use of a static machine can perform the following experiment that gives a striking result. A common tumbler is mounted on a revolving platform and a narrow strip of tinfoil is fastened with shellac varnish to the surface of the glass as follows: Starting beneath the foot of the glass from a point immediately below the stem, it is taken to the edge of the foot; it follows the edge for about 1 in. and then passes in a curve across the base, and ascends the stem. Then it passes around the bowl in a sinuous course to the rim, which it follows for about one-third of its circumference. After this, it descends on the inside and terminates at the bottom. The tinfoil on the outside of the glass is divided with a knife every ⅛ in., the parts inside and beneath the glass being left undivided. Current is then led from a static machine to two terminals, one terminal being connected to one end of the tinfoil strip, and the second terminal makes contact with the other end. As soon as the current is led into the apparatus, a spark is seen at each place where the knife has cut through the tinfoil. If the tumbler is rotated, the effect will be as shown in the illustration. A variety of small and peculiar effects can be obtained by making some of the gaps in the tinfoil larger than others, in which case larger sparks would be produced at these points. The experiment should be carried out in a darkened room, and under these circumstances when nothing is visible, not even the tumbler, the effect is very striking.

ELECTRICAL FUNDAMENTALS

— HOW TO MAKE A JUMP-SPARK COIL —

The induction coil is probably the most popular piece of apparatus in the electrical laboratory, and it is particularly popular because of its use in experimental wireless telegraphy. Once a miracle of science, telegraphy is the plaything of schoolboys and thousands of grownup boys as well.

Divested of nearly all technical phrases, an induction coil may be briefly described as a step-up transformer of small capacity. It comprises a core consisting of a cylindrical bundle of soft-iron wires cut to proper length. By means of two or more layers of No. 14 or No. 16 magnet wire, wound evenly about this core, the bundle becomes magnetized when the wire terminals are connected to a source of electricity.

Should we now slip over this electromagnet a paper tube upon which has been wound with regularity a great and continuous length of No. 36 magnet wire, we'll find that the lines of force emanating from the energized core penetrate the new coil-winding almost as though it

were but a part of the surrounding air itself. And when the battery current is broken rapidly, a second electrical current is said to be induced into the second coil or secondary.

All of the parts of an induction coil may be purchased readymade, and the first thing to do is to decide which of the parts the amateur mechanic can make and which would be better to buy readymade. If the builder has had no experience in coil-winding it would be probably pay to purchase the secondary coil readymade, as the operation of winding a mile or more of fine wire is very difficult and tedious, and the results are often unsatisfactory. In ordering the secondary it is always necessary to specify the length of spark desired.

The following method of completing a 1-in. coil illustrates the general details of the work. The same methods and circuits apply to small and larger coils. The readymade secondary is in cylindrical form, about 6 in. long and 2⅝ in. in diameter, with a hole through the winding 1¼ in. in diameter, as shown in *Figure 1*. The

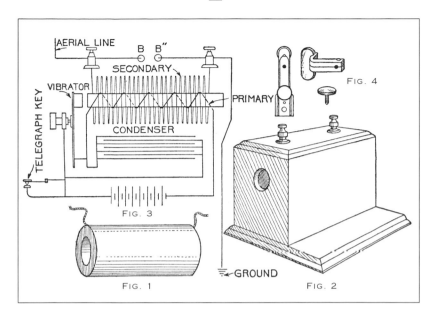

AERIAL LINE

B B″

SECONDARY

VIBRATOR

TELEGRAPH KEY

PRIMARY

CONDENSER

FIG. 4

FIG. 3

GROUND

FIG. 1

FIG. 2

JUMP-SPARK COIL.

secondary will stand considerable handling without fear of injury, and need not be set into a case until the primary is completed. The primary is made of fine annealed No. 24 iron wire cut 7 in. or 8 in. in length, as the maker prefers, and bundled to a diameter of ⅞ in. The wires may be straightened by rolling two or three at a time between two pieces of hardwood. If the amateur has difficulty in procuring this wire, the entire core may be purchased readymade.

After the core wires are bundled, the core is wrapped with one or two layers of Manila paper. The straighter the wire, the more iron will enter into the construction of the core, which is desirable. Beginning half an inch from one end, No. 16 cotton-covered magnet wire is wound from one end to the other evenly and then returned, making two layers. The terminals are tied down to the core with twine. Core and primary are then immersed in boiling paraffin wax to which a small quantity of resin and beeswax has been added. This same wax may be used later in sealing the completed coil into a box. Over this primary is now wrapped one layer of okonite tape, or the same thickness of heavily shellacked muslin. This completed primary will now allow for slipping the secondary into the hole.

Should the secondary have been purchased without a case, a wooden box of mahogany or oak is made large enough to contain the secondary with an inch to spare all around and with room for a small condenser. If it is not convenient to do this work, a box like that shown in *Figure 2* may be purchased at a small cost. A ⅞-in. hole is bored in the center of one end, through which the primary core projects ⅛ in. This core is to be used to magnetically attract the iron head of a vibrating interrupter, which is an important factor of the coil. This interrupter is shaped as in *Figure 4,* and is fastened to the box in such a way that the vibrator hammer plays in front of the core, and so that soldered connections may be made inside the box with the screws used in affixing the vibrator parts to the box. The condenser is made of four strips of thin paper, 2 yds. long and 5 in. wide, and a sufficient quantity of tinfoil. When cut and laid in one continuous length, each piece of tinfoil must overlap the adjoining piece a half-inch, so as to form a continuous electrical circuit.

In shaping the condenser, one piece of the paper is laid down, then the strip of tinfoil, then two strips of paper and another layer of foil, and finally the fourth strip of paper. This makes a condenser that may be folded, beginning at one end and bending about 6 in. at a time. The condenser is next wrapped securely with bands of paper or tape, and boiled in pure paraffin wax for one hour, after which it is pressed under considerable weight until firm and hard. One of the sheets of tinfoil is to form one pole of the condenser, and the other sheet, which is insulated from the first, forms the other pole or terminal. (This condenser material is purchased in long strips, ready for assembling.)

The wiring diagram, *Figure 3,* shows how the connections are made. This method of connecting is suitable for all coils up to 1½-in. spark. But for larger coils better results will be obtained by using an independent type of interrupter, in which a separate magnet is used to interrupt the circuit. Beside the magnetic vibrators, there are several other types, such as the mercury dash-pot and rotary-commutator types, but these will become better known to the amateur as he proceeds in his work and becomes more experienced in coil operations.

— ELECTRIC BLUE-LIGHT EXPERIMENT —

Take a jump-spark coil and connect it up with a battery and start the vibrator. Then take one outlet wire, *R*, and connect to one side of a 2-cp. electric lamp. Hold the other outlet wire, *B*, in one hand, and press all fingers of the other hand on the globe at point *A*. A bright, blue light will come from the wires in the lamp to the surface of the globe

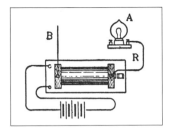

where the fingers touch. No shock will be perceptible.

— AN INTERESTING ELECTRICAL EXPERIMENT

The materials necessary for performing this experiment are: Telephone receiver, some wire and carbon paper, and a few pencils for arc lamps.

Run a line from the inside of the house to the inside of some other building and fasten it to one terminal of the receiver. To the other terminal fasten another piece of wire

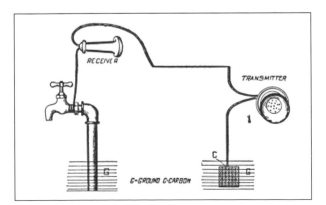

A UNIQUE BATTERY.

and ground it on the water faucet in the house. If there is no faucet in the house, ground it with a large piece of zinc.

Fasten the other end to one terminal of the transmitter and from the other terminal of the same run a wire into the ground. The ground here should consist either of a large piece of carbon, or several pieces bound tightly together.

If a person speaks into the transmitter, one at the receiver can hear what is said, even though there are no batteries in the circuit. It is a well-known fact that two telephone receivers connected up in this way will transmit words between two persons, because the vibration of the diaphragm causes an inductive current to flow and the other receiver copies these vibrations. But in this experiment, a transmitter that induces no current is used. Do the carbon and the zinc and the moist earth form a battery?

— HOMEMADE ARC LIGHT —

By rewinding an electric-bell magnet with No. 16 wire and connecting it in series with two electric-light carbons as shown in the sketch, a small arc will be formed between the carbon points when the current is applied. In the sketch, *A* is the electric-bell magnet, *B*, the armature, *C*, the carbon sockets, *D*, the carbons, and *E*, the binding posts. When connected with 10 to 12 dry batteries this lamp gives a fairly good light.

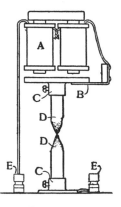

ARC LIGHT.

— WRITING WITH ELECTRICITY —

Soak a piece of white paper in a solution of potassium iodide and water for about a minute and then lay it on a piece of sheet metal. Connect the sheet metal with the negative or zinc side of a battery and then, using the positive wire as a pen, write your name or other inscription on the wet paper. The result will be brown lines on a white background.

ELECTROLYTIC WRITING.

— TO EXPLODE POWDER WITH ELECTRICITY —

A 1-in. hole is bored in the center of a 2-in. square block. Two finishing nails are driven in, as shown in the sketch. These are connected to terminals of an induction coil. After everything is ready, the powder is poured in the hole and a board weighted with rocks placed over the block. When the button is pressed or the circuit closed in some other way, the discharge occurs. The distance between the nail points—

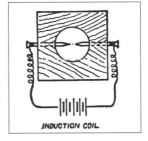

which must be bright and clean— should be just enough to give a good fat spark.

— HOW TO MAKE A SMALL RHEOSTAT —

In operating small motors there is, as a rule, no means provided for regulating their speed. This often is quite a disadvantage, especially in the case of toy motors such as those used on miniature electric locomotives. The speed, of course, can be regulated by changing the number of cells of a battery by means of a special switch, but then all the cells are not used the same amount, and some of them may be completely exhausted before the others show any appreciable depreciation. If a small transformer is used with a number of taps taken off the secondary winding, the voltage impressed upon the motor, and consequently the speed, can be changed by varying the amount of the secondary windings across which the motor is connected.

But in both these cases there is no means of varying the speed gradually. This can, however, be accomplished by means of a small rheostat placed in series with the motor. The rheostat acts in an electrical circuit in the same way a valve does in a hydraulic circuit. It consists of a resistance, which can be easily varied in value, placed in the circuit connecting the motor with the source of electrical energy. A diagram of the rheostat is shown in *Figure 1*, in which *A* represents the armature of the motor, *B*, the field, *C,* the rheostat, and *D,* the source of electrical energy. When the handle *E* is in such a position that the maximum amount of resistance is in circuit, there will be a minimum circuit through the field and armature of the motor, and its speed will be a minimum. As the resistance of

the rheostat is decreased, the current increases and the motor speeds up, reaching a maximum value when the resistance of the rheostat has been reduced to zero value. Such a rheostat may be used in combination with a special switch *F,* as shown in *Figure 2*. The switch gives a means of varying the voltage and the rheostat takes care of the desired changes in speed occurring between those produced by the variations in voltage.

A very simple and inexpensive rheostat may be constructed as follows: Procure a piece of thin fiber, about $^1/_{16}$ in. thick, ½ in. wide and approximately 10 in. long. Wind on this piece of fiber, after the edges have all been smoothed down, a piece of No. 22-ga. cotton-covered resistance wire. Start about ¼ in. from one end and wind the various turns fairly closely together to within ¼ in. of the other end. The ends of the wire may be secured by passing them through

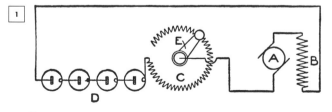

DIAGRAM SHOWING THE CONNECTIONS FOR A SMALL MOTOR
WHERE A RHEOSTAT IS IN THE LINE.

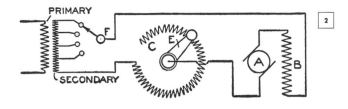

PRIMARY DIAGRAM OF A SMALL MOTOR WHERE A RHEOSTAT
AND SWITCH ARE IN THE LINE

several small holes drilled in the piece of fiber, and should protrude 3 or 4 in. for connecting to binding posts that will be mounted upon the base of the rheostat.

Now form this piece of fiber into a complete ring by bending it around some round object, the flat side being toward the object. Determine as accurately as possible the diameter of the ring thus formed, and also its thickness. Obtain a piece of well-seasoned hardwood, ½ in. thick and 4½ in. square. Round off the corners and upper edges of this block and mark out on it two circles whose diameters correspond to the inside and outside diameters of the fiber ring. The centers of these circles should be in the center of the block. Carefully saw out the two circles so that the space between the inside and outside portions will snugly fit around the fiber ring. Obtain a second piece of hardwood, ¼ in. thick

and 4¾ in. square, and round off its corners and upper edges. Mount the other pieces upon it by means of several small wood screws, which should pass up from the underside and be well countersunk. Place the fiber ring in the groove but, before doing so, drill a hole in the base proper for one end of the wire to pass through. Two small back-connected binding posts should be mounted in the corners. One of these should be connected to the end of the winding and the other to a small bolt in the center of the base that serves to hold the handle or movable arm of the rheostat in place. These connecting leads should all be placed in grooves cut in the under side of the base.

The movable arm of the rheostat may be made from a piece of 1/16-in. sheet brass, and should have the following approximate dimensions: length, 2 in.; breadth ½ in. at one end, and ¼ in. at the other. Obtain

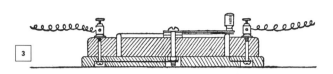

A CROSS SECTION OF THE RHEOSTAT, SHOWING
THE CONNECTIONS THROUGH THE RESISTANCE.

a ⅛-in. brass bolt, about 1 in. long, and several washers. Drill a hole in the larger end of the piece of brass to accommodate the bolt and in the center of the wooden base. Countersink the hole in the base on the under side with a ½-in. bit to a depth of ¼ in. On the underside of the piece of brass, and near its narrow end, solder a piece of thin spring brass so that its free end will rest upon the upper edge of the fiber ring. A small handle may be mounted upon the upper side of the movable arm. Now mount the arm on the base by means of the bolt, placing several washers between it and the upper surface of the base, so that its outer end will be raised above the edge of the fiber ring. Solder a short piece of thin brass to the nut that is to be placed

on the lower end of the bolt, and cut a recess in the countersunk portion of the hole in the base to accommodate it. When the bolt has been screwed down sufficiently tightly, a locknut may be put on, or the first nut soldered to the end of the bolt. If possible, it would be best to use a spring washer or two between the arm and base.

The insulation should now be removed from the wire on the upper edge of the fiber ring with a piece of fine sandpaper, so that the spring on the under side of the movable arm may make contact with the winding. The rheostat is now complete with the exception of a coat of shellac. A cross-sectional view of the completed rheostat is shown in *Figure 3*.

— A SMALL RHEOSTAT FOR EXPERIMENTS AND TESTING —

A rheostat made as shown in the sketch has been used successfully for calibrating a large number

of ammeters and wattmeters. One of the general designs suggested will be useful for many other purposes.

The dimensions given were used for obtaining a variation of from ½ to 5 amperes with a 6-volt source of electromotive force. For other capacities the proportions may be increased or decreased proportionately. A piece of pine, 7 x 9½ in., forms the base. For resistance wire No. 16-ga. was used, but wire of any material that will carry the maximum current without excessive oxidation may be employed instead. Nails support the resistance wire, which should be soldered to the nails to ensure good electrical contact. Leads of flexible cord are arranged as shown. These are soldered to the first and last nails in the series. To provide connection between the free ends of the cord and the resistance wire or the nails, 5-ampere test clips are soldered to the cord ends. The teeth of the clip jaws are filed off, and in their stead a short piece of brass wire is soldered to each jaw, as indicated in the detailed view. A nick is filed in each of the brass wires so that they will hold firmly onto the resistance wire or nail. Suspender or display-case clips, suitably modified, may be substituted for the commercial test clips.

In using the device, one clip is moved along the front span. The other is gripped to a nail in the rear row. Sliding the front clip along the span wire ensures a fine adjustment of resistance. Gripping the rear clip on the different nails provides the coarse adjustment.

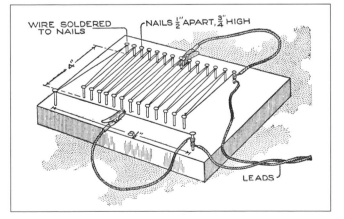

WIRE SOLDERED TO NAILS

NAILS ½" APART, ¾" HIGH

4"

8½"

LEADS

THIS HOMEMADE RHEOSTAT HAS A CAPACITY OF ONE-HALF TO FIVE AMPERES, ON A SIX-VOLT CIRCUIT.

— Carbon Rheostats
for Low-Amperage Current —

Model-railroad fans and other junior experimenters who would like a separate control for each block, but feel that the cost of such an installation is prohibitive, will find these rheostats just the thing. They are also handy for the electrical experimenter and for other uses where the current handled is of very low amperage. Of the two types shown below, the one in the lower detail is simpler, and gives steadier control. But it has the disadvantages of wearing quickly if it is used where the control must be adjusted frequently. The carbons for both rheostats are taken from flashlight cells. In the lower one, the carbon is mounted on a flameproof base by means of a bracket at one end. A sliding brass or copper contact brushes the carbon, and is controlled

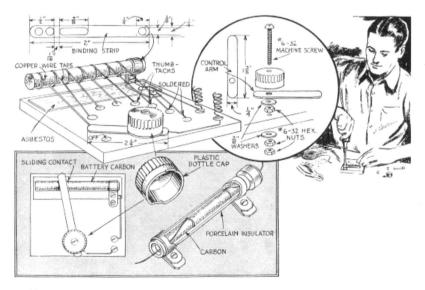

MOUNT SEVERAL OF THE RHEOSTATS IN A BOX LINED WITH FIREPROOF FOAM OR OTHER FIREPROOF MATERIAL, WITH THE KNOBS PROJECTING OUTSIDE. WIRE THEM TO THE BLOCKS IN YOUR MODEL RAILROAD AND YOU HAVE A REMOTE-CONTROL PANEL AT PRACTICALLY NO COST.

by a knob assembled as shown in the circular detail. The knob is a plastic bottle cap. The carbon in the rheostat in the upper detail is mounted in the same way, but it has several copper-wire taps leading to thumbtacks or screws which the control arm contacts as adjustment is made. This method avoids wear on the carbon, but control is likely to be a little jumpy unless care is taken to locate the tacks so that the arm contacts the next one the instant it breaks contact with the preceding one. If the carbons are used as permanently set resistors, it's a good idea to enclose them in a porcelain tube, because they are likely to heat up.

— Quick Capacitor Tester —

A quick capacitor tester can be made by connecting the positive lead of a 40-mfd. electrolytic capacitor to the metal cartridge of an old ballpoint pen and the negative lead to a length of wire with alligator clip attached. Tape the capacitor to the side of the pen. To use the tester, connect the clip to the set chassis and touch the pen tip to the capacitor contacts.

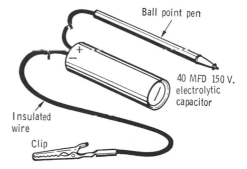

Ball point pen

40 MFD 150 V. electrolytic capacitor

Insulated wire

Clip

If the set works normally again, you know that the capacitor was bad.

— Another Interesting Electrical Experiment —

Anyone possessing a battery having an electromotive force of from 4 to 20 volts can perform this experiment. It is particularly interesting because of the variation of results within the same conditions.

Immerse two pieces of brass in a strong solution of common salt and water. Connect one of the pieces to the positive wire and the other to the negative, taking care that the brass pieces do not touch each other.

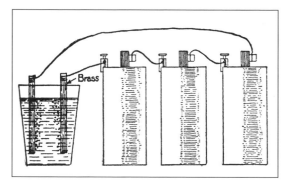

HOW THE WIRES ARE CONNECTED.

After the current has passed one or two minutes, the solution will become colored, and if the process is continued a colored pigment will be precipitated. The precipitate varies considerably in color and may be either yellow, blue, orange, green or brown, depending on the strength of the current, the strength of the solution, and the composition of the brass.

— LOCATING BREAKS IN ELECTRIC CORDS WITH A SPARK COIL —

When one of the wires of an electric cord is broken, the break can be found often by twisting the wires together at one end of the cord and connecting the other to a vibrator coil, such as used on model-T Fords. The connection is made as indicated, using three or four dry cells or a storage battery. The high-tension current passing through the cord will arc across the break in the wire, heating the insulation and causing it to smoke.

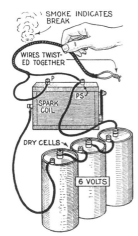

— HOW TO MAKE AN ELECTROLYTIC RECTIFIER —

Many devices that will change an alternating current to a direct current have been put on the market, but there are probably none that suits the amateur's needs and pocketbook better than the electrolytic rectifier.

Four 2-qt. fruit jars are required for the construction of such a rectifier. Place two electrodes, one of lead and one of aluminum, in each jar. The immersed surface of the aluminum should be about 15 sq. in. and the lead 24 sq. in. The immersed surface of the lead being greater than that of the aluminum, the lead will have to be crimped as shown in *Fig, 1.* In both *Figure 1* and *2,* the lead is indicated by *L* and the aluminum by *A.* The solution with which each jar is to be filled consists of the following:

> Water, 2 qt.
> Sodium Carbonate,
>   2 tablespoonfuls
> Alum, 3 tablespoonfuls

Care should be taken to leave the connections made as shown in *Figure 2.* The alternating current comes in on the wires as shown, and the direct current is taken from the point indicated.

The capacity of this rectifier is from 3 to 5 amperes, which is sufficient for charging small storage batteries, running small motors and lighting small lamps.

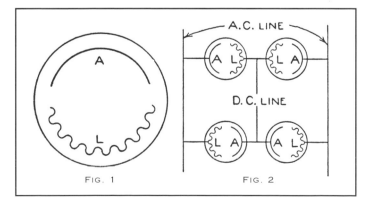

FIG. 1   FIG. 2

ELECTROLYTIC RECTIFIER AND CONNECTIONS.

— An Electrical Dancer —

The modification of the well-known mechanical dancer shown in the illustration is based on the principle of the electric bell. While the amusing antics of the mechanical dancer are controlled by the hand, the manikin shown is actuated by the electromagnet.

The mechanism is contained in a box. It consists of an electromagnet with a soft-iron armature carried by a spring. A wire from the battery goes to the magnet. The other terminal of the magnet connects with the armature spring at $L1$. The spring is bent at a right angle at its other end, $L2$, and carries a platform, $L3$, strengthened by a smaller disk underneath. The dancer performs upon this platform.

A contact spring, S, is carried by the armature spring. A contact screw, C, is adjustable in its contact with the spring S. A wire runs from the contact screw to the binding post B, to which the other battery wire is connected.

The current keeps the platform in constant vibration, causing the dancer to "dance." By means of the screw C, the action of the current may be varied, and the "dancing" will vary correspondingly.

The figure is designed to be made of wood with very loose joints and is suspended so that the feet barely touch the platform.

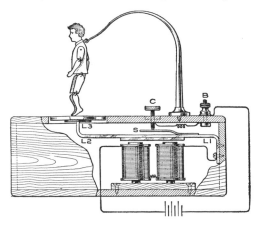

WHEN THE CONTACT IS MADE, THE FIGURE DANCES.

— ELECTRICAL EXPERIMENTS WITH BELL WIRE AND IRON —

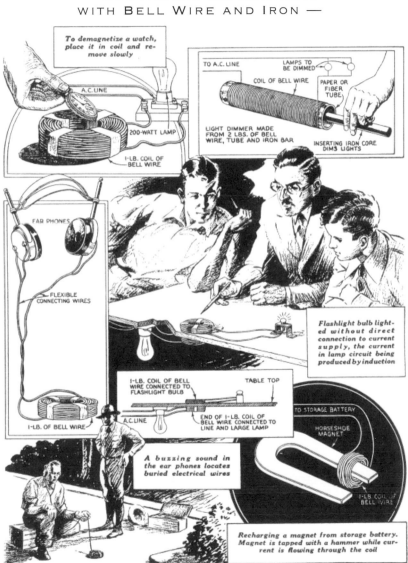

To demagnetize a watch, place it in coil and remove slowly

A.C. LINE

200-WATT LAMP

1-LB. COIL OF BELL WIRE

TO A.C. LINE — LAMPS TO BE DIMMED

COIL OF BELL WIRE

PAPER OR FIBER TUBE

LIGHT DIMMER MADE FROM 2 LBS. OF BELL WIRE, TUBE AND IRON BAR

INSERTING IRON CORE DIMS LIGHTS

EAR PHONES

FLEXIBLE CONNECTING WIRES

1-LB. OF BELL WIRE

Flashlight bulb lighted without direct connection to current supply, the current in lamp circuit being produced by induction

1-LB. COIL OF BELL WIRE CONNECTED TO FLASHLIGHT BULB

TABLE TOP

A.C. LINE

END OF 1-LB. COIL OF BELL WIRE CONNECTED TO LINE AND LARGE LAMP

TO STORAGE BATTERY

HORSESHOE MAGNET

1-LB. COIL OF BELL WIRE

A buzzing sound in the ear phones locates buried electrical wires

Recharging a magnet from storage battery. Magnet is tapped with a hammer while current is flowing through the coil

— PREVENT SHORT CIRCUIT BETWEEN DRY CELL BATTERIES —

To prevent short circuits between dry cell batteries in a damp place or where they are crowded together and liable to come in contact with one another, procure one or two inner tubes of quite large diameter from old bicycle tires. Cut them in lengths about 3 in. longer than the battery cell and pull the piece over the cell, leaving the connecting wires through the end of the tube. Wrap and tightly tie each end of the tube with a piece of strong cord. Place one of these on each cell and you will have no trouble with wet weather affecting your cells or short circuiting by cells coming in contact with one another.

ELECTRIC MEASURE TAKERS

— HOW TO MAKE A GALVANOSCOPE —

A galvanoscope for detecting small currents of electricity can be made from a coil of wire, *A*, a glass tube full of water, *B*, a core, *C*, and a base, *D*, with binding posts as shown. The core *C*, which is made of iron and cork, is a trifle lighter than the water it displaces and will therefore normally remain in the top of the tube. But as soon as a current of electricity passes through the coil, the core is drawn down out of sight. The current required is very small, because the core is so balanced that the least attraction will cause it to sink.

The glass tube may be a test tube, as shown in *Figure 1*, or an empty developer tube. If one has neither, an empty pill bottle may be used. The washers at the ends of the coil can be made of fiber, hard rubber, or wood, or can be taken from an old magnet. The base may be made of wood or any other insulating material and should have four short legs on the bottom. Make the coil of single-covered wire about No. 18, and then connect ends to binding posts as shown in *Figure 1*.

The core is made by pushing a small nail through a piece of cork. It should be made so that it will rise slowly when placed under water. Some filing may be necessary to get the weight just right, but it should

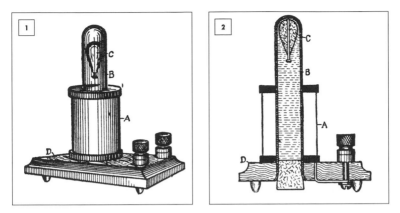

LEFT: THE COMPLETED GALVANOSCOPE.
RIGHT: INTERIOR VIEW.

be remembered that the buoyancy of the core can be adjusted after the parts are assembled. This is done by pressing the cork in the bottom of the test tube. This causes compression in the water so that some is forced into the upper cork, reducing its displacement and causing it to sink. The lower cork is then slowly withdrawn, by twisting, until the core slowly rises.

The instrument will then be adjusted ready for use.

Connect the binding posts to a single cell of battery—any kind will do, as a slight current will answer. On completing the circuit the core will descend; or put in a switch or push button on one of the battery wires. If the button is concealed where the operator can reach it, the core will obey his command to rise or fall, according to his control of the current. This is a mysterious looking instrument, the core being moved without visible connection to any other part.

— HOW TO MAKE A TANGENT GALVANOMETER —

Secure a piece of wood ½ in. thick and cut out a ring with an outside diameter of 10½ in., and an inside diameter of 9 in., and glue to each side two other rings ¼ in. thick with the same inside diameter as the

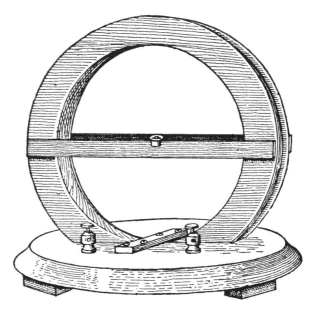

TANGENT GALVANOMETER.

first ring and 11 in. outside diameter, thus forming a ¼-in. channel in the circumference of the ring. If a lathe is at hand, this ring can be made from a solid piece and the channel turned out. Cut another circular piece 11 in. in diameter for a base. Make a hole in the center of this piece 1 in. wide and 6 5/16 in. long, into which the ring first made should fit so that its inner surface is just even with the upper surface of the baseboard. The ring is held upright in the hole by a small strip screwed to the base as shown. All screws and brads that are

used must be of brass. The cutting of these circular pieces is not so difficult if a band saw driven by power is used. The circular pieces may be cut by means of a keyhole saw if a band saw is not accessible.

Before mounting the ring on the base, the groove should be wound with 8 turns of No. 16 double cotton-covered magnet wire. The two ends may be tied together with a string to hold them temporarily.

Fasten two strips of wood ¼-in. thick, ⅝-in. wide, and 11 in. long across the sides of the ring with their upper edges passing exactly through the center of the ring. An ordinary pocket compass, about 1¼ in. in diameter, is fitted in these strips so that the center of the needle or pointer will be exactly in the center of the ring and its zero point mark at the halfway point between the two strips. Put the ring in place on the base, as shown in the sketch, and connect the two ends of the wire to two binding-posts that are previously attached to the base. Coat the entire surface with brown shellac. Deviation from the dimensions will cause errors in the results obtained by its use.

Remove all pieces of iron or steel and especially magnets in the near vicinity of the instrument when in use. Place the galvanometer on a level table and turn it until the needle, pointing north and south and swinging freely, lies exactly in the plane of the coil, as shown in the sketch. The needle then will point to zero if the directions have been followed closely. Connect one cell of battery to the instrument and allow the current to flow through the coils. The needle of the compass will be deflected to one side or the other, and will finally come to rest at a certain angle—let us say 45 deg. The dimensions of the instrument

ANGLES	CURRENT
10°	.088 amp.
20°	.182 amp.
30°	.289 amp.
40°	.420 amp.
45°	.500 amp.
50°	.600 amp.
55°	.715 amp.
60°	.865 amp.
70°	1.375 amp.

are such that when the deflection is 45 deg. the current flowing through the coils upon the ring is ½ ampere. The ampere is the unit chosen to designate the strength of the electric current. For other angles the value of the current may be found from the table above.

As the magnetic force that acts upon a magnet needle varies in different places, the values given for the current will not be true in all parts of the country. The table gives correct values for the immediate vicinity of Chicago and that part of the United States lying east of Chicago, and north of the Ohio river. The results given should be multiplied by 1.3 for places south of the Ohio river and east of the Mississippi.

— Detector for Slight Electrical Charges —

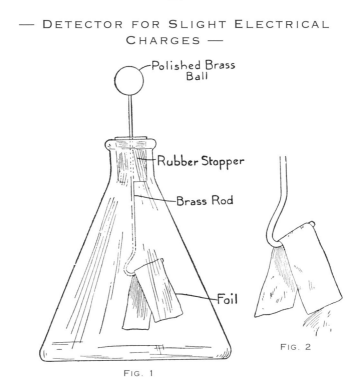

Polished Brass Ball

Rubber Stopper

Brass Rod

Foil

FIG. 1

FIG. 2

ALUMINUM FOIL IN A BOTTLE.

A thin glass bottle is thoroughly cleaned and fitted with a rubber stopper. A hole is made through the center of the stopper large enough to admit a small brass rod. The length of this rod will be governed by the shape of the bottle, but 3½ in. will be about right. The bottom of the rod is bent and two pieces of aluminum foil, each about ¼ in. wide and ½ in. long, are glued to it. The two pieces of foil, fastened to the rod, are better shown in *Figure 2*. Fasten a polished brass ball to the top of the rod and the instrument is ready for use. Place the article for testing near the ball, and if it holds a slight electrical charge, the two pieces of foil will draw together. If it does not hold a charge, the foils will not move.

— How to Make an Ammeter —

Every amateur mechanic who performs electrical experiments will find use for an ammeter, and for the benefit of those who wish to construct such an instrument the following description is given: The operative principle of this instrument is the same as that of a galvanometer, except that its working position is not confined to the magnetic meridian. This is accomplished by making the needle revolve in a vertical instead of a horizontal plane. The only adjustment necessary is that of leveling, which is accomplished by turning the thumbscrew shown at *A, Figure 1,* until the hand points to zero on the scale.

First make a support, *Figure 2,* by bending a piece of sheet brass to the shape indicated and tapping for the screws *CC.* These should have hollow ends, as shown, for the purpose of receiving the pivoted axle that supports the hand. The core, *Figure 3,* is made of iron. It is 1 in. long, ¼ in. wide and ⅛ in. thick. At a point a little above the center, drill a hole as shown at *H,* and through this hole drive a piece of knitting-needle about ½ in. long, or long enough to reach between the two screws shown in *Figure 2.* The ends of this small axle should be ground pointed and should turn easily in the cavities, as the sensitivity of the instrument

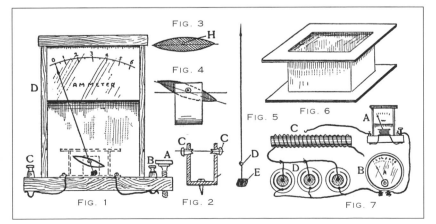

COMPLETE AMMETER AND DETAILS.

depends on the ease with which this axle turns.

After assembling the core as shown in *Figure 4*, it should be filed a little at one end until it assumes the position indicated. The pointer or hand, *Figure 5*, is made of wire. Aluminum is preferable, although copper or steel will do. Make the wire 4½ in. long and make a loop, *D*, ½ in. from the lower end. Solder to the short end a piece of brass, *E*, of such weight that it will exactly balance the weight of the hand. This is slipped on the pivot, and the whole thing is again placed in position in the support. If the pointer is correctly balanced it should take the position shown in *Figure 1*, but if it is not exactly right, a little filing will bring it near enough so that it may be corrected by the adjusting-screw.

Next, make a brass frame as shown in *Figure 6*. This may be made of wood, although brass is better, because the eddy currents set up in a conductor surrounding a magnet tend to stop oscillation of the magnet. (The core is magnetized when a current flows through the instrument.) The brass frame is wound with magnet wire, the size depending on the number of amperes to be measured. One wound with two layers of No. 14 wire, 10 turns to each layer, will be about right for ordinary experimental purposes. The ends of the wire are fastened to the binding posts *B* and *C, Figure 1.*

A wooden box, *D*, is then made and provided with a glass front. A piece of paper is pasted on a piece of wood, which is then fastened in the box in such a position that the hand or pointer will lie close to the paper scale. The box is 5½ in. high, 4 in. wide and 1¾ in. deep, inside measurements. After everything is assembled, put a drop of solder on the loop at *D, Figure 5*, to prevent it turning on the axle.

To calibrate the instrument connect as shown in *Figure 7*, where *A* is the homemade ammeter, *B*, a standard ammeter, *C*, a variable resistance, and *D*, a battery consisting of three or more cells connected in multiple. Throw in enough resistance to make the standard instrument read 1 ampere, and then put a mark on the paper scale of the instrument to be calibrated. Continue in this way with 2 amperes, 3 amperes, 4 amperes, etc., until the scale is full. To make a voltmeter out of this instrument, wind with plenty of No. 36 magnet wire instead of No. 14, or if it is desired to make an instrument for measuring both volts and amperes, use both windings and connect to two pairs of binding posts.

— MAKING A NEW TYPE OF AMMETER —

The outside case of this instrument is made of wood taken from old cigar boxes with the exception of the back. If carefully and neatly made, the finished instrument will be very satisfactory. The measurements here given need not be strictly followed, but can be governed by circumstances. The case should first be made and varnished and while this is drying, the mechanical parts can be put together.

The back is a board ⅜ in. thick, 6½ in. wide and 6¾ in. long. The outer edges of this board are chamfered. The other parts of the case are made from the cigar-box wood,

which should be well sandpapered to remove the labels. The sides are 3¼ in. wide and 5 in. long; the top and bottom, 3¼ in. wide and 4½ in. long. Glue a three-cornered piece, *A, Figure 1,* at each end on the surface that is to be the inside of the top and bottom pieces. Fasten the sides to the pieces with glue, and take care that the pieces are all square. When the glue is set, this square box is well sanded, then centered, and fastened to the back with small screws turned into each three-cornered piece.

The front, which is a piece 5¼ in. wide and 6½ in. long, has a circular opening cut near the top through

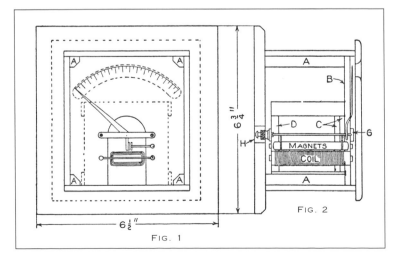

FIG. 1

FIG. 2

which the graduated scale may be seen. This front is centered and fastened the same as the back, and the four outside edges, as well as the edges around the opening, are rounded. The whole case can now be cleaned and stained with a light mahogany stain and varnished. Cut another piece of board, *B, Figures 2* and *3,* to just fit inside the case and rest on the ends of the three-cornered pieces, *A.* Glue to this board two smaller pieces, *C,* 3 in. square, with the grain of the wood in alternate directions to prevent warping. All of these pieces are made of the cigar-box wood. Another piece, *D,* ⅜ in. thick and 3 in. square, is placed on the other pieces and a U-shaped opening, 1¾ in. wide and 2½ in. high, is sawed out from all of the pieces as shown. The piece *D* is attached to the pieces *C* with four ½-in. pieces 2⅝ in. long.

A magnet is made from a soft piece of iron, *E,* about ⅜ in. thick, 1¼ in. wide and 2¾ in. long. Solder across each end of the iron a piece of brass wire, F, and make a turn in each end of the wires, forming an eye for a screw. These wires are about 2½ in. long. Wind three layers of about No. 14 double cotton-covered copper wire on the soft iron and leave about 5 or 6 in. of each end unwound for making connections.

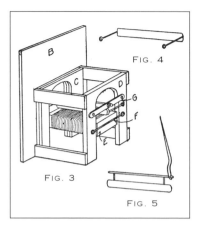

The pointer is made as shown in *Figure 5* from 1/16-in. brass wire filed to make a point at both ends for a spindle. About ½ in. from each end of this wire are soldered two smaller brass wires which in turn are soldered to a strip of light tin ¼ in. wide and 2⅝ in. long. The lower edge of this tin should be about ½ in. from the spindle. The pointer is soldered to the spindle ¼ in. from one end. All of these parts should be brass with the exception of the strip of tin. Another strip of tin, the same size as the first, is soldered to two brass wires as shown in *Figure 4.* These wires should be about 1 in. long.

The spindle of the pointer swings freely between two bars of brass, *G,* 1/16 in. thick, ¼ in. wide and 2½ in. long. A small hole is countersunk in one of the bars to receive one end of the spindle, and a hole ⅛ in. in diameter is drilled in the other. A thumb nut taken from the binding-post of an old battery soldered is over the hole, so the screw will pass through when turned into the nut. The end of the screw is countersunk to receive the other end of the spindle. A lock nut is necessary to fasten the screw when proper adjustment is secured. A hole is drilled in both ends of the bars for screws to fasten them in place. The bar with the adjusting screw is fastened on the back so it can be readily adjusted through the hole, *H*, bored in the back. The pointer is bent so it will pass through the U-shaped cutout and up the back of the board, *B*. A brass pin is driven in the board at *B* to hold the pointer from dropping down too far to the left. Place the tin, *Figure 4*, so it will clear the tin, *Figure 5*, and fasten in place. The magnet is next placed with the ends of the coil to the back and the top just clearing the tin strips. Two binding screws are fitted to the bottom of the back and connected to the extending wires from the coil.

The instrument is now ready for calibrating. This is done by connecting it in series with another standard ammeter which has the scale marked in known quantities. In this series is also connected a variable resistance and a battery or some other source of current supply. The resistance is now adjusted to show .5 ampere on the standard ammeter and the position of the pointer marked on the scale. Change your resistance to all points and make the numbers until the entire scale is complete.

When the current flows through the coil, the two tinned strips of metal are magnetized, and, being magnetized by the same lines of force, they are both of the same polarity. Like poles repel each other, and as the part is not movable, the part carrying the pointer moves away. The stronger the current, the greater the magnetism of the metal strips, and the farther apart they will be forced, showing a greater defection of the pointer.

— HOMEMADE BATTERY VOLTMETER —

Secure a piece of brass tube 3 in. long that has about a ¼-in. hole. Put ends, *A*, 1¼ in. square and cut from heavy cardboard on this tube. Make a hole in the center of each cardboard just large enough to allow the brass tube to fit tightly. Put two or three layers of stout paper around the brass tube and between the cardboard ends. Wind evenly about 2 oz. of No. 26 cotton covered magnet wire on the paper between the ends and leave about 2 in. of wire on each end extending from the coil. Use a board ½-in. thick, 3 in. wide, and 6 in. long for the base and fasten the coil to it, as shown in *Figure 1*. Bore holes for binding-posts, *B*, one on each side of the board, and connect the two wires from the coil to them. At the other end of the board and

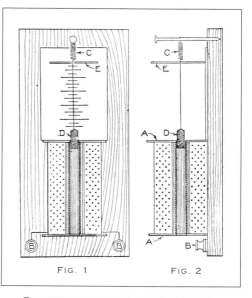

FIG. 1   FIG. 2

BATTERY VOLTMETER CONSTRUCTION.

in the center, drive a wire nail and attach a small spring, *C*, to it. The spring should be about 1 in. long. Take a small piece of soft iron, *D*, ½- in. long and just large enough to slip freely through the brass tube and solder a piece of copper wire to it. The other end of the copper wire is hooked to the spring, *C*. The copper wire must be just long enough to allow the piece of iron, *D*, to hang part way in the end of the coil and still hold the spring in place. A circular piece of cardboard, *E*, is slipped over the spring to where the spring

joins the wire. This cardboard is to serve as the pointer. A piece of paper 1½ in. wide and 2½ in. long is glued to the board so that it will be directly under the cardboard pointer and fit snugly up against the top of the coil.

The paper can be calibrated by connecting one cell of a battery to the binding-posts. The iron plunger, *D*, is drawn into the tube and consequently the pointer, *E*, is drawn nearer to the coil. Make a mark directly under the place where the pointer comes to rest. At that place mark the number of volts the cell reads when connected with a voltmeter. Do the same with two or three cells and mark down the result on the scale. By dividing off the space between these marks you may be able to obtain a surprisingly correct reading when connected with the battery cells to be tested.

— How to Make a Pocket Voltammeter —

Remove the works and stem from a discarded dollar watch. Drill two 3/16 in. holes in the edge, 3/4 in. apart, and insert two binding-posts, *Figure 1*, insulating them from the case with cardboard. Fold two strips of light cardboard, 1/2 in. wide, so as to form two oblong boxes, 1/2 in. long and 3/16 in. thick, open on the edges. On one of these forms, evenly wind the wire taken from a bell magnet to the depth of 1/8 in. On the other, wind some 20-ga. wire to the same depth. Fasten the wire with gummed label to keep it from accidentally unwinding.

Glue the coils to the back of the case and connect one wire from each binding-post as shown in *Figure 2*, while the other two wires are connected to an induction coil lead that is inserted in the hole from which the stem was removed. Fasten a brass-headed tack to the case at the point *F* with sealing wax or solder. Bend a wire in the shape shown in *Figure 3* to swing freely on the tack. Attach a piece of steel rod, 3/4 in. long, in the center coil, *C, Figure 2*.

A rubber band, *D*, connects the steel rod *C* with the top of the watch case. The ends of the rubber

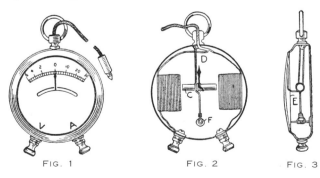

FIG. 1   FIG. 2   FIG. 3

VOLTAMMETER IN A WATCH CASE.

are fastened with sealing wax. The rubber keeps the pointer at zero or in the middle of the scale. Do not use too strong a rubber band. A dial may be made by cutting a piece of stiff, white paper so it will fit under the crystal of the watch. An arc is cut in the paper, as shown in *Figure 1,* through which the indicator works.

To calibrate the instrument, first mark the binding-post, *A,* which is connected to the coil of heavy wire, for amperes and the other post, V, to the coil of small wire for volts. Connect the lead and the post marked *A* to one, two, and three cells, and each time mark the place of the pointer on the dial. Take corresponding readings on a standard ammeter and mark the figures on the dial. The volt side of the dial may be calibrated in the same manner, using a voltmeter instead of the ammeter. The place where the indicator comes to rest after disconnecting the current is marked zero.

Battery Basics

— Connecting Up Batteries to Give Any Voltage —

Referring to the illustration: *A* is a five-point switch (may be homemade); *B* is a one-point switch, and *C* and *C1* are binding posts. When switch *B* is closed and *A* is on No. 1, you have the current of one battery. When *A* is on No. 2, you receive the current from two batteries; when it is on No. 3, you receive the current from three batteries. When *A* is on No. 4, the current flows from four batteries, and when on No. 5, from five batteries. More batteries may be connected to each point of switch *B*.

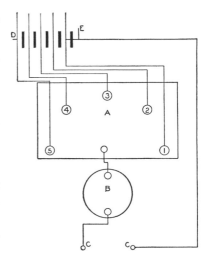

— RELAY SAVES BATTERY CURRENT —

A very weak line current may be used with the help of the device shown here. The relay, *A*, is connected with the main circuit and operates the local circuit, which may contain a bell, telegraph sounder, or any other electrical device by making a contact at the armature and completing the circuit of the local battery.

The relay may be made from an old bell magnet, *B*, rewound with fine wire about

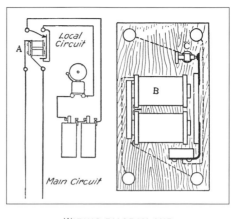

WIRING DIAGRAM AND CONSTRUCTION OF RELAY.

No. 28 or No. 30, single covered. It should be mounted on a wooden base, with the armature in position, as shown. The contact, *C*, can be made from the circuit breaker of the bell and should be so adjusted that the point nearly touches the contact when no current is flowing.

Then the least current flowing through the magnet will cause the armature to move and make contact, thereby closing the local circuit. Relays of a similar nature are in common use in telegraph and fire alarm lines and can also be used for battery cell telephones.

— HOW TO MAKE A THERMOELECTRIC BATTERY —

A novel way of producing an electric current by means of hot and cold water, heat from a match or alcohol lamp, is obtained from a device constructed as shown in the sketch. Place two 8 or 10 in.

long boards of hardwood, marble, or slate plates together, as in *Figure 1*, and mark and drill about 500 holes. These two pieces should be separated about 8 in. and fastened with boards across the ends, as shown in *Figure 2*.

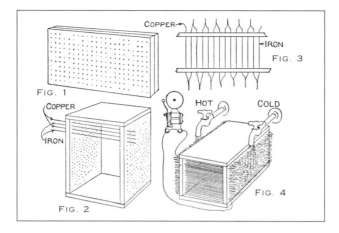

FIG. 1

FIG. 2

FIG. 3

FIG. 4

Cut lengths of soft copper wire, not smaller than No. 18 gauge. Pass these through the holes in the two boards, leaving sufficient end to make a tie. It will require about 70 ft. of wire to fill one-half the number of holes. Also, cut the same number of lengths from the same gauge galvanized-iron wire to fill the remaining holes. The wires are put through the holes in the boards alternately. That is: begin with copper, the next hole with iron, the next copper, the next iron, and so on, twisting the ends together as shown in *Figure 3*. The connections, when complete, should be copper for the first and iron for the last wire.

When the whole apparatus is thus strung, the connections—which must be twisted—can be soldered. Connect one copper wire to the bell and the other terminal, which must be an iron wire, to the other post of the bell. The apparatus is then short-circuited, yet there is no current in the instrument until a lighted match, or, better still, the flame of an alcohol lamp is placed at one end only.

Best results are obtained by putting ice or cold water on one side and a flame on the other. The experimenter may also place the whole apparatus under sink faucets with the hot water turned on at one terminal and the cold water at the other. The greater the difference of temperature in the two terminals, the more current will be obtained.

Very interesting experiments may thus be performed, and these may lead to the solving of the great thermo-electric problem.

— A Battery Switch —

The following device will be found most convenient in cases where batteries are used in series and it is desirable to change the strength and direction of the current frequently. In one inventor's case, he used four batteries, but any reasonable number may be used. Referring to the figure, it will be seen that by moving the switch, *A*, toward the left the

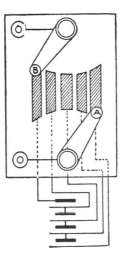

current can be reduced from four batteries to none. Then by moving the switch, *B*, toward the right, the current can be turned on in the opposite direction. In the various positions of these two switches, the current from each individual cell, or from any adjacent pair of cells, may be used in either direction. Experiment to see what else works.

— A Battery Rheostat —

In a board, 7 in. long and 5 in. wide, bore holes about ¼ in. apart, in a semicircle 2 in. from the bottom. Cut notches in the top end to correspond with the holes. From a piece of brass, cut a switch, *C*, with a knob soldered on at the end. Nails for stops are placed at *DD*. Two binding-posts are placed in the board at *A* and *B*. Using about 9 ft. of fine iron wire, attach one end to the bottom of post *A* and run the wire through the first hole and over in the first notch to the back of the board, then through the second hole and over the second

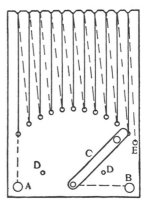

notch and so on, until *E* is reached, where the other end of wire is fastened. Connect switch to post *B*.

— Another Thermo Battery —

A thermo battery, for producing electricity direct from heat, can be made of a wooden frame, *A,* with a number of nails, *B,* driven in the vertical piece and connected in series with heavy copper wires, *C.* The connections should all be soldered to give good results, as the voltage is very low and the resistance of an unsoldered joint would stop the current. The heat may be supplied by an alcohol lamp or other device, and the current may then be detected by means of a simple galvanometer consisting of a square spool of No. 14 or No. 16 single-covered wire, *E,* with a pocket compass, *F,* placed on top. Turn the spool in a north and south direction, or parallel with the compass needle. Then, when the nail heads are heated and the circuit completed, the needle

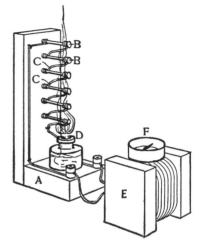

A THERMO BATTERY.

will swing around it at right angles to the coils of wire. Applying ice or cold water to the nail heads will reverse the current.

Lamp Illuminations

— Electric Lamp Experiments —

Incandescent electric lamps can be made to glow so that they may be seen in a dark room by rubbing the globe on clothing or with paper, leather, or tinfoil and immediately holding the globe near a ½-in. Ruhmkorff coil that is in action but not sparking. The miniature 16 cp., 20 and 22-volt lamps will show quite brilliantly, but the 110-volt globes will not glow. When experimenting with these globes, everything should be dry. A cold, dry atmosphere will give best results.

— Easy Experiments with an Electric-Light Circuit —

An electric-light circuit will be found much less expensive than batteries for performing electrical experiments. The sketch shows how a small arc light and motor may be connected to the light socket, *A*. The light is removed and a plug with wire connections is put in its place. One wire runs to the switch, *B*, and the other connects with the water rheostat, which is used for reducing the current.

A tin can, *C*, is filled nearly to the top with salt water, and a metal rod, *D*, is passed through a piece of wood fastened at the top of the can. When the metal rod is lowered, the current increases, and, as it is withdrawn, the current grows weaker. In this way the desired amount of current can be obtained.

By connecting the motor, *E*, and the arc light, *F*, as shown, either one may be operated by turning the switch, *B*, to the corresponding point. The arc light is easily made by fastening two electric light carbons in a wooden frame like that shown. To start the light, turn the current on strong and bring the points of the carbons together; then separate slightly by twisting the upper carbon while drawing it through the hole.

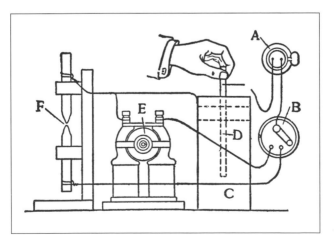

ARC-LIGHT MOTOR AND WATER RHEOSTAT.

— Experiment with Colored Electric Lamps —

To many, the following experiment may be much more easily performed than explained: Place a hand or other object in the light coming from two incandescent lamps, one red and one white, placed about a foot apart, and allow the shadow to fall on a white screen such as a table-cloth. Portions of the shadow will then appear to be a bright green. A similar experiment consists of first turning on the red light for about a minute and then turning it off at the same time that the white one is turned on. The entire screen will then appear to be a vivid green for

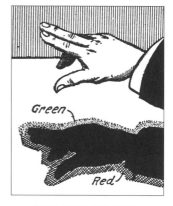

TWO-COLORED HAND.

about one second, after which it assumes its normal color.

— Electric Test for Fixtures —

A very useful device for testing fixtures before they are connected can be easily made as follows: Two wires are run from a plug, *A*, one to a socket, *B*, and the other to terminate at *C*. The line from the other side of the socket *B* terminates at *D*.

In testing a fixture, the plug *A* is turned into a socket of some source of current, and a lamp is turned into the socket *B*. The terminal *C* is held to the metal covering of the fixture, while the end *D* is held to one of the wires. If there is a leak of current, the lamp at *B* and those of the fixture will light up.

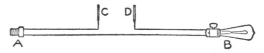

ONE LINE OF THE TWO CONNECTING WIRES IS BROKEN
AND THE ENDS USED AS TERMINALS ON THE FIXTURE.

— TESTING SMALL ELECTRIC LAMPS —

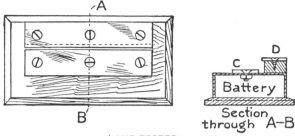

LAMP TESTER.

The accompanying sketch shows the construction of a handy device for testing miniature electric lights. The base is made to take in an electric flash lamp battery. Two strips of brass, *C* and *D,* are connected to the battery. The lamp is tested by putting the metal end on the lower brass strip and the side against the upper one. A great number of lamps can be tested in a short time by means of this device.

— ❖ ❖ ❖ —

{ CHAPTER 4 }

MOTORIZED
INVESTIGATIONS

— HOW TO MAKE A SMALL
ELECTRIC MOTOR —

The field frame of the motor, *Figure 1,* is composed of wrought sheet iron. It may be of any thickness so that, when several pieces are placed together, they will make a frame ¾ in. thick. It is necessary to lay out a template of the frame as shown, making it 1/16 in. larger than the dimensions given to allow for filing to shape after the parts are fastened together. After the template is marked out, drill the four rivet holes, clamp the template or pattern to the sheet iron, and mark carefully with a scriber. The bore can be marked

with a pair of dividers, set at ⅛ in. This will mark a line for the center of the holes to be drilled with a ¼-in. drill for removing the unnecessary metal. The points formed by drilling the holes can be filed to the pattern size. Be sure to mark and cut out a sufficient number of plates to make a frame ¾ in. thick, or even 1/16 in. thicker, to allow for finishing.

After the plates are cut out and the rivet holes drilled, assemble and rivet them solidly, then bore it out to a diameter of 2¾ in. on a lathe. If the thickness is sufficient, a slight finishing cut can be taken on the face. Before removing the field from the lathe, mark off a space 3⅜ in. in diameter for the field core with a sharp-pointed tool. Mark out another for the outside of the frame, 4½ in. in diameter, by turning the lathe with the hand. Then the field can be finished to these marks, which will make it uniform in size. When the frame is finished to this point, two holes, with 3⅜ in. between their centers, are drilled and tapped with a ⅜-in. tap. These holes are for the bearing studs. Two holes are also drilled and tapped for ¼-in. screws, which fasten the hold-down lugs or feet to the frame. These lugs are made of a piece of ⅛-in. brass or iron, bent at right angles as shown.

The bearing studs are now made as shown in *Figure 2*, and turned into the threaded holes in the frame. The bearing supports are made of two pieces of ⅛-in. brass, as shown in the sketch, *Figure 3*, which are fitted on the studs in the frame. A ⅝-in. hole is drilled in the center of

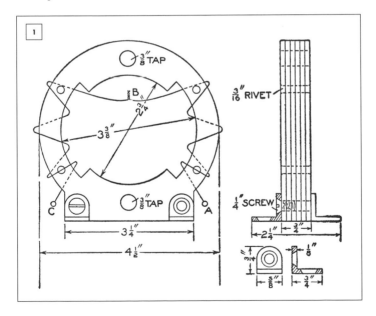

THE FIELD COIL CORE IS BUILT UP OF LAMINATED WROUGHT IRON RIVETED TOGETHER.

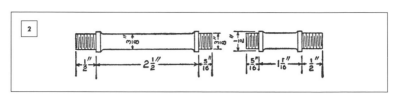

THE BEARING STUDS ARE TURNED FROM MACHINE STEEL
TWO OF EACH LENGTH BEING REQUIRED.

each of these supports, into which a piece of ⅝-in. brass rod is inserted, soldered into place, and drilled to receive the armature shaft. These bearings should be fitted and soldered in place after the armature is constructed. The manner of doing

this is to wrap a piece of paper on the outside of the finished armature ring and place it through the opening in the field; then slip the bearings on the ends of the shaft.

If the holes in the bearing support should be out of line, file them out to

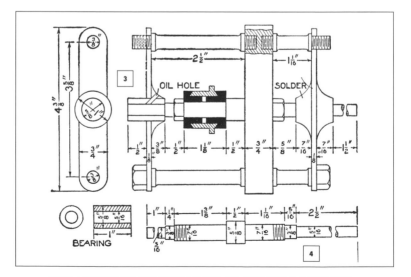

THE ASSEMBLED BEARING FRAME ON THE FIELD CORE AND
THE ARMATURE SHAFT MADE OF MACHINE STEEL.

make the proper adjustment. When the bearings are located, solder them to the supports, and build up the solder well. Remove the paper from the armature ring and see that the armature revolves freely in the bearings without touching the inside of the field at any point. The supports are then removed and the solder turned in a lathe, or otherwise finished. The shaft of the armature, *Figure 4,* is turned from machine steel, leaving the finish of the bearings until the armature is completed and fastened to the shaft. The armature core is made up as follows: Two pieces of wrought sheet iron, ⅛ in. thick, are cut out a little larger than called for by the dimensions given in *Figure 5* to allow for finishing to size. These are used for the outside plates, and enough pieces of No. 24-ga. sheet iron must be used to fill up the part between until the whole is over ¾ in. thick; these are cut like the pattern. After the pieces are cut out, clamp them together and drill six ⅛-in. holes through them for rivets. Rivet them together, and anneal the whole piece. When annealed, bore out the inside to 1 11/16 in. in diameter. Fit in a brass spider, which is made as follows: Procure a piece of brass, ¾ in. thick, and turn it to the size shown. File out the metal between the arms. Slip

the spider on the armature shaft and secure it solidly with the setscrew so that the shaft will not turn in the spider when truing up the armature core. File grooves or slots in the armature ring so that it will fit on the arms of the spider. Be sure that the inside of the armature core runs true. When this is accomplished, solder the arms of the spider to the metal of the armature core. The shaft with the core is then put in a lathe and the outside turned to the proper size. The sides are also faced off and finished. Make the core ¾ in. thick. Remove the core from the lathe and file out slots ¾ in. deep and ¼ in. wide.

The commutator is turned from a piece of brass pipe, ¾ in. inside diameter, as shown in *Figure 6*. The piece is placed on a mandrel and turned to ¾ in. in length and both ends chamfered to an angle of 60 deg. Divide the surface into 12 equal parts, or segments. Find the centers of each segment at one end, then drill a ⅛-in. hole and tap it for a pin. The pins are made of brass, threaded, turned into place and the ends turned in a lathe to an outside diameter of 1¼ in. Make a slit with a small saw blade in the end of each pin for the ends of the wires coming from the commutator coils. Saw the ring into the 12 parts on the lines between the pins.

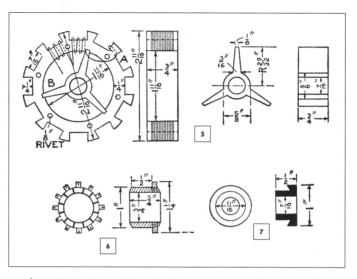

ARMATURE-RING CORE, ITS HUB AND THE CONSTRUCTION
OF THE COMMUTATOR AND ITS INSULATION.

The two insulating ends for holding these segments are made of fiber turned to fit the bore of the brass tubing, as shown in *Figure 7*. Procure 12 strips of mica, the same thickness as the width of the saw cut made between the segments, and use them as a filler and insulation between commutator bars. Place them on the fiber hub and slip the hub on the shaft, then clamp the whole in place with the nut, as shown in *Figure 3*. True up the commutator in a lathe to the size given in *Figure 6*.

The brush holder is shaped from a piece of fiber, as shown in *Figure 8*.

The studs for holding the brushes are cut from 5/16-in. brass rod, as shown in *Figure 9*. The brushes consist of brass or copper wire gauze, rolled up and flattened out to 1/8 in. thick and 1/4 in. wide, one end being soldered to keep the wires in place. The holder is slipped on the projecting outside end of the bearing, as shown in *Figure 3*, and held with a setscrew.

The field core is insulated before winding with 1/64-in. sheet fiber. Washers, 1 1/8 in. by 1 1/2 in., are formed for the ends, with a hole cut in them to fit over the insulation placed on the cores. A slit is cut through from the hole to the outside and then they are soaked in warm water until they become flexible enough to be put in place. After they have dried, they are glued to the core insulation.

The field is wound with No. 18-ga. double-cotton-covered magnet wire, about 100 ft. being required. Drill a small hole through each of the lower end insulating washers. In starting to wind, insert the end of the wire through the hole from the inside at *A, Figure 1,* and wind on four layers. This will take 50 ft. of the wire. Bring the end of the wire out at *B.* After one coil, or side, is wound, start at *C* in the same manner as at *A,* using the same number of turns and the same length of wire. The two ends are joined at *B.*

The armature ring is insulated by covering the inside and brass spider with 1/16-in. sheet fiber. Two rings of 1/16-in sheet fiber are cut and glued to the sides of the ring. When the glue is set, cut out the part within the slot ends and make 12 channel pieces from 1/64-in. sheet fiber, which are glued in the slots and to the fiber washers. Be sure to have the ring and spider covered so the wire will not touch the iron or brass.

Each slot of the armature is wound with about 12 ft. of No. 21-ga. double-cotton-covered magnet wire. The winding is started at *A, Figure 5,* by bending the end around one of the projections. Then wind the coil in one of the slots as shown, making 40 turns or four layers of 10 turns each, shellacking each layer as it is wound. After the coil is completed in one slot, allow about 2 in. of the end to protrude to fasten to

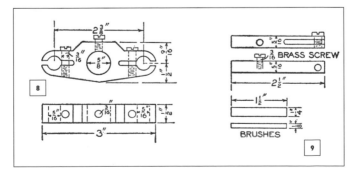

THE INSULATED BRUSH HOLDER AND ITS STUDS
FOR HOLDING THE BRUSHES ON THE COMMUTATOR.

the commutator segment. Wind the next slot with the same number of turns in the same manner and so on, until the 12 slots are filled. The protruding ends of the coils are connected to the pins in the commutator segments after the starting end of one coil is joined to the finishing end of the next adjacent coil. All connections should be securely soldered.

The whole motor is fastened with screws to a wood base, 8 in. long, 6 in. wide and 1 in. thick. Two terminals are fastened at one side on the base and a switch at the other side.

To connect the wires after the motor is on the stand, the two ends of the wire, shown at B, *Figure 1,* are

soldered together. Run one end of the field wire, shown at *A,* through a small hole in the base and make a groove on the under side so that the wire end can be connected to one of the terminals. The other end of the field wire *C* is connected to the brass screw in the brass brush stud. Connect a wire from the other brush stud, run it through a small hole in the base, and cut a groove for it on the underside so that it can be connected through the switch and the other terminal. This winding is for a series motor. The source of current is connected to the terminals. The motor can be run on a 110-volt direct current, but a resistance must be placed in series with it.

— A Disk-Armature Motor —

One of the simplest motors to make is the disk motor, its construction requiring a wood base, a brass disk, a 3-in. horseshoe magnet, and some mercury. In no case should the amateur scientist attempt to handle mercury. Only professionals should ever deal with this extremely toxic material, so the instructions given here are for information purposes only.

The base is made of hard wood, in the proportions shown in the sketch. The lead-in wires are connected to the

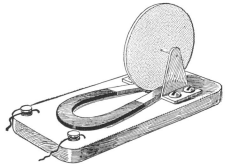

binding posts, *A* and *B*. From these, connections are made on the bottom of the base, from *A* to the groove *C* cut in the upper surface of the base for the

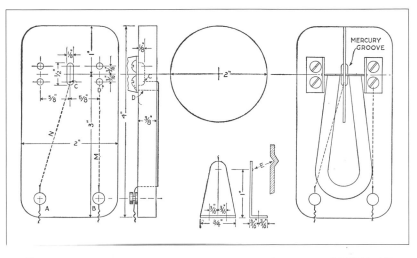

PARTS OF THE DISK MOTOR SHOWN IN DETAIL. ALSO THE LOCATION OF THE HORSESHOE MAGNET ON THE BASE. ENDS OF THE POLES ARE DIRECTLY UNDER THE CENTER OF THE SHAFT.

mercury, and from *B* to one screw, *D*, of one bearing. The end of the former wire must be clean and project into the end of the groove, where it will be surrounded with mercury.

The bearings consist of thin sheet brass, cut to the dimensions shown, the bearing part being made with a well-pointed center punch, as at *E*. The disk wheel is made of sheet brass, 2 in. in diameter. A needle, with the eye broken off and pointed, is used for the shaft. The needle shaft can be placed in position by springing the bearings apart at the top.

When the current is applied, the disk will revolve in a direction relative to the position of the poles on the magnet. The reverse can be made by turning the magnet over.

— How to Make a Small Single-Phase Induction Motor —

The following describes a small single-phase induction motor without an auxiliary phase. The problem to be solved was the construction of a motor large enough to drive a sewing machine or very light lathe, to be supplied with 110-volt alternating current from a lighting circuit, and to consume, if possible, no more current than a 16-cp. lamp. In designing, it had to be borne in mind that, with the exception of insulated wire, no special materials could be obtained.

The principle of an induction motor is quite different from that of the commutator motor. The winding of the armature, or "rotor," has no connection with the outside circuit, but the current is induced in it by the action of the alternating current supplied to the winding of the field-magnet, or "stator." Neither commutator nor slip rings are required, and all sparking is avoided. Unfortunately, this little machine is not self-starting. But a slight pull on the belt just as the current is turned on is all that is needed, and the motor rapidly gathers speed, provided no load is put on until it is in step with the alternations of the supply. It then runs at constant speed whether given much or little current, but stops if overloaded for more than a few seconds.

The stator has four poles and is built up of pieces of sheet iron used for stove pipes (which runs about 35 sheets to the inch). All the pieces are alike and cut on the lines with the dimensions as shown in *Figure 1*. The dotted line, *C*, is to be filed out after they are placed together. Each layer of four is placed with the pointed ends of the pieces alternately to the right and left, so as to break joints as shown in *Figure 2*. The laminations

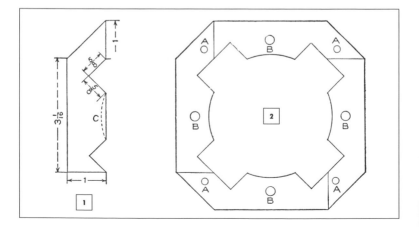

were carefully built up on a board into which heavy wires had been driven to keep them in place until all were in position and the whole could be clamped down. In the middle of the pieces, ¼-in. holes, *B*, were then drilled. Then, ¼-in. bolts were put in and tightened up, large holes being cut through the wood to enable this to be done. The armature tunnel was then carefully filed out and all taken apart again so that the rough edges could be scraped off and the laminations given a thin coat of shellac varnish on one side. After assembling a second time, the bolts were coated with shellac and put into place for good. Holes 5/32 in. in diameter were drilled in the corners, *A*, and filled with rivets, also varnished before they were put in. When put together, they should make a piece 2 in. thick.

This peculiar construction was adopted because proper stampings were not available, and because every bit of sheet iron had to be cut with a small pair of tinners' snips, it was important to have a very simple outline for the pieces. They are not particularly accurate as it is, and when

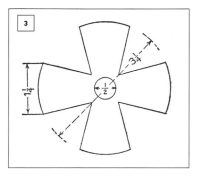

some of them got out of their proper order while being varnished, an awkward job occurred in the magnet that was never entirely corrected. No doubt some energy is lost through the large number of joints, all representing breaks in the magnetic circuit. But as the laminations are tightly held together and the circuit is about as compact as it could possibly be, the loss is probably not as great as it would appear at first sight.

The rotor was made of laminations cut from sheet iron, as shown in *Figure 3*. These were varnished lightly on one side and clamped on the shaft between two nuts in the usual way. A very slight cut was taken in the lathe afterwards,

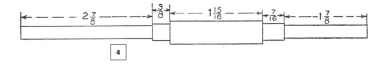

to true the circumference. The shaft was turned from ½-in. wrought iron, no steel being available, and is shown with dimensions in *Figure 4.* The bearings were cast of Babbitt metal, in a mold as shown in *Figure 5,* and bored to size with a twist drill in the lathe. They were fitted with ordinary wick lubricators. *Figures 6* and 7 are sections showing the general arrangement of the machine.

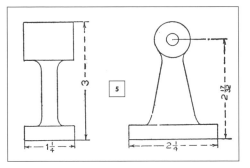

The stator was wound full with No. 22 double cotton-covered copper wire, about 2½ lb. being used. The connections were such as to produce alternate poles—that is, the end of the first coil was joined to the end of the second, the beginning of the second to the beginning of the third, and the end of the third to the end of the fourth, while the beginnings of the first and fourth coils connected to the supply.

The rotor was wound with No. 24 double cotton-covered copper wire, each limb being filled with about

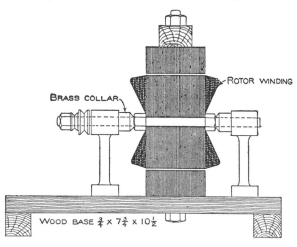

ROTOR WINDING

BRASS COLLAR

WOOD BASE ¾ x 7¾ x 10½

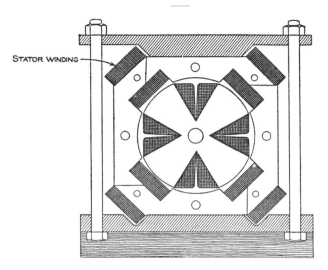

STATOR WINDING

200 turns, and all wound in the same direction. The four commencing ends were connected together on one side of the rotor and the four finishing ends were soldered together on the other. All winding spaces were carefully covered with two layers of cambric soaked in shellac. As each layer of wire was wound, it was well saturated with varnish before the next was put on.

This type of motor has drawbacks, as stated, but if regular stampings are used for the laminations, it would be very simple to build, having no commutator or brushes, and would not easily get out of order. No starting resistance is needed. And, because the motor runs at constant speed depending upon the number of alternations of the supply, a regulating resistance is not needed.

— A SIMPLE MOTOR CONTROLLER —

The controller described is very similar in operation to the types of controllers used on electric automobiles. Its operation may be easily followed by reference to the diagrammatic representation of its circuits, and those of a two-pole series motor to which it is connected, as shown in *Figure 1*. The controller consists of six flat springs, represented as small circles and lettered *A, B, C, D, E,* and *F,* which make contact with pieces of narrow sheet brass mounted on a small wood cylinder so arranged that it may be turned by means of a small handle located on top of the controller case in either direction from a point called neutral which is marked *N.* When the cylinder of the controller is in the neutral position, all six contact springs are free from contact with any metal on the cylinder. The contacts around the cylinder in the six different horizontal positions are lettered *G, H, J, K, L,* and *M.* There are three different positions of the controller in either direction from the neutral point. Moving the cylinder in one direction will cause the armature of the motor to rotate in a certain direction at three different speeds, while moving the cylinder in a reverse direction will cause the armature to rotate in the opposite direction at three different speeds, depending upon the

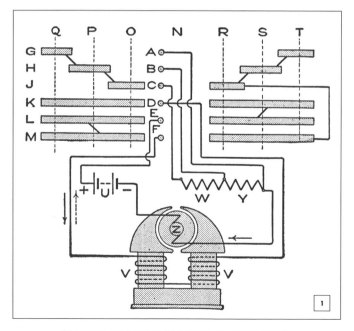

DIAGRAM OF THE ELECTRICAL CONNECTIONS
OF A CONTROLLER TO A TWO-POLE SERIES MOTOR.

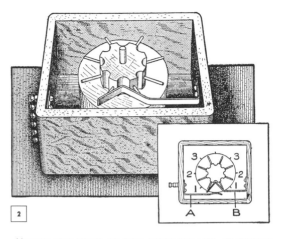

UPPER-END VIEW OF THE CONTROLLER, SHOWING
THE MANNER OF ATTACHING THE SPRINGS.

exact position of the cylinder. These positions are designated by the letters *O*, *P*, and *Q*, for one way and *R*, *S*, and *T*, for the other.

Supposing the cylinder is rotated to the position marked *O*, the circuit may be traced from the positive terminal of the battery *U*, as follows: To contact spring *E*, to strip of brass *L*, to strip of brass *M*, to contact spring *F*, through the field windings *VV*, to contact spring *D*, to strip of brass *K*, to strip of brass *J*, to contact spring *C*, through resistance *W* and *Y*, to armature *Z*, through armature to the negative terminal of the battery. Moving the cylinder to the position *P* merely cuts out the resistance *W*,

and to the position *Q*, cuts out the remaining resistance *Y*. The direction of the current through the armature and series field, for all positions of the cylinder to the left, is indicated by the full-line arrows. Moving the controller to the positions marked *R*, *S*, and *T*, will result in the same changes in circuit connections as in the previous case, except the direction of the current in the series field windings will be reversed.

The construction of the controller may be carried out as follows: Obtain a cylindrical piece of wood, 1¾ in. in diameter and 3⅛ in. long, preferably hardwood. Turn one end of this cylinder down to a diameter of

½ in., and drill a ¼-in. hole through its center from end to end. Divide the circumference of the small-diameter portion into eight equal parts and drive a small nail into the cylinder at each division point, the nail being placed in the center of the surface lengthwise and perpendicular to the axis of the cylinder. Cut off all the nail heads so that the outer ends of the nails extend even within the surface of the outer, or large size, cylinder. Divide the large part into eight equal parts so that the division points will be midway between the ends of the nails, and draw lines the full length of the cylinder on these points. Divide the cylinder lengthwise into seven equal parts and draw a line around it at each division point. Cut some ⅛-in. strips from thin sheet brass and mount them on the cylinder to correspond to those shown in *Figure 1*. Any one of the vertical division lines drawn on the cylinder may be taken as the neutral point. The pieces may be mounted by bending the ends over and sharpening them so that they can be driven into the wood. The various strips of brass should be connected electrically, as shown by the heavy lines in *Figure 1*. But these connections must all be made so that they will not extend beyond the outer surface of the strips of brass.

A small rectangular frame is made, and the cylinder is mounted in a vertical position in it by means of a rod passing down through a hole in the top of the rectangle, through the hole in the cylinder and partly through the bottom of the rectangle. The upper part of the rod may be bent so as to form a handle. The rod must be fastened to the cylinder in some convenient way.

Make six flat springs similar to the one shown at *A, Figure 2,* and mount them on the inside of the rectangle so that they will correspond in their vertical positions to the strips of brass on the cylinder. Six small binding posts mounted on the outside of the box and connected to these springs serve to make the external connections, and they should be marked so that they may be easily identified.

A flat spring, ¼ in. wide, is made similar to the one shown at *B, Figure 2.* Mount this spring on the inside of the rectangle so it will mesh with the ends of the nails in the small part of the cylinder. The action of this spring is to make the cylinder stop at definite positions. The top of the case should be marked so that the position of the handle will indicate the position of the cylinder. Stops should also be provided so that the cylinder case cannot be turned all the way around.

— Controller for a Small Motor —

An easy way of making a controlling and reversing device for small motors is as follows:

Cut a piece of wood (*A*) about 6 in. by 4½ in., and ¼ in. thick, and another piece (*B*) 6 in. by 1 in., and ¼ in. thick. Drive a nail through this near the center for a pivot (*C*). To the under side

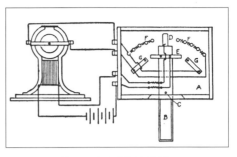

REVERSE FOR MOTOR.

of one end, nail a copper brush (*D*) to extend out about an inch. On the upper side, at the same end, nail another brush (*E*) so that it projects at both sides and is bent down to the level of the end brush. Then on the board put a semi-circle of brass-headed tacks as shown at *F*, leaving a small space at the middle and placing five tacks on either side, so that the end brush will come in contact with each one. Connect these tacks on the under side of the board with coils of

German-silver wire, using about 8 in. of wire to each coil. Fix these by soldering or bending over the ends of the tacks. Then nail two strips of copper (*G*) in such position that the side brush will remain on the one as long as the end brush remains on the tacks on that side.

Put sides about 1½ in. high around this apparatus, raising the board a little from the bottom to allow room for the coil. A lid may be added if desired. Connect up as shown.

— Direct-Connected Reverse for Small Motors —

A simple reverse for small motors can be attached directly to the motor as shown in *Figure 1. Figure 2* shows the construction of the reverse block: A is

a strip of walnut ⅝ in. square and ⅜ in. thick with strips of brass or copper (*BB*) attached as shown. Holes (*CC*) are drilled for the wire connections and they must be flush with the surface of the block. A hole for a ½ in. screw is bored in the block. In *Figure 1*, *D* is a thin strip of walnut or other dense, hard wood fitted to the binding posts of the brush holders, to receive the screw in the center.

Before putting the reverse block on the motor, remove all the connections between the lower binding posts and the brush holders and connect both ends of the field coil to the lower posts. Bend the strips *BB* (*Figure 2*) to the proper position to make a wiping contact with the nuts holding the strip of wood *D, Figure 1*. Put the screw in tight enough to make the block turn with a little resistance. Connect as shown in the illustration. To reverse, turn the block so the strips change connections and the motor will do the rest.

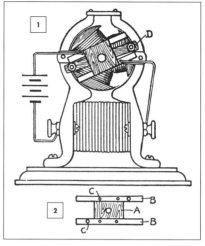

DIRECT-CONNECTED REVERSE.

— FOUR TOY MOTORS CONVEY BASIC IDEAS —

Here are four toy motors that, in spite of their small sizes and power, illustrate the principles of locomotion used in most engines.

Tin-and-nail motor: One of the simplest forms of an electric motor, where small electromagnets cause a tin rotor to spin, is shown in *Figures 2* and *6*. This motor runs on a couple of dry cells or will operate on 6 volts a.c. provided by a transformer. The rotor acts like a tiny switch as it wipes

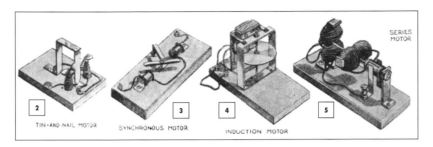

SERIES MOTOR

2

TIN-AND-NAIL MOTOR

SYNCHRONOUS MOTOR

3

4

INDUCTION MOTOR

5

against the brush lightly, turning on current momentarily just before its arms pass over the electromagnets. This current impulse, which occurs at each half rotation, is just enough to keep the rotor going. The rotor is cut from tin to the cross shape shown and the side arms are twisted at right angles. The electromagnets, or field coils, are wound in series on two nails, both windings being in the same direction. The nails are 2 in. apart. One end of the wire is scraped bare and twisted to form a tight coil that serves as a binding post; it is then tacked down to the baseboard at point *A, Figure 6*. At this point, connections to a transformer or battery are made. The other end of the wire is tacked to the yoke that

supports the upper end of the rotor. A length of bare copper wire is used as a brush, rubbing lightly against the edges of the rotor about ½ in. above the base. It is formed to a coil to provide flexibility. The other end of the brush wire is bared and formed

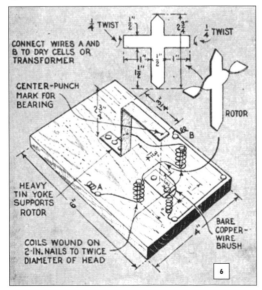

TIN-AND-NAIL MOTOR.

into a binding-post coil at point *B* to which the other side of the transformer or battery is connected. Center-punch marks are made to the yoke and in a small tin base plate half-way between the two nails. Then the rotor is set in place so that the arms are about ⅛ in. above the tops of the nails. The brush is adjusted so that it touches the edges of the rotor and

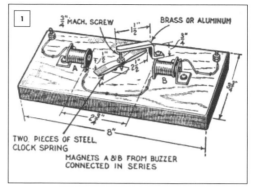

SYNCHRONOUS MOTOR.

also releases before the arms pass over the nail heads. After connecting the motor to the current supply, give the rotor a start by turning it and the motor should run.

Synchronous Motor: A synchronous motor is one that operates at a constant speed, which is equal to or a submultiple of the frequency of the alternating current supplied to it. A simple synchronous motor operating on low-voltage a.c. from a bell transformer is shown in *Figures 1* and *3*. The field coils *A* and *B* are two magnets from a buzzer or doorbell placed so that the windings run in the same direction. These are connected in series. The rotor consists of two pieces of steel clock spring and the shaft

is a No. 6-32 machine screw filed to a point at each end. Two nuts hold the springs to the shaft as shown. The shaft is pivoted between center-punched marks in the base plate and the supporting arms. There is no electrical connection to the rotor of

this motor. The motor will continue to operate about the speed at which it is started.

Series Motor: The motor shown in *Figure 1* runs on 6 volts d.c. or 8 to 12 volts a.c. from a toy transformer, and it can be fitted with a pulley to operate small models or other devices, delivering considerable power for its size. Details of construction are shown in *Figure 8.* The armature and field cores, *C* and *D,* as well as the end supports, *A* and *B,* are made of ⅛-in. strap iron. Armature and field coils are wound with bell wire that approximately should fill the space. The armature is slipped on the shaft and is held in place by peening or with a drop of solder. The commutator is made from a thread spool and two strips of copper. Slots are sawed in opposite sides of the spool, the edges of the copper strips are inserted into the slots, and the strips are bent around the spools. There should be about ¼ to ⅜-in. clearance between the two copper segments of the commutator,

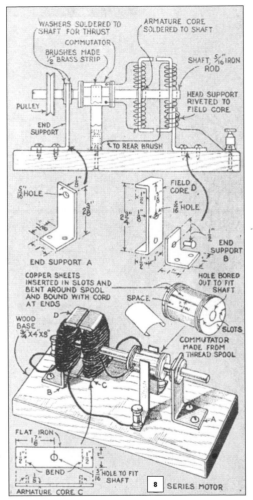

SERIES MOTOR.

and the armature is put in place. Two washers are soldered to the shaft on either side of the end support to limit end play. The brushes are made of spring brass, ½ in. wide. It may be necessary to give the motor a start by hand. If it does not run as first assembled, turn the commutator on the shaft to a position that will cause the motor to take hold.

Induction Motor: Operated on low-voltage a.c. from a toy transformer, the disk-type induction motor shown in *Figure 4* exemplifies a principle used in meters of various types. It will not operate on d.c. Details of parts are given in *Figures 9* to *12* inclusive. The laminations used are approximately of the dimensions shown in *Figure 12* and can be obtained from an old audio transformer used in a radio. Two stacks of laminations, each ⁹/₁₆ in. thick, are required for the lower and upper coil. The upper coil is wound with No. 28 d.c.c. wire, enough wire being wound on the coil to fill the winding space on the core. The lower coil is wound with No. 18 wire. The

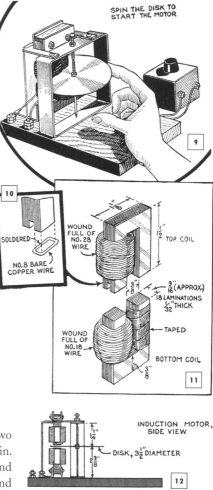

leads from each coil are brought out to a pair of binding posts on opposite sides of the motor. The core of the upper coil is drilled directly below the coil, and a single turn of No. 8 bare copper wire is inserted as shown in *Figure 10*. The ends of this wire should be lapped carefully and soldered together. The frame is made of No. 16-ga. sheet brass. The rotor is a disk of sheet copper or aluminum. It is moved up or down on the shaft until it is in the proper

position between the two cores. The upper coil terminals are connected to a radio rheostat and the lower coil is connected to the transformer supplying 6 volts. It will be necessary to shift the upper coil slightly to one side or the other in order to get the motor to operate properly. Once a proper position has been found, the speed can be controlled by adjusting the rheostat.

Radio On

— Simple Wireless System —

The illustrations will make plain a simple and inexpensive apparatus for wireless telegraphy by which operators have had no difficulty in sending messages across 1½ miles of water surface. It is so simple that the cuts scarcely need explanation.

Figure 1 shows the sending apparatus, consisting of a 40-cell battery connected with two copper plates 36 x 36 x ⅛ in. The plates are separated 6 in. by a piece of hard rubber at each end.

In *Figure 2* are seen duplicates of these insulated plates, connected

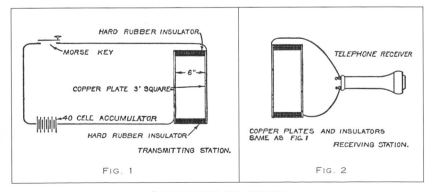

Fig. 1

Fig. 2

Simple wireless system.

with an ordinary telephone receiver. With this receiver the operator can hear distinctly the electric signals made by closing and opening the Morse key in *Figure 1*. Refer to any handbook for Morse Key codes.

— ONE-WIRE TELEGRAPH LINE —

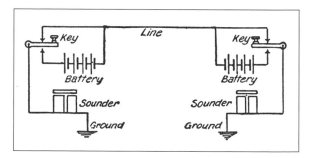

DIAGRAM OF ONE-WIRE LINE.

The accompanying wiring diagram shows a telegraph system that requires no switches and may be operated with open-circuit batteries on a one-wire line with ground connections at each end. Any telegraph set in which the key makes double contact can be connected up in this way.

— A SIMPLE RADIO-TRANSMITTING SET —

A simple spark-coil radio-transmitting set can be used where messages are to be sent over a short distance. The complete outfit can be put into a small suitcase, and is well adapted to the needs of those in motorcars or boats, and for boyscout field work.

The necessary instruments composing the set are the following: a high-tension jump-spark coil (of which different sizes can be obtained for distances up to 16 miles with the ignition coil from a standard light automobile), a key (an ordinary telegraph key answering the purpose), and a spark gap, which may be made from two zinc-battery electrodes mounted in two upright fiber posts. A condenser and helix will also be needed;

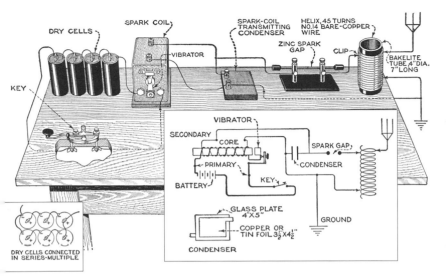

A VERY SIMPLE TRANSMITTING SET FOR THE RADIO AMATEUR.
IT CAN BE PACKED INTO A SUITCASE, MAKING IT SUITABLE FOR BOY
SCOUTS OR SIMILAR ORGANIZATIONS. ALL THE INSTRUMENTS MAY
BE MADE AT HOME, IF DESIRED, MAKING THIS A VERY CHEAP SET
AND ONE WELL-ADAPTED TO THE NEEDS OF THE BEGINNER.

the condenser stores up the energy, which is then discharged across the spark gap, and produces the oscillations that are thrown into space from the antenna in the form of waves.

The condenser can be made from a number of glass plates with sheets of tinfoil between them. Old 4 x 5-in. or 5 x 7-in. photographic negatives, from which the emulsion has been removed, will answer the purpose. The tinfoil sheets are cut ½ in. smaller than the plates and a tab, or ear, is left

projecting for connecting the lead wires to each sheet. In assembling the condenser, the tinfoil sheets are placed between the glass plates so that the tabs of alternate pieces will project from opposite sides. The condenser unit may consist of five sheets of foil and six glass plates. After assembling, bind the unit together and place in a cigar box, filling the surrounding space with melted paraffin, to make a compact article for a portable set. If the transmitter is to be stationary, the condenser may be supported on wooden blocks in a pan, into which enough insulating or transformer oil to cover the unit is poured. Any desired capacity can be obtained by adding the proper number of condensers.

The helix consists of 45 turns of No. 14 bare-copper wire, which is wound around a grooved Bakelite tube, 4 in. in diameter and 7 in. long. Spring clips are soldered to the wires from the aerial, ground, and spark gap, as shown in the diagram. Four dry cells give good results for short-distance work. When these are used, they may be connected in series, as shown in the upper part of the drawing. Another method of connecting them is in series-multiple, as shown in the insert. This distributes the load, and makes the battery last longer.

The already modest cost of the unit can be cut considerably by using materials that are usually available around the average workshop.

The aerial should be well insulated from the ground, but not with porcelain cleats, which should never be used for the aerial of a transmitting set. Solder all wire connections and make all leads short. The ground is important; make the ground wire as short as possible, and fasten it to a water pipe. Solder the wire to it or use a ground clamp.

If the set is to be used in the house as a stationary outfit, a lightening arrester, or ground switch, must be installed on the outside to prevent lightning from following the wire into the building.

An operator's license is necessary to operate a transmitting station. Full details of the necessary examination can be obtained from the radio inspector of the district in which the builder resides.

— How to Build an Adjustable Bridging Condenser —

An adjustable bridging condenser for wireless work that will serve as well as the high-priced manufactured articles on the market can be built easily and economically. It will work in the ground lead in C.W. transmission sets. But when used for this purpose, the mica should be of the best quality, and all units, when clamped together, should be tested out with 500 volts of direct current before installation. This condenser works nicely in receiving sets, and can be made in various capacities,

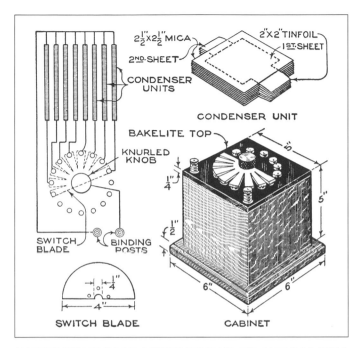

AN EFFICIENT BRIDGING CONDENSER THAT CAN EASILY BE BUILT
AT LOW COST AND THAT WILL WORK WELL IN THE GROUND LEAD
OF CONTINUOUS-WAVE SETS. IT WORKS NICELY IN RECEIVING
SETS AND CAN BE MADE IN VARIOUS CAPACITIES.

which are cut into and out of the circuit by the fan switch.

The eight condenser units are made
up of 2-in. squares of tinfoil, clamped
between 2½-in. square mica sheets.
Make one unit with five sheets of foil
and the remaining seven with three
sheets of foil each. The foil sheets are
cut out with a tab at one edge that projects beyond the mica plates.

In assembling the first unit, a
mica sheet is laid on the table. A
tinfoil sheet is placed on top of it
with the tab projecting to the right.
Another mica sheet is placed on top,
and the next tinfoil sheet placed with
the tab pointing to thc lcft, and so
on until the five sheets of foil and
six sheets of mica are assembled.
The remaining units are assembled

in the same manner, the tabs of the alternate sheets being brought out at opposite sides.

After assembling each unit, bind it with electrician's tape, or bolt the whole number of units together between metal plates and impregnate with paraffin. The foil tabs are all brought together at the ends and a lead wire soldered to each, the whole being bridged at the back, as shown. The leads are brought out to contacts in the Bakelite top of the cabinet; 16 points are used, eight of these are idle or dead taps, and merely serve to carry the switch blade smoothly. The switch blade is formed from sheet aluminum and screwed to the underside of the switch knob. If sheet aluminum is not to be had, use one of the fixed plates of an ordinary variable condenser, and saw out the radial teeth, as shown. The five-sheet unit is connected to the first point, shown at the left in the wiring diagram.

The cabinet is made from ¼-in. stock to the dimensions given, and the lead wires are brought to binding posts in the top. The cabinet should be finished to correspond to the finish of the other instruments. This condenser can also be back-mounted on the panel, instead of making it into a separate unit, if so desired.

— An Oscillation Transformer —

The oscillation transformer is an important part of an efficient radio-transmitting set, and there are many types on the market. However, the best kind for all practical purposes is the so-called "pancake" type. This transformer is simple to make and inexpensive. The advantages of this type of transformer over the helix type are many. It permits either direct or inductive coupling, ensures a pure and sustained wave that can be sharply tuned at the receiving station, and cuts out interference. All parts of the winding are accessible to the clips primary and secondary slide along a horizontal brass rod that makes quick changes in coupling possible, and the full energy of the transmitter can be utilized without under heating at the gap, as experienced with the old-style helix. The pancake transformer has made possible some remarkable records in amateur stations and nearly all of the record holders use it.

The woodwork may be any variety of wood stained and finished to the satisfaction of the maker; poplar or birch will be found easy to work and will take a mahogany finish well.

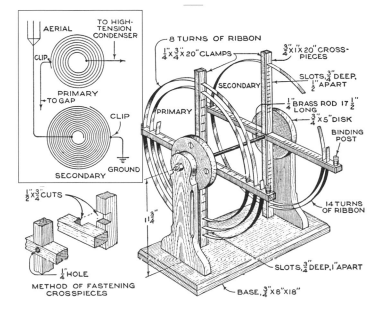

A SIMPLE AND EASILY MADE OSCILLATION TRANSFORMER, OF THE SO-CALLED "PANCAKE" TYPE. ALL MATERIAL, WITH THE EXCEPTION OF THE RIBBON, CAN BE PICKED UP AROUND THE RADIO LABORATORY.

The base and uprights are cut to the dimensions given, and assembled with 1¾-in. wood screws, driven through the bottom of the base. The brass rod is threaded and provided with a washer and nut at each end. Two wooden disks are screwed to the back of both primary and secondary crosspieces with 1-in. screws, and the crosspieces are slotted to take the required number of turns of ribbon. This ribbon may be of either copper or brass, about 1/16 in. thick by ¾ in. wide. It may be made up from a number of short pieces soldered together, or bought in one length, from any dealer in radio supplies. Clamps for holding the turns in place, in the form of light wooden strips, are fastened over the slots. So that there is no possibility of the ribbon working out of position, a binding post may be used at each outside ribbon terminal if desired, the lead wires to the condenser and aerial being soldered to standard helix clips, or clips can be used at all points. The clips from an old knife switch make ideal contacts.

— Dead-End Switch for Inductances —

The efficiency of a radio-receiving set can often be improved to a considerable extent by the use of a dead-end switch to short-circuit the unused turns of the inductance. The switch illustrated can be added to the set without disturbing the existing arrangement, and at a negligible cost. It consists simply of a piece of spring brass, bent as indicated, and soldered to the knob shaft at the back of the panel. Small pieces of brass, bent to right angles, are drilled and fastened under the head of each contact-point screw to provide positive contacts for the spring brass wiper. A little care is necessary to ensure that each contact piece is placed correctly, and that the wiper is in the proper position relative to the regular switch contactor, to short-circuit the unused turns and touch all the contact pieces.

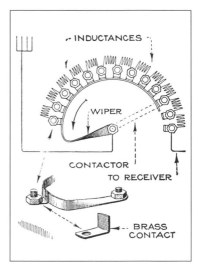

This switch can be used with any multi-point switch in which the points are arranged in an arc, and where contact is made by rotating switch arm.

— Making High-Frequency Oudin and Tesla Coils —

High-frequency coils are easy to make, and the materials are, for the most part, to be found around the average radio laboratory. Most experimenters want either an Oudin or a Tesla coil, and because they usually have all other necessary equipment on hand, such as transformers, high-tension condenser, and rotary gap, it is comparatively easy to gratify their ambition.

To make an Oudin coil, a cardboard tube, 6 x 11 in. is needed for the secondary tube. This tube is given two or three coats of shellac. When the last coat has dried, a single layer of No. 26 double silk-covered magnet wire is wound on. Start the winding ½ in. from the upper end of the tube, first fastening the end and allowing a loose end, of about 8 in., for connecting to the brass rod. Wind to within 1½ in. of the lower end. Small holes are made in the tube at the start and finish of the winding, and the loose ends of wire are pulled through and fastened. When the winding has been finished, it is given a coat of shellac, which is allowed to dry thoroughly before proceeding further.

The wooden disks shown in the drawing are made to fit into the ends of the secondary. The bottom disk is screwed to the base and the top one is drilled through the center to accommodate the brass rod leading to the ball. The top disk is then attached to the tube. A neat cap for the coil is

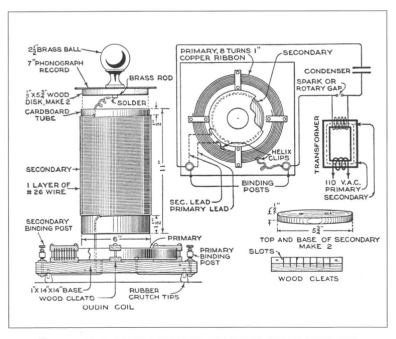

THE AMATEUR RADIO OPERATOR OF LIMITED MEANS NEED NOT DENY HIMSELF NECESSARY HIGH-FREQUENCY COILS.

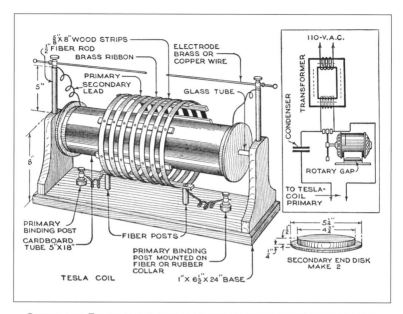

OUDIN AND TELSA COILS MAY BE MADE OF SUCH SIMPLE MATERIALS AS CARDBOARD TUBES, DISCARDED PHONOGRAPH RECORDS, SCRAPS OF BRASS, WOOD, AND FIBER.

made from a 7-in. phonograph record. The center hole is enlarged to take the brass rod, and small holes are drilled at opposite points for the small round-head wood screws that are used to fasten it to the wooden disk.

Almost any junkyard will yield the brass ball, which is of the type commonly used on metal bedsteads.

The base is preferably made of hardwood, which may be finished as desired. It is supported and, at the same time, insulated by rubber

crutch tips. These are fitted over wooden pegs, one at each corner.

The secondary having been completed and connections made, the maker must direct his attention to the primary winding. This winding consists of eight turns of 1-in. copper ribbon, which is held to the base by four wooden cleats, as indicated. These cleats are slotted, to separate the individual turns from each other. Flexible leads, with helix clips attached to one end, are connected to the building posts as indicated to complete the instrument. Using a ½-kw. transformer and a regular single-unit, oil-immersed, high-tension-type condenser, sparks from 10 to 16 in. long can be drawn from the coil, which is connected in circuit as shown in the diagram.

The Tesla-type coil is simple to make and operate. It consists of a secondary winding of a single layer of No. 28 single cotton-covered magnet wire over a well shellacked 5 x 18-in. cardboard tube. After the winding has been applied, it is given two coats of shellac, each of which is allowed to dry thoroughly. The wire is wound around the tube to within 1 in. of each end, and two small holes are punched through the cardboard at the terminals, for drawing the wire through and fastening it. After the wires have been looped and made fast to the tube, the ends are brought to the binding posts and soldered. The secondary end disks are turned to fit the ends of the tube snugly, and are drilled through their centers to receive the ¾-in. glass rod, or tube, which is supported in blind holes in the end pieces. This glass support is 21 in. long; if glass cannot be obtained, a wooden rod of the same dimensions will answer as well. The end blocks supporting

the coil are drilled at the center of their upper edges to take ½-in. rods of fiber. The upper ends of these are screwed to the secondary binding posts, as shown.

Seven turns of 1/16 x ⅝-in. brass ribbon form the primary, the separate turns of which are held apart by means of wooden strips, or cleats. The ribbon is fastened to these with small tacks or screws. The terminals of the primary are brought out and fastened to the bases of binding posts, which are elevated from the wooden base on short posts of hard rubber or fiber. Similar fiber posts, fastened to one of the cleats, are used to support the primary and keep it properly spaced with relation to the secondary. The wooden parts of the instrument are made from yellow pine to the dimensions shown in the drawing, and finished with black asphalt paint. The wire electrodes slide back and forth through the secondary binding posts, and regulate the length of spark as desired. A Tesla coil of this type is very powerful, and with it many interesting experiments with currents of high frequency can be performed without difficulty. The circuit in which a coil of this kind is used requires the same type of condenser as that shown in the wiring diagram of the Oudin coil.

ALTERNATIVE ENERGY

— HOW TO BUILD A WIND VANE WITH AN ELECTRIC INDICATOR —

Quite often it is practically impossible to ascertain the direction of the wind by observing an ordinary wind vane because the vane must be located so high up to give a true indication. By means of the device shown in *Figure 2,* the position of the vane may be determined without actually looking at the vane itself, and the indicating device may be located almost anywhere independently of the wind vane's position.

The principle upon which the device operates is that of the Wheatstone Bridge. The position of the moving contact *A, Figure 1,* is controlled by the wind vane. This contact is made

to move over a specially constructed resistance *R, Figure 2.* A second movable contact, *B,* is controlled by the observer and moves over a second resistance, identical with that over which the contact *A* moves. These two resistances are connected so as to form the two main branches of a Wheatstone Bridge; the points *A* and *B* are connected to the current-detecting device, which may be a galvanometer or telephone receiver, and current is supplied by a number of dry cells.

To obtain a balance—that is, no current through the receiver—the points *A* and *B* must occupy corresponding positions on their respective

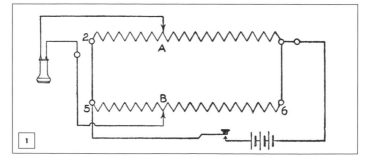

THE DIAGRAM OF A WHEATSTONE BRIDGE THAT SHOWS THE POINTS OF CONTACT SO PLACED THAT A BALANCE IS OBTAINED.

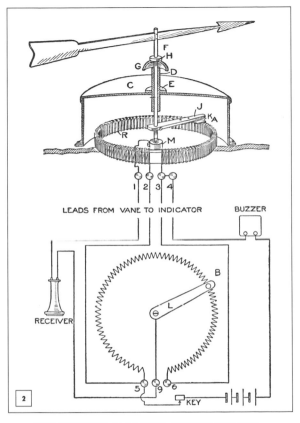

THE WEATHER VANE WITH RESISTANCE COIL,
AND DIAGRAM OF INDICATOR THAT
IS IDENTICAL WITH THAT OF THE VANE.

resistances. If the two resistances over which the points *A* and *B* move are mounted in the same position with respect to the cardinal points of the compass, then the points themselves will always be in the same position with respect to the cardinal points when a balance is obtained. The arrow head on the wind vane and the point *A* are made to occupy corresponding positions, and hence the position of the point *B*, when no current passes through the receiver, is an indication of the direction in which the wind vane is pointing.

The principal parts in the construction of the device are shown in the illustration, and the following description of their construction may be of interest to those who contemplate building the indicator.

Procure two pieces of $1/16$ in. hard rubber, $1\frac{1}{2}$ in. wide by 24 in. long. Clamp these, side by side, between two boards and smooth down their edges and ends, and then file small slots in the edges with the edge of a three-cornered file. These slots should all be equally spaced about 3/32 in. apart. Clamp the pieces together while filing the slots and mark one edge top and one end right so that the pieces may be mounted alike. Now procure a small quantity of No. 20-ga. bare manganin wire. Fasten one end of this wire to one end of the pieces of rubber by winding it in and out through three or four small holes. Then wind it around the piece, placing the various turns in the small slots that were filed in the edges. After completing the winding, fasten the end just as the starting end was attached. Wind a second piece of rubber in a similar manner and make sure to have the length of the free ends in each case

the same. Obtain a cylinder of some kind, about 8 in. in diameter, warm the pieces of rubber by dipping them in hot water, bend them around the cylinder, and allow them to cool.

A containing case, similar to that shown in cross section in the upper portion of *Figure 2,* should now be constructed from a good quality tin or copper. The inside diameter of this case should be about 1 in. more than the outside diameter of the resistance ring *R,* and it should be about 3 in. deep. The top, *C,* may be made curved as shown in the illustration, and should be fastened to the case proper by a number of small machine screws. The base of this case may be made so that the whole device can be mounted on the top of a pole.

Mount a piece of $\frac{1}{4}$ in. steel rod, about $\frac{1}{2}$ in. long and with a conical hole in one end, in the center of the bottom of the case as shown by *M.* A number of supports, similar to the one shown, should be made from some $\frac{1}{4}$ in. hard rubber and fastened to the sides of the case, to support the resistance ring. The dimensions of these supports should be such that the ends of the piece of rubber forming the ring are against each other when it is in place. The upper edge of the ring should be about 2 in. above the bottom of the case.

Next, mount a piece of brass tube, D, in the exact center of the top and perpendicular to it. A washer, E, may also be soldered to the top to aid in holding the tube. Procure a piece of steel rod, F, which will fit in the tube D and turn freely. Sharpen one end of this rod and mount a brass wind vane on the other end. A small metal cup, G, may be soldered to a washer, H, and the whole mounted on the steel rod, F, in an inverted position as shown. This will prevent water from getting down inside the case along the rod. The cup, G, may be soldered directly to the rod. Make a small arm, J, of brass, and fasten a piece of light spring, K, to one side of it, near the outer end. Then mount the arm on the steel rod so that it is parallel to the vane and its outer end points in the same direction as the arrow on the vane. The free end of the light spring on the arm J should be broad enough to bridge the gap between adjacent turns of wire on the resistance ring. Four bindings should

then be mounted on the inside of the case, and all insulated from it with the exception of number 1. Numbers 2 and 3 are connected to the ends of the winding, and number 4 is connected to number 3.

A second outfit should now be constructed, identical with the one just described except that it should have a flat top with a circular scale mounted on it, and the arm L should be controlled by a small handle in the center of the scale. The position of the contact B may be indicated on the scale by a slender pointer, attached to the handle controlling the arm L.

Four leads of equal resistance should be used in connecting the two devices and the connections made as shown. An ordinary buzzer placed in the battery circuit will produce an interrupted current through the bridge circuit and a balance will be obtained by adjusting the contact point B until a minimum hum is heard in the telephone receiver.

— WINDMILL FOR LIGHT POWER —

The windmill shown in the sketch is one that will always face the wind, and it never requires adjustment. It consists of a vertical shaft, A, provided with a number of

arms, B, on which are fixed hinged square sails, C. These sails are preferably made of wood frames covered with canvas. They are provided with hinges, D, attached to the ends of the

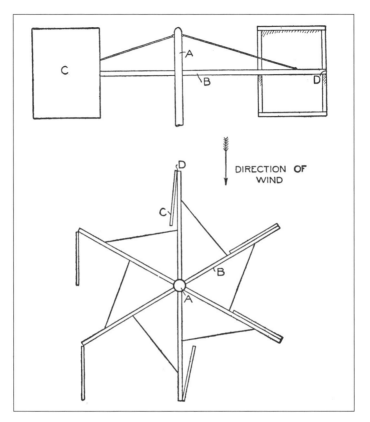

FRAMES HINGED TO THE ARMS.

arms in such a way that they offer resistance to the wind on one side of the wheel, while they move edgewise against the wind on the other side, as shown. The shaft of the mill can either be run in bearings set on an upright post, the lower end of the shaft turning on a conical bearing, or collars may be used on the bearings to keep it in position. The power can be transmitted with gears or by a flat belt over a pulley.

A wheel of this kind is not adapted for high speed; however, direct-connected to a pump or other slow-working machinery will prove very efficient.

— A Power Windmill —

The windmill shown is somewhat different from the ordinary kind. It is not a toy, nor does it approach in size the ordinary farm windmill, but is a compromise between the two. In a good strong wind, it will supply power enough to run a washing machine, a small dynamo, an emery wheel, or any other device used in the home workshop. The wheel is about 5 ft. in diameter, with eight blades. The overall length is about 6 ft.

The windmill is easily made and the cost is within the means of the average boy. There is not a part used in its construction that cannot be found in an ordinary manual-training shop. The most difficult parts of the construction will be described in detail. Symmetry and smoothness of design should be preserved, and the parts made as light as possible, consistent with strength and durability.

The Wheel. As shown in the drawings, the wheel has eight blades. Ordinarily the use of eight blades makes it difficult to construct a hub of sufficient strength to carry them.

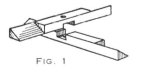

FIG. 1

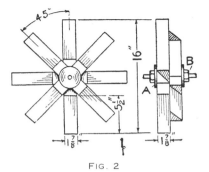

FIG. 2

THE HUB CONSISTS OF TWO PARTS, EACH HAVING FOUR ARMS FOR HOLDING THE BLADES

Where so many blades radiate from a common center, it is almost impossible to provide an anchorage for each blade. To provide a maximum of strength coupled with simplicity of design, the plan of using two hubs of four arms each was adopted in the construction of this mill. The ordinary hub of four arms is simple to make and quite strong. Four pieces of straight-grained oak, each 16 in. long and 1⅞ in. square, are used in constructing the hubs. The manner of notching each pair of pieces together is shown in *Figure 1*. The slope for the blades is made to run in opposite directions on the ends of each crosspiece. The slope is formed by cutting out a triangular piece, as shown.

The two hubs, thus formed, are mounted on the shaft, one behind the other, in such positions that the arms will be evenly divided for space in the wheel circle. These details are shown in *Figure 2*. The blades, *Figure 3*, are made of thin basswood or hard maple, and each is fastened in its place by means of two ⅜-in. bolts. A few brads are also driven in to prevent the thin blades from warping.

The Gears. This windmill was designed to transmit power by means of shafts and gear wheels, rather than with cranks and reciprocating pump rods, such as are used on ordinary farm mills. An old sewing machine head was used to obtain this result. Such a part can be obtained from a junk dealer or a sewing-machine agent. The head is stripped of its base plate with the shuttle gearing; likewise the needle rod, presser foot, etc., are taken from the front end of the head along with the faceplate. The

horizontal shaft and gear wheel are taken out and the bearings reamed out for a ½-in. shaft, which is substituted. The shaft should be 2 ft. in length, and 8 or 10 in. of its outer end threaded for the clamping nuts that hold the two hubs in place, as shown at *A* and *B, Figure 2*. The gear wheel is also bored out and remounted on the new shaft.

The supporting standard is constructed of oak with mortise-and-tenon joints, as shown in *Figure 4*. The width of the pieces will depend on the kind of sewing-machine head used. It may be necessary to slightly change the dimensions. The machine head is fastened on the support with bolts. A sleeve and thrust spring are mounted on the shaft, as shown. The sleeve is made of brass tubing of a size to fit snugly on the shaft. A cotter will keep it in place. The sleeve serves as a collar for the thrust spring, which is placed

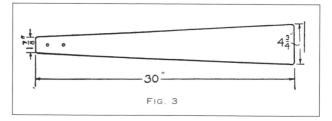

FIG. 3

THE LOWER END OF THE SHAFT HAS A HORIZONTAL
SHAFT GEARED TO IT FOR THE DRIVE PULLEYS.

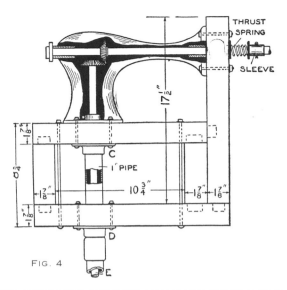

THRUST
SPRING

SLEEVE

$17\frac{1}{2}''$

C

1" PIPE

$10\frac{3}{4}''$

$1\frac{7}{8}''$

$1\frac{7}{8}''$ $1\frac{7}{8}''$

D

FIG. 4

E

THE SUPPORTING STANDARD HOLDS THE MACHINE HEAD
WITH THE WHEEL AND THE VANE ON AN AXIS.

between the sleeve and the standard. This arrangement acts as a buffer to take up the end thrust on the shaft caused by the varying pressure of the wind on the wheel.

The Vane. A vane must be provided to keep the wheel facing the wind at all times. It is made of basswood or hard maple, as shown in *Figure 5*. It is not built up solid, air spaces being left between the slats to reduce the wind resistance. Unless built in this manner, the vane is liable to twist off in a gale. The horizontal slats are ¼ in. thick, and the

upright and cross braces ⅜ in. thick, while the long arm connecting the vane to the supporting standard is ½ in. thick.

The supporting standard, carrying the wheel and the vane, must revolve about a vertical axis with the changes in the wind, and this vertical axis is supplied in the form of a piece of gas pipe that runs through the supporting standard at the points marked *C* and *D, Figure 4*. Ordinary pipe fittings, called flanges, are bolted to the frame at these points. The coupling in the gas pipe beneath

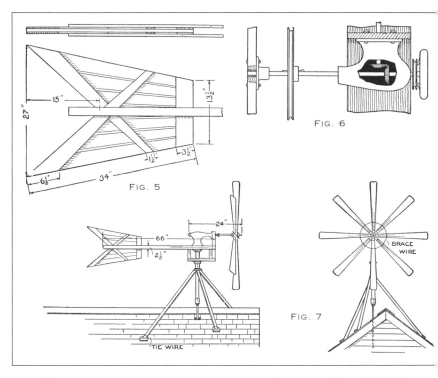

FIG. 6

FIG. 5

FIG. 7

BRACE WIRE

TIE WIRE

THE VANE CONSTRUCTION AND THE MANNER OF BUILDING THE TOWER.

the supporting standard serves as a stationary collar to support the weight of the whole mill. The vane should be placed correctly to balance the weight of the wheel.

The shaft passes through the framework of the mill on the inside of the pipe, as shown at *E*. A ⅜-in. soft-steel or wrought-iron rod is satisfactory for the shaft because no

weight is supported by it and only a twisting force is transmitted. The use of a larger rod makes the mill cumbersome and unwieldy. The upper end of the shaft is fastened to the shaft that projects from the under side of the machine head by means of a sleeve made of a piece of ⅜-in. pipe. Two cotters hold the shafts and sleeve together.

The device shown in *Figure 6* is installed at the lower end of the shaft, inside the workshop. The purpose of this appliance is to provide a horizontal shaft upon which pulleys, or driving gears, may be mounted. The device is constructed of another sewing-machine head similar to the one already described. The head is cut in two and the separate parts mounted on suitable supports. The gap between the sawed portions permits a pulley to be fastened on the shaft to serve as the main drive. The wheel propelled by the treadle of the sewing machine will make a good drive wheel. The small handwheel, originally mounted on the machine-head shaft, is left intact. This arrangement gives two sizes of drive wheels. Heavy sewing-machine belts will serve to transmit the power.

The tower can be built up in any manner to suit the conditions. Ordinary sticks, 2 in. square, are suitable. These are well braced with wire and fastened securely to the roof of the shop. The arrangement of the tower with the mill is shown in *Figure 7*.

— An Easily Constructed Ball-Bearing Anemometer —

An anemometer is an instrument that measures the velocity of the wind. The anemometers used by the weather bureau consist of four hemispherical cups mounted on the ends of two horizontal rods that cross at right angles and are supported on a freely turning vertical axle. Because the concave sides of the cups offer more resistance to the wind than do the convex sides the device is caused to revolve at a speed that is proportional, approximately, to that of the wind. The axle, to which the rotary motion is transmitted from the cups, is connected to a dial mounted at the foot of the supporting column. This dial automatically records the rotations. The reproduction of such a registering mechanism would be rather complicated. Hence, in the arrangement to be described none will be employed. Therefore, one of these improvised anemometers, when mounted on a high building, will indicate by the changing rapidity of its revolutions only the comparative, not the real, velocity of the wind.

In constructing the instrument, straight, dished vanes will be used instead of hollow cups. The vanes operate almost as effectively and may be combined more readily into

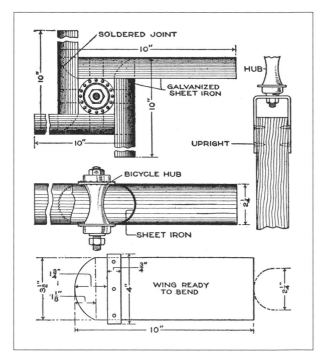

THIS ANEMOMETER IS MADE FROM GALVANIZED SHEET IRON, A BICYCLE HUB, AND A FEW IRON STRAPS. PRACTICE IN OBSERVING ITS MOTION WILL ENABLE ONE TO ESTIMATE FAIRLY CLOSELY THE WIND'S VELOCITY.

a sturdy rotating unit. A bicycle front hub is used to constitute a wear and noise-proof bearing having minimum friction. Each of the four wings is formed from a piece of galvanized iron, measuring 4½ by 10 in., which has one end cut to a curve as shown. To each wing is fastened, with tinner's rivets, a 4-in. length of ¾ by ¹⁄₁₆-in. strap iron. Form each

of the strips into a trough-shaped vane, measuring 2¼ in. from edge to edge—this being the distance between the spoke flanges of a bicycle hub. Some cylindrical object of suitable diameter will serve as a form for bending. Place the ends of the support strips between the spoke flanges and rivet them securely. The rivets pass through the spoke holes.

Some trying out may be required to ensure a symmetrical arrangement of the parts. Solder the curved end of each wing to the inner surface of the adjacent wing. Place a tin cap—a salve-box lid will do—under the upper lockout on the hub to exclude rain from the bearing.

The supporting upright may be a heavy wooden rod, or a piece of iron pipe. A yoke of 1 by ⅛-in. strap iron, held to the top of the upright with screws, is provided for the attachment of the hub. The locknut on the hub clamps it to the yoke. Apply a coat of metal paint to the iron parts that are exposed. Mount the device sufficiently high to give the wind free access to it from all directions. The curve at one end of each wing is an irregular one. Hence, its accurate construction involves a knowledge of sheet-metal pattern drawing. However, if it is made of a form similar to that shown, it will fit sufficiently well to permit a good soldered joint.

— AN ELECTRIC ANEMOMETER —

The construction of this instrument is so simple that any amateur can make one, and if accurate calibrations are desired, these can be marked by comparison with a standard anemometer, while both are placed in the wind.

The Indicator. The case of the indicator is built of thin wood—the material of an old cigar box will do—9 in. long, 6 in. wide and 1½ in. deep. If cigar-box material is used, it must first be soaked in warm water to remove the paper. If a cover is to be used on the box, a slot, on an arc of a circle, must be cut through it to show the scale beneath. The arc is determined by the length of the needle from a center over the axis on which the needle swings. When the box is completed, smooth up the outside surface with fine sandpaper and give it a coat of stain.

The core of the magnet is made by winding several layers of bond paper around a pencil of sufficient size to make an inside diameter of slightly over ¼ in. and a tube 2 in. long. Each layer of the paper is glued to the preceding layer.

Two flanges or disks are attached to the tube to form a spool for the wire. The disks are cut from thin wood, 1¼ in. square, and a hole bored through their centers so that each will fit on the tube tightly. One of them is glued to one end of the tube and the other fastened at a point ½ in.

from the opposite end. The space between the disks is filled with seven layers of No. 22-ga. insulated magnet wire, allowing sufficient ends of the wire to project for connections. The finished coil is located in the box, as shown at *A, Figure 1*.

The core for the coil is cut from a piece of ¼-in. iron rod, 1¼ in. long, and a slot is cut in each end, ¼ in. deep, into which brass strips are inserted and soldered, or otherwise fastened. The strips of brass are ³/₁₆ in. wide, one 1½ in. long and the other ¾ in. long. Two ¹/₁₆-in. holes are drilled in the end of the long piece, and one ¹/₁₆-in hole in the end of the short piece. The complete core with the brass ends is shown in *Figure 2*.

The needle *B, Figure 1,* is made of a copper or brass wire, about 6 in. long, and is mounted on an axis at *C*. The detail of the bearing for the axis is shown in *Figure 3*. The axis *D* is a piece of wood fitted in the U-shaped piece of brass and made to turn on brads as bearings, the center being pierced to receive the end of the needle. After locating the bearing for the axis *C, Figure 1*, it is fastened

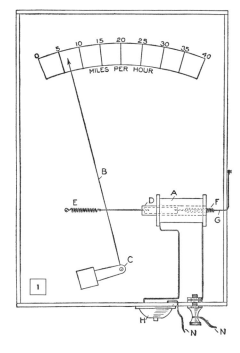

THE INDICATOR BOX WITH COIL, NEEDLE, AND SCALE, AS IT IS USED IN CONNECTION WITH THE ANEMOMETER.

in place so that the upper end, or pointer of the needle, will travel over the scale. The needle is then attached to the bearing after having been passed through the inner hole of the longer brass strip of the core, and the coil is fitted with core in the manner shown at *D*. A light brass coil spring is attached to each end of the core, as shown at *E* and *F*, the latter being held with a string, *G*, whose end is tied to a brad on the outside of the box for adjustment. A better device could be substituted by attaching the end of the spring *F* to a nut and using a knurled-head bolt passed through the box side. One of the wires from the coil is attached to a push button, *H*, to be used when a reading of the instrument is made. The connections for the instrument consist of one binding post and a push button.

The Anemometer. The anemometer resembles a miniature windmill and is mounted on top of a building or support where it is fully exposed to the air currents. It differs from the windmill in that the revolving wheel is replaced by a cupped disk, *A, Figure 4*, fitted with a sliding metal shaft, *B*, which is supported on crosspieces, *CC,* between the main

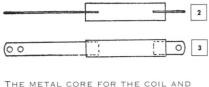

THE METAL CORE FOR THE COIL AND THE BEARING BLOCK FOR THE AXIS OF THE NEEDLE.

frame pieces *DD.* The latter pieces carry a vane at the opposite end. The frame pieces are ½ in. thick, 2¼ in. wide, and 36 in. long, and the cross-pieces have the same width and thickness and are 4 in. long.

A variable-resistance coil, *E*, is made as follows and fastened in the main frame. The core of this coil is a piece of wood, 2 in. square and 4 in. long, and wound with No. 18 gauge single-wound cotton-covered German-silver wire. The winding should begin ¼ in. from one end of the core and finish ¼ in. from

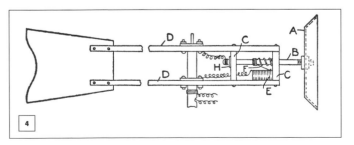

THE ANEMOMETER AS IT IS MOUNTED ON A STANDARD SIMILAR TO A SMALL WINDMILL WEATHER VANE.

the other, making the length of the coil 3½ in. The ends of the wire are secured by winding them around the heads of brads driven into the core. A small portion of the insulation is removed from the wire on one side of the coil. This may be done with a piece of emery cloth or sandpaper. A sliding spring contact, *F,* is attached to the sliding shaft, *B,* the end of which is pressed firmly on the bared portion of the wire coil. One end of a coil spring, which is slipped on the shaft between the pieces *CC,* is attached to the end crosspiece. The other end is fastened to the sliding shaft so as to keep the shaft and disk out and the flange *H* against the second crosspiece, when there is no air current applied to the disk *A.* The insulation of the standard upon which the anemometer turns is shown in *Figure 5.* The standard *J* is made of a piece of ½-in. pipe, suitably and rigidly attached to the building or support. The upper end, around which the anemometer revolves to keep in the direction of the air currents, is fitted with a plug of wood to insulate the ¼-in. brass rod *K.* A bearing and electric-wire connection plate, *L,* is made of brass, ⅛ in. thick, 2 in. wide, and 4 in. long. The bearing and connection plate *M* are made in a similar manner. The surface of the holes in

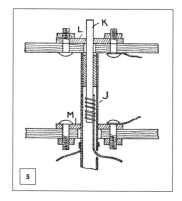

these plates, bearing against the pipe *J* and the brass rod *K,* make the two connections for the wires from the variable-resistance coil *E, Figure 4,* located on the main frame, to the wire connections between the two instruments. These wires should be weatherproof, insulated, attached as shown, and running to and connecting the indicator with the anemometer at *NN, Figure 1.*

Two or more dry cells must be connected in the line. When a reading is desired the button *H, Figure 1,* is pushed, which causes the current to flow through the lines and draw the magnet core *D* in the coil, in proportion to the magnetic force induced by the amount of current passing through the resistance in the coils on *E, Figure 4,* from the contact into which the spring *F* is brought by the wind pressure on the disk *A.*

{ CHAPTER 5 }

CHEMISTRY

POTENT INTERACTIONS

— THE HINDOO SAND TRICK —

This is one of the many tricks which was once kept secret by the Hindus, and for which they are famous. It consists of placing ordinary sand in a basin full of water, stirring the water, and taking out the sand in handfuls, perfectly dry. It need scarcely be said that without previous preparation, it is impossible to do so.

Take 2 lb. of fine silver sand, place it in a frying pan and heat well over a clear fire. When the sand is thoroughly heated, place a small piece of wax—the composition of a paraffin candle is preferred—in the sand, stirring it well to get it thoroughly mixed, then allow the sand to cool. When this sand is placed in a basin of water, it will be apparently dry when taken out. It is very important that only a small portion of the adherent be used so that it cannot be detected when the sand is examined by the audience. The explanation is that the grease or wax coating on each sand particle repels the water.

— CRYSTALLIZATION SHOWN ON A SCREEN —

The formation of chemical crystals can be shown in an interesting manner as follows: Spread a saturated solution of salt on a glass slide, or projection-lantern glass, and allow it to evaporate in the lantern's light or beneath a magnifying glass. The best substances to use are solutions of alum or sodium, alum being preferable. Ordinary table salt gives brilliant crystals that reflect the light to a marked degree. For regular formation, where the shape of the crystal is being studied, use a solution of hyposulphite of soda.

Many startling facts may be learned from the study of crystals in this manner, and watching them "grow" is great sport even to the seasoned chemist.

— EXPERIMENTS WITH CAMPHOR —

Place a few scrapings from gum camphor in a tumbler of water and watch the phenomenon. The scrapings will go through all kinds of rapid motions as if they were alive. A drop of turpentine, or any oil, will stop their maneuvers. This experiment will demonstrate to you how quickly oil will spread over the surface of water.

— THE PHANTOM FIRE EXTINGUISHER —

Because they are generally invisible, creating gases from chemical reactions can be a mysterious process, but simple experiments can reveal the nature of the gases you create. Try this simple experiment (or use it as a parlor trick) that sheds "light" on the properties of carbon dioxide (CO_2).

Put a teaspoon of baking soda in a small cup (1) and, after adding about the same amount of vinegar, put a saucer or other covering over the top of the cup (2). Now hold a cardboard tube at an angle, so that it is pointing downward at the flame of a lit candle (3). Uncover the cup and "pour" the invisible fire extinguisher slowly into the top end of the tube (4). You'll find that the flame will go out.

But why? Mixing "caustic" baking soda with acidic vinegar creates

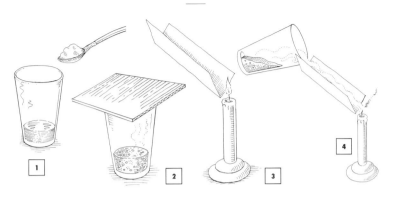

a chemical reaction (you'll see it as foam) that produces carbon dioxide. By covering the cup, you captured the gas until you poured it down the cardboard tube. As it poured over the top of the candle, the carbon dioxide essentially smothered the flame, because it prevented oxygen from reaching the lit wick. Without oxygen, the flame could not survive and your phantom fire extinguisher worked like magic!

— Cutting a Thread Inside a Glass Bottle —

This experiment can only be performed when the sun shines, but it is a good one. Procure a clear glass bottle and stick a pin in the lower end of the cork. Attach a thread to the pin and tie a small weight to the end of the thread so it will hang inside the bottle when the cork is in place.

All that is required to sever the thread is to hold a magnifying glass so as to direct the sun's rays on the

THE GLASS DIRECTS THE SUN'S RAYS.

thread. The thread will quickly burn and the weight fall.

— INSTANTANEOUS CRYSTALLIZATION —

Dissolve 150 parts of hyposulphite of soda in 15 parts of water and pour the solution slowly into a test tube which has been warmed in boiling water, filling the tube about one-half full. In another glass dissolve 100 parts of acetate of soda in 15 parts of boiling water. Pour this solution slowly on top of the first in such a way that it forms an upper layer, without mixing the solutions. The two solutions are then covered over with a thin layer of boiling water and allowed to cool.

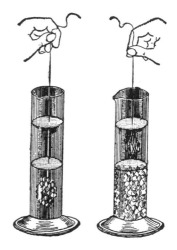

Lower into the test tube a wire, at the extremity of which is fixed a small crystal of hyposulphite of soda. The crystal transverses the solution of acetate without causing trouble, but crystallization will immediately set in as soon as it touches the lower hyposulphite of soda solution, as shown in the left of the sketch.

When the hyposulphite of soda solution becomes crystallized, lower into the upper solution a crystal of acetate of soda suspended by another wire, as shown in the right of the sketch, and this will crystallize the same as the other solution.

UNDER PRESSURE

— THE SUBSTANCE OF AIR —

We certainly know that any gas is a "something." Air, a combination of gases, definitely is a "something" when it hits us in a tornado, knocks us down and wipes out whole towns. Yet gases once were so mysterious that for many centuries many learned men thought that air not in motion was a "nothing"—just empty space. A

Sicilian philosopher who lived 450 years before Christ proved that air, even when not in motion, was "something" by showing that water would not flow into a bottle already filled with air, but would if the air were allowed to flow out.

You can perform that experiment by holding a glass with the opening down, and plunging it straight down into the water. The air in the glass will prevent the water from entering the glass. Tip the glass sideways a bit, so that the bubbles of air can escape. Water will fill the glass as the air leaves. You can use two glasses under water and actually pour air from one into the other.

Yet, so many gases, such as air, are invisible, tasteless, and odorless, so it is no wonder they were not identified for thousands of years and were thought of in terms of magic when their effects were felt.

— THE PRESSURE OF WATER —

Since water is a fluid, with its parts free to move in any direction, its pressure is exerted in all directions. The pressure against the side of a teakettle 5 in. below the water level is exactly the same as that against the bottom at a depth of five inches. The pressure against the bottom of a sloping dam is just as great as if the dam were a vertical wall.

You can see for yourself that water pressure pushes up, as well as down and sideways, by punching a hole in the bottom of a tin can and pushing the can, bottom-first, into a basin of water. The upward pressure will make a stream of water squirt into the can. If you push the can down four inches into the water, the pressure on the stream entering the can will be exactly the same as when you filled the can with water and watched water squirting out from the side of the can from a hole four inches down. In both cases the pressure was caused by the weight of four inches of water. In one case the water was in the can pushing out; in the other, it was outside the can pushing in.

In your teakettle, the water in the spout exactly balances the pressure against the lower opening. But suppose you fitted a plunger into the end of the spout and pushed on the water. This would upset the balance. You could push the water down through the spout and if the teakettle already were full, water would run out the top. Suppose the top were sealed shut and the water could not overflow.

In that case your plunger would be exerting an extra pressure on the water in the spout and on the water inside. Because in a fluid pressure acts in all directions, this pressure would push on the bottom of the teakettle, on the sides and upward on the lid. If the spout had an area of one square inch and you applied a 10-pound pressure on your plunger, obviously the pressure applied would be 10 pounds per square inch. Equally obvious, the pressure at the bottom of the spout, pushing against the rest of the water in the teakettle also would be 10 pounds on that square inch.

— THE DIVING BOTTLE —

This is a very interesting and easily performed experiment illustrating the transmission of pressure by liquids. Take a wide-mouthed bottle and fill almost full of water; then into this bottle place, mouth downward, a small vial or bottle having just enough air in the bottle to keep it barely afloat. Put a sheet of rubber over the mouth of the large bottle, draw the edge down over the neck and wrap securely with a piece of string thus forming a tightly stretched diaphragm over the top.

When a finger is pressed on the rubber, the small bottle will slowly descend until the pressure is released when the small bottle will ascend. The moving of the small bottle is caused by the pressure transmitted through the water, thus causing the volume of air in the small tube to decrease and the bottle to descend

PRESSURE EXPERIMENTS.

and ascend when released as the air increases to the original volume.

This experiment can be performed with a narrow-necked bottle, provided the bottle is wide, but not very thick. Place the small bottle in as before, taking care not to have too much air in the bottom. If the cork is adjusted properly, the bottle may be held in the hand and the sides pressed with the fingers, thus causing the small bottle to descend and ascend at will. If the small bottle used is opaque, or an opaque tube such as the cap of a fountain pen, many puzzling effects may be obtained.

— THE POWER OF AIR PRESSURE —

Even though we may not see it in our atmosphere, the air all around us is always pushing on us in a very powerful way. Even though you can't feel the pressure, it is constantly there. And there's a simple way to prove this.

Fill an ordinary drinking glass with water to the very rim. Now, cut a top out of a plastic take-out container or other sturdy waterproof material, and put it over the top of the drinking glass. Holding it tight to the rim of the glass, turn the glass over. Now remove your hand and see what happens! The plastic stays in place, and the reason is simple: the atmospheric pressure of the air pressure from the outside of the glass—including against the plastic because air pressure is exerted in all directions—is greater than the pressure of the weight of the water and gravity pushing against the other side of the plastic top. Now that's a lot of pressure—even if you can't see it.

— A MODEL STEAM ENGINE —

The sketch on the next page illustrates a two-cylinder single-acting, poppet valve steam engine of home construction.

The entire engine, excepting the flywheel, shaft, valve cams, pistons, and bracing rods connecting the upper and lower plates of the frame proper, is of brass; the other parts named are of cast iron and bar steel.

The cylinders, G, are of seamless brass tubing, 1½ in. outside diameter. The pistons, H, are ordinary 1½ in. pipe caps turned to a plug fit, and ground into the cylinders with oil and emery. This operation also finishes the inside of the cylinders.

The upright rods binding the top and bottom plates are of steel rod about ⅛-in. in diameter, threaded into the top plate and passing through holes in the bottom plate with hexagonal brass nuts beneath.

The valves, C, and their seats, B, are bored with a countersink bit and are plainly shown. The valves are

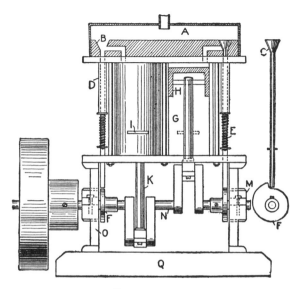

ENGINE DETAILS.

made by threading a copper washer, ⅜ in. in diameter, and screwing it on the end of the valve rod. Then a tapered mass of solder was roughly wiped on and ground into the seats *B* with emery and oil.

The valve rods operate in guides, *D*, made of ¼-in. brass tubing. This tubing passes through the top plate and into the heavy brass bar containing the valve seats and steam passages at the top, into which they are plug-fitted and soldered.

The location and arrangement of the valve seats and steam passages are shown in the sketch, the flat bar containing them being soldered to the top plate.

The steam chest, *A*, is constructed of 1-in. square brass tubing, one side being sawed out and the open ends fitted with pieces of 1/16 in. sheet brass and soldered in. The steam inlet is a gasoline pipe connection such as used on automobiles.

The valve-operating cams, *F*, are made of the metal ends of an old typewriter platen. One is finished to shape and then firmly fastened face to face to the other, and used as a pattern in filing the other to shape. Attachment to the shaft, *N*, is by means of setscrews which pass through the sleeves.

The main bearings, *M,* on the supports, *O,* and the crank-end bearings of the connecting rods, *K,* are split and held in position by machine screws with provision for taking them up when worn.

The exhausting of spent steam is accomplished by means of slots, *I,* sawed into the fronts of the cylinders at about ⅛ in. above the lowest position of the piston's top at the end of the stroke. At this position the valve rod drops into the cutout

portion of the cam and allows the valve to seat.

All the work on this engine was accomplished with a hacksaw, bench drill, carborundum wheel, files, taps and dies. The exceptions were turning the pistons, which was done in a machine shop, and the making of the flywheel, which was taken from an old dismantled model. The base, *Q,* is made of a heavy piece of brass.

The action is smooth and of high speed. Steam is supplied by a sheet brass boiler of about 3 pt. capacity, heated with a Bunsen burner.

— A HOMEMADE STEAM TURBINE —

Making a steam turbine is a good process for learning about the principles that go into any steam-driven motor.

To start, procure the following: brass measuring about ³/₁₆ in. thick and 4 in. square, 53 steel pens, not over ¼ in. in width at the shank, two enameled, or tin, saucers or pans with an inside diameter of about 4½ in., two stopcocks with ⅛ in. holes, one shaft, some pieces of brass, ¼ in. thick, and several ⅛-in. machine screws.

Lay out two circles on the ³/₁₆-in. brass, one with a diameter of 3½ in. and the other with a diameter of 2¾ in. The outside circle is the size of the

finished brass wheel, while the inside circle indicates the depth to which the slots are to be cut. Mark the point where a hole is to be drilled for the shaft and locate the drill holes, as shown at *A, Figure 1.* After the shaft hole and the holes *A* are drilled in the disk, it can be used as template for drilling the side plates *C.*

The rim of the disk is divided into 53 equal parts and radial lines drawn from rim to line *B,* indicating the depth of the slots. Slots are cut in the disk with a hacksaw on the radial lines. A small vise is convenient for holding the disk while cutting the slots.

When cutting the disk out of the rough brass, sufficient margin should be left for filing to the true line. The slots should be left in their rough state as they have a better hold on the pens that are used for the blades. The pens are inserted in the slots and made quite secure by forcing ordinary pins on the inside of the pens and breaking them off at the rim, as shown in *Figure 4.*

Once the pens are all fastened, two pieces of metal are provided, each about 1 in. in diameter and $1/32$ in. thick, with a $3/8$-in. hole in the center. These are used for filling pieces which are first placed around the shaft hole between the disk and side plates *C, Figure 1.* The side plates are then secured with some of the $1/8$-in. machine screws, using two nuts on each screw. The nuts should be on the side opposite the inlet valves. The shaft hole may also be filed square, a square shaft used, and the ends filed round for the bearings.

The casing for the disk is made of two enameled-iron saucers, *Figure 2.* These are bolted together with a thin piece of fireproof fiber matt between them to make a tight joint. A $3/4$-in. hole is cut near the edge of one of the saucers for the exhaust. If you want to carry the exhaust beyond the casing, a thin pipe can be inserted $1/4$ in. into the hole. Holes are drilled through the pipe on both inside and outside of the casing, and pins inserted, as shown in *Figure 5.* Solder is run around the outside pin to keep the steam from escaping. A $1/8$-in. hole is drilled at the lowest point of the saucer or casing to run off the water. A wood plug will answer for a stopcock.

If metal dishes—shaped from thick material with a good coating of tin—can be procured, it will be much easier to construct the casing than if enameled ware is used. The holes can be easily drilled and the parts fitted together closely. All seams and surfaces around fittings can be soldered.

Nozzles are made of two stopcocks with $1/8$-in. holes. These are connected to a $3/8$-in. supply pipe. The nozzles should be set at an angle of 20 deg. with the face of the disk. The nozzle or stopcock will give better results if the discharge end is filed parallel to the face of the disk when at an angle of 20 deg. There should be a space of $1/16$ in. between the nozzle and the blades to allow for sufficient play, *Figure 3.*

The bearings are made of $1/4$-in. brass and bolted to the casing with $1/8$-in. machine screws and nuts, as shown. Two nuts should be placed on each screw. The pulley is made by

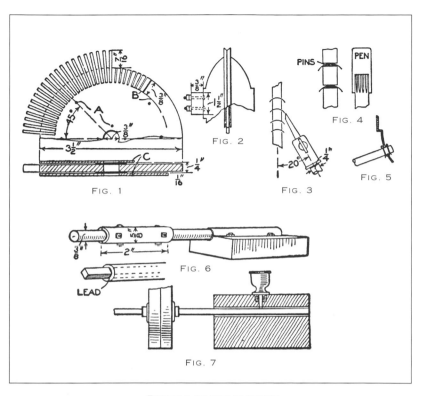

DETAILS OF THE TURBINE.

sliding a piece of steel pipe on the engine shaft and fastening it with machine screws and nuts as shown in *Figure 6*. If the shaft is square, solder should be run into the segments.

The driven shaft should have a long bearing. The pulley on this shaft is made of pieces of wood nailed together, and its circumference cut out with a scroll saw. Flanges are screwed to the pulley and fastened to the shaft as shown in *Figure 7*.

The bearings are made of oak blocks lined with heavy tin or sheet iron for the running surface. Motion is transmitted from the engine to the large pulley by a thin but very good leather belt.

— FORMULA FOR TOTAL HEAT OF SATURATED STEAM —

Values of the total heat of saturated steam, as given in the new steam tables of Marks and Davis, agree closely with the following formula derived from the tabular figures by Robert H. Smith:

$$H = 1826 + t - [1,250,000 / (1620 - t)]$$

in which H is the total heat above 32° F. in British thermal units (BTU), and t is the temperature in Fahrenheit degrees. Between 70° and 500° F the difference between the figures of the table and those computed by the formula does not exceed 0.9 BTU. Between 100° and 450° the difference does not exceed 0.4 BTU.

— A HOMEMADE WATER MOTOR —

In these days of modern improvements, most houses are equipped with a washing machine. The question that arises in the mind of the householder is how to furnish the power to run it economically. One homeowner built a motor that proved so very satisfactory that he has described it here.

A motor of this type will develop about ½ hp. with a water pressure of 70 lb. The power developed is correspondingly increased or decreased as the pressure exceeds or falls below this. In the latter case, the power may be increased by using a smaller pulley. *Figure 1* is the motor with one side removed, showing the paddlewheel in position. *Figure 2* is

an end view. *Figure 3* shows one of the paddles, and *Figure 4* shows the method of shaping the paddles. Several lengths of scantling, 3 in. wide by 1 in. thick (preferably of hard wood), are required to make the frame. Cut two of them 4 ft. long, to form the main supports of the frame, *AA, Figure 1*. Cut another 2 ft. 6 in. long, for the top, *B, Figure 1* and another, 26 in. long, to form the slanting part, *C, Figure 1*. Cut one, *D*, approximately 1 ft., according to the slant given at *C*. After nailing these together as shown in the illustration, nail two short strips on each side of the outlet, as at *E*, to keep the frame from spreading.

Cut two pieces 30 in. long. Lay these on the sides of the frame with

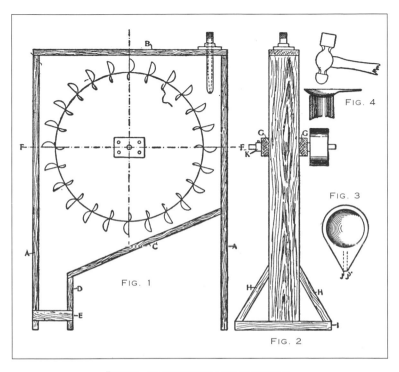

FIG. 4

FIG. 3

FIG. 1

FIG. 2

DETAIL OF HOMEMADE WATERWHEEL.

their centerlines along the line *FF,* which is 15 in. from the outside top of the frame. They are shown in *Figure 2* at *GG*. Do not fasten these boards now, but mark their position on the frame. Two short boards, 1 in. wide by 1 in. thick (*HH, Figure 2*), and another 1 in. by 1½ in. (*I, Figure 2*), form a substantial base.

Cut the wheel from sheet iron 1/16 in. thick, 24 in. in diameter. This can be done roughly with hammer and chisel and then smoothed up on an emery wheel. Then cut 24 radial slots ¾ in. deep on its circumference using a hacksaw. On each side of the wheel at the center fasten a rectangular piece of ½-in. iron 3 x 4 in., and secure it to the wheel by means of four rivets. Next, drill a ⅝ in. hole through the exact center of the wheel.

Cut 24 pieces of $1/32$-in. iron, 1½ x 2½ in. These are the paddles. Shape them by placing one end over a section of 1-in. pipe, and hammer bowl shapes with the peen of a hammer, as shown in *Figure 4*. Then cut them into the shape shown in *Figure 3* and bend the tapered end in along the lines *JJ*. Place them in the slots of the wheel and bend the sides over to clamp the wheel. Drill ⅛-in. holes through the wheel and sides of the paddles and rivet the paddles in place. Next, secure a ⅝-in. steel shaft 12 in. long to the wheel about 8 in. from one end by means of a key. This is done by cutting a groove in the shaft and a corresponding groove in the wheel, and fitting in a piece of metal in order to secure the wheel from turning independently of the shaft. Procure two collars or round pieces of brass (*KK, Figure 2*) with a ⅝-in. hole through them, and fasten these to the shaft by means of setscrews to prevent it from moving lengthwise.

Make the nozzle by filling a piece of ½-in. galvanized pipe 3½ in. long with Babbitt metal. Then drill a $3/16$-in. hole through its center. Make this hole conical, tapering from $3/16$ in. to a full ½ in. This is best done by using a square taper reamer. Then place the nozzle in the position shown in *Figure 1*, which allows the stream of water to strike the buckets full in the center when they reach the position farthest to the right. Take the side pieces, *G* and *G*, and drill a 1-in. hole through their sides centrally, and a ¼ -in. hole from the tops to the 1-in. holes. Fasten them in their proper position, with the wheel and shaft in place, the shaft projecting through the holes just mentioned. Now block the wheel. That is, fasten it by means of wedges or blocks of wood until the shaft is exactly in the center of the inch holes in the side pieces. Cut four disks of cardboard to slip over the shaft and large enough to cover the inch holes. Two of these are to be inside and two outside of the frames (one to bear against each side of each crosspiece). Fasten these to the crosspieces by means of tacks to hold them securely. Pour melted Babbitt metal into the ¼-in. hole to form the bearings. When it has cooled, remove the cardboard, take down the crosspieces, and drill a ⅛-in. hole from the top of the crosspieces through the Babbitt for an oil-hole.

Secure sufficient sheet zinc to cover the sides of the frame. Cut the zinc to the same shape as the frame and let it extend down to the crosspieces *EE*. Tack one side on. (It is wise to tack strips of heavy cloth—burlap will do—along the edges under the zinc to form a watertight joint.) Fasten the crosspiece over the zinc in its proper position. Drill a hole through the zinc, using the hole in the crosspiece as a guide. Then put the wheel in a central position in the frame, tack the other side piece of zinc in place and put the other crosspiece in place. Place the two collars mentioned before on the shaft and fasten so as to bear against the crosspieces in order to prevent the wheel and shaft from moving sidewise. If the bearings are now oiled, the shaft should turn easily and smoothly. Fasten a pulley 4 or 6 in. in diameter to the longest arm of the shaft.

Connect the nozzle to a water faucet by means of a piece of hose. Place the outlet over a drain, and belt the motor direct to the washing-machine, sewing machine, ice-cream freezer, drill press, dynamo or any other machinery requiring not more than ½ hp.

This motor has been in use for two years in all of the above ways, and has never once failed to give perfect satisfaction. It is obvious that, had the wheel and paddles been made of brass, it would be more durable, but as it would have cost several times as much, it is a question whether it would be more economical in the end. If sheet-iron is used, a coat of heavy paint would prevent rust and therefore prolong the life of the motor.

— How to Make a Steam Calliope —

A steam calliope can be a very interesting project for the young scientist looking to explore the science of hydrodynamics and of sound. The instructions for this device are as follows:

Secure ten gas jet valves, the part of the gas fixture shown in *Figure 1,* and prepare to place them in a piece of 1-in. pipe, 12 in.

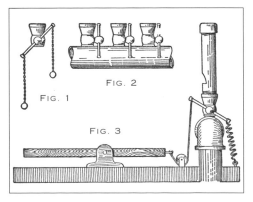

DETAILS OF THE CALLIOPE.

long. This is done by drilling and tapping 10 holes, each 1 in. apart, in a straight line along the pipe. The valves screwed into these holes appear as shown in *Figure 2*. The whistles are made from pipe of a diameter that will fit the valves. No dimensions can be given for the exact lengths of these pipes because they must be tried out to get the tone. Cut ten pieces of this pipe, each one of a different length, similar to the pipes on a pipe organ. Cut a thread on both ends, put a cap on the end intended for the top, and fit a plug in the other end. The plug must have a small portion of its side filed out, and a notch cut in the side of the pipe with its horizontal edge level with the top of the plug. This

part of each whistle is made similar to making a bark whistle on a green stick of willow. The pipes are then screwed into the valves.

The whistles may be toned by trying out and cutting off pieces of the pipe, or by filling the top end with a little melted solder. The 1-in. pipe must be equipped with a cap screwed on one end and the other attached to a steam pipe. The steam may be supplied by using an old range boiler, placed horizontally in a fireplace made of brick or sheet iron. If such a boiler is used, a small safety valve should be attached. The keys and valve operation are shown in *Figure 3*. This is so plainly illustrated that it needs no explanation.

— A SMALL HYDRAULIC TURBINE —

Considerable power and speed can be developed under ordinary water-supply pressure by the turbine, or water motor, shown in the sketch and detailed in the working drawings. The parts are of simple construction and the machine may be assembled or taken down easily. It is useful for either a belt or direct connection to electrical generators,

VIEW OF THE WATER TURBINE WITH THE COVER PLATE REMOVED, SHOWING INLET AND DRAIN.

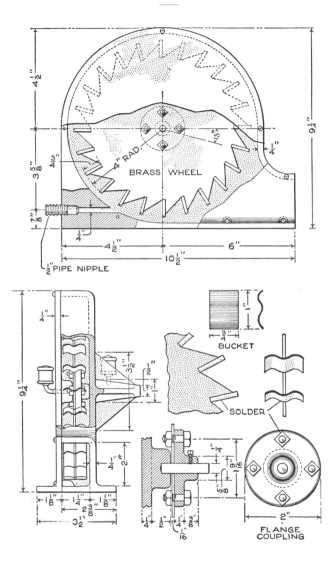

DETAILS OF A WATER TURBINE THAT WILL GIVE CONSIDERABLE POWER
AND SPEED FOR DRIVING A GENERATOR OR SMALL MACHINE.

small machines, etc. Direct connection is preferable for a generator. The wheel is built up of sheet metal and provided with curved buckets set in the saw-tooth edge. The water is admitted through an opening in the lower part of the housing and passes out at the opposite end into a suitable drainpipe. The housing is made of two sections, the main casting and a cover plate. Bearings for the shaft are cast into the housing, which is reinforced on the back by ribs radiating from the center.

Wooden patterns are made for the housing, the main casting and the cover plate being cast separately. The pattern for the cover plate should provide for the bearing lug, as shown in the sectional detail, and for the angle forming a support at the bottom. Special attention should be given to allowance for proper draft in making the pattern for the main casting. That is, the edges of the reinforcing ribs and the sides of the shell should be tapered slightly to make removal from the sand convenient. The advice of a patternmaker will be helpful to one inexperienced in this work although, many machine metalworkers are familiar with the process.

The finishing, machining, and assembling of the parts should be undertaken as follows: Clean the casting and file off rough parts. Smooth the cover plate and the shell to a close fit, and drill and tap the fastening holes for 8-32 machine screws. Drill ¼-in. holes for the bearings, through the bearing arm and ¼ in. into the lug on the cover plate. Drill and tap the two grease-cup holes for ⅛-in. pipe thread. Drill the nozzle hole ¼-in., and drill and tap it for a ½-in. pipe nipple.

Lay out the wheel of $1/16$-in. brass, making 24 notches in its edge. Fasten the wheel to the ¼-in. shaft with a flanged coupling, fixing it with a setscrew. Bolt the flange to the wheel with 8-32 steel bolts. Make the buckets of $1/32$-in. sheet brass, curved as detailed, and round off the edges. Solder them into place, using plenty of solder and making certain that the curve is set properly. Place drops of solder on the flange nuts to secure them. Place the ends of the shaft on two knife-edges, and balance the wheel by adding drops of solder to the lighter side. This is very important, as undue vibration from lack of balance will wear the bearings quickly.

Next, assemble the machine. Do this by using shellac between the cover plate and shell. Connect the turbine to the water supply with a ½-in. pipe. Bolt the machine down, and do not let it run at full speed without load.

— How to Make a Rotary Pump —

A simple rotary pump is constructed on the principle of creating a vacuum in a rubber tube and so causing water to rise to fill the vacuum. *Figs. 3, 4,* and *5* show all the parts needed, except for the crank and tubing. The dimensions and description given are for a minimum pump, but a larger one could be built in proportion.

Saw a circular opening 2⅞ in. in diameter through the center of a block of wood 4 in. square and ⅞ in. thick (*A, Figs. 1, 2* and *3*). On each side of this block cut a larger circle 3¼ in. in diameter, having the same center as the first circle (*Figure 3*). Cut

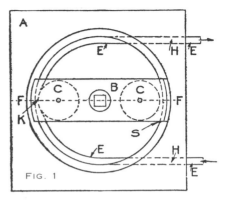

FIG. 1

PLAN OF PUMP. SIDES REMOVED

the last circles only ¼ in. deep, leaving the first circle in the form of a ridge or track ⅜ in. wide, against which the

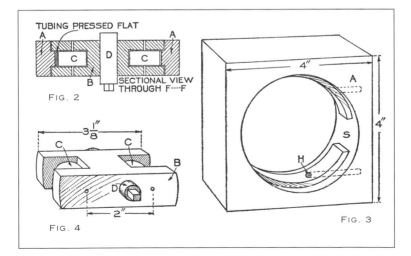

TUBING PRESSED FLAT

SECTIONAL VIEW THROUGH F----F

FIG. 2

FIG. 4

FIG. 3

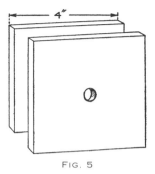

FIG. 5

rubber tubing, *E,* is compressed by wheels. Bore two ¼ in. holes (*HH, Figure 1*) from the outside of the block to the edge of the inner circle. Put the rubber tube, *E,* through one of these holes, pass it around the track and out through the other hole. Notice the break (*S*) in the track; this is necessary to place in position the piece holding the wheels.

Figure 4 shows the wheel-holder, *B.* Make it of hard wood 3⅛ in. long, 1 in. wide and a little less than ⅞ in. thick, so that it will run freely between the sides (*Figure 5*) when they are placed. Cut two grooves, one in each end, 1 in. deep and ½ in. wide. In these grooves place wheels, *CC,* to turn on pins of stout wire. These wheels should be ¾ in. in diameter. When placed in the holder their centers must be exactly 2 in. apart, or so arranged that the distance between the edge of the wheels and

the track (*K, Figure 1*) is equal to the thickness of the tubing when pressed flat. If the wheels fit too tightly, they will bind; if too loose, they will let the air through. Bore a hole through the middle of the wheel-holder and insert the crankpin, *D,* which should be about ½ in. in diameter. The crankpin should fit tightly. If necessary drive a brad through to keep it from slipping.

In the sides (*Figure 5*) bore a hole in the center of the crankpin to run in loosely. Now put all these parts together, as shown in the illustration. Do not fasten the sides too securely until you have tried the device and are sure it will run smoothly. For the crank, a bent piece of stout wire or a nail will serve, though a small iron wheel is better, because it gives steadiness to the motion. In this case, a handle must be attached to the rim

THE ASSEMBLED PUMP.

of the wheel to serve as a crank. The drive wheel from a broken-down eggbeater will do nicely. For ease in handling the pump, a platform should be added.

To use the pump, fill the tube with water and place the lower end of the tube in a reservoir of water. Make a nozzle of the end of a clay pipe stem for the other end of the tube. Then turn the crank from left to right. The first wheel presses the air out of the tube, creating a vacuum that is immediately filled with water. Before the first wheel releases the tube at the top, the other wheel is at the bottom, this time pressing along the water that was brought up by the first wheel. If the motion of the wheels is regular, the pump will give a steady stream. Two feet of ¼-in. tubing is all the expense necessary.

Vacuum Power

— The Fundamentals of a Vacuum

By now you've proven that air is all around us and that it exerts constant pressure. But we can create an area without air—and with subsequently much lower pressure—that we call a "vacuum." Several easy experiments can show us the properties of a vacuum. The first is the experiment of the egg and the bottle.

Procure a glass bottle with an opening just slightly smaller than the egg you'll use for this experiment. The egg should be hard-boiled and peeled. Now have an adult place a small piece of burning paper in the bottle, and wedge the egg in the bottle's opening. Suddenly, the egg will pop through the opening and into the bottle. The egg is simply responding to the vacuum beneath. As the fire burns the oxygen and gases in the bottle, it begins to create a vacuum. The outside air pressure pushing on the egg is much greater than the pressure of the vacuum, and it actually pushes the egg through the tiny opening.

This is actually a case of the negative pressure of a vacuum creating suction. See this in action by taking two drinking glasses or steel cups of exactly the same size. Cut a sponge or several thicknesses of paper towels in a ring that fits exactly around the rim of the cups. Wet the ring, and place it on one cup. Have an adult light a piece of paper on fire and drop it into the cup, then press the rim of the other cup onto the ring. In a minute, you can pick both cups up as if they were glued together.

The burning paper has again created a partial vacuum. The ring creates an airtight seal between the glasses, and so the air pressure outside of the glasses presses them together, against the much weaker pressure from the vacuum inside.

— Experiment with a Vacuum —

Take any kitchen utensil used for frying purposes— an ordinary skillet works best—having a smooth inner bottom surface, and turn in water to the depth of ½ in. Cut a piece of cardboard circular to fit the bottom

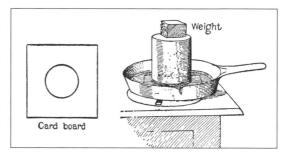

EXPERIMENTAL APPARATUS.

of the skillet and make a hole in the center 4 in. in diameter. The hole will need to correspond to the size of the can used. It should be 1 in. less in diameter than that of the can. Place this cardboard in the bottom of the skillet under the water. A 2-qt. syrup can or pail renders the best demonstration, although good results may be obtained from the use of an ordinary tomato can. The edge of the can must have no indentations, so it will fit perfectly tight all around on the cardboard. Place the can bottom side up and evenly over the hole in the cardboard. Put a sufficient weight on

the can to prevent it moving on the cardboard, but not too heavy, say, 1 lb.

Place the skillet with its adjusted contents upon a heated stove. Soon the inverted can will begin to agitate. When this agitation finally ceases remove the skillet from the stove, being careful not to move the can, and if the quickest results are desired, apply snow, ice or cold water to the surface of the can until the sides begin to flatten. The skillet with its entire contents may now be lifted by taking hold of the can. When the vacuum is complete the sides of the can will suddenly collapse, and sometimes, with a considerable report, jump from the skillet.

The cause of the foregoing phenomenon is that the circular hole in the cardboard admits direct heat from the surface of the skillet. This heat causes the air in the can to expand, which is allowed to escape by agitation. The water and the cardboard act as a valve to prevent its re-entrance. When the enclosed air is expelled by the heat and a vacuum is formed by the cooling, the above results are obtained as described.

— How to Make a Vacuum Pail —

As a substitute for a vacuum bottle, a very efficient pail can be made in the following manner. Procure a 1-gal. syrup pail for the outside and a ½-gal. size for the inside. Make a collar of tin, as shown, with projections. Bend these down, inside and outside. Then solder the collar to the inside of the larger pail, and the smaller pail to the inside of the collar. Be sure to make a perfectly airtight joint in the soldering. This gives a double wall with an airtight space all around the inner pail, or opening. To make vacuum covers for the pails, take two covers of each size and solder them together, as shown.

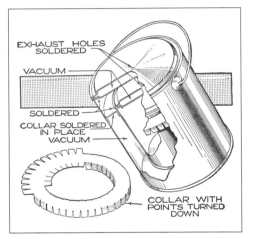

A TWO-WALL PAIL WITH COVERS IN WHICH A PARTIAL VACUUM IS MADE.

To produce a vacuum, make a small hole in the metal forming the collar, and one in each cover. Put a few drops of water in each vacuum compartment and set the parts on a heated surface. When the steam escapes, solder the holes. This will produce a partial vacuum in the space around the inner pail and the covers. This will make a very efficient vacuum pail.

— MAKE COINS STICK TO WOOD —

Take a quarter and place it flat against a vertical surface of wood such as the side of a bookcase, door facing, or door panel, and strike it hard with a downward sliding motion, pressing it against the wood. Take the hand away and the coin will remain on the woodwork. The striking and pressure expel the air between the quarter and the wood, thus forming a vacuum sufficient to hold the coin.

PROPERTIES OF H$_2$O

— THE WONDROUS WORKINGS OF WATER —

Water is truly an unusual substance. It can behave like a gas and like a solid. It is the basis for all life and we can't live long without it—our bodies are actually mostly water. Yet if we were to become entirely made of water, our bodies couldn't hold together. Let's look at a couple of experiments that illustrate properties of how water moves.

For the first experiment, you'll need large bottles with large mouths so that one bottle can be balanced on the other, mouth to mouth. Fill the bottom bottle with hot water and color the water with many drops of food coloring in your favorite color.

Now fill the other bottle with cold water. Cut a large disk of plastic, or laminated cardboard, and place it over the mouth of the bottle containing cold water. Turn the bottle upside down and place it directly on the mouth of the bottle containing the colored hot water. Once the bottles are properly balanced mouth-to-mouth, slide out the disk.

You notice something unusual. The hotter colored water begins to float up into the top bottle, while the cold water takes its place in the bottom bottle. This is because water reacts like most liquids and gases when heated—the molecules move quicker and take up more space, so that hot water is actually less dense and weighs less than cold water. Thus, in the bottles, since the cold water is heavier, it flows down, and the lighter, less dense hot water is forced up.

But another amazing thing about water is its surface tension. Although water seems like a very soft substance, sitting water actually has a "skin" of tension along its surface. To test this out, fill a drinking glass mostly full with water. Then put a small piece of paper towel, with a paper clip sitting on top, gently on the top of the water. As it becomes soaked and heavy, the paper will float to the bottom of the glass. But the surface tension will hold the paper clip on the surface of the water even though, if you dropped the paper clip into the water, you'd see that it's heavy enough to sink to the bottom of the glass.

— An Ice Water Experiment —

An especially interesting fact about heat is that when a material undergoes a change in state, large amounts of heat are required to pull the molecules far enough apart to create the new state—if a solid is changing to a liquid, or a liquid to a gas. On the other hand, large amounts of heat are given off if a gas is changing to a liquid, or if a liquid is changing to a solid, as the molecules push closer together.

This explains why ice is so good for cooling drinks. But to explain that further we need the following definition: The amount of heat required to raise the temperature of one pound of water one degree is a called a British Thermal Unit, or BTU.

If the temperature of a pound of ice is 31 degrees, one degree below the freezing point, one BTU of heat will raise its temperature to 32 degrees.

If you add another BTU, what happens? Instead of the temperature rising higher, part of the ice melts and the water resulting still has a temperature of only 32 degrees. In fact, you must add 144 BTUs (enough to raise the temperature of the same weight of water 144 degrees!) to melt that pound of ice. It took that much heat to push the molecules apart enough to change the state of the material from a solid, ice, to a liquid, water. The pound of melted water still has a temperature of only 32 degrees.

However, adding but one BTU after this change will raise the water temperature to 33 degrees, and so on up to the boiling point of 212 degrees Fahrenheit.

But this now involves another change of state, from water to steam. No matter how much heat is added to water boiling in an open vessel, we cannot make it hotter than 212 degrees. Cooks should remember this and save on the fuel bill. A small flame just high enough to keep the teakettle boiling slightly will keep the water just as hot as high flame that makes the water boil furiously. If you have a suitable thermometer, try it for yourself. The extra heat merely increases the vibration of more particles to the point where they become so far apart they are a gas and they pass off into the air.

But to change that pound of water to steam takes 970 BTUs, five times as much heat as was required to bring the water from the temperature just after the ice melted to the boiling point.

In melting, ice gets the needed heat from its surroundings. It cools your drink by taking heat from the water. You might find it interesting to put equal amounts of room-temperature water in two pans, then drop a pound of ice in one pan and a pound of ice water in the other. With a thermometer you readily will see that the ice cools the water in its pan much more than the ice water does in the other. Of course the reason is obvious. In melting, the pound of ice drew 144 BTUs of heat from the water before it became ice water. It then, as ice water, continued to absorb heat until all the water in the pan reached the same temperature.

— PECULIAR PROPERTIES OF ICE —

Of all the boys who make snow-balls, probably few know what occurs during the process. Under ordinary conditions water turns to ice when the temperature falls to 32°. But when in motion, or under pressure, much lower temperatures are required to make it a solid. In the same way, ice that is somewhat below the freezing point can be made liquid by applying pressure, and will remain liquid until the pressure is removed, when it will again return to its original state. Snow, being simply finely divided ice, becomes liquid in places when compressed by the hands. When the pressure is removed the liquid portions solidify and unite all the particles in one mass. In extremely cold weather it is almost impossible to make a snow-ball, because a greater amount of pressure is then required to make the snow liquid.

This process of melting and freezing under different pressures and a constant temperature is well illustrated by the experiment shown

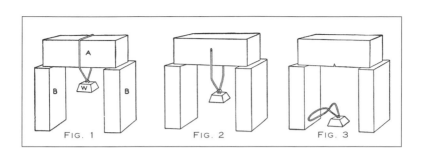

FIG. 1   FIG. 2   FIG. 3

in *Figs. 1, 2* and *3.* A block of ice, *A, Figure 1,* is supported at each end by boxes *BB.* A weight, *W,* is hung on a wire loop that passes around the ice as shown. The pressure of the wire will melt the ice and the wire will sink through the ice as shown in *Figure 2.* The wire will continue to cut its way through the ice until it passes all the way through the piece, as shown in *Figure 3.* This experiment not only illustrates how ice melts under pressure, but also how it solidifies when the pressure is removed, because the block will still be left in one piece after the wire has passed through.

Another peculiar property of ice is its tendency to flow. It may seem strange that ice should flow like water, but the glaciers of Switzerland and other countries are literally rivers of ice. The snow that accumulates on the mountains in vast quantities is turned to ice as a result of the enormous pressure caused by its own weight, and flows through the natural channels it has made in the rock until it reaches the valley below. In flowing through these channels it frequently passes around bends. When two branches come together, the bodies of ice unite the same as water would under the same conditions. The rate of flow is often very slow; sometimes only one or two feet a day. But no matter how slow the motion may be, the large body of ice has to bend in moving.

This property of ice is hard to illustrate with the substance itself, but may be clearly shown by sealing wax, which resembles ice in this respect. Any attempt to bend a piece of cold sealing-wax with the hands results in breaking it, but by placing it between books, as shown above, or supporting it in some similar way, it will gradually change from the original shape *A,* and assume the shape shown at *B.*

— MAKING A FIRE WITH THE AID OF ICE —

BEFORE   AFTER

FORMING THE ICE LENS

Take a piece of very clear ice and melt it down in the hollow of your hands so as to form a large lens. The illustration shows how this is done. With the lens-shaped ice used in the same manner as a reading glass to direct the sun's rays on paper or shavings you can start a fire.

— GOLDFISH TRAVEL FROM BOWL TO BOWL —

An interesting and entertaining experiment, that allows goldfish in one bowl to travel to another, is effected as shown in the drawing. An extra fish bowl is provided, and filled with water to the same height as the one containing the fish. Then a piece of glass tube, of large diameter,

AN ARRANGEMENT THAT PERMITS GOLDFISH IN ONE BOWL TO SWIM TO ANOTHER THROUGH A GLASS TUBE.

is made into an elongated "U," by heating where the bends are to be, and slowly bending. This U-shaped tube, after it has cooled, is filled with water and one end is placed in each bowl. The water will remain in the glass tube, even though it is above the level of the two bowls, so long as the water in both is kept above the ends of the tube.

{ CHAPTER 6 }

THE

PHYSICAL WORLD

AMAZING AUDIO

— THE SCIENCE OF SOUND —

Sound is nothing more than vibrations that disturb the air (that's why there is no sound in a vacuum such as outer space—there's no air to transmit the vibrations). There are many ways to explore how sound is created, and here are a few. The most basic experiment in sound involves a 2 ft. piece of thin waste wood, such as a broken picket and a solid table. Use one hand to hold the one end of the picket on the table and the other to snap the end (like a diving board) of the picket jutting out from the table. You'll hear the vibration, but you'll also be able to feel the vibrations that are creating the sound. Now move the picket further toward the center and out towards the rim. As you move the picket, you'll change the pitch of the vibrations—notice how the sound changes.

Now procure a tuning fork and tap it lightly on the edge of a table. You'll hear the constant note of the tuning fork because the metal is an excellent conductor of vibration and it maintains the same vibration for quite some time. If you tap the tuning fork and hold it lightly (too heavy and the vibration stops) to a finger, you'll feel the frequency of the vibrations, almost as a pulsing. This is how the vibration affects what you hear. The greater the frequency of the vibrations, the higher the pitch or note of the sound.

You can do other experiments with the transfer of sound vibrations, such as holding the tuning fork to a glass. The glass conducts the vibrations and changes the pitch or frequency of the vibration's "waves." Now add water to the glass and repeat the experiment—you'll notice the frequency has changed because your conductor is denser. Make up your own sound experiments by using many different liquids and solids in the glass and determining how those materials affect sound vibrations.

— Transmitting Sound —

If you hold a filled hot water bottle or a balloon filled with water against your ear, and hold a watch against the other side of the water bottle or balloon, you will hear how much better water carries the sound of the ticking than does the air.

Here is an even simpler experiment. You know the bones in your head are denser than the air that surrounds your head, or the flesh that covers the bone. From the above, you could expect that sound would travel through your cheeks better than through air, but better through your head bones than through your cheeks, because the particles in the bones are closer together.

Hold a pencil as if you were about to put one end in your mouth. Scratch the other end of the pencil, and note how loud the scratching sound is. Now close your lips over the end of the pencil and scratch the other end, but do not let your teeth touch the pencil. You will notice that the sound (now passing through your lips and cheeks to your ear, in addition to through the air) is somewhat louder. Now clamp your teeth tightly on the end of the pencil, pull your lips away, and scratch again. The sound is much louder! It now is passing through your teeth into the bone of your skull and then to your ears. To remind yourself how great the difference is, clamp the pencil in your teeth, then pull it out until it touches neither lips nor teeth, and keep on scratching the other end of the pencil all the while. When the pencil is out of your mouth, you are listening to sound through air. When your teeth are clamped on the pencil, you are listening to the same sound through bone, which is a good conductor of sound.

— A Telephone Experiment

If the small apparatus, as shown in the accompanying sketch, is attached to the underside of an ordinary dining table, it will, if connected to a telephone circuit, set the table in vibration, so that any number of people who put their ears flat upon the table will hear the voice of a person speaking from a distance, apparently coming out of the table.

A small piece of wood, *A, Figure 1,* is cut about 5 in. square, to the center of which is attached a small piece of soft iron wire, such as used for cores of induction coils, about 4 in. long and bent in the form of a hook at the lower end, as shown at *B.* This wire is attached to the block of wood, *A,* as shown in *Figure 2.* The end of the wire is soldered to a small brass plate that is set in the block so it will be level or flush with the top of the block, and then fastened with two screws. A small coil, *C,* is made

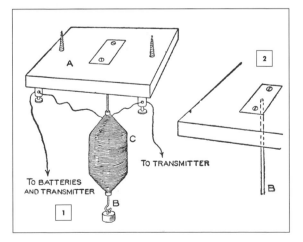

MECHANICAL TABLE TALK.

by winding No. 24 silk-or cotton-covered wire around a small tube, either a piece of glass, a short straw, or a quill. The coil is made tapering as shown without using wood ends. This coil is slipped over the wire *B* previous to soldering it to the small brass plate. The ends of the coil are connected to the two binding-posts that are fastened to the block *A*. A small lead weight weighing 2 or 3 oz. is hung on the hook made in the lower end of the wire *B*.

When all connections are made, as shown in *Figure 1*, and the block fastened to the underside of the table, the apparatus is ready for use and has only to be connected to an ordinary telephone transmitter and batteries as shown. The apparatus will work to a certain extent even if the weight is removed, though not as clear.

THE VISIBLE WORLD

— HOW LIGHT WAVES TRAVEL —

If you tie one end of a rope to a post and shake the other end, you see transverse waves (like light waves) move down the rope. No part of the rope itself moves to the other end— only the waves move. You can shake the rope in any direction and set up waves that vibrate in all directions at right angles to the rope.

Similarly, light coming to us directly from the sun or from a lamp vibrates in all directions at right angles to the direction of the ray.

But back to the rope: if you pass your rope through an up-and-down slit of some kind, and vibrate the rope in all directions, the slit stops sideways vibrations and will pass only up-and-down vibrations in the rope. The rope waves on the far side of the slit represent polarized light. Polarized light vibrates in one plane only. Light can be polarized by certain natural crystals. They act as the slit did on your rope. In glass that will polarize light, a thin film of synthetic crystals of this type is embedded in the glass. The crystals form a series of fine lines close together.

Back to your rope again: If you use two up-and-down slits, some distance apart, the first slit will pass only up-and-down vibrations and the second slit will pass them too. But if you turn the second slit sideways, this slit stops the up-and-down vibrations passed by the first slit. Beyond the second slit there is not vibration at all.

— How the Eye Works with Light —

If we understood everything there is to know about light before it strikes the eye, we still would not know everything about "seeing." As in the case of sound waves in the ear and the brain, "seeing" is a matter of light waves that originate "outside," being received by the eye, and interpreted by the brain as a sensation of seeing. Just how the brain gives us the sensation is something we know practically nothing about as yet. Indeed, we do not understand everything about the eye itself, but we know enough to realize what a marvelous instrument it is.

Light enters the eye and forms an inverted image against the back wall. Fortunately, the brain, in interpreting through the nerve fibers the signals from this wall, or sensitive screen, turns the image right-side-up. If we "saw" things as they actually appear inside the eye, everything would look upside down unless you walked around on your head.

You can duplicate the inverted image very easily. Paste narrow strips of tape or black paper to form a "T" on the side of the light bulb in a standing lamp around the house. Make a small hole in a piece of paper with the point of a pin. Hold the paper so light shining through hole will fall on another piece of white paper a short distance away. You will see an image of the bulb and the "T" on the second piece of paper, but the "T" will be upside down.

Light travels in straight lines. Light from the top of the bulb travels straight through the small hole in your paper and hits the second sheet of paper to form the bottom of the image. Light from the bottom of the bulb passes through the hole to the top of your image. So the image is upside down.

— The Coin-in-the-Cup Experiment —

One of the oldest parlor tricks in the world is the coin-and-cup-of-water trick. Place a coin in the bottom of a cup and step back until the rim of the cup just hides the coin from sight. Keep your eye in the same place and pour water in the cup. The coin magically will appear.

Ptolemy, the Greco-Egyptian astronomer, one of many who did believe that light rays travel toward the eye, figured out the coin trick nearly 1,800 years ago by deducing that light bends in passing from water into air.

Anything you can see either is a source of light itself (like a lamp) or reflects light from some source. Light itself is invisible unless one looks toward the source, or sees it reflected. You see a beam of sunlight cutting a sharp path in a dark room (or the beam of light from a movie projector in a theater) only because the light is reflected by particles of dust in the air. If the beam were passing through nothing, you could not see it. That is why space is black. Even in high-flying rocket-powered airplanes, pilots look up into a black sky (the absence of visible light) instead of a blue one (caused at lower altitudes by light reflected from particles in the air).

Thus we see the coin in the bottom of the empty cup, when we look straight down, because the coin is reflecting light from the sun or a lamp into our eyes. The rays travel in a straight line. Therefore we cannot see the coin when we move our eyes a certain distance to one side.

However, when the cup is filled with water, the rays reflected in a straight line through water from the coin to the rim of the cup now bend downward and enter our eyes, traveling, of course, in a straight line from the surface of the water to our eyes. Since the bent rays of light now enter our eyes, we see the coin as easily as if we had bent the rays by holding a mirror over the cup and reflected the rays into our eyes. You should try this for yourself.

— THE PRINCIPLES OF THE STEREOGRAPH —

Each of our eyes sees a different picture of any object; the one sees a trifle more to the right-hand side, the other to the left, especially when the object is near to the observer. The stereoscope is the instrument that effects this result by bringing the two pictures together in the senses. The stereograph produces this result in another way than by prisms as in the stereoscope. In the first place there is only one picture, not two mounted side by side. The stereograph consists of a piece of card, having therein two circular openings about 1¼ in. diameter, at a distance apart corresponding to the distance between the centers of the pupils. The openings are covered with transparent gelatin, the one for the left eye being blue, that for the right, orange. The picture is viewed at a distance of about 7 in. from the stereograph. As a result of looking at it through the stereograph, one sees a colorless black and white picture that stands out from the background. Try looking at the front cover of *Popular Mechanics* through these colored gelatin openings and the effect will be produced.

If one looks at the picture first with the right eye alone through the orange glass, and then with the left eye through the blue glass, one will understand the principle on which the little instrument works. Looking through the blue glass with the left eye, one sees only those portions that are red on the picture. But they seem black. The reason is that the red rays are absorbed by the blue filter. Through the orange gelatin, portions of the picture seem orange because of the rays coming from them which contain all the colors of the spectrum; only the orange rays may pass through. The red portions of the picture are not seen, because, although they pass through the screen, they are not seen against the red ground of the picture. It is just as though they were not there. The left eye therefore sees a black picture on a red background.

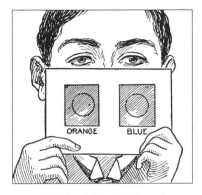

LOOKING THROUGH THE COLORED GELATIN.

In the same way the right eye sees through the orange screen only a black picture on a red background; this black image consisting only of the blue portions of the picture.

Any other part of complementary colors than blue and orange, as for instance red and green, would serve the same purpose.

The principle on which the stereograph works may be demonstrated by a very simple experiment. On white paper one makes a picture or mark with a red pencil. Looking at this through a green glass it appears black on a green ground; looking at it through a red glass of exactly the same color as the picture, it, however, disappears fully.

Through the glass one will see only a regular surface of the color of the glass itself without any picture.

Through a red glass, a green picture will appear black.

So with the stereograph, each eye sees a black picture representing one of the pictures given by the stereoscope; the only difference being that in the case of the stereograph, the background for each eye is colored while both eyes see a white background.

In the pictures the red and the green lines and dots must not coincide; neither can they be very far apart in order to produce the desired result. In order that the picture shall be "plastic," which increases the sense of depth and shows the effect of distance in the picture, they must be only a short distance apart. The arrangement of the two pictures can be so that one sees the pictures either in front of or on the back of the card on which they are printed. In order to make them appear before the card, the left eye sees through a blue screen, but the red picture which is seen by it is a black one, and lies to the right on the picture. The right eye sees the left-hand picture. The further apart the pictures are, the further from the card will the composite image appear.

In the manufacture of a stereoscope the difficulty is in the proper arrangement of the prisms; however, with the stereograph, in the proper choice of colors.

— HOW TO MAKE A HELIOGRAPH —

The heliograph, which is used in the army, provides a good method of sending messages by the reflection of the sun's rays. In the mountains there are stations from which messages are sent by the heliograph for great distances, and guides carry them for use in case of trouble or accident. The wireless telegraph delivers messages by electricity through the air, but the heliograph sends them by flashes of light.

The main part of the instrument is the mirror, which should be about 1 in. square, set in a wood frame, and swung on trunnions made of two square-head bolts, each ¼ in. in diameter and 1 in. long, which are firmly held to the frame with brass strips, ½-in wide, and 3 in. long. The strips are drilled centrally to admit the bolts, and then drilled at each end for a screw to fasten them to the frame. This construction is clearly shown in *Figure 1*.

A hole is cut centrally through the backing of the frame, and a small hole, not over ⅛ in. in diameter, is

THE HELIOGRAPH AS IT IS USED BY NEIGHBORING BOYS TO SEND MESSAGES ON A CLEAR DAY BY FLASHING THE SUN'S RAYS FROM ONE TO THE OTHER. THEY CAN BE READ AS FAR AS THE EYE CAN SEE THE LIGHT.

scratched through the silvering on the glass. If the trunnions are centered properly, the small hole should be exactly in line with them and in the center.

A U-shaped support is made of wood strips, ⅜ in. thick and 1 in. wide, the length of the uprights being 3 ½ in. and the crosspiece connecting their lower ends a trifle longer than the width of the frame. These are put together, as shown in *Figure 2*, with small brackets at the corners. A slot, 1½ in-deep and ¼ in. wide, is cut into the upper end of each upright to receive the trunnions on the mirror frame. Nuts are turned on the bolt

ends tightly to clamp the standard tops against the brass strips on the mirror frame. The cross strip at the bottom is clamped to the base by means of a bolt, 1½ in. long. The hole for this bolt should be exactly below the peephole in the mirror and run through one end of the baseboard, which is ¾ in. thick, 2 in. wide, and 10 in. long.

At the opposite end of the base, place a sighting rod, which is made as follows: The rod is ½ in. in diameter and 8 in. long. The upper end is fitted with a piece of thick, white cardboard, cut ¼ in. in diameter and having a projecting shank 1 in. long, as shown in *Figure 3*. The rod is placed in a ½ in. hole bored in the end of the baseboard, as shown in *Figure 2*. To keep the rod from slipping through the hole, a setscrew is made of a small bolt with the nut set in the edge of the baseboard, as shown in *Figure 4*.

The tripod head is formed of a wood disk, 5 in. in diameter, with a hole in the center, and three small blocks of wood, 1 in. square and 2 in. long, nailed to the under side, as shown in *Figure 5*. The tripod legs are made of light strips of wood, ⅜ in. thick, 1 in. wide, and 5 ft. long. Two of these strips, nailed securely together to within 20 in. of the top, constitute one leg. The upper unnailed ends are spread to slip over the blocks on the tripod top. These ends are bored to loosely fit over the headless nails driven part way into the block ends. One tripod leg is shown in *Figure 6*.

The screen, or shutter, is mounted on a separate tripod and is shown in *Figure 7*. Cut out two slats, ⅜ in. thick, 2½ in. wide, and 6 in. long,

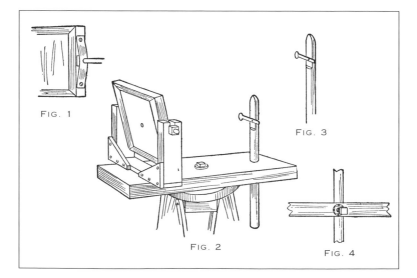

FIG. 1

FIG. 2

FIG. 3

FIG. 4

DETAIL OF THE PARTS FOR MAKING THE MIRROR AND SIGHT ROD, WHICH ARE PLACED ON A BASE SET ON A TRIPOD, TOP, THE WHOLE BEING ADJUSTED TO REFLECT THE SUN'S RAYS IN ANY DIRECTION DESIRED.

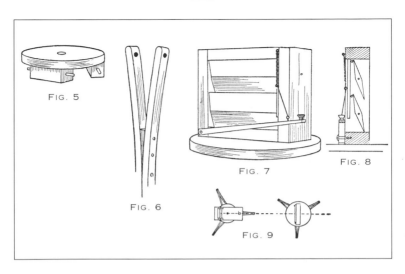

FIG. 5

FIG. 6

FIG. 7

FIG. 8

FIG. 9

THE PARTS IN DETAIL FOR MAKING THE TRIPODS AND THE SHUTTER
FOR FLASHING THE LIGHT. AND THE DIAGRAM SHOWING THE
LOCATION OF THE TRIPODS TO DIRECT THE LIGHT
THROUGH THE SHUTTER.

from hard wood, and taper both edges of these slats down to ³/₁₀ in. Small nails are driven into the ends of the slats, and the heads are filed off so that the projecting ends will form trunnions for the slats to turn on. Make a frame of wood pieces, ¾ in. thick and 2½ in wide, the opening in the frame being 6 in. square. Before nailing the frame together, bore holes in the side uprights for the trunnions of the slats to turn in. These holes are 1¾ in. apart. Then nail the frame together, and also nail it to the tripod top. The shutter is operated with a

key very similar to a telegraph key. The construction of this key is shown in *Figure 7*. A part of a spool is fastened to a stick that is pivoted on the opposite side of the frame. The key is connected to the slats in the frame with a bar and rod to which a coil spring is attached, as shown in *Figure 8. Figure 9* shows the positions of the tripods when the instrument is set to flash the sunlight through the shutter. The regular telegraph code is used in flashing the light.

To set the instrument, first turn the cardboard disk down to uncover the point of the sight rod. Then sight through the hole in the mirror and adjust the sight rod so that the tip end comes squarely in line with the receiving station. When the instrument is properly sighted, the shutter is set up directly in front of it, and the cardboard disk is turned up to cover the end of the sight rod. The mirror is then turned so that it reflects a beam of light with a small shadow spot showing in the center made by the peephole in the mirror, which is directed to fall on the center of the cardboard sighting disk. It will be quite easy to direct this shadow spot to the disk by holding a sheet of paper 6 or 8 in. in front of the mirror and following the spot on the paper until it reaches the disk. The flashes are made by manipulating the key operating the shutter in the same manner as a telegraph key.

— How to Find the Blind Spot in the Eye —

Make a small black circular dot ½ in. in diameter on a piece of cardboard, and about 3 in. from the center of this dot draw a star. Hold the cardboard so that the star will be directly in front of one eye, while the dot will be in front of the other. If the star is in front of the left eye, close the right eye and look steadily at the star while you move the cardboard until the point is reached where the dot disappears. This will prove the presence of a blind spot in a person's eye. The other eye can be given the same experiment by turning the cardboard end for end. The blind spot does not indicate diseased eyes, but it simply marks the point where the optic nerve enters the eyeball, which point is not provided with the necessary visual end organs of the sight, known as rods and cones.

— Optical Projection —

The earliest notice of the optical lantern is found in the writings of a Jesuit named Kircher, who resided in Rome in the seventeenth century. Kircher made a lantern of a large wooden box with an opening in the side for the lens, and with this he produced ghostly and shadowy forms, to the awe and amazement of his spectators, who were totally unable to perceive how the apparitions came about. Some authorities ascribe to this Jesuit the honor of the invention; others are inclined to believe that he rediscovered an old invention that dates back to the writings of one Cellini, a Florentine engraver, who flourished in the sixteenth century. Be this as it may, Kircher's writings form the first record of the existence of a "magic" lantern, as it was then called, and, indeed, as it is now most generally termed.

The lantern from that time onward gradually became better known and more and more generally used. It is, however, a strange thing that until comparatively recent years it was never looked upon as a scientific instrument, but was merely used as a toy to reproduce comic pictures for the purpose of amusing children. Some sixty years ago, it began to be recognized as of great value for the purpose of instruction, and as the science of photography advanced, so the lantern came more and more into general use, until today no school, college or technical institution can be considered up to date it if be without a lantern.

Although this writing deals with the lantern solely in respect of its purpose and utility to produce still pictures by means of glass slides, I must allude to that amazing development of photography known as "animatography," whereby the lantern is called upon to reproduce on the screen events as they actually occur. Just now we are on the threshold of a boom in this form of entertainment. What are called "electric theaters" are springing up in every district where the population justifies the outlay.

Now, the lantern comprises three essential factors, which we will briefly consider. They are (1) the illuminant, (2) the condenser, (3) the objective.

The Various Illuminants. We will first consider the illuminant, that being the most important factor of the three, for, however optically perfect the condenser and objective may be, they will be useless without the brilliant cooperation of their third partner. The various illuminants may be summarized as follows: Paraffin oil lamps, incandescent spirit lamps, incandescent gas burners, acetylene gas jets, blow-through limelight jets, mixed oxyhydrogen jets (either with both gases under pressure or with oxygen in conjunction with an ether saturator), electric lamps, on the Nernst principle or otherwise, where the current can be taken from an ordinary plug, and eclectic arc lamps, for which the current must be laid on specially to the lecture room.

Up to the comparatively recent years, oil and limelight were the only effective illuminants. In country places where gas and electric light are not available, we still find the Stocks 4-wick petroleum oil lamp in use. It gives an approximate candle power of 130, and illuminates a 6-ft. disc very well, which answers the purpose of a lecturer in a small schoolroom. As an alternative to a petroleum oil lamp, we have the incandescent spirit lamp, an ingenious apparatus that enables us to use the vapor of alcohol to incandesce an ordinary gas mantle. This does not produce a light so powerful as the Stocks lamp, the light so obtained only being equivalent to about 72 candle power.

Then, where gas exists, we find the incandescent gas burners used either with upright or inverted mantels, giving approximately 75 candle power. Acetylene gas, which comes next on the list, produces 128, 188, or 240 candle power with 2, 3, or 4 burners, respectively. This illuminant is very effective and satisfactory when the owner of the apparatus will take the trouble to thoroughly understand it, and also to clean it himself after each occasion of use. If he does not do this, he is sure to have trouble, and the lungs of his audience are inflated sooner or later with acetylene gas— not a pleasant experience.

With limelight we reach a very considerable candle power, ranging from 400 to 2,000, according to the jets employed (a blow-through jet giving you 400 candle power and a mixed jet, with both gases under pressure, giving anything between 700 and 2,000).

With the discussion of electric light we arrive at a progressive point that is still in its early youth. Here we have a great field for inventive skill. By means of electric light we can reach a light intensity of 2,000 candle power on a 200 voltage, each filament taking 1 ampere of current. With arc lamps we can reach yet a greater intensity, these being capable of producing light equivalent to between 1,000 and 5,000 candle power according to the current consumed.

Forms of Condensers. The form of condenser most generally in use in lanterns of the present day is that known as the "Herschel." This comprises a double convex lens next to the slide and a meniscus lens next to the source of light. This condenser is suitable for use with objectives of from 4-in. to 12½-in. equivalent foci. It is not often that one is called upon to operate a lantern in a hall so vast as to require an objective of longer focus than 12½ in.; but, should such occasion arise, then it will be necessary to replace the meniscus lens of the condenser by one of longer focus in order to be able to place the illuminant nearer to the condenser. This is because the longer the focus of the objective, the nearer the illuminant must be placed to the condenser.

Four-inch condensers are chiefly used in England because they are quite large enough to cover the standard English slide, which is 3¼ in. square. In America and in France, a 4½-in. condenser is used, because their slides are made 4 in. by 3¼ in. This is just one instance of the lack of international standardization.

The Objective. The objective is the final essential factor of our lantern. Some progress has certainly been achieved during the last few years, within which such vast improvements have been made in the manufacture of lenses generally. The use of this lens is to bring to a focus and project onto the screen the light that the condenser has caused to pass through the slide. The waves of light on arriving at the objective cross one another, with the result that an enlarged but inverted image of the slide appears on the screen. In the old days, a single convex lens was used, and with that, owing to spherical and chromatic aberration, a very imperfect image resulted, which even a diaphragm failed to improve in a marked degree. About the middle of the eighteenth century it was discovered that a combination of a double convex lens of crown glass with a concave-convex meniscus lens of flint glass solved the problem of chromatic aberration, and the achromatic lens was obtained.

In the modern lantern, the objective consists of a double achromatic combination, the outer, or front lens, being an achromatic plano-convex lens (the crown and flint lenses being cemented together), and the inner, or back, lens being of two separate lenses, one of them equi-convex and the other a meniscus concave lens. This double achromatic combination is mounted in a brass tube that, by means of a rack and pinion, can be moved backward and forward in an outer brass jacket. Comparatively recently, what is known as the "Petzval" system has been largely adopted on lanterns of standard make. This method arranges the objective lens combinations of varying foci in separate tubes, so that any combination can be slipped into the jacket of the objective, thereby giving the lantern operator the choice of any position in the lecture room at any distance from the screen.

— TESTING INCANDESCENT LIGHTS —

A convenient testing outfit is made of a generator, a bell from an old telephone box, and a wooden fork with metal tips. The tips of the fork are far enough apart to rest on the binding-screws of the rosette and are the terminals of the circuit containing the generator and the bells. Upon turning the generator crank while the fork tips are in contact with the rosette binding-screws, the ringing of the bells shows that the lamp and cord being

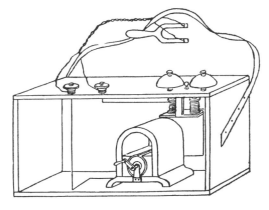

TESTING OUTFIT FOR INCANDESCENT LAMPS.

tested are in good order. Always open the switch or remove one or the other lamps before beginning testing.

RADIATION

— MAKE YOUR OWN CLOUD CHAMBER —

You can make your own cloud chamber quite simply, and in it, observe the tracks made by cosmic rays and other radiation. The simplest kind uses a wide-mouth glass fruit jar with a metal screw top. Cement a cloth pad or a piece of cardboard over the inside surface of the bottom of the jar. Cement a piece of black velvet on the inside of the lid. After the cement is dry, saturate the pad or cardboard with grain or rubbing alcohol and slightly moisten the velvet. Screw the top on the jar to make it airtight, and turn the jar upside down on a cake of dry ice. Cover any dry ice not covered by the metal cap with cloth to prevent vapor from rising around the outside of the jar.

Now project a beam of light through the side of the jar near the bottom. Soon clouds should form two or three inches above the black velvet. Look down on them so that the black velvet forms a background for observation. A miniature rain shower appears and in its midst the tracks of atomic particles appear as fine, silvery streaks lasting only a fraction of a second, then drift away. Tracks made by alpha particles are wider than those made by electrons, and gamma rays make numerous short paths. The particles, which penetrate the glass jar as if it weren't there, come either from cosmic radiation from space or from radioactive materials in your own neighborhood. Such radiation always is penetrating your body, just as it does the jar, although, in such amounts, it is no way harmful.

— RELATIVE ABSORPTION OF HEAT BY COLORS —

An easy method of demonstrating the relative heat-absorbing power of black and white, as well as other colors, is provided in this experiment. Black and white stripes are painted around the outside of an ordinary water tumbler. Small lumps of wax are softened and placed on the painted strips, and

pins are pushed into the wax, as shown in the drawing. A short length of candle is lighted and placed inside the tumbler; after a few minutes, it will be observed that the wax on the black strips begins to soften, and that the pins on these strips fall down on account of the large amount of heat absorbed.

— SIMPLE X-RAY EXPERIMENT —

The outlines of the bones of the hand may be seen by holding a piece of rice paper before the eyes and placing the spare hand about 12 in. behind the rice paper and before a bright light. The bony structure of your hand will be clearly distinguishable to your naked eye.

— Experiment with Heat —

Place a small piece of paper, lighted, in an ordinary water glass. While the paper is burning, turn the glass over and set it into a saucer previously filled with water. The water will rapidly rise in the glass, as shown in the sketch.

Magnetic Ideas

— The Basics of Magnetism in Action —

Most every schoolboy knows what magnetism is, but few could describe this strange phenomenon. Even scientists have a hard time saying precisely what magnetism is. We do know that it is an observable force of attraction created around certain ferrous (or iron-containing) bodies. The earth is one of these. There's a great big magnetic field around our planet, and, like all magnets, earth's magnetic field has a north and south pole. All magnets share this polarization.

You can see this for yourself with two simple bar magnets. To find which is which on your magnets, float the magnet on a piece of cork in water, in a large glass bowl. Use a compass to determine "North" and watch which end of the bar magnet points in that direction. That is the north end of your magnet. Mark that end with tape or a marking pen. Do this for both your bar magnets.

Now you can discover something else about magnetic poles. Try to push the two north poles of your magnets together. What happens? As you'll see, they want to move in the opposite direction. The simple rule for magnets is that "like" poles repel each other and "unalike" poles attract. Every magnet has a north and south pole and will maintain those poles no matter what. You can make a magnet out of a bar or rod of iron by repeatedly stroking it in one direction with your magnet. Once it's magnetized, the bar will have a north and south pole. But here's the really interesting part. Use bolt cutters or a hacksaw to cut the magnetized iron rod in half, and both halves are now magnets with their own north and south poles! Go ahead and test this by trying to put the different ends of the halves together.

— THE OPERATION OF THE COMPASS —

After trying to tell a few small boys what a compass is, they wanted a practical illustration, something they could see. Not having a compass or knowing where to locate one handily, the scientist used a piece of cork with

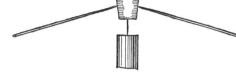

TWO LARGE NEEDLES IN A CORK BALANCED ON A CENTRAL NEEDLE TO MAKE THEM REVOLVE EASILY.

needles and a needle for a pivot and found it very satisfactory. The method used is shown in the sketch.

It is best not to magnetize both needles, unless care is exercised in maintaining pole relationship, or they will oppose each other and not point to the north. The extreme ends or the heads of the needles must be opposites, the head of one should be negative and the head of the other positive.

— DISCOVERING ELECTROMAGNETISM —

There is a special type of magnetism that you can create and control using an electric current. This is called electromagnetism and it has many useful applications. But the first step is to understand how electromagnets are created, and the best way to do that is to make one.

Secure a short piece of iron rod such as that used for welding. It only needs to be 4 or 5 in. long. Now wrap the rod from top to bottom, working in one direction only, with insulated copper wire (you can find this at most home centers or hardware stores). Strip the insulation off of each end of the wire, and connect the ends to the positive and negative terminals of a "D" battery. You'll now notice that your electromagnet attracts ferrous metals. The current flowing through the wire is working with the iron rod (or "core") to create a magnetic field. Just as with other magnets, this field has a north and south pole. You can try an easy experiment by either using a thicker iron rod or more tightly wound coils of wire. You should quickly discover that your electromagnet is more powerful.

— HOMEMADE MARINER'S COMPASS —

Magnetize an ordinary knitting needle, *A*, and push it through a cork, *B*, and place the cork exactly in the middle of the needle. Thrust a pin, *C*, through the cork at right angles to the needle, and stick two sharpened matches in the sides of the cork so that they will project downward as shown. The whole arrangement is balanced on a thimble with balls of wax stuck on the heads of the matches. If the needle is not horizontal, pull it through the cork

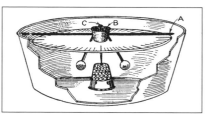

MAGNETIZED NEEDLE
REVOLVING ON A PIN.

to one side or the other, or change the wax balls. The whole device is placed in a glass berry dish and covered with a pane of glass.

— DESIGNING AND BUILDING ELECTROMAGNETS —

You can design and build electromagnets for almost any purpose without becoming involved in the difficulties of complicated mathematics. The information here brings the subject down to a few simple rules that, if followed carefully, will give results that are entirely satisfactory.

However, like any other piece of electrical apparatus in which iron is used, the final performance of an electromagnet will vary slightly from the figured value because it is not possible to look at iron and tell exactly how effective it will be. To make the work as accurate as possible, values for four grades of iron are given.

Direct-Current Magnets. Although the general principles are the same for A.C. or D.C. magnets, we will start with the D.C. types, a number of which are illustrated in *Figure 1*. To illustrate the method of design, we will show how to make a magnetic door latch, *Figures 2* and *3*. In this latch the bolt stroke need only be ¾ in. For long strokes, simple electromagnets are very inefficient. The first thing to do is to get a coil spring to hold the latch closed so that its tension can be tested. In the case illustrated, it was found that a pressure of 25 lbs. was required to compress it ¼ in. Now, as there will be considerable friction in operating the latch, it is advisable to design the magnet so that it will exert a pull of about 50 lbs.

The latch can be forged conveniently from wrought iron so we will make our magnet core and frame from the same material. Consulting *Figure 4* we find from the flag *B*, labeled "wrought iron," that the cross-sectional area of the core is found by dividing the pull required (50 lbs. in

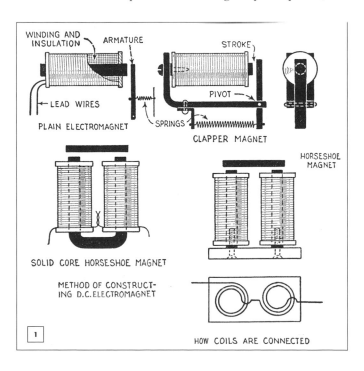

WINDING AND INSULATION ARMATURE STROKE

LEAD WIRES

PLAIN ELECTROMAGNET

PIVOT

SPRINGS

CLAPPER MAGNET

HORSESHOE MAGNET

SOLID CORE HORSESHOE MAGNET

METHOD OF CONSTRUCT-ING D.C. ELECTROMAGNET

1

HOW COILS ARE CONNECTED

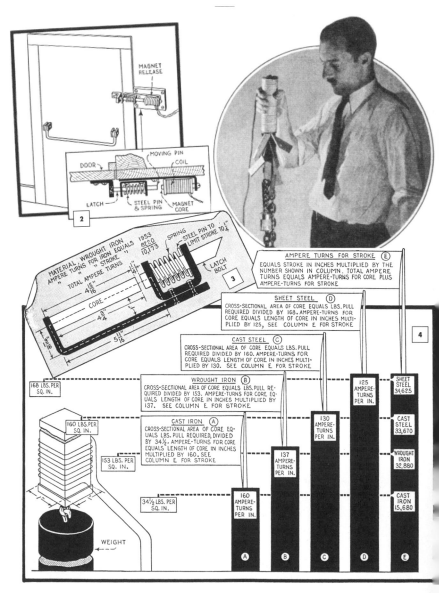

MAGNET RELEASE

DOOR — MOVING PIN — COIL

LATCH — STEEL PIN & SPRING — MAGNET CORE

2

3

MATERIAL WROUGHT IRON AMPERE TURNS FOR IRON EQUALS ""STROKE""
TOTAL AMPERE TURNS
1953 8220 10,173
SPRING STEEL PIN TO LIMIT STROKE TO 1/4"
LATCH BOLT

CORE
4 3/4"
4 5/16"
5 11/16"
9/16"

AMPERE TURNS FOR STROKE (E)
EQUALS STROKE IN INCHES MULTIPLIED BY THE NUMBER SHOWN IN COLUMN. TOTAL AMPERE TURNS EQUALS AMPERE-TURNS FOR CORE, PLUS AMPERE-TURNS FOR STROKE.

SHEET STEEL (D)
CROSS-SECTIONAL AREA OF CORE EQUALS LBS. PULL REQUIRED DIVIDED BY 168. AMPERE-TURNS FOR CORE EQUALS LENGTH OF CORE IN INCHES MULTIPLIED BY 125, SEE COLUMN E FOR STROKE.

4

CAST STEEL (C)
CROSS-SECTIONAL AREA OF CORE EQUALS LBS. PULL REQUIRED DIVIDED BY 160. AMPERE-TURNS FOR CORE EQUALS LENGTH OF CORE IN INCHES MULTIPLIED BY 130. SEE COLUMN E FOR STROKE.

168 LBS. PER SQ. IN.

WROUGHT IRON (B)
CROSS-SECTIONAL AREA OF CORE EQUIRED DIVIDED BY 153. AMPERE-TURNS FOR CORE EQUALS LENGTH OF CORE IN INCHES MULTIPLIED BY 137. SEE COLUMN E FOR STROKE.

125 AMPERE-TURNS PER IN.

SHEET STEEL 34,625

160 LBS. PER SQ. IN.

CAST IRON (A)
CROSS-SECTIONAL AREA OF CORE EQUALS LBS. PULL REQUIRED, DIVIDED BY 34 1/2. AMPERE-TURNS FOR CORE EQUALS LENGTH OF CORE IN INCHES MULTIPLIED BY 160, SEE COLUMN E FOR STROKE.

130 AMPERE-TURNS PER IN.

CAST STEEL 33,670

153 LBS. PER SQ. IN.

137 AMPERE-TURNS PER IN.

WROUGHT IRON 32,880

34 1/2 LBS. PER SQ. IN.

160 AMPERE-TURNS PER IN.

CAST IRON 15,680

WEIGHT

A **B** **C** **D** **E**

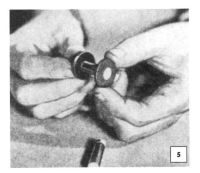

our case) by 153. Performing the division we get .327 sq. in. It is convenient to use iron rod of standard diameter for the core, so we will select a size of rod that has the nearest area over this required value. Accordingly, we will use ¾-in. rod for the core. Next we will again refer to flag *B,* labeled "wrought iron" in *Figure 4,* and figure the number of ampere turns that we will need to give our magnet the strength required. Here we find that the number of ampere turns required to magnetize the iron is found by multiplying the length of the magnet core by 137. Ampere turns is the name for the value found by multiplying the number of amperes flowing through a coil by the number of turns of wire in the coil. A coil, which passes 10 amperes and has 50 turns of wire, has 10 times 50, or 500 ampere turns. Similarly, a coil wound with 250 turns of wire and passing

2 amperes has 2 times 250, or 500 ampere turns. Before applying the formula to ascertain the number of ampere turns required, we will have to assume some reasonable value for the length of the coil and iron parts. A good rule to follow is given in *Figure 6.* Applying this, our coil will be wound to a depth of ¾ in. This means that the outside diameter of the coil will be 2¼ in. Multiplying ¾ in. by 6 gives 4½ in. as the length of the coil. To leave space for insulation, the iron core should be cut to a length of 4¾ in. Referring to the sketch of the magnetic latch shown in *Figure 3,* we can readily add up the total length of the iron core. The length of the dotted lines represents the length we will have to measure. In other words, we must find out how far the magnetism must travel through iron. This totals 14¼ in. Multiplying this by 137, as indicated in *Figure 4* under "wrought iron," we get 1,953 ampere turns. In addition, we must add a number of ampere turns to take care of the stroke. This amount is found by multiplying the length of the stroke, or ¼ in., by the number shown opposite "wrought iron" under the flag *E.* Multiplying this number, or 32,880, by ¼ in. we get 8,220 as the number of ampere turns to be added. Adding 1,953 to 8,220 we get 10,173 as the

WIRE TABLE

B & S or A.W.G. Number	Ohms per 1000 Ft at Coil Temperature	Circular Mils	TURNS PER SQUARE INCH				OHMS PER CUBIC INCH			
			Enamel Covered	Single Cotton Covered or Double Silk Covered	Double Cotton Covered	Enameled and Single Cotton Covered	Enamel Covered	Single Cotton Covered or Double Silk Covered	Double Cotton Covered	Enameled and Single Cotton Covered
8	764	16510	92.2	87.5	80	84.8	.00765	.00725	.00662	.00704
9	963	13090	116	110	97.5	105	.0121	.0115	.0102	.0110
10	1.215	10380	146	136	121	131	.0193	.0181	.0160	.0173
11	1.532	8234	184	170	150	162	.0308	.0283	.0250	.0271
12	1.931	6530	232	211	183	198	.0493	.0443	.0385	.0417
13	2.436	5178	293	262	223	250	.078	.0697	.0592	.0665
14	3.071	4107	365	321	271	306	.122	.107	.0907	.102
15	3.873	3257	460	397	329	372	.194	.168	.139	.157
16	4.884	2583	572	493	399	454	.304	.263	.213	.242
17	6.158	2048	718	592	479	553	.477	.397	.318	.370
18	7.765	1624	912	775	625	725	.774	.657	.530	.615
19	9.792	1288	1150	940	754	895	1.23	1.01	.806	.957
20	12.35	1022	1430	1150	910	1070	1.91	1.54	1.22	1.43
21	15.57	810	1780	1400	1080	1300	3.01	2.38	1.82	2.20
22	19.63	642	2240	1700	1260	1570	4.78	3.64	2.70	3.37
23	24.76	510	2820	2060	1510	1910	7.66	5.61	4.10	5.18
24	31.22	404	3560	2500	1750	2300	12.1	8.50	5.95	7.82
25	39.36	320	4420	3030	2020	2780	19.0	13.0	8.66	11.9
26	49.64	254	5580	3670	2310	3350	30.2	19.8	12.5	18.1
27	62.59	202	6900	4300	2700	3900	47.3	29.5	18.5	26.7
28	78.93	160	8700	5040	3020	4660	75.2	43.6	26.2	40.3
29	99.52	127	10700	5920		5280	116.	64.0		57.0
30	125.5	101	13500	7060		6250	185.	96.5		85.5
31	158.2	80	17000	8120		7360	293.	140.		127.
32	199.5	63	21100	9600		8310	460.	209.		181.
33	251.6	50	26300	10900		8700	721.	300.		266.
34	317.7	40	32000	12200		10700	1110.	422.		370.
35	400.1	32	39800				1740.			
36	504.5	25	49400				2710.			
37	636.2	20	61200				4250.			
38	802.2	16	76100				6660.			
39	1012	12								
40	1276	10								

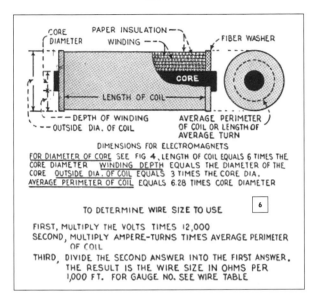

CORE DIAMETER · PAPER INSULATION · WINDING · FIBER WASHER

CORE

LENGTH OF COIL

DEPTH OF WINDING
OUTSIDE DIA. OF COIL

AVERAGE PERIMETER OF COIL OR LENGTH OF AVERAGE TURN

DIMENSIONS FOR ELECTROMAGNETS

FOR DIAMETER OF CORE SEE FIG 4, LENGTH OF COIL EQUALS 6 TIMES THE CORE DIAMETER   WINDING DEPTH EQUALS THE DIAMETER OF THE CORE OUTSIDE DIA. OF COIL EQUALS 3 TIMES THE CORE DIA. AVERAGE PERIMETER OF COIL EQUALS 6.28 TIMES CORE DIAMETER

TO DETERMINE WIRE SIZE TO USE   6

FIRST, MULTIPLY THE VOLTS TIMES 12,000
SECOND, MULTIPLY AMPERE-TURNS TIMES AVERAGE PERIMETER OF COIL
THIRD, DIVIDE THE SECOND ANSWER INTO THE FIRST ANSWER. THE RESULT IS THE WIRE SIZE IN OHMS PER 1,000 FT. FOR GAUGE NO. SEE WIRE TABLE

total number of ampere turns required for the coil. This same procedure may be used for any D.C. magnet. In all cases, the total length of the iron through which the magnetism must pass to make a complete circuit, must be measured. In case a core is used that does not have a return path for the magnetism, only the core length and length of stroke are considered in figuring the ampere turns required for magnets having short strokes. For long strokes, solenoids, or plunger magnets, should be used.

Next we figure the size of wire required to wind the coil. *Figure 6* shows a simple rule for doing this.

After figuring the average perimeter, which, according to the rule, is 6.27 times the core diameter, or in this case 4.71, we can then determine the wire size to use. If the coil is to be operated on 110 volts D.C., we first multiply this voltage (110) by 12,000, which gives us 1,320,000. Next we multiply the total number of ampere turns found as above, or 10,173, by the average perimeter (4.71), which gives us 47,915. Then we divide this number into 1,320,000, which gives us 27.55 ohms as the resistance of 1,000 feet of the size wire we need. Referring to the wire table, we find that this resistance corresponds to a

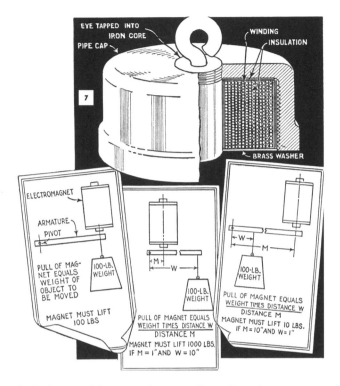

EYE TAPPED INTO IRON CORE
PIPE CAP
WINDING
INSULATION
7
BRASS WASHER

ELECTROMAGNET
ARMATURE
PIVOT
PULL OF MAGNET EQUALS WEIGHT OF OBJECT TO BE MOVED
100-LB. WEIGHT
MAGNET MUST LIFT 100 LBS

M
W
100-LB. WEIGHT
PULL OF MAGNET EQUALS WEIGHT TIMES DISTANCE W / DISTANCE M
MAGNET MUST LIFT 1000 LBS. IF M = 1" AND W = 10"

W
M
100-LB. WEIGHT
PULL OF MAGNET EQUALS WEIGHT TIMES DISTANCE W / DISTANCE M
MAGNET MUST LIFT 10 LBS. IF M = 10" AND W = 1"

size of wire between Nos. 23 and 24. We may choose either of these. The larger, or No. 23 wire, will increase the strength of the magnet slightly and cause it to become somewhat hotter; however, because this magnet is to be used intermittently, No. 23 wire may be used without danger of overheating. In winding the coil figured by these methods, it is not necessary to count the turns of wire because the selected size of wire will produce the correct number of ampere turns regardless of the exact number of turns wound. Changing either the voltage or the coil diameter will prevent the coil from performing as it should. The coil may be increased in length or shortened without changing the number of ampere turns or strength. If the coil is shortened it will run hotter and if it is lengthened it will run cooler and consume less current but will deliver the same pull. Washers of suitable size to slip over the core tightly as in *Figure 5* should be made from Bakelite or fiber. The outside diameter of the washers should be slightly over the outside diameter of the coil. With the end washers in place, the iron core between them is

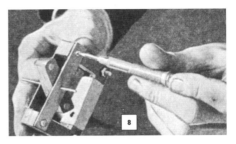

covered with two or three layers of heavy brown paper. This should be held in place with shellac, which also improves the insulating quality. One layer of paper should be placed between every two or three layers of wire for added insulation. Wire with any type of insulation may be used without changing the ampere turns in the coil. When the coil is finished, it is a good idea to coat it with shellac as shown in *Figure 14*.

Figure 7 shows a simple design for a lifting magnet. The frame for this type of magnet may be built from a pipe cap. The core is turned from a piece of cast iron or steel. The number of ampere turns required for a magnet of this type is figured exactly as explained above except that no allowance is made for stroke. Other special types of magnets may be worked out by similar methods. It must be remembered that enclosed windings or short coils tend to pull more amperes and therefore get hotter than long-exposed coils that can radiate their heat. Magnets used to operate systems of levers must be designed to allow for the variation in pull required due to the lever system. Some simple methods of figuring the pull required of lever magnets are given in the three details that are shown at left and on top of page 204.

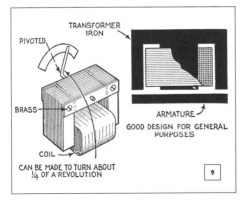

TRANSFORMER IRON

PIVOTED

BRASS

COIL

ARMATURE

GOOD DESIGN FOR GENERAL PURPOSES

CAN BE MADE TO TURN ABOUT ¼ OF A REVOLUTION

9

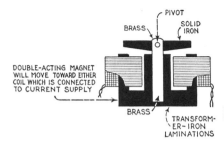

DOUBLE-ACTING MAGNET WILL MOVE TOWARD EITHER COIL WHICH IS CONNECTED TO CURRENT SUPPLY

PIVOT

BRASS

SOLID IRON

BRASS

TRANSFORMER-IRON LAMINATIONS

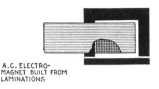

A.C. ELECTRO-MAGNET BUILT FROM LAMINATIONS

SIMPLE AND EFFICIENT DESIGN

Alternating-Current Magnets.
Alternating-current electromagnets may be designed for many purposes if care is taken to design the metal parts so that the iron makes a complete circuit around the coil when the magnet arm is closed. Plain magnets without a return path for the magnetism are not satisfactory for A.C. The cores for A.C. magnets must be built up from sheets of steel the same as the core of a transformer. *Figure 9* shows a number of A.C. magnets. Silicon steel or stovepipe iron, tightly assembled by means of stove bolts, as shown in *Figures 8* and *10,* may be used for the cores of this type of magnet. The moving part, or clapper as it is called, may be made from solid metal if it is small, but the core upon which the coil is wound must be built up from laminations as shown, otherwise trouble will be experienced from excessive heating.

To make clear the application of simplified methods for designing

A.C. magnets, we will construct an A.C. magnet suitable for closing an electrical switch. Magnets that are arranged to close or open electrical switches are called relays. Inasmuch as the core from an old transformer is usually available, we will use one of these for our magnet. A sketch of the core together with the mechanical arrangement is shown in *Figures 12* and *13.* From the sketch, we can see that the length of the iron face that will be effective in

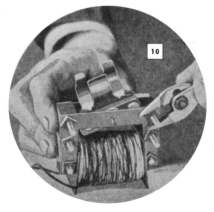

205

giving pull to the magnet is divided into three parts. The outside legs are ⅜ in. wide, and the center leg is ¾ in. long. Adding these together gives 1½ in. as the total length of the effective pulling surface. Multiplying this length by the thickness of the core, or ½ in., we get ¾ sq. in. as the cross-sectional area of the core that is effective in giving pull to the magnet. For A.C. magnets, it is safe to figure that each square

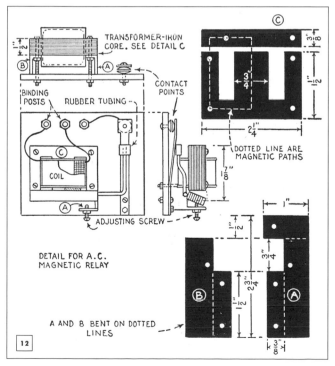

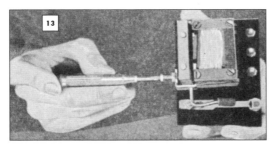

by the cross-sectional area, or .375, which gives us 1,352 as the required number of turns. The method of figuring the wire size is also indicated in *Figure 15.* Applying this rule, we first measure the length of the shortest path through which the magnetism must pass. This is indicated by dotted lines in *Figure 12,* and totals 4⅞ or 4.875 in. Applying the rule for wire size, we first multiply 4.875 times 50,000, which gives us 243,750. Dividing this number by the turns, or 1,352, gives us 180 circular mils as the wire size required. Referring to the wire table, we find that this falls between Nos. 27 and 28. Because we do not require the full power of the magnet for operat-

inch of pull surface will produce a pull of 88 lbs. The pull of our magnet will therefore be ¾ multiplied by 88 or 66 lbs. As this value is ample for our purposes, we will use the core as it is. The number of turns of wire required for the coil will depend upon the voltage to be used and upon the frequency or cycles of our current supply. If our magnet is to be operated on 110 volts, 60 cycles, A.C., we see from *Figure 15* that the turns are figured by multiplying the voltage by 4.7 and then dividing this answer by the cross-sectional area of the core. The cross-sectional area of the core in this case is the cross-sectional area of the leg upon which the coil is wound. Referring to *Figure 12* we see that this leg is ¾ in. wide and ½ in. thick. Multiplying these together gives us ⅜ or .375 sq. in. as the cross-sectional area. Then the turns are found by multiplying the voltage, or 110, by 4.7, which gives us 517. We then divide this number

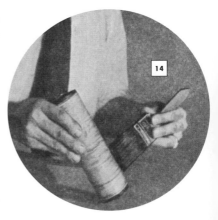

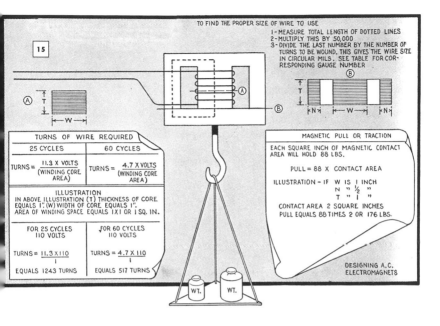

15

TO FIND THE PROPER SIZE OF WIRE TO USE

1 - MEASURE TOTAL LENGTH OF DOTTED LINES
2 - MULTIPLY THIS BY 50,000
3 - DIVIDE THE LAST NUMBER BY THE NUMBER OF TURNS TO BE WOUND. THIS GIVES THE WIRE SIZE IN CIRCULAR MILS. SEE TABLE FOR CORRESPONDING GAUGE NUMBER.

TURNS OF WIRE REQUIRED	
25 CYCLES	60 CYCLES
TURNS = $\dfrac{11.3 \times \text{VOLTS}}{\text{(WINDING CORE AREA)}}$	TURNS = $\dfrac{4.7 \times \text{VOLTS}}{\text{(WINDING CORE AREA)}}$

ILLUSTRATION
IN ABOVE ILLUSTRATION (T) THICKNESS OF CORE EQUALS 1". (W) WIDTH OF CORE EQUALS 1". AREA OF WINDING SPACE EQUALS 1 X 1 OR 1 SQ. IN.

FOR 25 CYCLES 110 VOLTS	FOR 60 CYCLES 110 VOLTS
TURNS = $\dfrac{11.3 \times 110}{1}$	TURNS = $\dfrac{4.7 \times 110}{1}$
EQUALS 1243 TURNS	EQUALS 517 TURNS

MAGNETIC PULL OR TRACTION

EACH SQUARE INCH OF MAGNETIC CONTACT AREA WILL HOLD 88 LBS.

PULL = 88 X CONTACT AREA

ILLUSTRATION – IF W IS 1 INCH
N " ½ "
T " 1 "

CONTACT AREA 2 SQUARE INCHES
PULL EQUALS 88 TIMES 2 OR 176 LBS.

DESIGNING A.C. ELECTROMAGNETS

ing the relay, we will select the smaller wire size, or No. 28. The coil may be wound on a form and installed on the core by the same methods as are used in transformer construction. Before the coils are fitted over the cores, the latter are covered with insulating paper.

Alternating-current magnets tend to hum badly unless they are equipped with what is termed a "shading coil," which is simply a turn

of very heavy copper wire wound into a slot in the core as shown in *Figure 16*. Either of the methods shown is effective. For the magnet

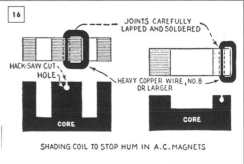

16

JOINTS CAREFULLY LAPPED AND SOLDERED

HACK-SAW CUT HOLE

HEAVY COPPER WIRE, NO.8 OR LARGER

CORE

CORE

SHADING COIL TO STOP HUM IN A.C. MAGNETS

just described a piece of No. 8 or larger copper wire should be used. The ends should be carefully lapped together and soldered as shown in *Figure 11.* Care must be taken to completely sweat the splice together, otherwise it will not be effective.

These methods for designing magnets may be applied to almost any kind of problem. In doing this kind of work it is best practice to figure out the design you need and then make minor variations by experimenting until you get exactly what you want.

— HOW TO BUILD SMALL ELECTROMAGNETS —

The first piece of electrical work to be attempted by most amateurs is the construction of some kind of electromagnet. Such magnets, besides being fundamental to almost every kind of electrical apparatus, are interesting in themselves.

Though almost any winding on any iron core constitutes a sort of magnet, far better results are to be had by correct proportioning. It is the purpose of this text to give an idea of what these proportions are, in the smaller sizes of magnets, for low voltages. These magnets can also be used on regular lighting circuits; the making of small magnets wound especially for such high voltages is a tedious proposition.

For use on a direct-current lighting circuit, connect the magnet in series with a lamp of slightly greater normal amperage. For example the ¼-ampere sizes will operate well

in series with a 40-watt lamp, on a 110-volt direct-current circuit, as diagrammed in the upper half of *Figure 1,* or on a 220-volt circuit, with a pair of 40-watt lamps connected as shown below. Likewise for the ½-ampere sizes, use two 40-watt or three 25-watt lamps on a 110-volt circuit. All lamps should be of regular voltage.

The general construction of electromagnets is familiar to almost everyone. The essential parts are a soft-iron core, surrounded by a winding of insulated copper wire. The bar magnet is the simplest type and is diagrammed in *Figure 2.* Here also is shown a turbogenerator rotor, which is also of the bar-magnet type. For increased power, a magnet core is more often bent into a "U," or horseshoe shape, so that both poles are brought to the load. A few forms are shown, with the method of winding indicated, in

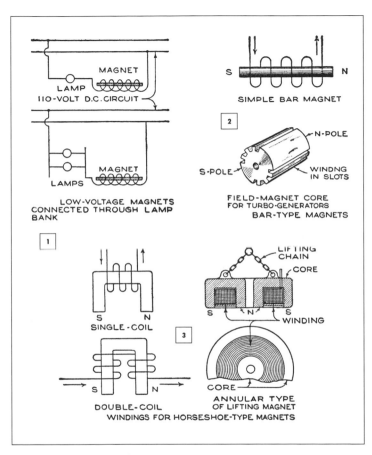

FIGURES 1, 2 AND 3 ILLUSTRATE DIAGRAMMATICALLY THE WAY
IN WHICH MAGNET WINDINGS ARE DIRECTED AND SHAPED.

Figure 3. The annular form is simply a modification of the horseshoe, often used in lifting magnets. *Figures 4, 5,* and *6* show three forms of core suitable for small magnets; the one in *Figure 6,* although more difficult to make than the others, gives complete protection to the winding, and is very suitable for a magnet to be used for practical purposes.

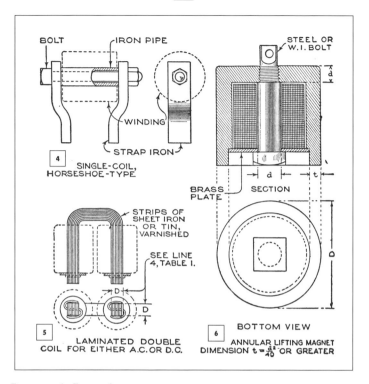

FIGURES 4, 5 AND 6 SHOW PRACTICAL METHODS OF CONSTRUCTION
FOR SMALL ELECTROMAGNETS OPERATED FROM BATTERIES.

A small current in a properly designed magnet will support a heavy weight. It will not, however, exert this force for any considerable distance from the pole faces. A great lifting magnet, capable of handling a 10-ton casing, will not disturb a knife in a pocket 10 ft. away— though it may disturb a watch very seriously. Even the scale on a rough casting may interfere with the ability of a magnet to hold it, and has to be considered in design. Neither can a magnet exert as great a force on comparatively small objects as on larger ones. For instance, a magnet capable of lifting a 20,000-lb. "skull-cracker" ball (such as is dropped some 20 ft. on a scrap pile, to break it up) cannot hold 1,000 lb. of scrap iron.

It will be seen, then, that although a magnet can be designed accurately for a specific purpose, it is impossible to give exact data for one to be used for general duty. Therefore, the data given in Tables I and II must be considered as suggestive, rather than hard and fast. It applies to magnets working under favorable conditions, that is, lifting flat, smooth iron objects, of a cross section at least equal to that of the core. Under these conditions, the rated holding power can be obtained. It will be noted that the smaller sizes are less economical of current than the larger, chiefly because of the resistance of the air gap between the poles and the load, which is about the same for all sizes.

Theoretically, a holding magnet does no work, and therefore should consume no power at all. The power used in the actual direct-current electromagnet is all lost in overcoming the resistance of the winding. Therefore, by using sufficient wire of proper size, the current may be made very small indeed. In practice, a balance is struck, determined by practical considerations. To avoid extremely heavy windings, a fairly high value of the current has been taken in the calculations in the tables below; but the current is not higher than can be drawn economically from a battery.

If a scientist wants to use a different winding and current on any size, it is

TABLE I.
General Data for Small Electromagnets of Any Voltage

Pull, or Holding Force, in Lb.	2	5	10	20	50	100
Ampere Turns	175	225	300	400	800	1,500
Area of Core (Minimum) in Sq. In.	.04	.1	.2	.4	1.0	2.0
Diameter of Round Core in In.	¼ to ⅜	⅜ to ½	½	¾	1⅛	1½

TABLE II.
For Finding Dimensions of a Winding

Voltage	Holding Power in Pounds	Current in Amperes	Number of Turns in Winding	Gauge of Wire	Diameter of Wire in Decimals of One Inch	Length of Wire Needed
1½	2 5 10 10	¼ ¼ ¼ ⅓	700 900 1,200 900	28 25 23 23	.012 .018 .022 .022	105 180 300 225
3	2 5 10 10	¼ ¼ ¼ ⅓	700 900 1,200 900	31 28 26 26	.008 .012 .016 .016	100 170 300 225
6	2 5 10 10 20 20	¼ ¼ ¼ ⅓ ⅓ ½	700 900 1,200 900 1,200 800	34 31 29 29 26 26	.006 .008 .011 .011 .016 .016	100 170 300 225 425 280
12	10 10 20 20 50 100	¼ ⅓ ⅓ ½ ½ 1	1,200 900 1,200 800 1,600 1,500	32 32 29 29 24 21	.008 .008 .011 .011 .020 .028	300 225 425 280 850 1100

only necessary that the product of the turns of wire times the current should be the same as that given as ampere turns in Table I. For example, the 10-lb. magnet can be wound by either of the two methods in Table II. Both give 300 ampere turns; in one case, ¼ ampere by 1,200 turns, in the other, ⅓ ampere by 900 turns. It would develop the same pull with 1 ampere and 300 turns, or .1 ampere and 3,000 turns. So one can suit himself in the matter of windings, given sufficient wire, and patience in winding it on.

The core is the same in any given size, whatever the winding.

The windings are best made up of cotton-covered magnet wire. In fact, this is about the only form in which such small sizes of wire can be had in most places. Rather than wind the wire directly on the core, it is better to make up the winding on a false core of wood or paper, wrapping it with tape before placing it on the iron core. The winding may be made up in two coils, if desired.

The core may be of any shape of section, but where the coils rest upon it, it should be round or nearly so, or a waste of wire will result. In any case, its area should be at all points equal to or greater than that of the round core listed in the table. Other dimensions are made to suit the winding.

These magnets will operate, after a fashion, on alternating current if the voltage is high enough. But they will heat up from core losses. This heating can be much reduced by making the core of iron wire or of a bundle of sheet-iron strips, insulated with paper or varnish, as shown in *Figure 5*. To get sufficient voltage it will be necessary to connect through lamps to the lighting circuit, exactly as outlined above. It will be impossible to get as much holding power as can be had with direct current, without overheating.

Closely allied with the subject of electromagnets is that of solenoids for use with a core that is to be pulled into the coil, thus operating some mechanism. Such cores necessarily have a large air gap; that is, there is no nearly complete magnetic circuit of iron, as in a horseshoe magnet. For this reason, it is hardly possible to give very definite data for the pull to be expected from a certain winding. The table will give suggestions for the windings of such solenoids, though the pull will of course be much less than that given for magnets. In general, the pull depends on the cross section of the core and the ampere turns of the coil, so that a greater pull can be obtained by increasing either factor. For best operation, however, a reasonable proportion should be maintained between the two. With a solenoid and plunger, a motion of an inch or more is readily obtained, though this involves, of course, a corresponding reduction of the pulling force.

Note: Pull is calculated for a cast-iron armature of area equal to that of the core; the air gap is assumed, .005 in. for smallest size. Other core dimensions should be determined to suit the form and size of the windings, making the core as short as convenient.

— A Floating Electromagnet —

A piece of iron placed in a coil of wire carrying a current of electricity becomes an electromagnet. If such a coil and iron core are made small enough, they can be attached to a cork and the cork, floating on a solution, will allow the magnet to point north and south. The sketch shows how to make such an instrument. A coil of insulated wire is wrapped around a small iron core, leaving a few inches of each end free for connections. The insulation is removed from these ends and they are run through a piece of cork. Attach to the wires, on the underside of the cork, a piece of zinc to one end and a piece of copper to the other. The cork is then floated on an acidic solution, with the zinc and copper hanging in the solution. If zinc and

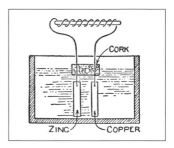

copper are used, the solution is made from water and blue vitriol. If zinc and carbon are used, the solution is made from sal ammoniac and water.

The float will move about on the solution until the magnet iron will point north and south. If two of them are floating on the same solution, they will move about and finally arrange themselves end to end with the coils and magnet cores pointing north and south.

— Demagnetizing a Watch —

A test can be made to know if your watch is magnetized by placing a small compass on the side of the watch nearest the escapement wheel. If the compass pointer moves with the escapement wheel, the watch is magnetized. A magnetized watch must be placed in a coil that has an alternating current of electricity

flowing through it to remove the magnetism. A demagnetizer can be made as shown in the illustration. Two end pieces for the coil are made as shown in *Fig. 1* from ¼-in. wood. These ends are fastened together, *Fig. 2*, with cardboard 3 in. long glued to the inside edges of the holes cut in them. Upon the newly formed spool, wind about 2 lb. of No. 16 cotton-covered copper wire. As it will be necessary to place a 16-cp. lamp in series with the coil, both the coil and lamp can be mounted on a suitable base and connected as shown in *Fig. 3*. The current, which must be 110-volt alternating current, is turned on the lamp and coil and the magnetized watch slowly drawn through the opening in the center of the coil.

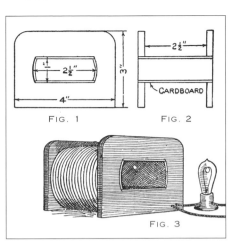

FIG. 1

FIG. 2

FIG. 3

— MAKING PERMANENT MAGNETS BY USE OF ALTERNATING CURRENT —

In the amateur's laboratory it often happens that he desires permanently to magnetize steel parts, but is not able to do so without means of rectifying the commonly used alternating current. This difficulty can be easily overcome if the coil used to magnetize the parts is placed in circuit with a fairly heavy fuse, of 5 or 10 amperes, or with a piece of light copper wire, as shown in the sketch. When the switch is closed, the fuse, of course, is blown, but the instantaneous surge of current in the coil is very great, and the break so sudden that the steel is left magnetized. The result is secured only if the current

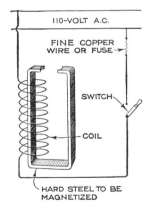

happens to break near the peak of a wave, or alternation; if not successful the first time, the process must be repeated.

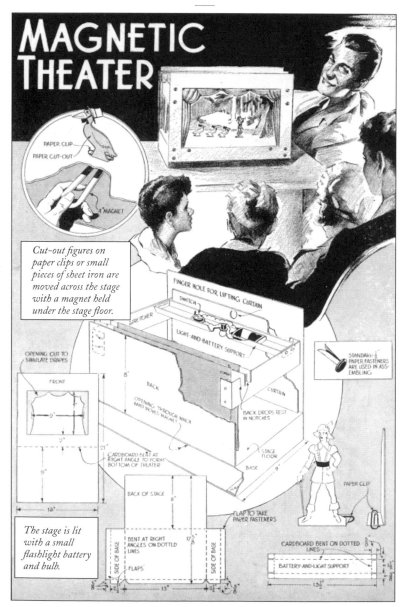

MAGNETIC THEATER

PAPER CLIP

PAPER CUT-OUT

A MAGNET

Cut-out figures on paper clips or small pieces of sheet iron are moved across the stage with a magnet held under the stage floor.

FINGER HOLE FOR LIFTING CURTAIN

SWITCH

STRETCHER

LIGHT-AND-BATTERY SUPPORT

STANDARD PAPER FASTENERS ARE USED IN ASSEMBLING

OPENING CUT TO SIMULATE DROPS

FRONT

BACK

OPENING THROUGH WHICH HAND MOVES MAGNET

8"

CURTAIN

BACK DROPS REST IN NOTCHES

9"

2"

21"

CARDBOARD BENT AT RIGHT ANGLE TO FORM BOTTOM OF THEATER

STAGE FLOOR

9"

BASE

9"

PAPER CLIP

BACK OF STAGE

8"

The stage is lit with a small flashlight battery and bulb.

SIDE OF BASE

BENT AT RIGHT ANGLES ON DOTTED LINES

17⅝"

SIDE OF BASE

FLAP TO TAKE PAPER FASTENERS

CARDBOARD BENT ON DOTTED LINES

FLAPS

BATTERY-AND-LIGHT SUPPORT

13½"

13"

— THE CONSTRUCTION
OF A POLARIZED RELAY —

The trend of amateur construction is to utilize standard parts of easily obtained apparatus in making other devices with a minimum of work. A good example of this is the very sensitive polarized relay described here.

The permanent magnet used in this relay is from an old telephone magneto. The pivot for the armature is from a polarized ringer. The long ends of the ringer-pivot bar are cut off, and holes are drilled in it at such a distance from the center that two bolts inserted in them will straddle one leg of the magnet. A short piece of brass, or iron, is similarly drilled for mounting the armature pivot to the magnet as shown.

The armature is made of soft iron, just wide enough to fit between the pivot screws, and its length should be about two-thirds of the distance between the ends of the magnet. A center punch is used to make recesses on the edges of the armature for pointed pivot screws. The rest of the armature may be cut down to the same width as the cores of the electromagnets. A short piece of brass is riveted at the lower end of the armature with small rivets made from copper wire. The free end of this brass strip is provided with a silver contact point, made by drilling a small hole in the brass, into which a piece of silver wire is riveted.

The electromagnets, wound for a resistance of about 75 ohms each, are from single–pole telephone receivers. These coils are mounted at the ends of a U-shaped iron yoke, so as to leave a space of about ¼ in. between the cores. The legs of the yoke should be long enough to bring the coils midway between the legs of the magnet. The coils are mounted with machine screws, through holes in the end of the yoke.

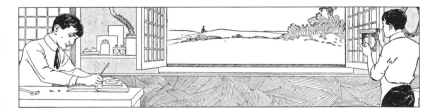

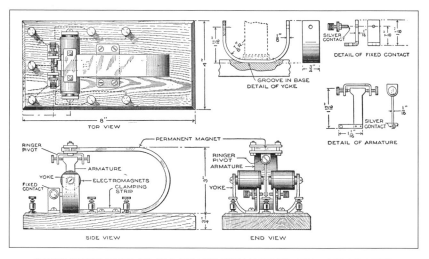

PARTS TAKEN FROM AN OLD TELEPHONE MAGNETO ARE USED TO MAKE THIS VERY SENSITIVE POLARIZED RELAY, THE RESISTANCE OF WHICH CAN BE VARIED TO SUIT OPERATING CONDITIONS. BY USING THE PROPER POSTS THE COILS CAN BE USED ALONE, IN SERIES, OR IN PARALLEL.

The stationary contacts are made from brass strips, bent as shown. Holes for attaching to the base and to the adjusting screws are drilled. The holes for the adjusting screws should be tapped to accommodate the screws, which should be provided with locknuts. Silver contacts are soldered to the ends of these screws.

A groove is made in the wooden base to fit the yoke supporting the coils, as shown in the drawing. The yoke is held in place by the magnet, which is attached to the base by the brass clamping strip, as shown. A short length of fine copper wire is soldered to the brass strip on the armature, to carry the current. Each coil should be connected to a separate set of binding posts; the two stationary contacts and the armature contact being connected to the other three posts.

By using the proper posts, the resistance of the relay may be altered as found necessary. With both coils in series, the resistance is about 150 ohms; using one coil alone, 75 ohms; and with both coils in parallel, about 32 or 33 ohms. In making connections, care should be taken to have the magnets form opposite poles on the different sides of the armature.

Science in Motion

— Why Gravity Batteries Fail to Work —

Many amateur electricians and some professionals have had considerable trouble with gravity batteries. They follow directions carefully and then fail to get good results. The usual trouble is not with the battery itself, but with the circuit. A gravity battery is suitable only for a circuit which is normally closed. It is therefore undesirable for electric bells, induction coils, and all other open-circuit apparatus. The circuit should also have a high resistance. This makes it impractical for running fan motors, as the motor would have to be wound with a fine wire and it would then require a large number of batteries to give a sufficiently high voltage.

To set up a gravity battery: Use about 3½ lb. of blue stone, or enough to cover the copper element 1 in. Pour in water sufficient to cover the zinc ½ in. Short-circuit for three hours, and the battery is ready for use. If desired for use immediately, do not short-circuit, but add 5 or 6 oz. of zinc sulphate.

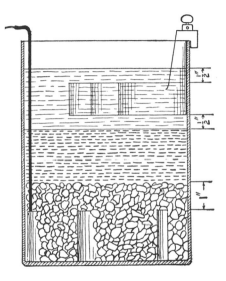

SETTING UP
A GRAVITY BATTERY.

Keep the dividing line between the blue and white liquids about ½ in. below the bottom of the zinc. If too low, siphon off some of the white liquid and add the same amount of water, but do not agitate or mix the two solutions. This type of battery will give about 0.9 of a volt, and should be used on a circuit of about 100 milli-amperes.

— FEAT OF BALANCING ON CHAIRS —

Among the numerous experiments of gravity is the feat of balancing on the two rear legs of a chair while one foot rests on the front part of the seat and the other on the back of the chair. This may appear to be a hard thing to do, yet with a little practice it may be accomplished. This is an exercise practiced by the boys of a boys' home for an annual display given by them. A dozen of the boys will mount chairs at the same time and keep them in balance at the word of a commanding officer.

— WHY A POUND OF SUGAR IS A POUND OF SUGAR —

If you go to the grocery store and buy one pound of sugar, you get an amount of sugar that weighs one pound on the grocer's scales where you live. It "weighs" one pound because gravity pulls down on it with a force of one pound.

In the sack is a certain amount of sugar made up of molecules that, in turn, are made of atoms. There is a certain number of atoms in that sack, and the parts of the atoms make up the so-called "solid" part of the sugar. That is its "mass."

If you were going on a camping trip you might put that sugar in your pack, without ever opening the sack, and climb a high mountain. If you weighed your sugar there it would weigh less than a pound. Was the grocer at home dishonest? Not at all. The force of gravity has changed. As you climbed the mountain as Newton's theory tells us, the force of gravity lessened. The force gets smaller as the square of the distance elongates.

The sack of sugar honestly no longer weighs a pound, because "weight" is merely a measure of the force of gravity, and the force of gravity becomes less the farther away you get from the center of the earth. On the other hand, there still are as many atoms in the sack as when you started. The amount of solid material, the "mass," remains the same.

Of course, if you had a sack twice as large, with twice as much sugar in it, it would weigh twice as much as the smaller sack, regardless of whether you weighed it back home on the grocer's scales, or on your own at the top of a mountain. It would weigh twice as much at home, or two pounds. On the mountain it would not weigh two pounds, but it still would weigh twice as much as the small sack of sugar.

So "weight," or the force of gravity, depends both on distance and on "mass"—the height of the mountain and the number of atoms of a certain kind in the sack.

— CENTER OF GRAVITY EXPERIMENT —

This experiment consists of suspending a pail of water from a stick placed upon a table as shown in the accompanying sketch. In order to accomplish this experiment, which seems impossible, it is necessary to place a stick, *A*, of sufficient length, between the end of the stick on the table and the bottom of the pail. This makes the center of gravity somewhere near the middle of the stick on the table, thus holding the pail as shown.

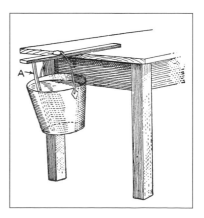

— A Perpetual-Motion Puzzle —

The fallacy of perpetual motion is now so generally understood that the description of a new scheme for attaining it is only justified in so far as it may be instructive. The sketch illustrates such a device, apparently successful, and the discovery of the error in it is both instructive and interesting.

Mount a horseshoe magnet on a wooden base, and into the latter cut a continuous groove along the three sides of a triangle opposite the poles of the magnet, *N* and *S*. Suspend a long narrow bar magnet on a universal joint from a standard. A pin projects into the groove from the lower end, which is its north pole, and can move only along the triangular course.

Start the device with the suspended magnet in the position shown. The lower end will tend to move in the direction of the arrows because in so doing it is getting farther away from the repelling north pole of the horseshoe magnet and nearer the attracting south pole, which action will bring it to the corner of the triangle in the foreground. It will next move down the side as indicated by the arrow because along that line it is nearer the attracting south than

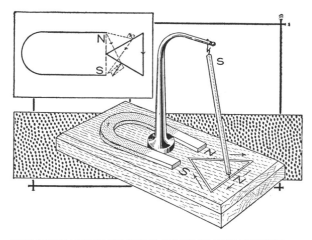

THE INTERACTION BETWEEN POLES OF THE MAGNETS
CAUSES THE TRAVELER TO MOVE AROUND THE TRIANGLE.

the repelling north pole. When it reaches the end of its trip, at the angle between the poles of the magnet, the attraction and repulsion will be balanced, but a slight jar will carry the traveler beyond the angle.

The third leg of the triangle will be covered similarly, the north pole repelling the traveler. On this basis,

the motion should continue indefinitely, but a test will show that it will not do so.

The corners of the triangle should be rounded slightly and it would be better to use several hanging magnets, flexibly connected, so that when one is at the dead center, the others will carry the traveler on.

— REVOLVING SHAFT WITHOUT POWER —

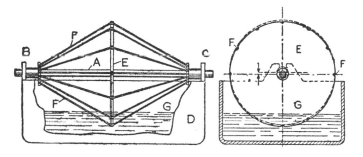

THE EXPANSION AND CONTRACTION OF THE ROPES KEEP
THE DISK UP AND TO ONE SIDE OF THE CENTER.

The device illustrated seems paradoxical, for it apparently works without any power being applied to it, making from two to three revolutions per hour, which, though slow, is nevertheless motion, requiring energy.

The shaft *A* is supported on the edges, in the bearings *B* and *C,* of a tank, *D.* A disk, *E,* having a central hole larger in diameter than the shaft, is located at the middle of the

latter. The disk is supported by 12 or more cotton ropes, *F.* The tank is filled to the level *G* with water. The lower ropes, being immersed in the water, shrink and lift the disk slightly above the center in the position of an eccentric, as shown by the dotted lines in the sketch. The center of gravity of the disk in this position, being higher and slightly to one side of the shaft, the disk has a tendency to turn around. The motion drives the next rope into the water where it becomes soaked and shrinkage takes place again, lifting the disk to a higher position, while the rope coming out of the water dries out. The ropes, emerging from the water but not yet thoroughly dry, cause the upper part of the disk to be in an eccentric position laterally with reference to the center of the shaft, thus causing the center of gravity to be not only above, but also slightly to one side.

— Experiment with Two-Foot Rule and Hammer —

An example of unstable equilibrium is shown in the accompanying sketch. All that is needed is a 2-ft. rule, a hammer, a piece of string, and a table or bench. The experiment works best with a hammer having a light handle and a very heavy head. Tie the ends of the string together, forming a loop, and pass this around the hammer handle and rule. Then place the apparatus on the edge of the table, where it will remain suspended as shown.

AN EXPERIMENT IN EQUILIBRIUM.

— Galileo's Pendulum Experiment —

Galileo, a scientist of the Italian Renaissance and one of the greatest mathematical thinkers of all time, was armed only with such mathematics as then existed (algebra, which so completely simplifies so many complex matters, came in common usage only during the last years of his life).

So he came up with many wonderful experiments to test his theories.

He did an experiment that you can do. He drove a nail into a wall, hung a string on the end of the nail, and fastened a weight to the end of the string. (If you do this, it is suggested you not drive the nail into the living room plaster. Any wall will do, and if there is no wall that cannot be harmed, you can drive the nail into any other flat surface, such as a board or a piece of heavy cardboard.)

The weight (which can be anything—a stone, a marble, a piece of lead or iron) now replaces the chandelier that Galileo saw swinging in the Cathedral of Pisa. First, we should make sure (as Galileo did) that what he thought he observed in the cathedral was true. When we swing the weight back and forth, does it really make one complete swing, when it is swinging high, in the same time that it does when it is swinging only enough to be barely moving?

If you have a stopwatch, you can do this experiment easily. You can pull the weight way out, let loose of it, start the watch when it passes the bottom spot, let it swing both ways, and stop the watch as it passes the bottom again after swinging both ways. Then you can pull the weight out just a little bit, and let it swing in a small arc. If you press the buttons

on the watch at just the right times, you will find the weight (or pendulum) swings back and forth in exactly the same length of time, regardless off how far back you pull when you let it loose. If you make a mistake in pushing the buttons at the right time, repeat the experiment many times to make sure your timing is right.

If you do not have a stopwatch, you or somebody around the house has a watch or clock with a second hand on it (which is something Galileo did not have). You can hold the weight back some distance so that it will swing through a long arc. Let it swing 50 times and check on the watch or clock how many seconds 50 swings take. Then, if you divide the total time by 50 (mathematics, already) you will have the average time it took your weight to swing once, and the value you get should be quite accurate. Now you can repeat the experiment many times, but each time hold the weight out a different distance, so that the arc through which the weight swings will be different.

— FURTHER INVESTIGATION INTO THE PENDULUM —

Galileo discovered other things about pendulums. He discovered that any one pendulum

will vibrate or oscillate (swing back and forth) only a certain number of times in a given period of time. You can prove that for yourself by letting your homemade pendulum swing for 30 seconds. Count the number of oscillations in 30 seconds, repeat the experiment, and the number always comes out the same.

However, if you lengthen the string and count again, you will find that the pendulum now makes fewer oscillations in 30 seconds. Further experiment will show that this new number always applies, no matter how far back you hold the weight to start the pendulum swinging.

If you shorten the string, the pendulum will oscillate more often in 30 seconds. But for each length of the string, the number of oscillations is always the same. No matter what you do, you cannot change the number so long as the length of the string remains the same. Try it. Blow on the weight, hit the string, stop the weight at different points and let it swing free again. You cannot change the natural frequency of that particular pendulum with that length of string.

"Natural frequency," you will find later, plays a big part in physics. The tiniest parts of matter vibrate with natural frequencies also. This is related, for example, to the reason things have different colors.

Galileo watched his pendulums so long and timed them so carefully, that he discovered that he could tell how long the string was even if it were so long that the top of it was out of sight. He did this merely by counting and comparing oscillations.

He found that the length of the string was in inverse (backwards) proportion to the square of the number of oscillations in a given time.

For example, if one pendulum with a string 20 in. long oscillates 40 times while another pendulum oscillates 20 times, Galileo figured out mathematically that the other pendulum had to have a string 80 in. long.

First he squared the number of oscillations in both cases (multiplied the numbers by themselves)—40 squared is 1,600 (40 times 40) and 20 squared is 400 (20 times 20). The proportion or ratio between 1,600 and 400 is 4 to 1 (1600 divided by 400 equals 4). Therefore the longer string would be four times as long as the short one. Since the short one was 20 in., the long one would be 4 times that, or 80 in.

You can rig up a second pendulum and find out for yourself whether Galileo was right. You can be sure that he would have done that to determine whether you were right, if the tables were reversed. Make one string 20 in. long and the other 80 in. long. Start both pendulums swinging.

While you count 40 oscillations of the short pendulum, have a friend count the oscillations of the long pendulum. Did your friend count 20 while you counted 40? If so, Galileo was right.

Change the length of the longer string. You count 40 oscillations again. While you are doing that, how many oscillations of the longer pendulum did your friend count? Was it still 20? If it was, Galileo was wrong. If you are a true scientist and want to work a while longer, test your new results against Galileo's theory. He said the lengths of the strings would be in inverse proportion to the squares of the number of oscillations.

If you multiply the new length of the longer string by the square of the number of oscillations your friend counted while you counted 40, the answer should be 32,000. Do you know why? If not, be patient. You will understand it when mathematics becomes easier for you.

Of course, even if Galileo's theory was right, your problem will come out right only if the two pendulums swing for exactly the same length of time. Your friend must count the oscillations of the longer one during exactly the same time that it takes you to count 40 oscillations of the shorter one.

— A MYSTERIOUS WATCH —

A very interesting experiment may be made with the ordinary dollar watch in illustrating the law of the pendulum. A pendulum 39.1 in. long will make 60 one-way swings per minute, the number of swings varying inversely as the square root of the length. By actual count it was found that the balance wheel of the watch in question made 240 one-way swings per minute, which is just 4 times as fast as the 39-in. pendulum. Therefore, according to the foregoing law, a pendulum $\frac{1}{16}$ as long, or about 2½ in., would swing in

unison with the wheel of the watch. The question then arises as to what would happen if the watch itself were suspended so as to swing as a pendulum of the latter length. The experiment was made as illustrated, with the result that the watch keeps on swinging continuously. The swing amounts to about ⅜ in., and appears so vigorous that it is almost incomprehensible that the small spring in a watch should be able to maintain so much weight in continuous motion for 24 hours.

— THE PARADOX OF THE FALLING BODIES —

During his tenure as a teacher, Galileo discovered the laws of falling bodies. He defied the ancient Aristotle and proved that if a heavy stone and a light stone are dropped, both hit the ground at the same time.

Even though you easily can prove that this is true, it may not seem logical to you. It may still seem to you, as it did to Aristotle, that one body twice as heavy as another ought to fall faster.

Try reasoning it out this way. Suppose we divide the heavy body into two parts. Imagine we have a big ball of molding clay and we divide it equally into two smaller balls. Each weighs the same as the other. If we drop the two smaller balls at the same time, one from each hand, with out hands three feet apart, it is reasonable to expect them to hit the ground at the same time.

Now if we hold our hands so close together that the balls almost touch, and drop them again, we again would expect them to hit the ground at the same time. If we do this a third time, with the balls closer still—in fact, so close that they touch and we press them together into one big ball again, is it not reasonable to expect them to drop at the same speed as before? Does it matter whether they drop separately or as two parts of a bigger ball? Not at all.

What we have said about falling bodies would be true in every case if there were no air. But, of course, air resists the movement of any object through it. The air does not "like" being pushed aside—any more than water "likes" being pushed aside when a boat passes through it.

An empty rubber balloon will fall faster than one filled with air. This is not because it is lighter. In fact, the air inside the balloon has weight, and therefore the balloon filled with air is heavier than the empty balloon. You can prove this for yourself by weighing an empty balloon and a full balloon on postal scales.

The reason that the filled balloon falls more slowly than the empty one is that the filled balloon is larger and therefore presents more surface to air resistance, which slows it down.

You know from your own experience that the bigger the surface pushing against the air, the greater the resistance. If you hold your hand out the window of a moving car, you have to use force to keep it from being pushed backward. But if you hold your hand flat, palm downward, you feel less air resistance then if you turn your hand palm forward, presenting a larger surface in the direction of motion. Any falling body, falling in air, has a surface pushing against the air.

— A SIMPLE ACCELEROMETER —

A simple accelerometer for indicating the increase in speed of a train is described below. The device consists of an ordinary 2-ft. ruler, A, with a piece of thread tied to the 22-in. mark, as shown in the sketch, and supporting the small weight, which may be a button or other small object.

The device thus arranged, and placed on the windowsill of the car, will indicate the acceleration and retardation as follows: Every ½ in. traveled by the thread over the bent portion of the rule, indicates an increase or decrease of

velocity to the extent of 1 ft. per second for each second. Thus, if the thread moved 2¼ in. in a direction opposite to the movement of the train, then the train would be increasing its speed at the rate of 4½ ft. per second.

If the thread is tied at the 17-in. mark, then each half inch will represent the mile per hour increase for each second. Thus if the thread moves 1 in., it shows that the train is gaining 2 miles an hour each second.

— LIFTING POWER WITH PULLEY BLOCKS —

A man pulling with a force of 100 lbs. can lift only that amount with a single block, as shown in *Figure 1*, but by using two single blocks he can lift double that amount, as indicated in *Figure 2*. By using a double block above and a single block below, as shown in *Figure 3*,

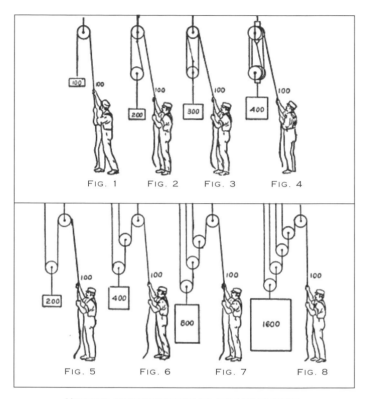

FIG. 1 FIG. 2 FIG. 3 FIG. 4

FIG. 5 FIG. 6 FIG. 7 FIG. 8

VARIOUS ARRANGEMENTS OF PULLEY BLOCKS
SHOWING LIFTING POWER.

100 lb. pull on the rope will lift 300 lb. and by using two double blocks, as indicated in *Figure 4*, 100 lb. will lift 400 lb.

In *Figure 1* the load is supported directly by one rope; in *Figure 2* by two ropes; in *Figure 3* by three and in *Figure 4* by four ropes. The weight is 100, 200, 300 and 400 lb. respectively. Thus with pulley blocks arranged in this way the weight that can be raised is in direct proportion to the number of ropes that support it. In these calculations the portion of rope that the man holds is ignored, as he pulls in a direction opposite to the movement of the weight, but should he take his position above the pulleys and pull up, then the rope that he holds should be counted also.

Another system of arranging pulleys is shown in *Figures 5, 6, 7,* and *8,* the pulley blocks being all single. In an arrangement of this kind, the power is just doubled by the addition of each pulley as indicated by the figures. In all these calculations no allowance has been made for friction so that the actual force required to lift the given weights will be somewhat greater, the exact amount depending on the flexibility of the rope, diameter of the pulleys, smoothness of the bearings, and other conditions.

INDEX